Disability KEY ISSUES AND FUTURE DIRECTIONS

EMPLOYMENT
AND **WORK**

The SAGE Reference Series on Disability: Key Issues and Future Directions

Series Editor: Gary L. Albrecht

Arts and Humanities, by Brenda Jo Brueggemann
Assistive Technology and Science, by Cathy Bodine
Disability Through the Life Course, by Tamar Heller and Sarah Parker Harris
Education, by Cheryl Hanley-Maxwell and Lana Collet-Klingenberg
Employment and Work, by Susanne M. Bruyère and Linda Barrington
Ethics, Law, and Policy, by Jerome E. Bickenbach
Health and Medicine, by Ross M. Mullner
Rehabilitation Interventions, by Margaret A. Turk and Nancy R. Mudrick

Disability KEY ISSUES AND FUTURE DIRECTIONS

EMPLOYMENT
AND WORK

Susanne M. Bruyère
Cornell University

Linda Barrington
Cornell University

SERIES EDITOR
Gary L. Albrecht
University of Illinois at Chicago

⑤SAGE reference

Los Angeles | London | New Delhi
Singapore | Washington DC

Los Angeles | London | New Delhi
Singapore | Washington DC

FOR INFORMATION:

SAGE Publications, Inc.

2455 Teller Road

Thousand Oaks, California 91320

E-mail: order@sagepub.com

SAGE Publications Ltd.

1 Oliver's Yard

55 City Road

London EC1Y 1SP

United Kingdom

SAGE Publications India Pvt. Ltd.

B 1/I 1 Mohan Cooperative Industrial Area

Mathura Road, New Delhi 110 044

India

SAGE Publications Asia-Pacific Pte. Ltd.

3 Church Street

#10-04 Samsung Hub

Singapore 049483

Publisher: Rolf A. Janke

Acquisitions Editor: Jim Brace-Thompson

Assistant to the Publisher: Michele Thompson

Project Development, Editing, & Management: Kevin Hillstrom,
    Laurie Collier Hillstrom

Production Editor: David C. Felts

Reference Systems Manager: Leticia Gutierrez

Reference Systems Coordinator: Laura Notton

Typesetter: C&M Digitals (P) Ltd.

Proofreader: Annie Lubinsky

Indexer: Sylvia Coates

Cover Designer: Gail Buschman

Marketing Managers: Kristi Ward, Carmel Schrire

Printed in the United States of America.

Library of Congress Cataloging-in-Publication Data

Bruyère, Susanne M. Employment and work / Susanne M. Bruyère, Linda Barrington.

p. cm.—(The SAGE reference series on disability: key issues and future directions)
Includes bibliographical references and index.

ISBN 978-1-4129-9292-3 (cloth)

1. People with disabilities—Employment.
2. Work environment. I. Barrington, Linda.
II. Title.

HD7255.B78 2012
331.5'9—dc23   2012020493

12 13 14 15 16 10 9 8 7 6 5 4 3 2

Contents

Series Introduction

The SAGE Reference Series on Disability appears at a time when global attention is being focused on disability at all levels of society. Researchers, service providers, and policymakers are concerned with the prevalence, experience, meanings, and costs of disability because of the growing impact of disability on individuals and their families and subsequent increased demand for services (Banta & de Wit, 2008; Martin et al., 2010; Mont, 2007; Whitaker, 2010). For their part, disabled people and their families are keenly interested in taking a more proactive stance in recognizing and dealing with disability in their lives (Charlton, 1998; Iezzoni & O'Day, 2006). As a result, there is burgeoning literature, heightened Web activity, myriad Internet information and discussion groups, and new policy proposals and programs designed to produce evidence and disseminate information so that people with disabilities may be informed and live more independently (see, for example, the World Institute of Disability Web site at http://www.wid.org, the Center for International Rehabilitation Research Information and Exchange Web site at http://cirrie .buffalo.edu, and the Web portal to caregiver support groups at http:// www.caregiver.com/regionalresources/index.htm).

Disability is recognized as a critical medical and social problem in current society, central to the discussions of health care and social welfare policies taking place around the world. The prominence of these disability issues is highlighted by the attention given to them by the most respected national and international organizations. The *World Report on Disability* (2011), co-sponsored by the World Health Organization (WHO) and the World Bank and based on an analysis of surveys from over 100 countries, estimates that 15% of the world's population (more than 1 billion people) currently experiences disability. This is the best prevalence estimate available today and indicates a marked increase over previous epidemiological calculations. Based on this work, the British medical journal *Lancet* dedicated an entire issue (November 28, 2009) to disability, focusing attention on the salience of the problem for health care systems worldwide. In addition, the WHO has developed community-based rehabilitation principles and strategies which are applicable to communities of diverse cultures and at all levels of development (WHO, 2010). The World Bank is concerned because of the link between disability and poverty (World Bank, 2004). Disability, in their view, could be a major impediment to economic development, particularly in emerging economies.

Efforts to address the problem of disability also have legal and human rights implications. Being disabled has historically led to discrimination, stigma, and dependency, which diminish an individual's full rights to citizenship and equality (European Disability Forum, 2003). In response to these concerns, the United Nations Convention on the Rights of Persons with Disabilities (2008) and the European Union Disability Strategy embodying the Charter of Fundamental Rights (2000) were passed to affirm that disabled people have the right to acquire and change nationalities, cannot be deprived of their ability to exercise liberty, have freedom of movement, are free to leave any country including their own, are not deprived of the right to enter their own country, and have access to the welfare and benefits afforded to any citizen of their country. As of March 31, 2010, 144 nations—including the United States, China, India, and Russia—had signed the U.N. Convention, and the European Union Disability Strategy had been ratified by all members of the European Community. These international agreements supplement and elaborate disability rights legislation such as the Americans with Disabilities Act of 1990 and its amendments, the U.K. Disability Discrimination Act of 1995, and the Disabled Person's Fundamental Law of Japan, revised in 1993.

In the United States, the Institute of Medicine of the National Academy of Sciences has persistently focused attention on the medical, public health, and social policy aspects of disability in a broad-ranging series of reports: *Disability in America* (1991), *Enabling America* (1997), *The Dynamics of Disability: Measuring and Monitoring Disability for Social Security Programs* (2002), *The Future of Disability in America* (2007), and *Improving the Presumptive Disability Decision-Making Process for Veterans* (2008). The Centers for Disease Control have a long-standing interest in diabetes and obesity because of their effects on morbidity, mortality, and disability. Current data show that the incidence and prevalence of obesity is rising across all age groups in the United States, that obesity is related to diabetes, which is also on the rise, and that both, taken together, increase the likelihood of experiencing disability

(Bleich et al., 2008; Gill et al., 2010). People with diabetes also are likely to have comorbid depression, which increases their chances of functional disability (Egede, 2004).

Depression and other types of mental illness—like anxiety disorders, alcohol and drug dependence, and impulse-control disorders—are more prevalent than previously thought and often result in disability (Kessler & Wang, 2008). The prevalence of mental disorders in the United States is high, with about half of the population meeting criteria (as measured by the *Diagnostic and Statistical Manual of Mental Disorders,* or DSM-IV) for one or more disorders in their lifetimes, and more than one-quarter of the population meeting criteria for a disorder in any single year. The more severe mental disorders are strongly associated with high comorbidity, resulting in disability.

Major American foundations with significant health portfolios have also turned their attention to disability. The Bill and Melinda Gates Foundation has directed considerable resources to eliminate disability-causing parasitic and communicable diseases such as malaria, elephantiasis, and river blindness. These efforts are designed to prevent and control disability-causing conditions in the developing world that inhibit personal independence and economic development. The Robert Wood Johnson Foundation has a long-standing program on self-determination for people with developmental disabilities in the United States aimed at increasing their ability to participate fully in society, and the Hogg Foundation is dedicated to improving mental health awareness and services. Taken in concert, these activities underscore the recognized importance of disability in the present world.

Disability Concepts, Models, and Theories

There is an immense literature on disability concepts, models, and theories. An in-depth look at these issues and controversies can be found in the *Handbook of Disability Studies* (Albrecht, Seelman, & Bury, 2001), in the *Encyclopedia of Disability* (Albrecht, 2006), and in "The Sociology of Disability: Historical Foundations and Future Directions" (Albrecht, 2010). For the purposes of this reference series, it is useful to know that the World Health Organization, in the International Classification of Functioning, Disability and Health (ICF), defines disability as "an umbrella term for impairments, activity limitations or participation restrictions" (WHO, 2001, p. 3). ICF also lists environmental factors that interact with all these constructs. Further, the WHO defines impairments as "problems in body function or structure such as significant deviation or loss"; activity limitations as "difficulties an individual may have in executing activities"; participation as "involvement in a life situation"; and environmental factors as those components of "the physical, social and attitudinal environment in which people live and conduct their lives" (WHO, 2001, p. 10). The U.N. Convention on the Rights of Persons with Disabilities, in turn, defines disability as including "those who have long-term physical, mental, intellectual or sensory impairments which in interaction with various barriers may hinder their full and effective participation in society on an equal basis with others." In the introduction to the *Lancet* special issue on disability, Officer and Groce (2009) conclude that "both the ICF and the Convention view disability as the outcome of complex interactions between health conditions and features of an individual's physical, social, and attitudinal environment that hinder their full and effective participation in society" (p. 1795). Hence, disability scholars and activists alike are concerned with breaking down physical, environmental, economic, and social barriers so that disabled people can live independently and participate as fully as possible in society.

Types of Disability

Interest in disability by medical practitioners has traditionally been condition specific (such as spinal cord injury or disabilities due to heart disease), reflecting the medical model approach to training and disease taxonomies. Similarly, disabled people and their families are often most concerned about their particular conditions and how best to deal with them. The SAGE Reference Series on Disability recognizes that there are a broad range of disabilities that can be generally conceived of as falling in the categories of physical, mental, intellectual, and sensory disabilities. In practice, disabled persons may have more than one disability and are often difficult to place in one disability category. For instance, a spinal-cord injured individual might experience depression, and a person with multiple sclerosis may simultaneously deal with physical and sensory disabilities. It is also important to note that disabilities are dynamic. People do experience different rates of onset, progression, remission, and even transition from being disabled at one point in time, to not being disabled at another, to being disabled again. Examples of this change in disability status include disability due to bouts of arthritis, Guillain-Barré Syndrome, and postpartum depression.

Disability Language

The symbols and language used to represent disability have sparked contentious debates over the years. In the *Handbook of Disability Studies* (Albrecht, Seelman, & Bury, 2001) and the *Encyclopedia of Disability* (Albrecht, 2006), authors from different countries were encouraged to use the terms and language of their cultures, but to explain them when necessary. In the present volumes, authors may use "people with disabilities" or "disabled people" to refer to individuals experiencing disability. Scholars in the United States have preferred "people with disabilities" (people-first language), while those in the United Kingdom, Canada, and Australia generally use "disabled people." In languages other than English, scholars typically use some form of the "disabled people" idiom. The U.S. version emphasizes American exceptionalism and the individual, whereas "disabled people" highlights the group and their minority status or state of being different. In my own writing, I have chosen "disabled people" because it stresses human diversity and variation.

In a recent discussion of this issue, DePoy and Gilson (2010) "suggest that maintaining debate and argument on what language is most correct derails a larger and more profound needed change, that of equalizing resources, valuation, and respect. Moreover, . . . locating disability 'with a person' reifies its embodiment and flies in the very face of the social model that person-first language is purported to espouse. . . . We have not heard anyone suggest that beauty, kindness, or even unkindness be located after personhood." While the debate is not likely over, we state why we use the language that we do.

Organization of the Series

These issues were important in conceiving of and organizing the SAGE Reference Series on Disability. Instead of developing the series around specific disabilities resulting from Parkinson's disease or bi-polar disorder, or according to the larger categories of physical, mental, intellectual, and sensory disabilities, we decided to concentrate on the major topics that confront anyone interested in or experiencing disability. Thus, the series consists of eight volumes constructed around the following topics:

- Arts and Humanities
- Assistive Technology and Science

- Disability Through the Life Course
- Education
- Employment and Work
- Ethics, Law, and Policy
- Health and Medicine
- Rehabilitation Interventions

To provide structure, we chose to use a similar organization for each volume. Therefore, each volume contains the following elements:

Series Introduction

Preface

About the Author

About the Series Editor

Chapter 1. Introduction, Background, and History

Chapter 2. Current Issues, Controversies, and Solutions

Chapter 3. Chronology of Critical Events

Chapter 4. Biographies of Key Contributors in the Field

Chapter 5. Annotated Data, Statistics, Tables, and Graphs

Chapter 6. Annotated List of Organizations and Associations

Chapter 7. Selected Print and Electronic Resources

Glossary of Key Terms

Index

The Audience

The eight-volume SAGE Reference Series on Disability targets an audience of undergraduate students and general readers that uses both academic and public libraries. However, the content and depth of the series will also make it attractive to graduate students, researchers, and policymakers. The series has been edited to have a consistent format and accessible style. The focus in each volume is on providing lay-friendly overviews of broad issues and guideposts for further research and exploration.

The series is innovative in that it will be published and marketed worldwide, with each volume available in electronic format soon after it appears in print. The print version consists of eight bound volumes. The electronic version is available through the SAGE Reference Online platform, which hosts 200 handbooks and encyclopedias across the social sciences, including the *Handbook of Disability Studies* and the *Encyclopedia of Disability*. With access to this platform through college, university, and public libraries, students, the lay public, and scholars can search these interrelated disability and social science sources from their computers or handheld and smart phone devices. The movement to an electronic platform presages the cloud computing revolution coming upon us. Cloud computing "refers to 'everything' a user may reach via the Internet, including services, storage, applications and people" (Hoehl & Sieh, 2010). According to Ray Ozzie (2010), recently Microsoft's chief architect, "We're moving toward a world of (1) cloud-based continuous services that connect us all and do our bidding, and (2) appliance-like connected devices enabling us to interact with those cloud-based services." Literally, information will be available at consumers' fingertips. Given the ample links to other resources in emerging databases, they can pursue any topic of interest in detail. This resource builds on the massive efforts to make information available to decision makers in real time, such as computerizing health and hospital records so that the diagnosis and treatment of chronic diseases and disabilities can be better managed (Celler, Lovell, & Basilakis, 2003). The SAGE Reference Series on Disability provides Internet and Web site addresses which lead the user into a world of social networks clustered around disability in general and specific conditions and issues. Entering and engaging with social networks revolving around health and disability promises to help individuals make more informed decisions and provide support in times of need (Smith & Christakis, 2008). The SAGE Reference Online platform will also be configured and updated to make it increasingly accessible to disabled people.

The SAGE Reference Series on Disability provides an extensive index for each volume. Through its placement on the SAGE Reference Online platform, the series will be fully searchable and cross-referenced, will allow keyword searching, and will be connected to the *Handbook of Disability Studies* and the *Encyclopedia of Disability*.

The authors of the volumes have taken considerable effort to vet the references, data, and resources for accuracy and credibility. The multiple Web sites for current data, information, government and United Nations documents, research findings, expert recommendations, self-help, discussion groups, and social policy are particularly useful, as they are being continuously updated. Examples of current and forthcoming data are the results and analysis of the findings of the U.S. 2010 Census, the ongoing reports of the Centers for Disease Control on disability, the World Health Organization's *World Report on Disability* and its updates, the World Bank reports on disability, poverty, and development, and reports from major foundations like Robert Wood Johnson, Bill and Melinda Gates, Ford, and Hogg. In terms of clinical outcomes, the evaluation of cost-effective interventions, management of disability, and programs that work, enormous attention is being given to evidence-based outcomes (Brownson, Fielding, & Maylahn, 2009; Marcus et al., 2006; Wolinsky et al., 2007) and comparative effectiveness research (Etheredge, 2010; Inglehart, 2010). Such data force a re-examination of policymakers' arguments. For example, there is mounting evidence that demonstrates the beneficial effects of exercise on preventing disability and enhancing function (Marcus et al., 2006). Recent studies also show that some health care reform initiatives may negatively affect disabled people's access to and costs of health care (Burns, Shah, & Smith, 2010). Furthermore, the seemingly inexorable rise in health care spending may not be correlated with desirable health outcomes (Rothberg et al., 2010). In this environment, valid data are the currency of the discussion (Andersen, Lollar, & Meyers, 2000). The authors' hopes are that this reference series will encourage students and the lay public to base their discussions and decisions on valid outcome data. Such an approach tempers the influence of ideologies surrounding health care and misconceptions about disabled people, their lives, and experiences.

SAGE Publications has made considerable effort to make these volumes accessible to disabled people in the printed book version and in the electronic platform format. In turn, SAGE and other publishers and vendors like Amazon are incorporating greater flexibility in the user interface to improve functionality to a broad range of users, such as disabled people. These efforts are important for disabled people as universities, governments, and health service delivery organizations are moving toward a paperless environment.

In the spirit of informed discussion and transparency, may this reference series encourage people from many different walks of life to become knowledgeable and engaged in the disability world. As a consequence, social policies should become better informed and individuals and families should be able to make better decisions regarding the experience of disability in their lives.

Acknowledgments

I would like to recognize the vision of Rolf Janke in developing SAGE Publications' presence in the disability field, as represented by the *Handbook of Disability Studies* (2001), the five-volume *Encyclopedia of Disability* (2006), and now the eight-volume SAGE Reference Series on Disability. These products have helped advance the field and have made critical work accessible to scholars, students, and the general public through books and now the SAGE Reference Online platform. Jim Brace-Thompson at SAGE handled the signing of contracts and kept this complex project coordinated and moving on time. Kevin Hillstrom and Laurie Collier Hillstrom at Northern Lights Writers Group were intrepid in taking the composite pieces of this project and polishing and editing them into a coherent whole that is approachable, consistent in style and form, and rich in content. The authors of the eight volumes—Linda Barrington, Jerome Bickenbach, Cathy Bodine, Brenda Brueggemann, Susanne Bruyère, Lana Collet-Klingenberg, Cheryl Hanley-Maxwell, Sarah Parker Harris, Tamar Heller, Nancy Mudrick, Ross Mullner, and Peggy Turk—are to be commended for their enthusiasm, creativity, and fortitude in delivering high-quality volumes on a tight deadline. I was fortunate to work with such accomplished scholars.

Discussions with Barbara Altman, Colin Barnes, Catherine Barral, Len Barton, Isabelle Baszanger, Peter Blanck, Mary Boulton, David Braddock, Richard Burkhauser, Mike Bury, Ann Caldwell, Lennard Davis, Patrick Devlieger, Ray Fitzpatrick, Lawrence Frey, Carol Gill, Tamar Heller, Gary Kielhofner, Soewarta Kosen, Jo Lebeer, Mitch Loeb, Don Lollar, Paul Longmore, Ros Madden, Maria Martinho, Dennis Mathews, Sophie Mitra, Daniel Mont, Alana Officer, Randall Parker, David Pfeiffer, Jean-François Raveau, James Rimmer, Ed Roberts, Jean-Marie Robine, Joan Rogers, Richard Scotch, Kate Seelman, Tom Shakespeare, Sandor Sipos, Henri-Jacques Stiker, Edna Szymanski, Jutta Traviranus, Bryan Turner, Greg Vanderheiden, Isabelle Ville, Larry Voss, Ann Waldschmidt, and Irving Kenneth Zola over the years contributed to the content, logic, and structure of the series. They also were a wonderful source of suggestions for authors.

I would also like to acknowledge the hospitality and support of the Belgian Academy of Science and the Arts, the University of Leuven, Nuffield College, the University of Oxford, the Fondation Maison des Sciences de l'Homme, Paris, and the Department of Disability and Human

Development at the University of Illinois at Chicago, who provided the time and environments to conceive of and develop the project. While none of these people or institutions is responsible for any deficiencies in the work, they all helped enormously in making it better.

Gary L. Albrecht
University of Illinois at Chicago
University of Leuven
Belgian Academy of Science and Arts

References

Albrecht, G. L. (Ed.). (2006). *Encyclopedia of disability* (5 vols.). Thousand Oaks, CA: Sage.

Albrecht, G. L. (2010). The sociology of disability: Historical foundations and future directions. In C. Bird, A. Fremont, S. Timmermans, & P. Conrad (Eds.), *Handbook of medical sociology* (6th ed., pp. 192–209). Nashville, TN: Vanderbilt University Press.

Albrecht, G. L., Seelman, K. D., & Bury, M. (Eds.). (2001). *Handbook of disability studies.* Thousand Oaks, CA: Sage.

Andersen, E. M., Lollar, D. J., & Meyers, A. R. (2000). Disability outcomes research: Why this supplement, on this topic, at this time? *Archives of Physical Medicine and Rehabilitation, 81,* S1–S4.

Banta, H. D., & de Wit, G. A. (2008). Public health services and cost-effectiveness analysis. *Annual Review of Public Health, 29,* 383–397.

Bleich, S., Cutler, D., Murray, C., & Adams, A. (2008). Why is the developed world obese? *Annual Review of Public Health, 29,* 273–295.

Brownson, R. C., Fielding, J. E., & Maylahn, C. M. (2009). Evidence-based public health: A fundamental concept for public health practice. *Annual Review of Public Health, 30,* 175–201.

Burns, M., Shah, N., & Smith, M. (2010). Why some disabled adults in Medicaid face large out-of-pocket expenses. *Health Affairs, 29,* 1517–1522.

Celler, B. G., Lovell, N. H., & Basilakis, J. (2003). Using information technology to improve the management of chronic disease. *Medical Journal of Australia, 179,* 242–246.

Charlton, J. I. (1998). *Nothing about us without us: Disability, oppression and empowerment.* Berkeley: University of California Press.

DePoy, E., & Gilson, S. F. (2010). *Studying disability: Multiple theories and responses.* Thousand Oaks, CA: Sage.

Egede, L. E. (2004). Diabetes, major depression, and functional disability among U.S. adults. *Diabetes Care, 27,* 421–428.

Etheredge, L. M. (2010). Creating a high-performance system for comparative effectiveness research. *Health Affairs, 29,* 1761–1767.

European Disability Forum. (2003). *Disability and social exclusion in the European Union: Time for change, tools for change.* Athens: Greek National Confederation of Disabled People.

European Union. (2000). *Charter of fundamental rights.* Retrieved from http://www.europarll.europa.eu/charter

Gill, T. M., Gahbauer, E. A., Han, L., & Allore, H. G. (2010). Trajectories of disability in the last year of life. *The New England Journal of Medicine, 362*(13), 1173–1180.

Hoehl, A. A., & Sieh, K. A. (2010). *Cloud computing and disability communities: How can cloud computing support a more accessible information age and society?* Boulder, CO: Coleman Institute.

Iezzoni, L. I., & O'Day, B. L. (2006). *More than ramps.* Oxford, UK: Oxford University Press.

Inglehart, J. K. (2010). The political fight over comparative effectiveness research. *Health Affairs, 29*, 1757–1760.

Institute of Medicine. (1991). *Disability in America.* Washington, DC: National Academies Press.

Institute of Medicine. (1997). *Enabling America.* Washington, DC: National Academies Press.

Institute of Medicine. (2001). *Health and behavior: The interplay of biological, behavioral and societal influences.* Washington, DC: National Academies Press.

Institute of Medicine. (2002). *The dynamics of disability: Measuring and monitoring disability for social security programs.* Washington, DC: National Academies Press.

Institute of Medicine. (2007). *The future of disability in America.* Washington, DC: National Academies Press.

Institute of Medicine. (2008). *Improving the presumptive disability decision-making process for veterans.* Washington, DC: National Academies Press.

Kessler, R. C., & Wang, P. S. (2008). The descriptive epidemiology of commonly occurring mental disorders in the United States. *Annual Review of Public Health, 29*, 115–129.

Marcus, B. H., Williams, D. M., Dubbert, P. M., Sallis, J. F., King, A. C., Yancey, A. K., et al. (2006). Physical activity intervention studies. *Circulation, 114*, 2739–2752.

Martin, L. G., Freedman, V. A., Schoeni, R. F., & Andreski, P. M. (2010). Trends in disability and related chronic conditions among people ages 50 to 64. *Health Affairs, 29*(4), 725–731.

Mont, D. (2007). *Measuring disability prevalence* (World Bank working paper). Washington, DC: The World Bank.

Officer, A., & Groce, N. E. (2009). Key concepts in disability. *The Lancet, 374*, 1795–1796.

Ozzie, R. (2010, October 28). *Dawn of a new day.* Ray Ozzie's Blog. Retrieved from http://ozzie.net/docs/dawn-of-a-new-day

Rothberg, M. B., Cohen, J., Lindenauer, P., Masetti, J., & Auerbach, A. (2010). Little evidence of correlation between growth in health care spending and reduced mortality. *Health Affairs, 29*, 1523–1531.

Smith, K. P., & Christakis, N. A. (2008). Social networks and health. *Annual Review of Sociology, 34,* 405–429.

United Nations. (2008). *Convention on the rights of persons with disabilities.* New York: United Nations. Retrieved from http://un.org/disabilities/convention

Whitaker, R. T. (2010). *Anatomy of an epidemic: Magic bullets, psychiatric drugs, and the astonishing rise of mental illness in America.* New York: Crown.

Wolinsky, F. D., Miller, D. K., Andresen, E. M., Malmstrom, T. K., Miller, J. P., & Miller, T. R. (2007). Effect of subclinical status in functional limitation and disability on adverse health outcomes 3 years later. *The Journals of Gerontology: Series A, 62,* 101–106.

World Bank Disability and Development Team. (2004). *Poverty reduction strategies: Their importance for disability.* Washington, DC: World Bank.

World Health Organization. (2001). *International classification of functioning, disability and health.* Geneva: Author.

World Health Organization. (2010). *Community-based rehabilitation guidelines.* Geneva and Washington, DC: Author.

World Health Organization, & World Bank. (2011). *World report on disability.* Geneva: World Health Organization.

Preface

I t is fitting that this SAGE Reference Series on Disability includes a volume on *Employment and Work.* Engaging in meaningful work not only provides each of us the means for economic self-sufficiency and independence, but it also affords us the forum whereby we can utilize our talents and skills and contribute to the community as a whole. All of these benefits of the ability to work are important to everyone, yet people with disabilities historically have been disproportionately underrepresented in the American, and more broadly the global, workforce. The importance of work globally to the well-being of people with disabilities has been confirmed in its inclusion in the United Nations Convention on the Rights of People with Disabilities, adopted in 2006, as Article 27: Work and Employment. It is the purpose of this volume to further elaborate on the importance of work, to individuals with disabilities and society at large, by providing an overview of the employment landscape for people with disabilities over time to the present date, offering an introductory "big picture" overview of selected major areas for consideration and exploration, and suggesting resources where readers might go next in pursuing further information on this topic.

In Chapter 1, *Introduction, Background, and History,* we further explore the importance of work, but we also discuss how work limitation has been used over time to actually define disability, and how changing definitions affects the way we count people with disabilities. We provide an overview of factors that affect finding a job in the American job market, including the art of matching supply and demand and the impact of public policy and other factors on the motivation of individuals to seek work. We discuss the Great Recession's impact on the employment of people with disabilities, including resulting economic disparities, as well as inequities in access to health care. This chapter also includes an historical overview of how we have dealt with employment for people with disabilities in America, including services to veterans, industrialization and job injuries, and the expansion of civil rights for people with disabilities.

In Chapter 2, *Current Issues, Controversies, and Solutions,* we discuss the factors contributing to continuing economic disparities and employment discrimination for individuals with disabilities, as well as their resulting impact, including failure to accommodate in the workplace, pay gaps, and other compensation disparities beyond wages and salary. Additional disparities experienced by specific populations, such as the aging workforce, ethnic/racial minorities with disabilities, and people with particular types of disabilities, are also discussed. This chapter also includes discussion of some current controversies that scholars, policy-makers, and advocates struggle with in their respective work to improve employment outcomes for people with disabilities, including conflicting policy incentives, the extent of employer efforts at inclusiveness versus litigation-avoidance, and equal opportunity versus quota requirements. We end this chapter with a discussion of possible solutions to address continuing challenges.

In Chapter 3, *Chronology of Critical Events,* we trace the legislation, systems formulation, public policies, and changing philosophical approaches that have etched their mark into the landscape of employment and work for people with disabilities over the past six centuries, from the 1500s to the present time.

In Chapter 4, *Biographies of Key Contributors in the Field,* we provide information on 40 of the scholars, policymakers, and disability advocates who have been instrumental thinkers and leaders in shaping our understanding of the employment status of people with disabilities, and also in creating public policies which address the employment disparities we are confronted with. Biographical sketches and selected key writings are provided for each person.

In Chapter 5, *Annotated Data, Statistics, Tables, and Graphs,* we provide information on employment and disability data sources, and how disability and employment are defined across a number of national survey and administrative data sources. We discuss employment and economic disparities, including U.S. employment rates over time, international employment rates, income and earning disparities, and resulting higher poverty levels for people with disabilities. In this chapter, we also provide information on where people with disabilities work, in terms of occupation, class of jobs, and industries. Workplace discrimination information is provided through the U.S. Equal Employment Opportunity Commission's charge data on disability employment discrimination, comparing it to rates of employment discrimination charges under laws affording protections on the basis of age, gender, and race/ethnicity. We end this chapter with information about statistics available on who is out of the workforce, including those displaced through occupational illness and injury and now on workers' compensation; those on public benefits because of disability, such as Social Security Disability Insurance (SSDI) and Social Security Insurance (SSI); and those receiving vocational rehabilitation (VR) services through state agencies.

Chapter 6, *Annotated List of Organizations and Associations,* and Chapter 7, *Selected Print and Electronic Resources,* include extensive reference material to afford the reader ample opportunity for further research on select topics, as their interests might lead them. In these chapters, we provide a brief description, contact information, and Web sites for almost 200 organizations and associations, and 100 print and electronic resources.

It is our hope that this volume will contribute to the thinking of college and university students, people with disabilities and their advocates and family members, and the general public about the importance of work for people with disabilities. Without employment, many of us do not have the means to live independently, and often feel—if we are not in fact—alienated from the mainstream of American life. Meaningful work, where we are fairly compensated and valued as a contributing member of a work unit and of society more broadly, not only contributes to the American economy, but contributes to our sense of self and self-worth. Everyone deserves to have the opportunity to be an active part of the American workforce. This volume is about how we can make that dream a reality for people with disabilities in America and around the world.

Acknowledgments

An effort such as this volume in the SAGE Reference Series on Disability requires the significant work of many people to bring about a successful outcome. We would like to thank Gary Albrecht, series editor, and Jim Brace-Thompson, senior editor at Sage Reference, for their vision, and our publishers at SAGE for conceptualizing and shepherding this series to completion. We would also like to thank Kevin Hillstrom and Laurie Collier Hillstrom of Northern Lights Writers Group for their excellent editorial support and for helping us make sure that our volume aligned with and added value to the overarching series.

Support for our time to contribute to this series has been funded by a grant from the U.S. Department of Education National Institute on Disability and Rehabilitation Research (NIDRR) to Cornell University for a Rehabilitation Research and Training Center on Employment Policy and Individuals with Disabilities (Grant No. H133B040013). Our thanks go to our NIDRR Project Director, David Keer, for his ever-supportive and collegial guidance and encouragement.

Closer to home, we would like to acknowledge the contributions of many of our Cornell University ILR School and Employment and Disability Institute (EDI) colleagues whose writing, research, and knowledge added insight and content to this volume.

Sarah von Schrader and **Bill Erickson**, researchers from the Employment and Disability Institute, drew upon their robust expertise in disability statistics and national survey and administrative data sets to provide the material presented in Chapter 5, *Annotated Data, Statistics, Tables, and Graphs.* Their contribution to this volume enables us to provide the reader with up-to-date information on available employment and disability data sources, employment and economic disparities, where people with disabilities work, workplace discrimination, and data detailing who is in and out of the workforce due to disability.

Thomas Golden, Associate Director of the Employment and Disability Institute, has long-standing expertise in Social Security benefits, as well as employment and disability public policy more broadly. He added substantive insights on legislative history and contemporary public policy issues as well as overall contextual structure to our Chapter 1, *Introduction, Background, and History.*

Arun Karpur, EDI research associate, whose specialties include epidemiological research and program evaluation, contributed on the topics of health care policy and employer wellness practices.

Sara Furguson, Cornell University student research associate, assisted us in identifying events for inclusion for our Chapter 3, *Chronology of Critical Events,* as well as the related associations and information resources provided in Chapter 6, *Annotated List of Organizations and Associations,* and Chapter 7, *Selected Print and Electronic Resources.*

Margaret Waelder, EDI administrative and research assistant, was of great assistance in tracking down information on individual experts' publications included in our Chapter 4, *Biographies of Key Contributors in the Field.*

Melissa Bjelland, EDI economist and researcher, provided excellent technical editing assistance on final versions of our work. **Kevin Hallock**, Joseph R. Rich '80 Professor and Director of the Institute for Compensation Studies, offered guidance on the topic of pay gaps.

Finally, our sincerest thanks must go to **Nancy Elshami** and **Sara VanLooy,** research assistants from the Employment and Disability Institute and the Institute for Compensation Studies, who were our partners and collaborators throughout this process, helping us to conduct literature reviews and identify needed references, and providing excellent overarching editorial support.

Without these terrific colleagues, this effort would not have been possible, and we are most grateful for their substantive assistance.

Susanne M. Bruyère and Linda Barrington

About the Authors

Susanne M. Bruyère, Ph.D., CRC, is currently Professor of Disability Studies, Director of the Employment and Disability Institute, and Associate Dean of Outreach at the Cornell University ILR (Industrial and Labor Relations) School in Ithaca, New York.

Dr. Bruyère is currently Project Director and Co-Principal Investigator of numerous federally sponsored research, dissemination, and technical assistance efforts focused on employment and disability policy and effective workplace practices for people with disabilities, including the U.S. Department of Labor Office of Disability and Employment Policy National Technical Assistance, Policy, and Research Center for Employers on Employment of People with Disabilities; the Rehabilitation Research and Training Center on Employer Practices to Improve Employment Outcomes for Persons with Disabilities; and Organizational Practices to Increase Employment Opportunities for People with Disabilities: The Power of Social Networks. She is a past president of the American Rehabilitation Counseling Association, National Council on Rehabilitation Education, and Division of Rehabilitation Psychology (22) of the American Psychological Association, and past Chair of GLADNET (the Global Applied Disability Research and Information Network on Employment and Training) and the CARF (Committee on Accreditation of Rehabilitation Facilities) Board of Directors.

Dr. Bruyère holds a doctoral degree in Rehabilitation Psychology from the University of Wisconsin-Madison. She is a Fellow in the American Psychological Association, a member of the National Academy of Social Insurance, and currently serves as an Executive Board Member of the Division of Rehabilitation Psychology (22) of the American Psychological Association.

Linda Barrington, Ph.D., is Managing Director of the Institute for Compensation Studies (ICS) in the ILR School at Cornell University. ICS is an interdisciplinary initiative that analyzes, teaches, and communicates broadly about monetary and nonmonetary rewards from work.

Dr. Barrington's work appears in the *Review of Economics and Statistics,* the *Journal of Economic History,* and the *Historical Statistics of the U.S.,* as well as in numerous business/practitioner reports. She is editor and contributing author to *The Other Side of the Frontier: Economic Explorations into Native American Economic History.*

Dr. Barrington has received underwriting for her research from various sources, including the Atlantic Philanthropies, Rockefeller Foundation, Russell Sage Foundation, Gates Foundation, and most recently the U.S. Department of Education's National Institute on Disability and Rehabilitation Research.

Dr. Barrington comes to the Institute for Compensation Studies from The Conference Board, a global business membership and research organization. There, she held several positions over the past 10 years, including economist, special assistant to the CEO, research director, and most recently Managing Director of Human Capital. Prior to The Conference Board, Dr. Barrington served on the economics faculty at Barnard College of Columbia University. There she published several articles on gender economics, poverty measurement, and economic history.

Dr. Barrington earned a Ph.D. in economics from the University of Illinois, and a B.S. in economics from the University of Wisconsin.

About the Series Editor

Gary L. Albrecht is a Fellow of the Royal Belgian Academy of Arts and Sciences, Extraordinary Guest Professor of Social Sciences, University of Leuven, Belgium, and Professor Emeritus of Public Health and of Disability and Human Development at the University of Illinois at Chicago. After receiving his Ph.D. from Emory University, he has served on the faculties of Emory University in Sociology and Psychiatry, Northwestern University in Sociology, Rehabilitation Medicine, and the Kellogg School of Management, and the University of Illinois at Chicago (UIC) in the School of Public Health and in the Department of Disability and Human Development. Since retiring from the UIC in 2005, he has divided his time between Europe and the United States, working in Brussels, Belgium, and Boulder, Colorado. He has served as a Scholar in Residence at the Maison des Sciences de l'Homme (MSH) in Paris, a visiting Fellow at Nuffield College, the University of Oxford, and a Fellow in Residence at the Royal Flemish Academy of Science and Arts, Brussels.

His research has focused on how adults acknowledge, interpret, and respond to unanticipated life events, such as disability onset. His work, supported by over $25 million of funding, has resulted in 16 books and over 140 articles and book chapters. He is currently working on a longitudinal study of disabled Iranian, Moroccan, Turkish, Jewish, and Congolese immigrants to Belgium. Another current project involves working with an international team on "Disability: A Global Picture," Chapter 2 of the *World Report on Disability,* co-sponsored by the World Health Organization and the World Bank, published in 2011.

He is past Chair of the Medical Sociology Section of the American Sociological Association, a past member of the Executive Committee of the

Disability Forum of the American Public Health Association, an early member of the Society for Disability Studies, and an elected member of the Society for Research in Rehabilitation (UK). He has received the Award for the Promotion of Human Welfare and the Eliot Freidson Award for the book *The Disability Business: Rehabilitation in America.* He also has received a Switzer Distinguished Research Fellowship, Schmidt Fellowship, New York State Supreme Court Fellowship, Kellogg Fellowship, National Library of Medicine Fellowship, World Health Organization Fellowship, the Lee Founders Award from the Society for the Study of Social Problems, the Licht Award from the American Congress of Rehabilitation Medicine, the University of Illinois at Chicago Award for Excellence in Teaching, and has been elected Fellow of the American Association for the Advancement of Science (AAAS). He has led scientific delegations in rehabilitation medicine to the Soviet Union and the People's Republic of China and served on study sections, grant review panels, and strategic planning committees on disability in Australia, Canada, the European Community, France, Ireland, Japan, Poland, South Africa, Sweden, the United Kingdom, the United States, and the World Health Organization, Geneva. His most recent books are *The Handbook of Social Studies in Health and Medicine,* edited with Ray Fitzpatrick and Susan Scrimshaw (SAGE, 2000), the *Handbook of Disability Studies,* edited with Katherine D. Seelman and Michael Bury (SAGE, 2001), and the five-volume *Encyclopedia of Disability* (SAGE, 2006).

One

Introduction, Background, and History

Why Work? Employment Outcomes of People With Disabilities in America

"Work keeps us from three great evils: boredom, vice, and poverty."

—Voltaire, *Candide*, 1759

"What we do is a large part of what we are."

—Alan Ryan, British political philosopher, 1996

Introduction: Why Work?

Importance of Employment and Work

Our view of work and the jobs we do has evolved from Voltaire's articulation of work as a means to avert moral defect and starvation to Ryan's definition of work as effectively defining one's identity or core being. Today, to a

1

large extent, we are what we "do." This evolving emphasis on work has not bypassed people with disabilities. Improving employment outcomes for persons with disabilities has, in parallel, increased in importance.

Studies have shown that employment is not only important for monetary and personal fulfillment, but also for the maintenance of health and even happiness. Sullivan and von Wachter (2009), whose research matched quarterly earnings and employment records to death certificates, found that job loss leads to a 10% to 15% increase in annual death rates during the subsequent 20 years. People who lose their jobs are also more prone to developing depression symptoms. Dooley, Catalano, and Wilson (1994) found that people who become unemployed have over twice the risk of depressive symptoms than those who remain employed (see also Hallock, 2009).

Research shows that having a job is an important determinant of self-esteem and provides a critical link between an individual and society (Doyle, Kavanagh, Metcalfe, & Lavin, 2005). According to the World Health Organization (WHO), "although it is difficult to quantify the impact of work alone on personal identity, self-esteem and social recognition, most mental health professionals agree that the workplace environment can have a significant impact on an individual's mental well-being" (Harnois & Gabriel, 2000, p. 5). The WHO notes that employment provides time structure, social contact, collective effort and purpose, social identity, and regular activity, which are all essential factors to maintaining a healthy lifestyle. The absence of any of these factors can pose a major psychological burden.

The sense of purposefulness and life meaning that work can provide contributes to a sense of overall well-being that results in improved health status and rehabilitation outcomes. Increased purpose in life has been shown to be associated with positive adaptation following spinal cord injury (deRoon-Cassini, de St. Aubin, Valvano, Hastins, & Horn, 2009), to affect the risk of death from all causes, stroke, and cardiovascular disease (Koizumi, Ito, Kaneko, & Motohashi, 2008), and to contribute to a substantially reduced risk of Alzheimer's disease (Boyle, Buchman, Barnes, & Bennett, 2010).

Gainful and meaningful employment are not synonymous, but achieving both involves two considerations: the employment process (being hired for a particular position that is appropriate to one's skills and abilities); and the workplace experience (what happens once an employee is on the job). Clearly, both of these considerations underpin successful work outcomes for all individuals, and for people with disabilities in particular. The lead actors in both the employment process and the workplace experience are the employers and the individual job seekers and employees, but they are not acting alone. Policymakers, service delivery providers, and even profit incentives of employers combine to motivate, force, or influence employers, job seekers, and employees.

In this chapter we discuss the definition of and framework for analyzing employment outcomes, the employment process, important factors in the workplace experience, indicators of disparities in employment outcomes for people with disabilities, and how consideration of employment for people with disabilities has evolved and continues to evolve.

Does Work Limitation Define a Person With a Disability?

Assessing how we are doing in the employment of people with disabilities necessitates being able to measure employment outcomes in some manner. To measure the employment outcomes of people with disabilities requires defining both who is a person with a disability and who is employed, and neither has a unique characterization. To confound matters, the ability to work is so integral to the discussion of people with disabilities that "work limitation" has commonly, and in some cases continues to be, integral to defining who is a person with a disability.[1]

Not surprisingly, overlaying different definitions of disability and employment affect the estimates of employment outcomes. Lower employment rates for people with disabilities are estimated when the threshold for being defined as employed is higher or the definition of disability is stricter (limited to more severe disabilities).

"Official" Definition of a Person With a Disability

How disability is defined officially by the U.S. government varies according to the purpose for which the definition is being used, and it is often connected to a particular federal or state program or service. The Americans with Disabilities Act, the Rehabilitation Act of 1973 (Section 503), and the Workforce Investment Act (Section 188) define a person with a disability as someone who (a) has a physical or mental impairment that substantially limits one or more "major life activities," (b) has a record of such an impairment, or (c) is regarded as having such an impairment. But, for purposes of qualifying for Social Security disability benefits, individuals must have a severe disability (or combination of disabilities) that has lasted, or is expected to last, at least 12 months or result in death, and which prevents working at a "substantial gainful activity" level. State vocational rehabilitation (VR) offices, on the other hand, will find a person with a disability to be eligible for VR services if he or she has a physical or mental impairment that constitutes or results in a "substantial impediment" to employment for the applicant (U.S. Department of Labor, n.d.).

Distinctions also exist for the degree of disability. The Rehabilitation Act defines an individual with a significant disability, for example, as an individual with a disability who "has a severe physical or mental impairment which seriously limits one or more functional capacities (such as mobility, communication, self-care, self-direction, interpersonal skills, work tolerance, or work skills) in terms of an employment outcome" whose "vocational rehabilitation can be expected to require multiple vocational rehabilitation services over an extended period of time" and who "has one or more physical or mental disabilities" resulting from a number of serious causes[2] (Rehabilitation Act of 1973, as amended).

In the context of employment and work outcomes, broader or narrower definitions of who is a person with a disability can produce notable variation in the count of persons with disabilities in the United States. For example, among the working-age U.S. population between the ages of 25 and 61[3], there exists a range of estimates from a handful of the most reputable sources of disability data available during the first decade of the 21st century, the highest, 26.6 million (in 2002), from the Survey of Income and Program Participation (SIPP) and the lowest, 11.2 million (in 2003), based on the work limitation disability definition in the Annual Social and Economic Supplement to the Current Population Survey (CPS-ASEC). (See Chapter 5 for more thorough discussion of definitions and measures of prevalence.)

Concern about improving the measurement of employment outcomes for people with disabilities was evidenced by President Bill Clinton in 1998, when he issued Executive Order 13078. It mandated "the development of an accurate and reliable measure of the employment rate of people with disabilities, to be published as frequently as possible." The definition of disability stated in the Executive Order is an adult "with a physical or mental impairment that substantially limits at least one major life activity."

After a decade of governmental workgroups and content testing of various survey questions, a six-question query to identify disability status was introduced into the Current Population Survey (CPS) beginning in June 2008.[4] The CPS is administered on a monthly basis. It provides the official source of labor force data (e.g., unemployment rates) for the United States, with results released the last Friday of every month by the Commissioner of the Department of Labor in the *Employment Situation* report. While government definitions of disability still vary according to program and service needs, the fulfillment of Executive Order 13078 has meant that persons with disabilities now receive the same broad visibility in official employment statistics as other major demographic groups (e.g., gender, race/ethnicity, and veteran status). The CPS continues to contain, and has contained since 1981, a work limitation measure on the CPS-ASEC.

The disability questions used in the CPS give respondents six disability types under which to categorize themselves and members of their households aged 15 and older: hearing, visual, cognitive, ambulatory, self-care, and independent living. People recorded as having a limitation in any of the six areas are those defined as having disabilities. People reported as having difficulty with self-care or other routine actions (dressing, bathing, shopping alone, visiting the doctor) are considered to have "limitations in daily activities, a more significant level of disability that may require help from other people to perform such activities" (Kaye, 2010, p. 20). The importance of this richer definition being included in the CPS is well-articulated by Kaye, who wrote, "It is now possible to track month-to-month changes in the employment levels of people with various types of disabilities, with only a few weeks' lag between data collection and analysis. The new survey measures even allow for tracking individual respondents as their labor force status changes from month to month"[5] (2010, p. 20). This more detailed information on disability has just begun to contribute to better understanding of employment outcomes for people with disabilities.

When comparing employment outcomes for people with disabilities to those of their nondisabled peers, defining disability by a "work limitation" may seem an obvious weakness in the statistical record, bordering on tautology. Executive Order 13078 and the inclusion of the set of six disability questions in the ACS and CPS have been a significant improvement in the availability of reliable disability data. Despite this change, the "work limitation" question nonetheless remains a commonly used definition in investigating employment outcomes for people with disabilities, because it is the only disability status question that has been in continuous use in a governmental survey for several decades. The Annual Social and Economic

Supplement of the CPS-ASEC has used the work limitation question for over 30 years, dating back to 1981. It therefore continues to provide the continuity so crucial for establishing credible time series of data (for more information on how different surveys define disability, see Brault, 2008).

The recent decades of scientific advances in new technologies and medicines have allowed more persons with disabilities the opportunity to work. For example, voice recognition software has improved dramatically (evident in Siri, the "voice function" of the 2011 iPhone). Recently, "sip and puff" technology has allowed the person with little or no upper-limb function to operate a wheelchair or other devices by sucking or blowing air through a tube. Highly sensitive touch pads for the mouth have also very recently been developed. By touching different keys with the tongue, someone with spina bifida, for example, is able to operate any number of electronic devices (Cooper, 1999; Huo, Wang, & Ghovanloo, 2008; Voice of America, 2007).

As scientific advances continue to expand the scope of medical as well as technological knowledge, definitions of people with disabilities will likely grow to include a wider array of both the population at large and those employed. One indicator of how society's awareness of disability changes over time can be found in what categories appear in documentation of the employment discrimination charges filed with the Equal Employment Opportunity Commission (EEOC). Numbers of charges against employers involving post-traumatic stress disorder (PTSD), genetic testing, or genetic discrimination were not broken out into separate categories in reports by the EEOC until after 2000 (S. von Schrader, personal communication regarding calculations from EEOC Integrated Mission System, 2011).

See the *Assistive Technology and Science* volume in this series for more information on changing medical and scientific knowledge of disabilities.

Defining Employment

Definitions of employment in official statistics also vary; some are more and some less strict in terms of how much one must work in order to be counted as employed. Under some official U.S. definitions (e.g., the American Community Survey and the Current Population Survey) a respondent who reports having worked at all during the previous week is defined as employed. Other surveys stipulate that having worked during the past two weeks (e.g., Survey of Income and Program Participation) or the past month (e.g., National Health Interview Survey) defines one as employed.

Definitions of employment may take a longer view and include anyone who worked at least 52 total hours in a year's time (working an hour a week throughout the year or just one intense 52-hour work week in a whole year would count the same). The strictest definition may limit employment to include only full-time year-round workers (at least 35 hours a week and 50 or more weeks per year). Weathers and Wittenburg (2009) define employment in their research using three levels of work intensity, or attachment to the labor force: "reference period employment," "any annual employment", and "full-time annual employment." Further considerations about what are really meaningful and truly integrated employment opportunities are discussed in this chapter in a later section ("The Art of Matching Supply and Demand").

Varying the Definitions Changes the Numbers

The specifics of the variation between diverse definitions of "employment" and "disability" in official statistics may seem superfluous; however, estimates of statistics important to understanding employment outcomes of people with disabilities do range dramatically as various definitions are applied. And, importantly, the *variability* in the measured employment rates under these differing definitions of employment and disability is far greater for persons with disabilities than for their nondisabled peers (see Table 2, Chapter 5; see also Weathers & Wittenburg, 2009, Table 4.2, p. 114).

Using the "reference period employment" definition, the U.S. employment rate among persons aged 21 to 64 years and defined as having no disability in the 2008 CPS-ASEC, for example, is 79.7% (see Figure 7, Chapter 5). Compare this to the parallel 2008 ACS rate of 79.9% for respondents with no disability, but where disability is defined as reporting one or more of the following six disability types: visual, hearing ambulatory, cognitive, independent living or self-care (see Figure 2, Chapter 5). The spread in employment rate for those with no disability under two different definitions of disability is less than one percentage point. Using the same reference period and again considering these two definitions of disability, the U.S. employment rate among persons with a disability is 17.7% in the 2008 CPS-ASEC, but 39.5% in the 2008 ACS. This is a spread of over 20 percentage points in the estimates of the employment rate of persons with disabilities when the definition of employment is held constant, but the definition of disability changes.

A similar pattern is seen using Any Annual Employment or Full-Time Annual Employment definitions of work attachment (see Table 2,

Chapter 5). Measures of employment outcome vary significantly for persons with disabilities based on the criteria used to define disability. The same volatility does not surface among the employment data for people without a disability.

Not surprisingly perhaps, for those with no disabilities, the employment rate is more affected by changing the definition of employment than by changing the definition of disability. But for those *with* a disability, changing the definition of employment has an even greater effect than it did for the nondisabled population. The employment rates drop by about one-third for those with no disability when the definition of employment is tightened from Any Annual Employment to Full-Time Annual Employment (from 86%–90% down to 58%–65%, depending on the survey). The size of the drop is closer to one-half when the employment definition is tightened equivalently for people with disabilities (see Table 2, Chapter 5).

Not surprisingly, the lowest measure of employment for persons with disabilities in recent U.S. data is reported for Full-Time Annual Employment using the "work limitation disability" definition used by the CPS-ASEC in 2003. Under this definition, fewer than 1 in 10 (9.4%) persons with a (work-limiting) disability were employed (full-time), compared to 65% of their nondisabled peers (see Table 2, Chapter 5).

While varying definitions certainly have far greater impact on the employment rate for persons with disabilities than for their nondisabled peers, it is most notable how much lower the employment rate is for persons with disabilities under any commonly used definitions of disability or employment.

Background: Finding Work in the American Job Market

The Art of Matching Supply and Demand

Securing employment is a matching game between individuals and employers—supply and demand. In its simplest form, employment happens in a "marketplace" where people looking for work bring themselves and their talents and skills to the market (supply) and employers come looking to acquire or hire the talents and skills they need (demand). If what a person offers matches what an employer is looking for, and both agree on the salary or wage (price), then employment happens.

Figure 1   Matching Market

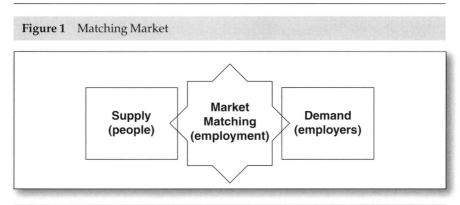

Source: Authors.

This simple story is merely the foundation for what really happens in the job market. The landscape actually encountered when people look for work and employers seek to hire is far more complex, and this is especially true for people with disabilities. To discuss the employment and career advancement of people with disabilities, it is important to understand this complexity, including the roles played by public (regulatory) policy, market-based incentives, and service delivery providers. All three of these factors can influence the employment matching process in general and among people with disabilities specifically.

Public (Regulatory) Policy

At its most basic, public policy in the realm of employment is about maintaining a balance of fairness between people on one hand and employers on the other (see Figure 2). It is important to note that while the discussion here focuses on federal policy, there is a myriad of state and local legislations regulating workplaces and employment markets as well.

Policy disproportionately favoring employers might tip the balance to allow for exploitation of employees, such as the historical but now banned use of child labor in the United States (Child Labor Public Education Project, 2010). On the other hand, policy established in the pursuit of protection of individuals could also have undesirable repercussions. For example, legislation of the early 20th century that sought to protect women from unsafe work conditions initially resulted in exclusion of women from higher paying manufacturing or construction jobs.

Figure 2 Matching Market and Policy

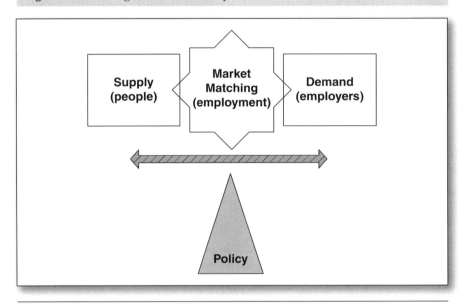

Source: Authors.

The Fair Labor Standards Act (FSLA) is the current public (federal regulatory) policy that most broadly defines the rules for employment of people in the United States, and it includes setting standards for wages (e.g., minimum wage) and work hours (e.g., 40-hour work week). It also is the most recent example of the continuing dynamics of labor market regulation. A controversial clause within the Fair Labor Standards Act of 1938, 14(c), allows the Secretary of Labor to grant special wage certificates to employers of people with disabilities, allowing them to pay sub-minimum commensurate wages.[6] On October 4, 2011, a bill was introduced in Congress to repeal the 14(c) clause. Disability advocates argue that 14(c) encourages the placement of people with disabilities in employment that does not optimize their lifetime opportunities and achievements. As the bill to repeal 14(c) states, "While some employers possessing special wage certificates claim to provide rehabilitation and training to disabled workers to prepare them for competitive employment, the fact that such employers can pay their workers less than the Federal minimum wage gives them an incentive to exploit the cheap labor provided by their disabled workers rather than to prepare those workers for integrated employment in the mainstream economy" (Fair Wages for Workers with Disabilities Act, 2011).

The goal of this legislative effort, and the subject of ongoing public debate over all labor market regulation (at the federal, state, and local levels), is determining how to set balanced policy that levels the playing field on which the game of employment matching (including pay levels) takes place.

Forcing Versus Motivating Individuals and Employers to Match Up

Viewpoints vary as to how much any person seeks employment for noble aspirations such as self-realization and doing good in the world, versus for personal enrichment or because the person is simply financially forced to work for survival. Similarly, viewpoints vary as to how much any employer seeks to provide employees with opportunities for self-advancement and improving the world, versus work environments and jobs designed to exploit and suppress individuals for the good of the organization or its leaders.

Public policy has been described as setting rules that *force* certain behaviors in the employment marketplace, presumably because collectively society does not believe that individuals or employers always "do right." These rules induce behaviors of both employers and individuals. Regulatory policies such as the Americans with Disabilities Act *require* employers to provide reasonable accommodation to an employee with a disability. Rules surrounding government-provided unemployment benefits *require* individuals to actively seek employment to qualify for such benefits.

Policies also seek to encourage or influence rather than force better behavior. Earned Income Tax Credits and Work Opportunity Tax Credits motivate, respectively, individuals in lower-paying jobs to work more and employers to hire additional employees who face employment barriers.

Motivations to "do right" also come from private sources. Many employers realize that more success will come to their businesses if they are viewed as an employer of choice in the marketplace for talent, and if they demonstrate to customers in the marketplace for goods and services that they are benevolent corporate citizens and contribute or give back to the communities where they operate.

Skilled and talented people seek out employers of choice in the employment marketplace. With estimates of average hiring costs ranging from $3,000 to over $50,000 per employee,[7] many argue it is good business to be sought out by quality job seekers because it can lower recruiting costs. Evidence for this assertion can be found in the large number of companies that spend time and resources seeking honors such as *DiversityInc*'s

Top 10 Companies for People with Disabilities and *CAREERS & the disABLED* magazine's Private-Sector Employer of the Year.

In the products and services marketplace, surveys by private-sector and nonprofit organizations support the claim that customers direct their dollars toward businesses viewed as model corporate citizens, although little academic research documents this finding. Some examples of opinion surveys cited in business publications that suggest customers do consider whether the businesses they patronize are good corporate citizens and "give back" include the following:

- Almost two-thirds of chief executives surveyed by the Business Council and the Conference Board said "sustainability had become a mainstream concern for business. In fact, 81% agreed that business leadership will increasingly be judged by the ability to create enterprises that are economically, socially, and environmentally sustainable" (Wright, 2009, p. 1).
- Eighty-seven percent of consumers "agree" or "strongly agree" that they prefer to patronize companies that employ people with disabilities (Siperstein, Romano, Mohler, & Parker, 2006).
- According to Cone Communications, a public relations and marketing agency, 83% of American survey respondents reported wanting "more of the products, services and retailers they use to support causes" (2010, p. 5).
- Forty percent of respondents in a national opinion survey of 3,500 Americans reported that they would "recommend a company for its products or services because of good corporate citizenship," and that they would "be willing to try the company's products for the first time" (GolinHarris, 2005, p. 2).
- An international survey of 11,000 senior executives of large privately held businesses found that over half (56%) felt that corporate responsibility could keep business costs down, while the same percentage reported that these practices were important to gain public support for their brands (Grant Thornton, 2011).
- A survey by the Conference Board found that 46% of the responding companies "view corporate citizenship and sustainability issues primarily as sources of business opportunity" (Vidal, 2006, p. 3).

The practice of classifying the employment and advancement of people with disabilities as "a cause" rather than business as usual, however, has its critics. If not done respectfully and carefully, appearing to place one's employees with disabilities into a "we do good" campaign can backfire and damage the engagement of the exact employees that the company is seeking to promote. What is agreed on, however, is that the marketplace provides incentives for employers to do better and not become known as an employer that discriminates against people with disabilities.

Once people with disabilities become employees with disabilities, the profit incentive can also motivate employers to invest in effective training, management, and promotion of employees with disabilities, the same as it does for their nondisabled peers, to maximize employees' abilities and output.

Much business literature extols the productivity and profit gains that also result from building a workplace that stimulates an employee to be "engaged" at work, a state embodied in "a heightened emotional and intellectual connection . . . [to] his/her job, organization, manager, or coworkers that, in turn, influences him/her to apply additional discretionary [work] effort" (Gibbons, 2007, p. 3). But obtaining an engaged workforce is not simple. As Saks (2006) states, "managers should understand that employee engagement is a long-term and on-going process that requires continued interactions over time in order to generate obligations and a state of reciprocal interdependence" (p. 614). See Chapter 2 for further discussion of how workplace organization and culture can contribute to more fully productive and engaged employees with disabilities.

Employing, managing, and investing in people with disabilities on par with all other employees can align with and support employer strategies to maximize the success of their operations, regardless of regulatory requirements.

The U.S. Federal Government as "Model Employer"

During the 1990s and 2000s, representation of people with disabilities among federal government employees fell (U.S. Equal Employment Opportunity Commission, 2008a). To address this slide, EEOC Management Directive 715 (MD-715), which became effective on October 1, 2003, provided policy guidance and standards for establishing and maintaining an effective affirmative action program for the hiring, placement, and advancement of people with disabilities in the federal sector (U.S. Equal Employment Opportunity Commission, 2008a). The directive requires each federal agency to establish explicit numerical hiring goals for people with disabilities and incorporate those goals into its strategic mission. In addition, to help meet these hiring targets, preferential hiring is allowable and encouraged, taking disability into account as a selection factor for federal-sector job candidates. In other words, "favoring an individual with a disability over a non-disabled individual for purposes of affirmative action in hiring or advancement is not unlawful disparate treatment based on disability, and therefore does not violate the Rehabilitation Act. This rule stands in stark contrast to the legal standards under Title VII for making employment decisions based on race, color, sex, or national origin" (U.S. Equal Employment Opportunity Commission, 2008b).

The means by which federal-sector employers are motivated to preferentially hire applicants with targeted disabilities into governmental positions is provided by Schedule A. A person with a targeted disability who has a Schedule A certification and is qualified for the job can be selected to fill a position without the government agency competitively advertising for candidates (U.S. Office of Personnel Management, n.d.). In addition to enabling an agency to obtain a qualified employee and fulfill model employer goals, Schedule A allows agencies to reduce the time it may take to fill a vacancy.

Supporting Supply and Demand Matching: Disability Service Providers as Catalysts for Employment

While government action and market forces can *motivate* positive behaviors on the part of employers seeking workers, and public policy can set rules that *force* certain behaviors in the employment marketplace, disability service providers try to *facilitate* employment through more (and ideally better) matching, serving as a catalyst between supply and demand. If regulatory policy requires that the gears of the employment engine be of certain dimensions, then community rehabilitation programs hope to add more lubricants so that the engine's system works easier and faster—with less friction for people with disabilities.

Disability service providers can take many forms and be generally classified by different terms. For example, a disability service provider may specialize in providing services and supports to a specific disability population (e.g., individuals with autism or mental illness). Disability service providers may also specialize in certain types of services and supports. For example, one provider might specialize in providing independent living services, while another may focus exclusively on employment, provide peer counseling services, or offer a range or combination of other specialized services. Disability service providers can also be state-operated (as part of a state/ federal partnership), not-for-profit community-based, or for-profit community-based. They may also be under contract to provide services and supports under some state/federal partnership, such as the vocational rehabilitation program outlined in the Rehabilitation Act of 1973. For our purposes, we will refer to the network of disability service providers that serve as catalysts in the supply/demand employment matching process as community rehabilitation programs (CRPs). It is important to clarify that One-Stop Centers, operating under the Workforce Investment Act and stemming from its local Workforce Development Systems, also serve in a catalyst capacity in the employment matching process. However, it is a universal system that to this point has not prioritized service delivery for individuals with disabilities, and has primarily served a nondisabled population.

Community rehabilitation programs are nongovernmental organizations that exist to facilitate employment of people with disabilities through a range of work-related services (see Figure 3). The employment-related services of CRPs are generally categorized as (a) assessment of employment talents, skills, and training needs; (b) training; (c) community job placement; (d) affirmative business placement; (e) supported employee placement; (f) sheltered employment; and (g) day habilitation for non-employment activity.

CRPs work as catalysts, matching people with disabilities to employers in the labor market by providing assessment, training, job referral, and on-the-job coaching support. They can also become employers themselves. Funding to provide these community rehabilitation services most often comes through state-level grants and contracts from state offices of vocational rehabilitation (VR), developmental disabilities (DD), and mental health (MH), as well as some county-based offices, community

Figure 3   Community Rehabilitation Programs (CRPs)

Source: Authors.

programs, and private charitable donations. Most CRPs have nonprofit charitable status.

In some cases, services to assess individuals' employment talents, skills, and training needs are provided by CRP-hired professionals who administer testing and complete structured assessment processes. These assessments focus on identification of work capacity, skills, and support needs, and can take many forms, including formal psychometric and standardized testing, functional capacity assessments, and person-centered approaches. Individuals often come to the CRP for assessment through referral from a related state agency (e.g., VR, DD, or MH). Such an individual, once the CRP has completed its assessment, would then typically be referred by the sponsoring state agency for services and supports that maximize the individual's employment potential.

Training services provided by CRPs (as defined in the Rehabilitation Act of 1973) typically take one of two approaches to preparing individuals with disabilities for employment—"train then place," or "place then train" (Nazarov, Golden, & von Schrader, in press). The train then place approach is typically focused on closing gaps in basic workforce readiness—including pre-vocational preparation (e.g., resume drafting, interview-appropriate dress, development of work behaviors) and short-term and job-specific skill development (e.g., data entry, food preparation)—and provided in a sheltered or segregated work setting. This workforce readiness approach often requires an individual to demonstrate his/her readiness for work prior to being placed in the competitive job market. While the model is purported to reinforce positive employment outcomes, recent research has shown that pre-vocational services have a negative impact on earning potential (Nazarov, Golden, & von Schrader, in press).

CRP workforce readiness training targeting immediate job search and employment often disproportionately directs people toward jobs that may not provide long-run career advancement into higher-paying occupations. Referrals from state agencies can provide for more formal and extensive educational training by providing access to higher-level educational institutions such as two- and four-year colleges. In addition to the Title II and Title III requirements of the ADA, any college or university receiving federal funding of any kind (e.g., research grants, federal student aid) must provide equal access to its programs under Section 504 of the Rehabilitation Act.[8]

In contrast to the train then place approach, the place then train approach builds from the perspective that skills developed in isolation may not transfer effectively to the work setting. Over the past 40 years, CRP job placement services have been evolving notably, providing a range of employment services and supports in the competitive job market. These services have placed increased emphasis on quickly identifying work capacities of the individuals to be served, matching them to competitive jobs, placing them in employment, and providing onsite training that may be needed to ensure their long-term success. As evidenced by the approaches described earlier, CRPs offer services across a continuum of employment involvement.

Subsequent models of employment have also emerged from CRPs, including affirmative businesses, supported employment, customized employment, supported self-employment, and self-employment. We present these models in ascending order by level of integration in the competitive job market.

- Sheltered employment is a line of business operated by the CRP that directly employs people with disabilities. These sheltered workplace businesses create goods and services that are sold in the marketplace, but often through specific contractual or outsourcing agreements with local businesses or government agencies. Typically these work environments also have 14(c) wage certificates allowing them to pay sub-minimum wage.
- Affirmative businesses provide community-based employment training settings that are owned and operated by the CRP, providing an intermediate employment step to competitive or individualized supported job placement. In this way, the affirmative business placement provides a training-ground employment environment where the individual can acquire further skills and work experience that improve his/her resume for a follow-on job. Recently, some affirmative business models have begun to evolve into cooperatively owned businesses—demonstrating either a partnership between the CRP and the employees or a partnership between employees.
- Supported employment is provided by specially trained CRP personnel. As a model, it represents a major deviation from the traditional train then place approach in that it provides onsite job training and support, including job coaching and other support services, to improve the likelihood of long-term employment success in the actual competitive job market.
- Supported self-employment is a hybrid model, providing critical employment supports that a person with a significant disability may need to operate his/her own business. Similar to supported employment, it provides the critical services and supports necessary to enable the individual to manage and operate an independent business venture.

Facilitating more mainstream employment, CRPs also provide placement-only services and self-employment/small business development services to assist individuals with disabilities who require minimal training supports for long-term employment success in securing a job or starting a business. CRPs can also provide day-habilitation services, which fall outside of the employment realm, as these services provide non-employment activity for those individuals who have been determined to currently be unable to function in an employment setting.

Businesses whose employees include a majority of people with disabilities qualify for special government support labeled set-aside contracts. Set-aside contracts are government contracts that have been exempted from the normal competitive bid process and reserved to award to "worthy organizations" that employ individuals with disabilities. Federal, state, and local governments have varying regulations and definitions regarding set-asides. For-profit companies seek to contract with diverse suppliers and may also give preferential consideration to suppliers in which employees with disabilities compose a majority of the workforce. (The set-aside and supplier-diversity preferences are also used to benefit minority-owned, women-owned, veteran-owned, disabled-owned, and service-disabled veteran-owned businesses.)

In the case of sheltered workshops where employees with disabilities are a majority or the entirety of the workforce, controversy exists over set-aside contracts for two reasons. Critics argue that the set-aside can encourage segregated rather than integrated or mainstreaming employment of people with disabilities. The potential conflict arises where the CRP is both advising and directing the person with a disability into employment while at the same time operating sheltered workshops receiving set-aside contracts. This situation has the potential to create disincentives to providers for promoting more integrated employment. Some existing state policies may create conditions that provide legitimate incentives to CRPs for keeping people with disabilities in more segregated settings—thus reducing the individuals' optimal achievement. For example, in most states, providers can earn considerably more by providing day-habilitation services than they can by placing an individual in a job, which might provide a short stream of revenue to the provider. It is important to note that sheltered workshops and businesses receiving set-aside contracts have always been able to pay (and many have paid) market or prevailing wages or salaries.[9]

Workplace Experience

Once a person with a disability is hired and becomes an employee with a disability, the challenge changes from optimal job matching of individuals and employers to optimizing work performance and rewards.

People with disabilities report experiencing lower levels of subjective fit between their abilities and the demands of their jobs. Recent work suggests that people with disabilities are less likely to experience workplace conditions that enhance retention and career advancement, and more likely to experience workplace discrimination (Nishii & Bruyère, 2009).

Universe of Regulatory Policies: General and Disability-Specific

As mentioned earlier, the FLSA establishes the regulatory landscape of employment law and, with the exception of 14(c), is not specific to persons with disabilities. Also applying to employment and the workplace in general (for all persons) are seven EEO/anti-discrimination statutes and regulations: EEOC Regulations (29 CFR Part 1614), Title VII of the Civil Rights Act of 1964, the Age Discrimination in Employment Act of 1967, the Rehabilitation Act of 1973, the Equal Pay Act of 1963, Executive Order 11478 (Equal Employment Opportunity in the Federal Government), and the Notification and Federal Employee Antidiscrimination and Retaliation Act of 2002 (No FEAR Act). These acts collectively articulate the rules that employers must follow to support an employment market and workplaces that prohibit discrimination, reprisal, or workplace harassment against employees or those applying for a job, whether they be persons with disabilities or not.

The Americans with Disabilities Act (ADA) is a disability-specific regulation that explicitly protects the employment rights of people with disabilities. The complete ADA gives civil rights protections to individuals with disabilities similar to those provided to individuals on the basis of race, sex, national origin, and religion. The ADA guarantees equal opportunity for individuals with disabilities in areas of employment, public accommodations, transportation, state and local government services, and telecommunications. The term "disability" within the ADA is defined to mean "(a) a physical or mental impairment that substantially limits one or more major life activities of such individual; (b) a record of such an impairment; or (c) being regarded as having such an impairment" (Americans with Disabilities Act of 1990).

Title I of the ADA specifically addresses employment. Title I stipulates the following:

- Employers with 15 or more employees may not discriminate against qualified individuals with disabilities.
- Employers must reasonably accommodate the disabilities of qualified applicants or employees, unless an undue hardship would result.
- Employers may not discriminate against a qualified applicant or employee because of the known disability of an individual with whom the applicant or employee is known to have a relationship or association.

Limits of protection are delineated within the ADA as well.

- Employers may reject applicants or fire employees who pose a direct threat to the health or safety of other individuals in the workplace.
- Applicants and employees are not protected from personnel actions based on their current illegal use of drugs. Drug testing is not affected.
- Religious organizations may give preference in employment to their own members and may require applicants and employees to conform to their religious tenets.

Following court rulings that interpreted the definition of disability more narrowly than Congressional supporters intended, amendments were made to the ADA in 2008.[10] The purpose of these amendments as specifically stated in the 2008 legislation was to reinstate "a broad scope of protection" and clarify a looser, more inclusive definition of disability than some court decisions had rendered. Namely, the amendments were intended "to reject . . . that the terms 'substantially' and 'major' in the definition of disability under the ADA 'need to be interpreted strictly to create a demanding standard for qualifying as disabled'" (Americans with Disabilities Act of 1990, as amended).

Under the ADA, employees or job applicants who believe they have been discriminated against based on any mental or physical disability (including reasonable accommodation) or subjected to reprisal or workplace harassment for participating in an activity that is protected by the related EEO statutes and regulations can file a complaint (called a "charge"). The individual who perceives discrimination, retaliation, or harassment by an employer on the basis of disability must first file a charge (citing the ADA) at the administrative level with either an office of the Equal Employment Opportunity Commission (EEOC) or a state or local Fair Employment Practice Agency (FEPA). If such a charge is eventually substantiated, remedies can include back pay and/or court injunctions ordering the employer to cease the discriminatory behavior. Table 1 presents the most common issues cited on ADA charges between 2005 and 2010.

While the costs to employers of making reasonable accommodations as required under the ADA are often discussed as a regulatory burden, charges to the EEOC are only half as likely to be made because of complaints relating to insufficient accommodation as complaints relating to discharge. Between 2005 and 2010, roughly 60% of ADA charges cited discharge in the complaint. Reasonable accommodation, while the second most common issue cited, averaged closer to a 30% share (von Schrader, 2011a).[11]

Of concern is also an apparently increasing perception of a hostile work environment by persons with disabilities. Between 2005 and 2010, the

Table 1   Most Common Issues Cited on ADA Charges, 2005–2010

Condition	Percent of Charges
Discharge	58.4
Reasonable Accommodation	28.2
Terms and Conditions	19.8
Harassment	14.8
Discipline	8.6
Hiring	6.7

Source: Adapted from "Calculations from EEOC Integrated Mission System," by S. von Schrader, 2011, Ithaca, NY: Cornell University Rehabilitation Research and Training Center on Employer Practices Related to Employment Outcomes among Individuals with Disabilities.

Note: A charge may cite one or more issues.

share of ADA charges citing retaliation in the complaint has risen sharply, from under 15% of all charges to 23.2% (von Schrader, 2011a). By virtue of the size of their workforces, larger firms and agencies are likely to have larger numbers of employees with disabilities who could potentially file charges with the EEOC under the ADA.

Culture and Engagement

Changing attitudes of managers and co-workers to create work environments that are fully inclusive of employees with disabilities is among the most difficult tasks in accommodating people with disabilities. In surveys of both private- and public-sector human resource managers, the vast majority identified visible top management commitment as the best method for reducing employment and advancement barriers (81% of private-sector and 90% of public-sector respondents) (Bruyère, 2000).

Many barriers to the inclusion of employees with disabilities, however, are under the direct control of the employees' immediate manager: job empowerment, participation in decision-making, fair treatment, and work climate. The role and impact of the manager in fostering inclusion, minimizing employment disparities, and implementing disability practices will be central. Although middle managers are generally expected to maintain the status quo while diversity professionals are expected to challenge it, middle managers have the capacity to play a critical role in promoting diversity in terms of "hiring, development and promotion decisions." However, middle managers can also become "a roadblock to inclusion initiatives as when they fail to support their employees' efforts to participate in affinity group programs" (Conference Board, 2007). Gates (2000) argues that supervisors are the essential link between the employee and the organization and thus are responsible for carrying out the accommodation process. Supervisors are most familiar with job requirements and most able to monitor the impact of the accommodation on the employee with a disability.

Self-Identification

The business world's adage "what gets measured, gets done" runs up against a challenge in advancing employment outcomes for people with disabilities. Nearly 30% of people with disabilities have "hidden" disabilities that are not easily observable by others, such as mental and emotional disabilities (U.S. Census Bureau, 2010). Without express self-disclosure of a disability to the employer, the employer may never know a given employee has a disability. A literature review by Goldberg, Killeen, and O'Day (2005) reveals that people who have visible disabilities are more comfortable disclosing their disability at work than people who have non-evident disabilities. "Researchers who have studied disclosure issues among people with hidden disabilities have often found that disclosure poses significant challenges for people with hidden disabilities" (p. 468).

The decision to self-disclose rests to a large degree on the company culture within which the employee with a disability works. If the work environment is supportive and embracing of employees with disabilities, then disclosure is likely easier for the employee with a disability. Such an environment likely requires education, employee and supervisor training programs, and various other programs and processes. For example, employers whose health insurance plans do not provide coverage for mental health may be sending the message that their workplace is not supportive of employees with mental health conditions, discouraging those employees from self-disclosing. According to Gates (2000, pp. 86–87), "Evidence is mounting . . . that successful employment is not just a function of individual disability symptoms and characteristics. It is also a function of the responsiveness of the work environment to the needs of the employees with disabilities."

Interestingly, a recent survey reveals a gap for persons with disabilities between feeling comfortable to discuss their disability at work and taking formal action to "disclose" the disability to human resources or other institutional structures at work. In a nationally representative Harris Interactive Survey (2010), 78% of respondents with disabilities who are employed answered "yes" to the question, "Does anyone at your organization know that you have a disability?" Of these, 83% reported that the manager or supervisor knows he/she has a disability. But only 55% of those who reported that someone at work knows of their disability said that "other . . . supervisors [know], for example Human Resources." This gap of more than 25 percentage points indicates the important role managers play in creating an inclusive workforce for employees with disabilities. It also suggests that human resource departments are not as fully informed as front-line managers about the needs of the employees with disabilities, and that those employees may not feel comfortable disclosing through formal processes.

Disparities in Employment Outcomes

The employment and workplace experiences of people with disabilities ultimately combine to produce more or less successful employment outcomes. In other words,

$$Employment + Workplace\ Experience = Outcome$$

People with disabilities experience lower overall rates of workforce participation, pay, full-time employment, and post-layoff reemployment.[12] As a result of these differences in employment and workplace experiences, significant disparities in employment outcomes can be measured using any number of economic yardsticks, including employment rates, household income, and poverty rates. People with disabilities have significantly lower household income and are far more likely to be living in poverty (Erickson, Lee, & von Schrader, 2010; Mechanic, Bilder, & McAlpine, 2002).

Employment

The employment-to-population ratio, or the employment rate, is calculated across all persons: those working, those actively seeking employment, and those neither employed nor seeking work. It is simply the number of employed people in a given group divided by the total number of people in that same group. Comparing employment rates between those with and without disabilities provides a more inclusive or comprehensive account of the employment situation for the population with disabilities than comparing unemployment rates, because many people with disabilities are not actively seeking employment and are therefore excluded from the tabulation of unemployment (see the section called Unemployment that follows). Note that all estimates provided as follows are limited to the noninstitutionalized population.

In 2009, the employment-to-population rate for people with disabilities aged 16 years and older was 14.5% compared to 64.5% for their nondisabled peers. Narrowing the age range to the prime working years of 21 to 64 reduces the employment gap slightly. The 2009 employment-to-population rate of people with disabilities ages 21 to 64 years was 36.0%, compared to 76.8% for their nondisabled peers (Erickson, Lee, & von Schrader, 2010). The slight narrowing in the employment gap is due in large part to the fact that people with disabilities are more than three times as likely to be 65 years or older (Bureau of Labor Statistics, 2010). Those persons with ambulatory, cognitive, self-care, and independent living disabilities experience even lower employment rates (Erickson, Lee, & von Schrader, 2010).

Full-Time Versus Part-Time

Tightening the definition of employment to consider only those of prime working age (21 to 64 years old) and working full-time/full-year (FT/FY), rates of employment drop, and more so for people with disabilities than for those without. According to the 2008 ACS, a person is considered employed FT/FY if he or she worked 35 hours or more per week (full-time) and 50 or more weeks per year (full-year). Using this criterion compared to Any Annual Employment drops the employment rate for people with a disability from 39.5% to 25.4% (Erickson, Lee, & von Schrader, 2010). For persons without a disability, 60.4% are employed full-time versus 80% using the Any Annual Employment definition. Employment level differs *among* people with disabilities as well, based on the type of disability. Persons with a hearing disability have the highest FT/FY employment rate at 40.9%, followed by those with visual disability at 29%. Only about one in ten persons with self-care or independent living disabilities are employed FT/FY. See Figure 2 in Chapter 5 for a full comparison of employment rates by disability type and FT/FY vs. Any Annual Employment.

Labor Force Participation

According to figures published by the Bureau of Labor Statistics (2011, November 4), the labor force participation rate in October 2011 for people ages 16 years and older with a disability was 21.3%, versus 69.6% for those without disabilities ages 16 years and older. The labor force participation rate is the number of persons "in the labor force" divided by the population count as defined by the CPS. The number in the labor force does have some particular specifications that are important to note, especially with regard to people with disabilities.

The number of persons in the labor force excludes anyone who is without employment and is not seeking work. It also excludes persons on active duty in the armed forces or confined to institutions such as nursing homes and prisons. Collectively, only those civilians not in institutional settings who have a job, who are on layoff, or who actively searched for work in the last four weeks are counted as being in the labor force. These details of the construction of the labor force population are also important for understanding other measures such as the unemployment rate, the calculation of which includes the labor force count in the denominator.

Unemployment

The unemployment rate is the number of unemployed persons divided by the number of persons determined to be in the labor force. People are classified by the U.S. Bureau of Labor Statistics as unemployed if they do not have a job, have actively looked for work in the prior four weeks, and are currently available for work (Bureau of Labor Statistics, 2009).

The unemployment rate in October 2011 for people with disabilities ages 16 years and older was 13.2%, as compared to 8.3% for those without disabilities. In other words, the percentage of people with disabilities in the labor force who were not working but were actively looking for work (unemployment rate) was more than 1.5 times that of people without disabilities (Bureau of Labor Statistics, 2011, November, Table A6).

Not in the Labor Force, but Only "Marginally Attached"

The unemployment rate only includes persons *in* the labor force who are without a job and are actively looking for work. It excludes individuals who are "marginally attached" to the labor force and those "discouraged workers" who have given up trying to find work. People with disabilities who are not working may often fall into these excluded categories.

The Bureau of Labor Statistics (2009) classifies individuals as outside of the labor force and therefore excluded from the unemployment counts for three reasons. They

1. are marginally attached (including discouraged workers);
2. are not working but have not looked for a job in the past 12 months (suggesting they are not interested in working); and
3. do not meet the requirements for inclusion in the labor force survey (see next section).

In the October 2011 Current Population Survey, people with disabilities who were not in the labor force accounted for roughly 68% of the civilian noninstitutionalized population with disabilities ages 16 to 64. In comparison, only 24% of their nondisabled peers ages 16-64 were not in the labor force (Bureau of Labor Statistics, 2011, November, Table A6). Without imposing an age restriction to account for those retiring, the percentages for those 16 and over are 80% and 30%, respectively, for people with and without disabilities.

The Bureau of Labor Statistics (2008) defines a person to be marginally attached to (but not in) the labor force if they report wanting a job, being available to work, and having looked for a job in the past 12 months but not during the immediate four weeks preceding the survey. Unemployment figures therefore ignore many persons with disabilities who are employable but not working because they are not considered to be in the labor force. If a "marginally attached" person reports that she did not look for work recently because she believes "there are no jobs available or there are none for which [she] would qualify," that person is further defined as a "discouraged worker." The 2010 annual average number of discouraged workers with a disability ages 16 to 64 was 85,000 (Bureau of Labor Statistics, 2011, June, Table 5). This is separate from (and in addition to) the annual average of 786,000 persons with disabilities ages 16-64 formally classified as unemployed in 2010 (Bureau of Labor Statistics, 2011, June, Table A). If a broader definition were adopted that included discouraged workers in the enumeration of unemployed people, the 2010 annual average count of unemployed persons with a disability would increase by almost 11%.[13]

Not in the Labor Force and Not Surveyed

As previously stated, the labor force is made up of all the employed and unemployed persons not on active duty in the armed forces and not confined to institutions such as nursing homes and prisons. This is because the U.S. labor force survey (the Current Population Survey) tabulations are based on a population of respondents who are 16 years or older, civilians, and not residing in institutional settings. In other words, persons under 16 years old, on active duty in the armed forces, or confined to group quarters (GQ) such as nursing homes and prisons are not included in U.S. employment statistics, whether they are actively working or not. Those determined to be marginally attached or not interested in working are excluded from the labor force as well.

Excluding the GQ population from consideration in the employment statistics disproportionately excludes people with disabilities. Using the 2006 and 2007 American Community Survey to identify the distribution of the working-age population with and without disabilities by major residence type, Stapleton, Honeycutt, and Schechter (2009) found that about one in 13 males and one in 33 females with disabilities live in GQ. Moreover, 40% of male and 62% of female GQ residents have a disability. Younger males with disabilities are more likely to reside in GQ, particularly institutional GQ. Stapleton et al. conclude that the inclusion of the total GQ population (institutionalized and noninstitutionalized) would significantly lower employment rate estimates for males with disabilities.

Education and Employment

Educational attainment greatly affects employment rates for people with and without disabilities. Just as employment rates for people with disabilities are lower than those of people without disabilities, so are levels of educational attainment. Nearly one-quarter (23.9%) of working-age persons with disabilites have less than a high school education, as compared to 11.1% of persons without disabilites. Moreover, only 12.3% of working-age persons with disabilities have a bachelor's degree or higher education level, as compared to nearly one-third (30.6%) of those without a disability (Erickson, Lee, & von Schrader, 2010).

These findings are troubling in part because of the positive relationship between education and employment opportunities. A person with a disability who has a bachelor's degree or higher is more than twice as likely to be employed (54.8%) as a person with a disability who never graduated high school (22.8%, a 32.3% difference). The employment gap between those with more (bachelor's degree or higher) and less (less than a high school) education is smaller for people without disabilities. Among people without disabilities, a 20 percentage point difference exists in the employment rate between those holding a bachelor's degree (83.6%) and those without a high school diploma (62.8%) (Erickson, Lee, & von Schrader, 2010).

It is also clearly the case that the employment rate increases more noticeably with higher levels of education for people with disabilities than it does for people without disabilities. Education thus reduces the employment gap between those with and without disabilities. The employment rate gap for people with and without disabilities who have a bachelor's degree or higher is less than 30 percentage points (54.8% and 83.6%, respectively). For those without a high school diploma, meanwhile, the gap in the employment rate between people with and without disabilities is 40 percentage points (22.8% and 62.8%, respectively) (Erickson, Lee, & von Schrader, 2010).

Table 2   Economic Disparities, 2009

Noninstitutionalized Persons in the U.S. Aged 21–64 Years	With Disabilities	Without Disabilities
Employment rate of working-age persons	36.0%	76.8%
With less than a high school degree	22.8	62.8
With a bachelor's degree or higher	54.8	83.6
Pay (median annual earnings of those employed Full-Time/Full-Year)	$35,000	$40,700
Household income (median)	$37,200	$60,000
Poverty rate	26.4%	10.8%
Without health insurance	17.4%	20.5%

Source: Adapted from "Disability statistics from the 2008 American Community Survey (ACS)," by W. Erickson, C. Lee, & S. von Schrader, 2010, Ithaca, NY: Cornell University Rehabilitation Research and Training Center on Disability Demographics and Statistics (StatsRRTC). Retrieved from http://www.disabilitystatistics.org.

In surveys conducted by Cornell University of federal and private-sector human resource representatives, lack of related experience and lack of requisite skills and training in the applicant or employee with a disability were cited as the most common barriers for people with disabilities (Bruyère, 2000). The disparity in employment between people with disabilities and people without disabilities is a function of many inequities, including access to education, training, and employment, as well as society's attitudes toward people with disabilities (see Table 2).

Household Income

Differences in the ability of persons with disabilities to find work and advance in the workplace, not surprisingly, create income disparities. In the United States, household income is lower for those households that include an individual with a disability. And, among working people, the earnings of people with disabilities fall below the level of their nondisabled peers.

The median annual earnings for persons working full-time/full-year (FT/FY) were $35,000 for people with disabilities and $40,700 for their nondisabled peers in 2009 (Erickson, Lee, & von Schrader, 2010). The reason that figures on earnings are limited to FT/FY workers is to standardize the number of hours worked to produce the income, as much as possible. It is important to remember that this criterion excludes all persons working part-time and/or part of the year. Given this limitation, it is essential to examine this data in concert with the FT/FY employment levels. When considering these differences, it is important to note that only a small proportion of people with disabilities actually work FT/FY (25.4%); therefore the overall earnings discrepancy is even greater than these estimates indicate. Median income also varies across different types of disability: persons with hearing disabilities have the highest median income, and those with cognitive disabilities have the lowest.

Median household income can be a better reflection of the economic status of a certain group of people, as it includes all household members regardless of their individual employment status and reveals total income resources available. Household income includes the total income of all household members from all sources, including any public assistance. The median income of households that include any working-age people with disabilities in the United States in 2009 was $37,200, compared to $60,000 for households that did not include any working-age people with disabilities (Erickson, Lee, & von Schrader, 2010). This represents a significant income gap of $22,800. In other words, typical households with working-age persons with disabilities have roughly one-third less income than typical households without any working-age persons with disabilities.

Poverty

The calculation of poverty compares the sum of total income from each family member living in the household to the appropriate poverty threshold given the household's composition. Poverty thresholds are adjusted to take account of the size of the family, the age of the householder, and the number of related children under the age of 18. Over one-quarter (26.4%) of working-age persons with disabilities are living in poverty. This poverty rate is nearly 2.5 times higher than that of persons without disabilities (10.8%) (Erickson, Lee, & von Schrader, 2010). As Figure 10 in Chapter 5 shows, persons with cognitive, self-care, and independent living disabilities have the highest poverty rates. Persons with hearing disabilities have much lower rates but still are nearly twice as likely to live in poverty as persons without any disability.

The Great Recession's Impact on Employment of People With Disabilities

The recession that hit at the end of 2007 was characterized by the largest four-quarter decline in the gross domestic product since World War II and historic unemployment rates within every age cohort of workers. Recent inclusion of disability status questions in the monthly CPS has allowed analysis of this recession's impact on people with disabilities that has not been possible in the past. As Kaye (2010) wrote, "research on the effect of recessions on workers with disabilities has been limited by lack of data collection on the employment experiences of people with disabilities . . . [but the new CPS data allow analysis of] whether workers with disabilities are indeed the first to be fired and the last to be hired in bad economic times" (p. 19).

Kaye found that labor force participation among persons with disabilities fell from 5.4 million to 4.9 million during the recession, but no significant similar decline existed among persons without disabilities. And, while the unemployment rate rose for persons both with and without disabilities, people with disabilities "experienced a 12.3 percent decline [in raw employment numbers], from 4.7 million to 4.2 million [employed individuals], compared with a 3.4 percent drop for working-age adults without disabilities" (p. 19).

While people with disabilities and African American and Latino workers were all hit harder by the recession than nondisabled, nonminority Americans, for people with disabilities "job exit has a larger magnitude and occurs earlier" (Kaye, 2010, p. 29). (See Table 3 for a summary of Kaye's data.) An important contributor, the proportion of working-age people with disabilities dropping out of the labor force (reporting that they are unable to participate in the labor force), rose almost three percentage points from 44.9% to 47.6% (Kaye, 2010, p. 21).

Disparities in Access to Health Care

Prior to the enactment of the health care reform program through the Affordable Care Act of 2010, the type of health care coverage available to working-age persons with disabilities was tied almost exclusively to their employment status. The pre-reform system resulted in a significant dependence among persons with disabilities on public health coverage (such as Medicaid) due to their (a) relatively high rates of unemployment and underemployment; (b) lack of access to employer-paid health insurance resulting from higher likelihood of being employed in temporary or transitional jobs; (c) high incidence of pre-existing conditions that many

Table 3   Demographic and Socioeconomic Characteristics of U.S. Adults Ages 18–64, by Disability Status, October 2008 and June 2010

	With Disability		Without Disability	
	Oct-08	Jun-10	Oct-08	Jun-10
Population (millions)	14.7	14.3	173.3	[1]175.9
Percentage of working-age population	7.8	[2]7.5	92.2	[2]92.5
Age and sex				
Mean age	47.7	[1]48.0	39.8	[2]39.9
Percentage female	50.4	51	50.7	50.7
Race/ethnicity[3] (percent)				
White	80.6	80.9	81.5	[1]81.2
African American	16.4	[2]16.0	12.6	[1]12.9
Asian/Pacific Islander	2.2	2.2	5.7	5.9
American Indian/Alaska Native	2.8	3.3	1.5	1.5
Latino/Hispanic	10.4	[1]11.3	15.4	[2]15.6
Education				
College graduates (percent)	13.4	[1]14.6	29.7	29.7
Labor force participation				
Participants (millions)	5.4	[1]4.9	140.9	141.3
Employed	4.7	[1]4.2	132.8	[1]128.3
Unemployed (looking for work)	0.6	[1]0.8	8.2	[1]13.0
Perceives unable to participate (percent)	44.9	[1]47.6	2	[1]2.3

Source: Adapted from "Table 1: The impact of the 2007–09 recession on workers with disabilities," by H. S. Kaye, *Monthly Labor Review,* 2010, October, p. 21.

Notes: (1) Difference is statistically significant at $p < .01$.

(2) Difference is statistically significant at $p < .05$.

(3) Racial/ethnic categories are not mutually exclusive.

insurance companies refused to cover; and (d) lifetime caps on benefits that insurance companies agreed to pay. Adding to this dependence on public coverage was the rising cost of health care premiums that encouraged employers to limit health coverage or, more drastically, discouraged them from employing or retaining employees with high health care needs (Stapleton & Liu, 2009). This link between employment status and health care coverage prevented many persons with disabilities from entering the labor force for fear of losing health care coverage they had under public programs (Goodman, Stapleton, Livermore, & O'Day, 2007). Eligibility for Medicaid has restricted employment, due to the requirement that beneficiaries prove an inability to work to receive public benefits.[14]

The most significant provision in the Affordable Care Act is the mandate for universal coverage (Section 1501). Under this provision, all Americans must have a minimum level of health care coverage or be subject to a penalty. The Affordable Care Act, in essence, strengthens the ADA as it applies to employer-sponsored health insurance and other private plans, and vastly expands health coverage options for persons with pre-existing and chronic conditions (Powers, Pyles, Sutter, & Verville PC, Attorneys at Law, 2010).

The future of the Affordable Care Act is in no way secure. For people with disabilities, the forces pushing health care reform forward and backward will be important currents to observe.

Geographic Differences

Despite the U.S. historical claim to having some of the greatest domestic labor mobility among industrialized economies, regional disparities in many measures still exist. Disability prevalence rates as well as employment rates of people with disabilities vary across U.S. geographies. For example, the state with the lowest disability prevalence rate according to the 2008 American Community Survey is Hawaii at 7.2%. West Virginia has the highest disability prevalence rate at 18.7% (Erickson, Lee, & von Schrader, 2010). (See Chapter 5 for further discussion of state-by-state differences.)

History: An Evolution of the Modern Landscape

Throughout U.S. history, various waves of change have altered the balance around the employment market and work opportunities for people with disabilities. The evolving national philosophy about the ability and right of people with disabilities to have access and opportunity to work has been influenced by significant numbers of veterans with disabilities returning home from war, industrial advances in the workplace, deinstitutionalization, and the modern civil rights movement.

"Official" Perception Through the Lens of the U.S. Census

The U.S. Decennial Census of the Population is the longest continuous survey in the United States. Commencing in 1790, the Census is required by the Constitution to be conducted every 10 years. As such, the evolving terminology and definitions of the U.S. Census form provide a unique lens through which to view the changing social perceptions of disability and employment.

The first time the U.S. Decennial Census included a count of individuals with disabilities was in 1830. From 1830 through 1880 the enumeration question(s) regarding disability status of each member of the household expanded to include more categories and specific references to work or employment. In 1830 and 1840, counts of household members were made separately for those who were "deaf and dumb" and/or blind. In 1850 and 1860, cognitive disabilities were recognized, but the distinction of disability type (albeit rough as it had been) was lost by asking a single yes/no question as to whether the household member was "deaf, dumb, blind, insane, idiotic, pauper, or convict?"[15] The forced lumping of disability with poverty and criminal status was removed in 1870 (U.S. Census Bureau, 2011).

The Census of 1880 was a progressive high-water mark for early data collection on the population of Americans with disabilities. Separate questions were asked to allow for distinct counts of persons who were "blind," "deaf and dumb," "idiotic," "insane," and "maimed, crippled, bedridden or otherwise disabled." Another question linked disability to work limitation. For each household member, it was asked if on that day the person was "sick or disabled so as to be unable to attend to ordinary business or duties? If so, what was the sickness or disability?" (U.S. Census Bureau, 2011).

Almost a century passed before regular enumeration of disability status returned to the U.S. Census, although the intermittent and sporadic questions that were included were as likely as not to relate disability to work. The 1930 Census, for example, would only have enumerated a person as having a disability if his/her disability was noted as the reason the person was "not at work" or "out of a job."

In 1990, a milestone year for persons with disabilities due to the passage of the ADA, the Census questions expanded, and the specificity of the disability status increased again in the 2000 Decennial Census. But in the 2010

Decennial Census, a single questionnaire asking only 10 questions in total was instituted, with no disability question. Coverage of more detailed questions that had been included on the long-form questionnaire (and asked of just a sample of Americans), including those on disability status, were transferred to the annual American Community Survey beginning in 2001. The six disability-status questions included in the annual ACS and monthly CPS, discussed previously, now provide continually updated nationally representative disability data for the U.S. population.

Evolution of Service Delivery and Employment Models

After the advances in civil rights, desegregation, and deinstitutionalization in the 1950s and 1960s, the 1970s and 1980s represented a critical time in policymaking in the United States. Disability advocates advanced the theories of normalization, protection and advocacy, independent living, and civil rights and empowerment for people with disabilities. Activists worked to shift policymakers from a viewpoint of persons with disabilities that was based on a medical model of disability and rehabilitation to one based on functional supports, a move that helped make disability be seen as something as much environmental as residing in an individual.

The burgeoning independent living movement was a driving force for many changes, as it helped in making the voices of people with disabilities heard during the design and implementation of public policy. "Nothing about without us" (Charlton, 1998) was the motto of this time. The early 1970s saw a push toward the removal of physical barriers in architecture and transportation, which was later expanded to include efforts to remove communication barriers by implementing accessible telecommunication technologies for people with visual and hearing impairments. This movement toward universal design and accessible communities and technologies drove the early removal of disability discrimination from air carriers and housing, and the expansion of access to assistive technology, even prior to the passage of the Americans with Disabilities Act in 1990.

In these crucial two decades, protection and advocacy was greatly expanded. The Rehabilitation Act of 1973 established a Client Assistance Program, which provided representation and advocacy support for clients of the Vocational Rehabilitation (VR) system. The Developmental Disability Bill of 1975, the 1980 Civil Rights of Institutionalized Persons Act, and the Mental Illness Bill of Rights Act of 1985 all continued to expand provision of protection and advocacy services.

Many believe that Justin Dart's 1987 testimony to Congress was key to the advancement of this new paradigm. Dart, then Commissioner of the Rehabilitation Services Administration, testified that "an inflexible federal system, like the society it represents, still contains significant portions of individuals who have not yet overcome obsolete, paternalistic attitudes toward disability" (Levy, 1988, p. 80). One year later the Congress created a Task Force on the Rights and Empowerment of Americans with Disabilities, to build support for the passage of the Americans with Disabilities Act (ADA), enacted in 1990.

In an attempt to create a more "customer-focused" system of employment training and placement support, the Workforce Investment Act (WIA) was enacted in 1998. It reformed federal job training programs by incorporating the Rehabilitation Act Amendments of 1998 (as Title IV) along with superseding or amending other employment support programs not specifically targeting people with disabilities, namely, the Job Training Partnership Act (JTPA), the Wagner-Peyser Act, and the Adult Education and Family Literacy Act (included as Title II). The goal of embedding rehabilitation programs for people with disabilities into the same legislative framework as employment programs serving the nondisabled population was to create a consolidated, non-duplicative workforce investment system that more comprehensively served Americans seeking employment and employers looking to hire.

An important philosophical shift in service delivery over the recent decades is found in "person-centered approaches" (Blessing, Golden, & Bruyère, 2009). Person-centered planning as an innovation and technology was designed for the express purpose of evolving how people who have disabilities can become contributing members within the natural community, beyond the real and artificial barriers of the disability service system. Philosophically, person-centered planning holds at its core a capacity view of people. It believes that the expression and expansion of an individual's innate talents, interests, and skills leads to opportunities for sharing space with people who have similar interests, talents, and skills, and consequently to the development of purposeful associations and valued community membership roles, including employment. It assumes that the potential to make meaningful contributions and connections already exists within the person; its intentional practice is to look for and bring forth this potential.

Clearly the past three to four decades have seen a tremendous growth in the areas of economic, technological, medical, and rehabilitative developments. These changes have enhanced opportunities for people with disabilities to live, learn, and earn in more integrated and competitive settings and pursue greater economic success. Adding to these expanded opportunities are the ramifications of social and legislative change and judicial decisions supporting the increased community integration of people with disabilities. This movement has continued to grow in momentum, pushing the design of inclusive and integrated, demand-driven policies, procedures, and practices to promote full employment for Americans with disabilities.

Veterans

Throughout history, veterans who sustained service-related disabilities have helped to raise awareness of the needs of all people with disabilities. The large numbers of aging Civil War veterans with disabilities, along with the advent of the Progressive Era, likely spurred national interest in late-19th-century Census enumeration of people with disabilities.

Federally supported vocational rehabilitation finds its 20th-century roots strongly linked to veterans with disabilities. The influx of World War I veterans with disabilities brought public attention to the employment needs of those with disabilities. In fact, Henry Ford, interested in the reemployment of the returning World War I veterans, instructed his plant managers throughout the country to make surveys of their communities and determine how many persons, in proportion to the population, had physical disabilities. From these surveys, the Ford Motor Company instituted a policy of hiring 10% of its employees from the local pools of disabled workers (Spears, 1945). Simultaneously, the Smith-Sears Soldiers Rehabilitation Act of 1918 created a federal funding mechanism of work rehabilitation for veterans with disabilities (see also Elliott & Leung, 2005). In 1921, the Veterans Bureau was created, and within three years it had published a manual of procedure for the vocational rehabilitation of veterans of World War I.

World War II provided another stimulus for government action on vocational rehabilitation. In the midst of the war in 1943, both the Barden-LaFollette Act (or Vocational Rehabilitation Amendments) and the Welsh-Clark Act, also known as the World War II Disabled Veterans Rehabilitation Act, were passed. These acts expanded the coverage of federally funded rehabilitation programs and authorized the Veterans Administration to carry out rehabilitation programs to help veterans with disabilities find employment again. The Servicemen's Readjustment Act of 1944, better known as the G.I. Bill of Rights, provided tuition and subsistence for up to 48 months for veterans who underwent and completed training and vocational assessment/counseling services.

In 1945, as veterans with disabilities looking for reemployment in the U.S. workforce were becoming more visible, Congress passed House Joint Resolution 23 establishing the first week in October as "National Employ the Physically Handicapped Week." Further recognition was evident in the creation of a Presidential Committee in 1947.

Beginning in the 1990s with the first Persian Gulf War, and continuing into the second decade of the 21st century with the Iraq and Afghanistan wars, another generation of veterans with disabilities raised public awareness and influenced public policy in the United States. Veterans' education and rehabilitation programs were expanded again. The American Jobs Act proposed economic stimulus strategies that included tax breaks for businesses hiring veterans with disabilities (Title 2, Section 201, Returning Heroes and Wounded Warriors Work Opportunity Tax Credits) (White House, 2011).

Industrialization and On-the-Job Injuries

The arrival home of World War I veterans with disabilities followed the mass adoption of Industrial Revolution technologies in the late 1800s and the passage of early federal workplace safety legislation during the Progressive Era of the early 1900s. Increasing mechanization of the workplace swelled the numbers of workers injured on the job. In the railroad industry alone, the number of (nonfatal) accidents rose some 40% over the first decade of the 20th century (see Table 4) (Fishback & Kantor, 1996).

Progressives responded by bringing government policy into the fray, moving from state-level to federal action. States across the nation experimented first with workers' compensation legislation to assist those whose disability was obtained on the job. In 1911, Wisconsin established the first workers' compensation law to be declared constitutional and spawned the employers' insurance industry in the United States. By 1929, all but four states had passed workers' compensation laws.

In 1920, the federal government passed the Vocational Rehabilitation Act (commonly called the Smith-Fess Act), which was originally conceived as a vocational training and counseling program for those injured on the job (Social Security Online, n.d.). This initiative marked the beginning of public rehabilitation programs, initially only for veterans and now extended to all people with disabilities. It established a civilian vocational rehabilitation program funded with equal shares from the federal and state governments. The funding could be used for vocational guidance, training, occupational adjustment services, and job placement (Henderson & Bryan, 2011). Rehabilitation and treatment for

Table 4   Rise in Accident Risk in the Early Twentieth Century

Year	Railroad Nonfatal Accidents per Million Man-Days
1892	114.9
1893	119.8
1894	98.8
1895	108.5
1896	119.7
1897	110.6
1898	121.0
1899	126.1
1900	130.6
1901	134.3
1902	141.3
1903	159.5
1904	168.4
1905	165.0
1906	176.9
1907	179.4
1908	179.2
1909	170.2
1910	192.3

Source: Adapted from "The adoption of workers' compensation in the United States, 1900–1930," by P. V. Fishback & S. E. Kantor, 1996, November, NBER Working Paper 5840, Table 1, p. 46.

medical and physical ailments were not included in the program until 1943 (Social Security Online, n.d.).

State-level vocational rehabilitation programs were also becoming better organized and operated. In 1923, State Administrators of Vocational Rehabilitation banded together to form the National Civilian Rehabilitation Conference. Within a few years, discussion at the fourth National Conference on Vocational Rehabilitation had shifted to technical and administrative considerations from "plans and philosophy" that had dominated their earlier convenings (Obermann, 1965, p. 249). For government bureaucrats, the focus had shifted from whether to provide large rehabilitation agencies to how to run them.

Civil Rights Movement

Following the milestone passage of the Social Security Act in 1935, and important amendments to the Vocational Rehabilitation Act in 1943 and 1954, the 1960s brought further advancements for people with disabilities as the civil rights movement swept the United States. In 1965, the Medicaid and Medicare Acts brought health care to the poor and elderly, including those with disabilities, and in 1968, the Architectural Barriers Act (ABA) required buildings "designed, built, altered, or leased with federal funds" to be accessible to those with disabilities. The Access Board, created to enforce the ABA, develops and maintains accessibility guidelines (U.S. Access Board, n.d.).

In 1975, the Education for All Handicapped Children Act (EAHCA) was passed, requiring free, appropriate public education in the least restrictive setting for children with disabilities. In 1980, the Civil Rights of Institutionalized Persons Act was established to protect the constitutional rights of persons confined in state and local institutions (including patients in mental health facilities, prisoners in detention and jail settings, and elderly enrollees in nursing homes).

By the mid-1970s, the movement for the rights of people with disabilities assumed a more global position of importance. In 1975, the United Nations adopted the "Declaration on the Rights of Disabled Persons," which proclaims the equal civil and political rights of people with disabilities. While it was not a binding resolution, it provided a global framework for crafting international and domestic law, and was the first international document attempting to define the term "disability."

Expanding Rights for Work Opportunities

In 1983, the President's Council on the Employment of the Handi-capped further developed its focus on employment of people with dis-abilities through legislative action to establish the Job Accommodation Network (JAN). JAN's consultants formed a network that could offer one-on-one guidance on workplace accommodations and self-employment and entrepreneurship options for people with disabilities. This network aimed to assist private employers, government agencies, employee repre-sentatives, service providers, and people with disabilities and their fami-lies (Job Accommodation Network, n.d.).

The Americans with Disabilities Act, arguably one of the most impor-tant legislative initiatives enacted to protect the rights of people with disabilities, passed in 1990. Ironically, the passage of the ADA does not seem to have increased the labor force participation of people with dis-abilities, and some researchers argue it has had a negative impact. Much of the debate focuses on the unintended consequences of other disability benefit programs on return to work. For example, individuals who receive Social Security Disability Insurance and begin working at gainful and substantial levels may lose their cash benefit over time. Similarly, individuals who receive means-tested cash benefits like Supplemental Security Income (SSI) and increase their income through work may have such benefit amounts lowered. Concern is also raised about the differing definitions of disability used in the major data sources of record.[16]

The wide-ranging scope of the ADA initially incited criticism for being too costly to business. With regard to the burden ADA regulations place on employers, a survey conducted by Cornell University in both the fed-eral and private sectors revealed that the costs of training, supervision, and accommodations for applicants or employees with disabilities were least likely to be rated as significant barriers to the employment of people with disabilities. Overall, three-quarters of the respondents did not feel that the cost considerations of accommodations, such as those required by the ADA, posed significant barriers (Bruyère, 2000).

The Family and Medical Leave Act (FMLA), another important piece of legislation supporting the employment of people with disabilities, was signed into law in 1993. The FMLA establishes, for employers with 50 or more employees, a minimum labor standard with regard to leaves of absence for family or medical reasons. Under the FMLA, an eligible employee may take up to 12 work weeks of leave during any 12-month period due to a serious health condition that makes the employee unable to perform one or more of the essential functions of his or her job, or due to the employee's need to care for a spouse, son, daughter, or parent with a serious health condition. Unrelated to disability, FMLA leave is also allowed for the birth of a child, caring for a newborn child, or placement of a child with the employee through adoption or foster care (U.S. Department of Labor, Wage and Hour Division, 2011).

The 1999 Ticket to Work and Work Incentive Improvement Act (TWWIIA) is another major law that targeted the improvement of employment options for people with disabilities. It acknowledged the importance of health care to people with disabilities and the adverse incentives created by the loss of Medicare or Medicaid coverage in case of successful employment. The act made it possible for Americans with disabilities to join the workforce without fear of losing their Medicare or Medicaid coverage (Legal Information Institute, 2011).

Struggles Along Many Dimensions of Diversity

Barriers to Employment

Barriers to the employment of people with disabilities parallel those of other minority populations—namely, attitudes/stereotypes of supervisors and co-workers, and lack of work experience and skills. A number of studies focusing on employment discrimination claims have found that alleged unlawful discharge complaints are the most common among employees with disabilities. However, like other underrepresented or protected groups, people with disabilities perceive discrimination across the employment process—from hiring to on-the-job harassment and disparate treatment (see Figure 4) (Bjelland et al., 2010; McMahon, Shaw, & Jaet, 1995).

Employers' Diversity Practices and Discrimination Charges

Perhaps the greatest shared employment experience between various underrepresented demographic minorities is employers' fear of increasing employee discrimination claims and lawsuits following every legislative advance or awareness-raising campaign. Installation of workplace training and expanded roles of compliance officers indicate that employers do seriously seek to avoid litigation risk and also to incorporate into business practice the enlightenment that underpins the inclusion of

Figure 4 Number of Charges Citing the ADA Compared to Other Statutes

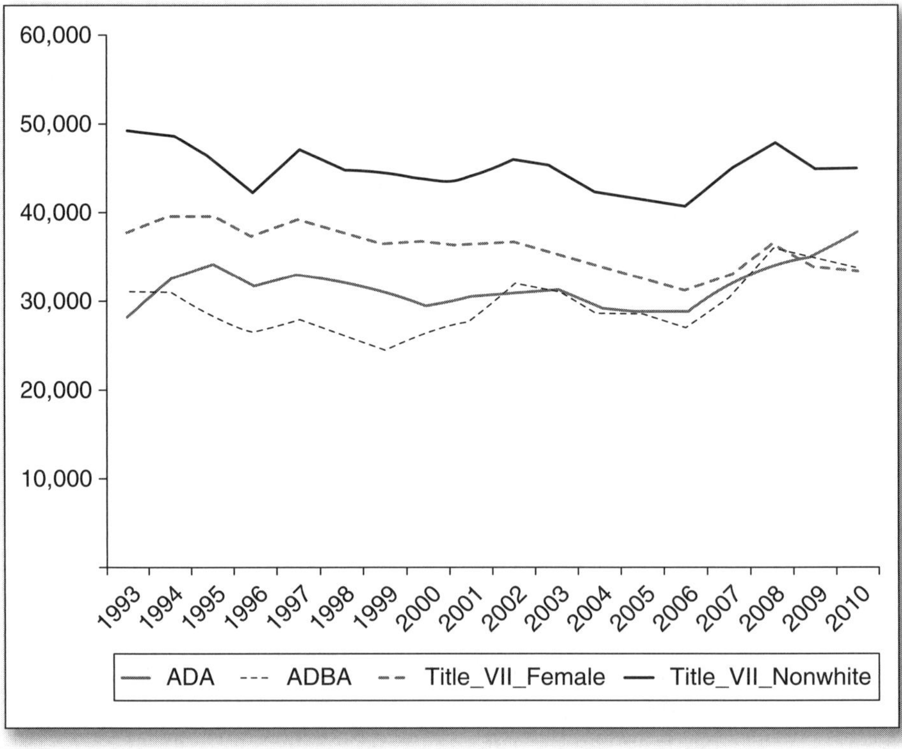

Source: Adapted from "EEOC charge data: What we can learn about the employment of persons with disabilities," presentation made for the EARN webinar series by S. von Schrader, 2011, October 20.

employees of all dimensions of diversity: women, African Americans, lesbian/gay/bisexual/transgender (LGBT), generational, and people with disabilities. However, Hirsh and Kmec (2009) found that when an EEO office is established within the workplace or employees are provided diversity training at work, discrimination charges increase, suggesting that awareness-raising expands utilization of workforce protections through legal action. They also found strong evidence to indicate that if the training is for *managers* rather than employees at large, the opposite (and intended consequence) occurs—discrimination charges fall. Adopting some affirmative-action plans had no significant impact on charges.

Similarities in Difference

The lesbian, gay, bisexual, transgender (LGBT) population is one demographic group to which the challenges of inclusion for people with disabilities are compared. Many LGBT employees struggle with the decision to acknowledge their sexual orientation to workplace colleagues or supervisors for fear of discrimination in promotion or retention. This parallels those with nonobvious disabilities who struggle with revealing or disclosing their disability at work. Some employers striving to improve the culture of inclusion for employees with disabilities are looking to successes they had in increasing the inclusion of LGBT employees through employee resource/affinity groups (ERGs) and involvement of LGBT "allies" (on success of workplace "allies" for LGBT employees, see Martinez & Hebl, 2010).

This parallel between people with nonobvious disabilities and the LGBT population is sometimes drawn in distorted ways. In drafting the Rehabilitation Act, lawmakers felt the need to clarify that one's sexual orientation is not a determinate of disability. The Rehabilitation Act specifically states that the term "impairment" does not include homosexuality or bisexuality, and therefore the term "individual with a disability" does not include an individual on the basis of homosexuality or bisexuality.

It is important to acknowledge there are many obvious differences in the experiences and struggles of each minority and underrepresented group. The fear of violence related to workplace inclusion, for example, has threatened different populations differently.

Securing appropriate accommodations at work is one challenge people with disabilities face that sets them apart. Supervisors' lack of knowledge about providing accommodations and the perceived cost of accommodations surfaces repeatedly as a barrier to successful employment outcomes for people with disabilities although, even with regard to accommodation challenges, there are allies to be found among other underrepresented populations. Some of religious faith also require workplace accommodations, for example, and also struggle with workplace accommodation rights and protocols.

Globalization

U.N. Convention on the Rights of People with Disabilities

Several global initiatives, like the United Nations Convention on the Rights of People with Disabilities, have aimed to protect fundamental rights of people with disabilities. The text was adopted by the UN in 2006 and put into effect on May 3, 2008. While the text offers a comprehensive discussion of the different issues concerning people with disabilities, Articles 26 and 27 in particular focus on rehabilitation and employment.

The main objective of Article 26 is to reaffirm states parties' responsibility toward habilitation and rehabilitation of persons with disabilities. States are expected to take the appropriate measures to support persons with disabilities in order for them to "attain and maintain maximum independence, full physical, mental, social and vocational ability, and full inclusion and participation in all aspects of life" (United Nations, 2006, p. 19). This goal is to be achieved through the organization of rehabilitation services and programs in different areas, like health, employment, education, and social services. The article also stresses that states parties should promote the availability of and knowledge about assistive devices and technologies that are designed to rehabilitate people with disabilities.

Article 27 of the Convention speaks more directly to issues of employment and the right of people with disabilities to participate equally in the labor force with their nondisabled peers. It calls for states parties to "safeguard and promote the realization of the right to work, including for those who acquire a disability during the course of employment" (p. 19), by passing legislation and taking other appropriate steps to do the following:

a. Prohibit discrimination on the basis of disability with regard to all matters concerning all forms of employment, including conditions of recruitment, hiring, and employment, continuance of employment, career advancement, and safe and healthy working conditions;

b. Protect the rights of persons with disabilities, on an equal basis with others, to just and favorable conditions of work, including equal opportunities and equal remuneration for work of equal value, safe and healthy working conditions, including protection from harassment, and the redress of grievances;

c. Ensure that persons with disabilities are able to exercise their labor and trade union rights on an equal basis with others;

d. Enable persons with disabilities to have effective access to general technical and vocational guidance programs, placement services and vocational and continuing training;

e. Promote employment opportunities and career advancement for persons with disabilities in the labor market, as well as assistance in finding, obtaining, maintaining and returning to employment;

f. Promote opportunities for self-employment, entrepreneurship, the develop-
    ment of cooperatives and starting one's own business;

g. Employ persons with disabilities in the public sector;

h. Promote the employment of persons with disabilities in the private sector
    through appropriate policies and measures, which may include affirmative
    action programmes, incentives and other measures;

i. Ensure that reasonable accommodation is provided to persons with disabili-
    ties in the workplace;

j. Promote the acquisition by persons with disabilities of work experience in
    the open labor market;

k. Promote vocational and professional rehabilitation, job retention and
    return-to-work programs for persons with disabilities. (United Nations,
    2006, pp. 19–20)

The Convention also stresses that persons with disability should not be
held in compulsory labor.

Variation in Employment Outcomes Across the Globe

Figure 8 and Table 5 in Chapter 5 demonstrate that the low employment rate for people with disabilities is not an issue unique to the United
States. While the measurement of disability and employment varies
across the countries presented in Figure 8, it is clear that the rate of
employment for people with disabilities is low and in several cases has
fallen over time. Table 5 further demonstrates that people with disabilities
are employed at a far lower rate than people without disabilities, with relative employment ratios ranging from a low of 0.28 in Poland, to a high of
0.72 in Finland.

In transitional countries especially, disabled adults are far less likely to
work in the formal economy. For example, in Moldova they are 60% less
likely to work than their nondisabled peers, and in Bosnia and Herzegov-
ina they are 20% less likely to work (Morris, 2011). Moreover, in these
kinds of economies, policies promoting employment of people with disabilities may not have much of a positive effect due to the large informal
work sector in such countries. In India, for example, 87% of people with
disabilities who work do so in the informal sector (World Health Organization, 2011). The prominence of the informal sector in these countries
also makes data on the employment of people with disabilities scarce. In a
study conducted by the United Nations, for example, only 13 governments

Table 5 Employment Rates, Proportion of Disabled and Not Disabled Respondents

	Percent					
	Low-Income Countries		High-Income Countries		All Countries	
Individuals	Not Disabled	Disabled	Not Disabled	Disabled	Not Disabled	Disabled
Male	71.2	58.6*	53.7	36.4*	64.9	52.8*
Female	31.5	20.1*	28.4	19.6*	29.9	19.6*
18–49	58.8	42.9*	54.7	35.2*	57.6	41.2*
50–59	62.9	43.5*	57	32.7*	60.9	40.2*
60 and over	38.1	15.1*	11.2	3.9*	26.8	10.4*

Source: Adapted from *World report on disability,* by the World Health Organization, 2011, Geneva, Switzerland: Author.

Note: Estimates are weighted using World Health Survey post-stratified weights, when available (probability weights otherwise), and age-standardized.

*t-test suggests significant difference from "Not disabled" at 5%.

in Asia and the Pacific provided data on the employment of people with disabilities" (Morris, 2011).

For both high-income and low-income countries, significant differences in employment exist across all categorizations between disabled and non-disabled persons (see Table 5) (World Health Organization, 2011). For more information on employment rates and changes over time, see Chapter 5.

Disparities exist not only in employment rates, but in wages as well. In Russia, for example, "a one-step deterioration in health status, as from very good to good, results in a 14% wage decrease, but a one-step deterioration in disability ranking results in a 30% wage decrease" (Morris, 2011). Wage differences span across gender as well. According to a report by the World Health Organization (2011, p. 239), disabled women earn less than disabled men. While these disparities in wage differences are less apparent in industrialized countries, notable exceptions are the United States, Sweden, and Portugal, where "disabled employees earn at or below 70% of nondisabled employees" (Morris, 2011, p. 7).

Global Trends in Workplace Models

The goal of disability policy is to encourage active workforce participation while providing a safety net to meet basic living needs. Different countries adopt different methods for the integration of people with disabilities into the job market. Different kinds of policies include "cash payments, job-related services and supports, anti-discrimination laws, quotas, and even separate employment" (Mont, 2004, p. 14).

In China, for example, a shift in policy approach to the employment of people with disabilities has drastically increased employment rates within the past couple of decades. Before 1978, China had a "concentration" approach to disability employment (wherein people with disabilities are employed in "welfare workshops" in which people with disabilities should account for at least 35% of the entire staff body). Beginning in 1990, when the Law on the Protection of Disabled Persons (LPDP) was passed, China began pursuing a different strategy of "dispersion" (wherein people with disabilities are employed through self-employment or through a quota scheme where all employers are required to have a certain percentage of people with disabilities in their workforce). According to the China Disabled Persons' Federation (CDPF), the nation's employment rate for working-age disabled populations rose from 60% in 1988 to 70% in 1995 and to 82.5% in 2000—an increase of more than 20 percentage points in just over a decade (Huang, Guo, & Bricout, 2009).

U.S. Businesses as Cross-Border Employers in a Global Labor Market

As globalization blurs international borders, the question of preserving the employment rights of people with disabilities takes on a new dimension. Do U.S. multinational corporations have a responsibility to promote employment for people with disabilities in the different countries where they operate? According to the U.S. Equal Employment Opportunity Commission (2003), "Individuals who are not U.S. citizens are not protected by U.S. EEO laws when employed outside the U.S. or its territories." Employees of these corporations are only protected if there are similar laws for the specific country in which they work.

While concerned with compliance around the world, employers are also interested in leveraging diversity. U.S. employers devote energy and resources to improving their workplace diversity and inclusion because they believe in the business case for diversity that comes both from reduced litigation costs and noncompliance fines and from the profits to be gained from diversity-stimulated innovation and total employee engagement. Increasingly, employers in the United States are recognizing people with disabilities around the world as part of their diverse workforce mosaic.

Notes

1. The Annual Social and Economic Supplement of the Current Population Survey (CPS-ASEC) continues to include what is referred to as a "work limitation" disability status question. The work limitation is determined by the following question: "Does anyone in this household have a health problem or disability which prevents them from working or which limits the kind or amount of work they can do?" (U.S. Census Bureau, Housing and Household Economics Statistics Division, n.d.).

2. The list of causes includes "amputation, arthritis, autism, blindness, burn injury, cancer, cerebral palsy, cystic fibrosis, deafness, head injury, heart disease, hemiplegia, hemophilia, respiratory or pulmonary dysfunction, mental retardation, mental illness, multiple sclerosis, muscular dystrophy, musculoskeletal disorders, neurological disorders (including stroke and epilepsy), paraplegia, quadriplegia, and other spinal cord conditions, sickle cell anemia, specific learning disability, end-stage renal disease, or another disability or combination of disabilities determined on the basis of an assessment for determining eligibility and vocational rehabilitation needs to cause comparable substantial functional limitation" (Rehabilitation Act of 1973, as amended).

3. Note that although the "working age" population is often as broad as 16 to 64 years in official data, and often limited to ages 21 to 64 to exclude the youngest

ages of the population, the age group used in these comparisons is ages 25 to 61. This range is chosen because it falls within the period after most people have completed their schooling and before they have reached the age of retirement currently allowed without penalty by the Social Security Administration.

4. To enhance the enumeration of people with disabilities, six disability questions were first included in the 2000 Decennial Census Long Form. These were subsequently adopted by the Census Bureau's American Community Survey (ACS). To address dissatisfaction with these disability questions, in 2004 the Office of Management and Budget (OMB) Interagency Committee created an ACS Subcommittee on Disability Measurement with the National Center on Health Statistics taking the lead in determining the adequacy of the Census disability questions. Eventually a new set of six disability questions was developed and tested and found to be an improvement over the previous set (Brault, Stern and Raglin, 2007). These new disability questions were first included in the ACS in 2008 and slightly modified versions were adopted into the monthly Current Population Survey (CPS) in June 2008. (See McMenamin, Kruse, Hale, & Kim, 2005, for a discussion of this process.) Several other major national surveys now also utilize the six-question query to identify disability status.

5. Though Kaye also notes (p. 22) that in the June 2010 CPS, "4.0 million people cited disability as a reason for not participating in the labor force but did not endorse any of the six newly added functional measures. In fact, of those people whose labor force status is listed as 'disabled' in the [CPS] dataset, only 67.5 percent are captured by the new disability measure."

6. The Department of Labor defines a commensurate wage as "a special minimum wage paid to a worker with a disability that is based on his or her individual productivity (no matter how limited) in proportion to the productivity of experienced workers who do not have disabilities performing essentially the same type, quality, and quantity of work in the vicinity where the worker with a disability is employed. The commensurate wage in the context of work subject to Section 14(c) is always less than the applicable minimum wage required by section 6(a) of the FLSA, or where applicable, the prevailing wage required by a McNamara-O'Hara Service Contract Act (SCA) Wage Determination" (U.S. Department of Labor, 2009).

7. In a survey of nearly 300 organizations representing 12 industry sectors, PwC Saratoga reports cost-per-hire (calculated as total hiring costs divided by total hires) at $3,375 in 2009 (PricewaterhouseCoopers, 2011, p 12). The latest Compensation Planning Outlook published by the Conference Board of Canada calculates the average cost-per-hire as follows: Executive $43,000, Management/Professional $17,000, Technical $13,300, Clerical/Support $ 3,300. Quoting the Compensation Outlook 2002 by the Conference Board of Canada, the average time-to-hire has been calculated as: Executive 15 weeks, Management/Professional 9 weeks, Technical 7 weeks, Clerical Support 4 weeks (Canada Human Resources Centre, 2011).

8. See Volume 2: *Education* for more information on education and disability.

9. The prevailing wage for a particular job performed by a worker with a disability who receives a special minimum wage is defined by the Department of Labor as "the wage paid to experienced workers who do *not* have disabilities performing essentially the same type of work in the vicinity." An employer paying a special minimum wage must be able to demonstrate that the prevailing wage rate used to determine a commensurate wage was objectively determined. Employers usually conduct surveys to establish the prevailing wage, as they are required to demonstrate that their commensurate wage was objectively determined. The Department of Labor states that, normally, prevailing wage rates are based on the results of surveys conducted by the employer. The prevailing wage "is not an entry-level wage or a training wage, but the wage rate paid to experienced employees after completion of any training or probationary periods. An experienced worker is one who has learned the basic elements or requirements of the work to be performed, ordinarily by completion of a probationary or training period. Typically, such a worker will have received at least one pay raise after successful completion of the probationary or training period. The prevailing wage may not be lower than the applicable statutory minimum wage as established by Ssection 6(a)(1) of the FLSA or, where applicable, a higher state minimum wage" (U.S. Department of Labor, 2009).

10. For discussion of major court cases and their impacts, see the National Council on Disability's 2002 report, "Supreme Court Decisions Interpreting the Americans with Disabilities Act," and their 2004 report, "Righting the ADA."

11. A charge may cite one or more issues.

12. See also Acemoglu & Angrist, 2001; Burkhauser, Houtenville, & Wittenberg, 2001; Burkhauser & Stapleton, 2003; DeLeire, 2000a, 2000b; Hotchkiss, 2004; Houtenville & Burkhauser, 2005; Jolls & Prescott, 2004.

13. This percentage increase is calculated as $[(786{,}000+85{,}000)/786{,}000]-1$. For purposes of comparison and also using data from Bureau of Labor Statistics (2011, June, Table 5 and Table A), the same computation would increase the count of unemployed people without a disability by 7%, calculated as $[(13{,}590{,}000+ 986{,}000)/13{,}590{,}000]-1$.

14. To be eligible for disability benefits, Social Security Administration rules state that a person "must be unable to engage in substantial gainful activity (SGA)." SGA is defined as a monthly income level, and the exact amount of a person who is earning more than a certain monthly amount (net of impairment-related work expenses) is ordinarily considered to be engaging in SGA. The amount of monthly earnings considered as SGA depends on the nature of a person's disability. The SGA amount is higher for statutorily blind individuals than for people without visual disabilities, and federal regulations specify a lower SGA amount for sighted individuals. Both SGA amounts generally increase with increases tied to the national average wage index. According to SSA Online, "The monthly SGA amount for statutorily blind individuals for 2010 was $1,640. For

nonblind individuals, the monthly SGA amount for 2010 was $1,000. SGA for the blind does not apply to Supplemental Security Income (SSI) benefits, while SGA for the nonblind disabled applies to Social Security and SSI benefits" (Social Security Online, 2011).

15. The wording "pauper or convict" was only included for free persons. The Census of 1870 was the first without separate enumeration questions for slaves (U.S. Census Bureau, 2011).

16. For more information on this debate, see Acemoglu and Angrist (1998; 2001); Bagenstos (2004); Beegle and Stock (2003); Bound and Waidmann (2000); Burkhauser, Daly, Houtenville, and Nargis (2001); Burkhauser, Houtenville, and Wittenburg (2001); Burkhauser and Stapleton (2003); DeLeire (2000a; 2000b); Goodman and Waidman (2003); Hotchkiss (2004); Houtenville and Burkhauser (2005); Jolls and Prescott (2004); Lehman (2006); and Schwochau and Blanck (2000).

References

Acemoglu, D., & Angrist, J. (1998). *Consequences of employment protection? The case of the Americans with Disabilities Act* (Working paper 6670). Cambridge, MA: National Bureau of Economic Research.

Acemoglu, D., & Angrist, J. (2001, October). Consequences of employment protection? The case of the Americans with Disabilities Act. *Journal of Political Economy, 109,* 915–957.

Americans with Disabilities Act of 1990, as Amended, 42 U.S.C. § 12101 *et seq.* (2009). Retrieved from http://www.ada.gov/pubs/adastatute08.htm

Americans with Disabilities Act of 1990, Pub. L. No. 101-336, § 2, 104 Stat. 328 (1991).

Bagenstos, S. (2004). Has the Americans with Disabilities Act reduced employment for people with disabilities? *Berkeley Journal of Employment and Labor Law, 25,* 527–563.

Beegle, K., & Stock, W. A. (2003). The labor market effects of disability discrimination laws. *The Journal of Human Resources, 38*(4), 806–859.

Bjelland, M., Bruyère, S., von Schrader, S., Houtenville, A., Ruiz-Quintanilla, A., & Webber, D. (2010). Age and disability employment discrimination: Occupational rehabilitation implications. *Journal of Occupational Rehabilitation, 20,* 456–471.

Blessing, C., Golden, T., & Bruyère, S. (2009). Evolution of U.S. employment and disability policies and practices: Implications for global implementation of person-centered planning. In C. Marshall, E. Kendall, M. Banks, & R. Gover (Eds.), *Disability: Insights from across fields and around the world.* Westport, CT: Praeger.

Bound, J., & Waidmann, T. (2000). *Accounting for recent declines in employment rates among the working-aged disabled* (Working paper 7975). Cambridge, MA: National Bureau of Economic Research. Retrieved from http://www.nber .org/papers/w7975

Boyle, P. A., Buchman, A. S., Barnes, L. L., & Bennett, D. A. (2010). Effect of a purpose in life on risk of incident: Alzheimer Disease and mild cognitive impairment in community-dwelling older persons. *Archives of General Psychiatry, 67*(3), 304–310.

Brault, M. (2008, December). *Americans with disabilities: 2005. Household Economic Studies* (Current Population Reports, No. P70-117). Washington, DC: U.S. Bureau of the Census. Retrieved from http://www.census.gov/prod/2008 pubs/p70-117.pdf

Bruyère, S. (2000). *Disability employment policies and practices in private and federal sector organizations.* Ithaca, NY: Cornell University, School of Industrial and Labor Relations Extension Division, Program on Employment and Disability.

Bureau of Labor Statistics (2008). *BLS Information: Glossary.* Retrieved from http:// www.bls.gov/bls/glossary.htm

Bureau of Labor Statistics (2009, February). *How the government measures unemployment.* Retrieved from http://www.bls.gov/cps/cps_htgm.htm

Bureau of Labor Statistics (2010, August 25). *Persons with a disability: Labor force characteristics–2009* (USDL-10-1172). Retrieved from http://www.bls.gov/ news.release/archives/disabl_08252010.pdf

Bureau of Labor Statistics (2011, June 24). *Persons with a disability: Labor force characteristics–2010* (USDL-11-0921). Retrieved from http://www.bls.gov/news .release/pdf/disabl.pdf

Bureau of Labor Statistics. (2011, November 4). *The employment situation—October, 2011* (USDL-11-1576). Retrieved from http://www.bls.gov/schedule/ archives/empsit_nr.htm

Burkhauser, R. V., Daly, M., Houtenville, A., & Nargis, N. (2001). *Employment of working age people with disabilities in 1980s and 1990s: What current data can and cannot tell us.* Ithaca, NY: Cornell University, Rehabilitation Research and Training Center for Economic Research on Employment Policy for Persons with Disabilities.

Burkhauser, R. V., Houtenville, A., & Wittenburg, D. (2001). *A user guide to current statistics on the employment of people with disabilities.* Ithaca, NY: Cornell University/Urban Institute, Rehabilitation Research and Training Center for Economic Research on Employment Policy for People with Disabilities.

Burkhauser, R. V., & Stapleton, D. (2003). A review of the evidence and its implications for policy change. In D. Stapleton & R. V. Burkhauser (Eds.), *The decline in employment of people with disabilities: A policy puzzle* (pp. 369–405). Kalamazoo, MI: W. E. Upjohn Institute for Employment Research.

Canada Human Resources Centre. (2011). *Calculating cost vs. time vs. loss.* Retrieved from http://www.canadahrcentre.com/solutions/calculating-cost

Charlton, J. I. (1998). *Nothing about us without us: Disability, oppression and empowerment.* Berkeley: University of California Press.

Child Labor Public Education Project. (2010). *Child labor in U.S. history.* Retrieved from http://www.continuetolearn.uiowa.edu/laborctr/child_labor/about/us_history.html

Cone Communications. (2010). *2010 Cone Cause Evolution Study.* Boston, MA: Author. Retrieved from http://www.coneinc.com/2010-cone-cause-evolution-study

Conference Board. (2007, April*). Middle managers: Engaging and enrolling the biggest roadblock to diversity and inclusion* (The Conference Board Executive Action Series, No. 234). New York, NY: Author.

Cooper, R. (1999). Technologies for disabilities. *British Medical Journal, 319*(7220), 1290–1293.

DeLeire, T. (2000a). The wage and employment effects of the Americans with Disabilities Act. *The Journal of Human Resources, 35*(4), 693–715.

DeLeire, T. (2000b). The unintended consequences of the Americans with Disabilities Act. *Regulation, 23*(1), 21–24.

deRoon-Cassini, T. A., de St. Aubin, E., Valvano, A., Hastins, J., & Horn, P. (2009). Psychological well-being after spinal cord injury: Perception of loss and meaning making. *Rehabilitation Psychology, 54*(3), 306–314.

Dooley, D., Catalano, R., & Wilson, G. (1994). Depression and unemployment: Panel findings from the Epidemiologic Catchment Area Study. *Journal of Community Psychology, 22*(6), 745–765.

Doyle, C., Kavanagh, P., Metcalfe, O., & Lavin, T. (2005). *Health impacts of employment: A review.* Dublin, Ireland: The Institute of Public Health in Ireland. Retrieved from http://www.hiaconnect.edu.au/files/Health_Impact_of_Employment.pdf

Elliott, T., & Leung, P. (2005). Vocational rehabilitation: History and practice. In W. Walsh & M. Savickas (Eds.), *Handbook of vocational psychology: Theory, research, and practice* (3rd ed., pp. 319–343). Mahwah, NJ: Erlbaum.

Erickson, W., Lee, C., & von Schrader, S. (2010). *Disability statistics from the 2008 American Community Survey* (ACS). Ithaca, NY: Cornell University Rehabilitation Research and Training Center on Disability Demographics and Statistics (StatsRRTC). Retrieved from http://www.disabilitystatistics.org

Exec. Order No. 13078, 3 C.F.R. 13078. Retrieved from the FDSYS Web site: http://www.gpo.gov/fdsys/pkg/CFR-1999-title3-vol1/pdf/CFR-1999-title3-vol1-eo13078.pdf

Fair Wages for Workers with Disabilities Act of 2011, H.R. 3086, 112th Cong. (2011). Retrieved from the Thomas Web site: http://thomas.loc.gov/cgi-bin/bdquery/z?d112:h3086:

Fishback, P., & Kantor, S. (1996). *The adoption of workers' compensation in the United States, 1900–1930* (Working paper 5840). Cambridge, MA: National Bureau of Economic Research. Retrieved from http://www.nber.org/papers/w5840

Gates, L. (2000). Workplace accommodation as a social process. *Journal of Occupational Rehabilitation, 10*(1), 85–98. doi:10.1023/A:1009445929841

Gibbons, J. (2007). *Finding a definition of employee engagement* (The Conference Board: Executive Action Series No. 236). New York, NY: The Conference Board.

Goldberg, S., Killeen, M., & O'Day, B. (2005). The disclosure conundrum: How people with psychiatric disabilities navigate employment. *Psychology, Public Policy, and Law, 11*(3), 463–500.

GolinHarris (2005). *Doing well by doing good 2005: The trajectory of corporate citizenship in American business.* Retrieved from http://www.brandchannel.com/images/papers/102_Corporate_citizen_2005.pdf

Goodman, N., Stapleton, D., Livermore, G., & O'Day, B. (2007). *The health care financing maze for working age people with disabilities.* Ithaca, NY: Cornell University, Rehabilitation Research and Training Center on Employment Policy for People with Disabilities. Retrieved from http://digitalcommons.ilr.cornell.edu/edicollect/1234

Goodman, N., & Waidmann, T. (2003). Social Security Disability Insurance and the recent decline in the employment rate of people with disabilities. In D. C. Stapleton & R. V. Burkhauser (Eds.), *The decline in employment of people with disabilities: A policy puzzle* (pp. 339–367). Kalamazoo, MI: Upjohn Institute.

Grant Thornton. (2011). *Corporate social responsibility: The power of perception* (Grant Thornton International Business Report 2011). Retrieved from http://www.internationalbusinessreport.com/Reports/2011/Reports/CSR.asp

Hallock, K. (2009). Job loss and the fraying of the implicit employment contract. *Journal of Economic Perspectives, 23*(4), 69–93.

Harnois, G., & Gabriel, P. (2000*). Mental health and work: Impact, issues, and good practices* (Nations for mental health). Geneva, Switzerland: World Health Organization. Retrieved from http://www.who.int/mental_health/media/en/712.pdf

Harris Interactive. (2010). *The ADA 20 years later—Kessler Foundation/NOD Survey of Americans with Disabilities.* New York, NY: Author. Retrieved from http://www.2010disabilitysurveys.org/pdfs/surveyresults.pdf

Henderson, G., & Bryan, W. (Eds.). (2011). *Psychosocial aspects of disability* (4th ed.). Springfield, IL: Charles C. Thomas.

Hirsh, E., & Kmec, J. (2009). Human resource structures: Reducing discrimination or raising rights awareness? *Industrial Relations, 48*(3), 512–32.

Hotchkiss, J. L. (2004). A closer look at the employment impact of the Americans with Disabilities Act. *The Journal of Human Resources, 39*(4), 887–911.

Houtenville, A., & Burkhauser, R. (2005). *Did the employment of people with disabilities decline in the 1990s, and was the ADA responsible? A replication and robustness check of Acemoglu and Angrist (2001).* Ithaca, NY: Cornell University, Rehabilitation Research and Training Center for Employment Policy for Persons with Disabilities.

Huang, J., Guo, B., & Bricout, J. (2009). From concentration to dispersion: The shift in policy approach to disability employment in China. *Journal of Disability Policy Studies, 20*(1), 46–54.

Huo, X., Wang, J., & Ghovanloo, M. (2008). Introduction and preliminary evaluation of the Tongue Drive System: Wireless tongue-operated assistive technology for people with little or no upper-limb function. *Journal of Rehabilitation Research & Development, 45*(6), 921–930. Retrieved from http://www.rehab.research.va.gov/jour/08/45/6/pdf/huo.pdf

Job Accommodation Network. (n.d.). *About JAN.* Retrieved from https://askjan.org/links/about.htm

Jolls, C., & Prescott, J. J. (2004). *Disaggregating employment protection: The case of disability discrimination* (Working paper 10740). Cambridge, MA: National Bureau of Economic Research. Retrieved from http://www.nber.org/papers/w10528

Kaye, H. S. (2010). The impact of the 2007–09 recession on workers with disabilities. *Monthly Labor Review, 133*(10), 19–30. Retrieved from http://www.bls.gov/opub/mlr/2010/10/home.htm

Koizumi, M., Ito, H., Kaneko, Y., & Motohashi, Y. (2008). Effect of having a sense of purpose in life on the risk of death from cardiovascular diseases. *Journal of Epidemiology, 18*(5), 191–196.

Legal Information Institute. (2011). *20 CFR 411: The Ticket to Work and Self-Sufficiency Program.* Retrieved from http://www.law.cornell.edu/cfr/text/20/411

Lehman, I. S. (2006). Minimum wage rates and employment of individuals with disabilities. *Journal of Rehabilitation, 72*(2), 50–57.

Levy, C. (1988). *A people's history of the independent living movement. Lawrence: The University of Kansas Research and Training Center on Independent Living.* Retrieved from http://www.rtcil.org/products/Advocacy.shtml

Martinez, L. R., & Hebl, M. R. (2010). Additional agents of change in promoting lesbian, gay, bisexual, and transgendered inclusiveness in organizations. *Industrial and Organizational Psychology: Perspectives on Science and Practice, 3,* 82–85.

McMahon, B. T., Shaw, L. R., & Jaet, D. N. (1995). An empirical analysis: Employment and disability from an ADA litigation perspective. *NARPPS Journal, 10*(2), 3–14.

McMenamin, T., Kruse, D., Hale, T., & Kim, H. (2005). *Designing questions to identify people with disabilities in labor force surveys: The effort to measure the employment level of adults with disabilities in the CPS.* Washington, DC: U.S. Department of Labor, Bureau of Labor Statistics. Retrieved from http://www.bls.gov/osmr/abstract/st/st050190.htm

Mechanic, D., Bilder, S., & McAlpine, D. (2002). Employing persons with serious mental illness. *Health Affairs, 21*(5), 242–253. doi:10.1377/hlthaff.21.5.242

Mont, D. (2004*). Disability Employment Policy* (Social Protection Discussion Paper Series). Washington DC: Social Protection Unit, Human Development Network, The World Bank. Retrieved from http://digitalcommons.ilr.cornell.edu/gladnetcollect/431

Morris, M. (2011, July 1). *Disability and economics: The nexus between disability, education and employment* (DESA Briefing Seminar Series). Retrieved from http://www.un.org/disabilities/default.asp?id=1575

National Organization on Disability. (2002). *Supreme Court decisions interpreting the Americans with Disabilities Act*. Washington, DC: Author. Retrieved from the NOD Web site: http://www.ncd.gov/publications/2002/Sept172002

National Organization on Disability. (2004). *Righting the ADA*. Washington, DC: Author. Retrieved from the NOD Web site: http://www.ncd.gov/publications/2004/Dec12004

Nazarov, Z., Golden, T., & von Schrader, S. (in press). Prevocational services and supported employment wages. *Journal of Vocational Rehabilitation*.

Nishii, L., & Bruyère, S. (2009, August). *Protecting Employees with disabilities from discrimination on the job: The role of unit managers*. Symposium conducted at the 117th annual convention of the American Psychological Association, Toronto, Canada.

Obermann, C. E. (1965). *A history of vocational rehabilitation in America*. Minneapolis, MN: Denison Press.

Powers, Pyles, Sutter, & Verville PC Attorneys at Law. (2010, April 16). *Highlights of the new health reform law—H.R. 3590 as modified by H.R. 4872*. Retrieved from http://www.ppsv.com/assets/attachments/98.pdf

PricewaterhouseCoopers. (2011). *PWC Saratoga 2011/2012 human capital effectiveness report: Executive summary*. Retrieved from http://www.pwc.com/us/en/hr-saratoga/publications/human-capital-effectiveness-report.jhtml

Rehabilitation Act of 1973, as Amended, 29 U.S.C. § 701. Retrieved from http://www.law.cornell.edu/uscode/html/uscode29/usc_sup_01_29_10_16.html

Saks, A. M. (2006). Antecedents and consequences of employee engagement. *Journal of Managerial Psychology, 21*(7), 600–619.

Schwochau, S., & Blanck, D. (2000). The economics of the Americans with Disabilities Act, part III: Does the ADA disable the disabled? *Berkeley Journal of Employment and Labor Law, 21*(27), 271–313.

Siperstein, G., Romano, N., Mohler, A., & Parker, R. (2006). A national survey of consumer attititudes towards companies that hire people with disabilities. *Journal of Vocational Rehabilitation, 24*(1), 3–9.

Social Security Online. (2011). *Automatic determinations: Substantial Gainful Activity*. Retrieved from http://www.ssa.gov/oact/cola/sga.html

Social Security Online. (n.d.). *Special collections: Chronology, 1900s-1920s*. Retrieved from http://www.ssa.gov/history/1900.html

Spears, E. (1945). Reemployment of veterans. *Conference Board Reports: Studies in Personnel Policy* (No. 69). New York, NY: National Industrial Conference Board.

Stapleton, D., Honeycutt, T., & Schechter, B. (2009). *Out of sight, out of mind: Including group quarters residents with household residents can change what we know about working-age people with disabilities.* MPR Report No. 6061–780. Princeton, NJ: Mathematica Policy Research.

Stapleton, D., & Liu, S. (2009, November). *Will health care reform increase the employment of people with disabilities? Policy Brief 09–04.* Washington, DC: Mathematica Policy Research, Center for Studying Disability Policy. Retrieved from http://www.mathematica-mpr.com/publications/redirect_PubsDB.asp?strSite=PDFs/disability/healthcarereform.pdf

Stern, S., & Brault, M. (2005). *Disability data from the American Community Survey: A brief examination of the effects of a question redesign in 2003* (U.S. Census Bureau, Housing and Household Economic Statistics Division Working Paper). Retrieved from http://www.census.gov/hhes/www/disability/ACS_disability.pdf

Sullivan, D., & von Wachter, T. (2009). Job displacement and mortality: An analysis using administrative data. *The Quarterly Journal of Economics, 124*(3), 1265–1306. doi:10.1162/qjec.2009.124.3.1265

United Nations. (2006). *Convention on the Rights of Persons with Disabilities.* Retrieved from the UN Enable Web site: http://www.un.org/disabilities/default.asp?navid=14&pid=150

U.S. Access Board (n.d.). *The Architectural Barriers Act (ABA) of 1968.* Retrieved from http://access-board.gov/about/laws/ABA.htm

U.S. Census Bureau. (2010, May 26). *20th anniversary of Americans with Disabilities Act: July 26* (U.S. Census Bureau News: Facts for Features. CB10-FF.13). Retrieved from http://www.census.gov/newsroom/releases/archives/facts_for_features_special_editions/cb10-ff13.html

U.S. Census Bureau. (2011). *History: Through the decades: Index of questions.* Retrieved from http://www.census.gov/history/www/through_the_decades/index_of_questions

U.S. Census Bureau, Housing and Household Economics Statistics Division. (n.d.). *Definition of disability differs by survey.* Retrieved from http://www.census.gov/hhes/www/disability/disab_defn.html

U.S. Department of Labor. (2009, May). *Fact sheet #39B: Prevailing wages and commensurate wages under Section 14(c) of the Fair Labor Standards Act (FLSA).* Retrieved from http://www.dol.gov/whd/regs/compliance/whdfs39b.pdf

U.S. Department of Labor. (n.d.). *Frequently asked questions: How does the federal government define "disability?"* Retrieved from http://www.dol.gov/odep/faqs/federal.htm

U.S. Department of Labor, Wage and Hour Division. (2011). *Family and Medical Leave Act.* Retrieved from http://www.dol.gov/whd/fmla/index.htm

U.S. Equal Employment Opportunity Commission. (2003). *Employee rights when working for multinational employers.* Retrieved from http://www.eeoc.gov/facts/multi-employees.html

U.S. Equal Employment Opportunity Commission. (2008a). *Improving the participation rate of people with targeted disabilities in the federal work force.* Washington, DC: Author. Retrieved from http://www.eeoc.gov/federal/reports/pwtd.html#ExecSum

U.S. Equal Employment Opportunity Commission. (2008b). *Questions and answers: Promoting employment of individuals with disabilities in the federal workforce.* Retrieved from http://www.eeoc.gov/federal/qanda-employment-with-disabilities.cfm#affirm

U.S. Office of Personnel Management. (n.d.). *Federal employment of people with disabilities: How to hire people with disabilities.* Retrieved from http://www.opm.gov/disability/mngr_3-13.asp

Vidal, D. (2006, November). *Reward trumps risk: How business perspectives on corporate citizenship and sustainability are changing* (The Conference Board Executive Action Series No. 216). New York, NY: The Conference Board.

von Schrader, S. (2011a). *Calculations from EEOC Integrated Mission System.* Ithaca, NY: Cornell University, ILR School, Employment and Disability Institute, RRTC on Employer Practices Related to Employment Outcomes Among Individuals with Disabilities.

von Schrader, S. (2011b, October 20). *EEOC charge data: What we can learn about the employment of persons with disabilities.* Presentation made for the EARN webinar series.

Voice of America. (2007, March). *How technology can help disabled people live more normal lives.* Retrieved from http://www.voanews.com/learningenglish/home/a-23-2007-03-04-voa2-83133247.html

Weathers, R., & Wittenburg, D. (2009). Employment. In A. Houtenville, D. Stapleton, R. Weathers, & R. Burkhauser (Eds.), *Counting working age people with disabilities: What current data can tell us and options for improvement* (pp. 101–129). Kalamazoo, MI: W. E. Upjohn Institute for Employment Research.

White House. (2011, September 12). *The American Jobs Act.* Retrieved from http://www.whitehouse.gov/sites/default/files/omb/legislative/reports/american-jobs-act.pdf

World Health Organization. (2011). *World report on disability.* Geneva, Switzerland: Author. Retrieved from http://www.who.int/disabilities/world_report/2011/en/index.html

Wright, M. (2009). *Integrating improving employment outcomes for those with disabilities into the corporate social responsibility agenda* (Paper produced under subcontract to Cornell University through Department of Labor funding for the National Employer Technical Assistance, Policy, and Research Center on Employment of People with Disabilities). New York, NY: The Conference Board.

TWO

Current Issues, Controversies, and Solutions

Problems: Continuing Economic Disparities and Employment Discrimination Despite Changes

In Chapter 1 we provide a broad overview of why the topic of employment and work is an important one for people with disabilities. We discuss the challenges for people with disabilities in finding work in America and trace the evolution of service delivery and employment models for people with disabilities across American public policy history. In this chapter, we examine the problem of continuing economic disparities and employment discrimination, along with the often conflicting and competing incentives to both employers and individuals with disabilities presented in public policy, and explore possible disability employment policy and employer practice solutions to address these challenges.

Disparities in employment rates and other employment outcomes between people with disabilities and people without are well documented (Erickson, Lee, & von Schrader, 2010; Mechanic, Bilder, & McAlpine, 2002). Baldwin and Schumacher (2002) find that the rate of involuntary job change is 38% higher for workers with disabilities compared to their nondisabled counterparts. More recently, Mitra and Kruse (2008) find that the job loss rate is two to three times higher for persons with disabilities compared to persons without disabilities, depending on the measure used for job loss.

These disparities are not limited to the private sector. In 2008, people with "targeted disabilities"[1] represented only 0.96% of the federal workforce, yet individuals with disabilities (more broadly defined) represented over 10% of the U.S. working-age population (Erickson, Lee, & von Schrader, 2010).

Charges of Discrimination and Failure to Accommodate at Work

A survey of the human resources (HR) representatives of 43 businesses (Unger, Wehman, Yasuda, Campbell, & Greene, 2002) found that most felt their organizations were doing an adequate job of creating a more inclusive work culture. Areas in which respondents felt their organizations were doing well included returning employees who become disabled to work and retaining existing employees with disabilities. On the other hand, recruiting new applicants with disabilities and providing workers with disabilities with advancement opportunities were not perceived to be as high a priority. Attitudes toward people with disabilities were not felt to be a significant barrier, and neither were costs associated with accommodation.

One indirect way to study workplace outcomes for persons with disabilities is to look at what employers are being accused of doing (or not doing) that is in violation of disability employment nondiscrimination law, referred to as "charges" or "charge data." Charge data are the records of individuals' claims that employers' actions are in violation of the Americans with Disabilities Act (ADA). These data are available by special research request from the Equal Employment Opportunity Commission and can be used to see where job seekers and employees believe discrimination is occurring.

Charge data exist for people with disabilities because people with disabilities are a "protected class" under specific antidiscrimination legislation. Charge data also exist for other protected classes of people in the United States. Three specific legislative statutes define the civil rights protections related to employment of these Americans.

Charges or claims of employment-related discrimination filed under these statutes provide one measure of perceived inequity in the workplace.

In making any comparison between the numbers of claims of discrimination under these various legislative acts, it is important to recognize that the number of people in each protected class varies notably. There are

Table 1 Legislation and Protected Class

Legislation	Full Legislative Title	Protected Class
ADA (and ADAAA)	Americans with Disabilities Act (and ADA Amendments Act)	People with disabilities
ADEA	Age Discrimination in Employment Act	People aged 40 years or older
Title VII	Title VII of the Civil Rights Act	Women and people of color

Source: Authors.

71,904,000 women ages 16 and older in the civilian labor force, for instance, and only 5,795,000 people with disabilities (Bureau of Labor Statistics, 2011a, 2011c). Even if women and people with disabilities experienced the same rate of employment-related discrimination, the fact that there are more women in the labor force means that there would be more claims of gender discrimination.

To account for the differing numbers of people in the labor force in the various protected classes defined under civil rights statutes, the number of claims needs to scaled and put on a comparable base. When this is done, people with disabilities file claims of employment discrimination at a much higher rate than other protected groups (Bjelland et al., 2010). Over the 15-year period from 1993 to 2007, the average number of ADA charges per 10,000 people with disabilities in the labor force was 81.6 (see Figure 11 in Chapter 5). This is 15 times the rate of charges under Title VII of the Civil Rights Act of 1964 among females in the labor force (5.6 charges per 10,000). The rate of charges for people with disabilities is also 20 times the rate of charges under the Age Discrimination in Employment Act (ADEA) among people aged 40 and over in the labor force (4.3 charges per 10,000) and 4 times the rate under Title VII among people of color in the labor force (19.5 charges per 10,000) (Bjelland et al., 2010).

Charges of disability discrimination filed with the U.S. Equal Employment Opportunity Commission (EEOC) and state and local Fair Employment Practices agencies arise most commonly from issues relating to discharge, reasonable accommodation, terms/conditions, harassment, and hiring (Bjelland et al., 2010). The top five most common specific impairments cited on ADA charges are: orthopedic/structural back impairment (12.23%), nonparalytic orthopedic impairment (7.5%), depression (5.8%), diabetes (3.8%), and other psychiatric disorders (3.6%) (see Chapter 5 for additional data tables).

Clearly, work remains to be done toward increasing equal employment opportunities for Americans with disabilities.

Pay Gaps for People With Disabilities

Unequal pay as a form of discrimination is illegal under several federal laws, including the following enforced by the U.S. Equal Employment Opportunity Commission: the Equal Pay Act of 1963 (EPA), Title VII of the Civil Rights Act of 1964 (Title VII), the Age Discrimination in Employment Act of 1967 (ADEA), and Title I of the Americans with Disabilities Act of 1990 (ADA). Compensation discrimination on the basis of race, color, religion, sex, national origin, age, or disability is prohibited by Title VII, the ADEA, and the ADA. In addition, the EPA requires that men and women be given equal pay for equal work in the same establishment. The jobs under consideration need not be identical (for example, they may have different titles), but they must be substantially equal in job content, requiring substantially equal skill, effort, and responsibility under similar working conditions (U.S. Equal Employment Opportunity Commission, 2010).

Charge statistics compiled from the EEOC's Charge Data System provide one measure of pay discrimination, but further evidence of pay discrimination is sought through scholarly research, typically employing sophisticated statistical analysis of pay or income data. One of the first studies to examine directly the job experiences of a larger number of individuals with disabilities was conducted by Schur, Kruse, and Blanck (2005), who surveyed a nationwide sample of 30,000 adults. They found that compared to their peers without disabilities, people with disabilities continued to face disparities in pay, job security, training, and participation in decision making. They estimated that the disparity in pay, specifically, was 8%, even after removing the effects of other pay-impacting job and demographic characteristics.

A disparity or difference in pay between two different groups is termed a wage[2] or pay gap by scholarly researchers. In using statistical techniques to identify and measure the size of wage gaps, researchers seek to identify what are "explanatory factors" (also called "control variables") of the observed gap and what is left as an "unexplained residual." The explanatory or control variables are the reasonable factors that may "explain" the gap, such as education levels or years of experience or occupation. Schur et al. (2005), for example, include hours worked, age, sex, race, education, years of tenure at the company, occupation, and union status among their control variables. The wage gap shrinks as these factors are included in the analysis and "controlled for" statistically. The entire remaining "unexplained" gap is interpreted by some as discrimination, but not everyone agrees with this interpretation. While the cause of the gap could be discrimination, it is very plausible that some share of the unexplained gap is due to other factors not included in or controlled for in the study, such as interpersonal skills or unrecorded absenteeism.

At the same time, however, it is important to understand that even if all statistically relevant control variables are included to the point where the gap is fully "explained away" and a pay gap is no longer measured between two groups of people, this lack of pay gap does not prove the absence of workplace discrimination. For example, adding control variables to take account of the different occupations in which people work could explain away a large share of the wage gap. Discriminatory practices, however, could still limit who gets access to the higher-paying jobs. It must be remembered that pay gap analysis ignores, by definition, the degree of discrimination in non-pay practices. It does identify, however, which non-pay practices and characteristics contribute most to explaining (away) any observed pay gap. If occupation is an important control variable to explain a pay gap, then we have learned that ensuring equal and merit-based opportunity to all occupations is very important to equalizing earnings.

Regarding the wage gap between individuals with disabilities and those without, research reveals notable inequities. Baldwin and Johnson (2006) reviewed more than 100 studies and distilled the 12 most robust, empirical articles. They found that the quantitative evidence supported the contention that employees with disabilities did systematically receive lower pay. Schur, Kruse, Blasi, and Blanck (2009), however, do note that employees with disabilities are as likely as nondisabled workers to be eligible for performance-based pay. Workplace inequalities revealed in the research to date do contribute to differences in employment outcomes that ultimately culminate in income gaps (see Chapters 1 and 5).

Compensation Beyond Wages and Salary

Income from wages or salaries for paid employment is only part of total compensation or remuneration received for work. On average, 30 cents of every dollar that employers spend per employee in the United States is not spent on wages or salaries, but rather on other compensation benefits such as health care, paid vacation, or unemployment taxation.[3]

Table 2   Relative Importance of Employer Costs for Employee
Compensation, September 2011

Compensation Component	Civilian Workers
Wages and salaries	69.4%
Benefits	30.6%
Paid leave	6.9%
Supplemental pay	2.4%
Insurance	8.9%
Health benefits	8.4%
Retirement and savings	4.6%
Defined benefit	2.8%
Defined contribution	1.8%
Legally required	7.8%

Source: U.S. Department of Labor, Bureau of Labor Statistics, Employer Costs for Employee Compensation, USDL-11-1718, December 7, 2011.

More research on the broader compensation gap between people with and without disabilities is needed. Results from the few existing studies that have gone beyond remuneration dollars from wages or salaries to explore the broader definition of compensation confirm that considering compensation more broadly is important (see Burton & Spieler, 1998). Interestingly, Schur et al. (2009), despite showing an 8% pay gap, find no statistically significant gap in total compensation between employees with disabilities and their nondisabled peers.[4] In Colella, DeNisi, and Varma (1998), it is suggested that persons without disabilities may not want to be in "group pay" programs with those with disabilities because the two groups may value non-cash components of total compensation, like health care or flexible work arrangements, differently. Colella et al. do not, however, specifically discuss the pay "mix" issue. Many questions remain regarding the manner in which the mix of pay for persons with disabilities compares to their nondisabled peers. The Cornell University ILR School's Institute for Compensation Studies has published a series of working papers, available at http://digitalcommons.ilr.cornell.edu/ics/, which includes research related to compensation gaps for people with disabilities.

Health Care Insurance

Health care benefits are a notable part of compensation costs for employers. In the United States, concerns over access to and the value of health insurance benefits are inexorably linked to employment outcomes. Roughly one in six Americans is uninsured.[5] Of those who are insured, about 65% are insured through work-based health care insurance or directly purchased private insurance. The military is providing for 4% of insured Americans, while Medicaid covers 16% and Medicare almost 15% of the remaining individuals officially classified as insured (DeNavas-Walt, Proctor, & Smith, 2011). Greater shares of working-age people with disabilities have insurance coverage through government-provided pro-grams, namely Medicaid (29.0%), Medicare (22.5%), and the military/ Veterans Administration (7.2%). Employer/union-sponsored programs reportedly cover 39.0% of working-age people with disabilities, while 9.9% have privately purchased coverage (Erickson, Lee, & von Schrader, 2009). It should be noted that a person may have more than one type of coverage. If the person has previously been eligible for publicly funded health insurance, the increase in income from employment can often result in a loss of eligibility. Therefore, maintaining access to health care is a major concern for people with disabilities who are seeking employment or looking to change jobs. The Institute for Compensation Studies work-ing papers (http://digitalcommons.ilr.cornell.edu/ics) also includes information on the value of health insurance in employment decisions made by people with disabilities.

In the U.S. system of private and public insurance, states, the federal government, employers, and individuals have often sought to reduce their own costs by shifting liabilities to each other. Most private coverage is obtained through employers, while public coverage is linked to the inability to work, making "it difficult for people with disabilities to move into and out of the labor market" (Goodman, Stapleton, Livermore, & O'Day, 2007, p. 1).

Many small employers do not offer health insurance, and if an employer does not provide group private coverage, the cost of obtaining a personal insurance policy can be prohibitive to a person whose disability requires ongoing medical care or assistive technologies (Stapleton & Liu, 2009). Furthermore, many people with disabilities work on a part-time basis and/or in low-wage jobs, increasing their likelihood of not having access to employer-based health insurance (Seshamani & Montz, 2009). The fear of increasing costs associated with providing health insurance to workers with disabilities could manifest as discriminatory practices in hiring and retaining people with disabilities (Schur, 2002).

Even for people who are willing and able to pay for health insurance coverage, in many states insurers may deny or limit coverage to people with pre-existing medical conditions. In 2009, approximately 15% of applicants (ages 18 to 64) undergoing medical underwriting were denied insurance coverage (AHIP Center for Policy and Research, 2009).

Health Care Reform in the United States

It is extremely important to understand the link between employment and health insurance in the United States in the context of the health care reform debate and the Patient Protection and Affordable Care Act of 2010 (ACA). While no mandate exists in the ACA that employers provide employee health insurance, financial incentives do exist. "In 2014, as a matter of fairness, the Affordable Care Act requires large employers to pay a shared responsibility fee only if they don't provide affordable coverage and taxpayers are supporting the cost of health insurance for their workers through premium tax credits for middle to low income families" (Healthcare.gov, 2010).

Small businesses, on the other hand, will be eligible for tax credits of up to 35% of the premium costs for providing health insurance, rising to up to 50% starting in 2014 (Healthcare.gov, 2010). The ACA also attempts to increase workplace wellness programs through employer-directed outreach and subsidies (Karpur & Bruyère, 2012).

Much remains to be learned about the potential impact of the ACA in general and for people with disabilities in particular.[6] For example, from the time of its passage, the ACA prohibited job-based and new individual plans from denying or excluding coverage to children based on a pre-existing condition, including a disability. Starting in 2014, excluding adults from coverage or charging a higher premium for a pre-existing condition, including a disability, is also prohibited (Healthcare.gov, 2011). Such rules regarding pre-existing conditions will impact people with disabilities in a much greater way than the population at large. At the time of publication, pending political elections and court challenges to the health care reform law make its future uncertain.

Age, Disability, and Employment

Older workers make up one of the fastest-growing subsets of the workforce in America. Between 2006 and 2016, the size of the workforce aged

55 and older is projected to increase by 47% (Toosi, 2007). It is not surprising, then, that mature-worker claims being filed with the EEOC are the fastest-growing category of discrimination cases.

The characteristic of age interacts with other individual demographic characteristics, and it may influence certain employment outcomes (Bjelland et al., 2010). One of the most prominent demographic characteristics associated with age is disability, especially since the prevalence of disability increases with age. Of adults aged 40 years and younger, 10% report a work-limiting disability. Among 60-year-olds, 25% report a work-limiting disability (Stock & Beegle, 2004). It is also true that, if properly accommodated, many disabilities do not have to result in a work reduction.

The aging of the U.S. (and the global) baby-boom population has created some workplace issue tensions. Many advocates within the maturing workforce movement do battle with the stereotype that an older employee means a feebler and therefore less productive employee. However, the increasing odds of needing accommodation as one ages suggest that those advocating to reduce misperceptions and discrimination against mature workers would likely do better to align with, rather than separate from, those working to improve work outcomes for employees with disabilities.

In the discrimination claims charged by American workers under the Americans with Disabilities Act (ADA) or Age Discrimination in Employment Act (ADEA), patterns between age and claims are clear. In their analysis of trends in discrimination claims across the aging and disability populations, Bjelland et al. (2010) found that individuals over the age of 40 filed nearly 60% of ADA charges. Those ages 50 and older filed 72% of the ADA/ADEA jointly filed charges. Among the jointly filed charges by older workers, the most commonly cited bases were orthopedic/structural back impairment, nonparalytic orthopedic impairment, and heart conditions.

The willingness of employees with disabilities to acknowledge their need for accommodation is always a concern. But this unwillingness to disclose an accommodation need may only be greater when compounded by a mature worker's additional fear of suffering from age discrimination (McMullian & Shuey, 2006). To help maintain the productivity and job satisfaction of older workers, employers will need to increasingly design jobs and working conditions with the capabilities, limitations, needs, and preferences of older workers in mind. The increase in the number of dually filed (under both age and disability) employment discrimination claims confirms the importance of proactively addressing this needed change in workplace practice (Corthell & McAlees, 1991). It will be imperative for employers to educate their workplaces on the characteristics of aging workers in order to decrease discrimination in the workplace (Bruyère, von Schrader, Bjelland, & Coduti, 2011).

Productivity and Age

New research on productivity and age is revealing a need for businesses to focus on disability management rather than age, per se (Allen, Woock, Barrington, & Bunn, 2008; Gobel & Zwick, 2010). Proactive employers are looking to instate more effective accommodation practices and disability case management services to assist them in retaining older workers and maximizing their longer-term productivity.

Disability management, as defined by the Certification of Disability Management Specialists Commission (CDMSC), "is a workplace program that seeks to reduce the impact of injury and disability and to accommodate employees who experience functional work limitations" (CDMSC, 2008, p. 1). Disability management affords a comprehensive set of skills and services (including case management) that can help employers to better address the health care planning and resource management needs of their aging workforce (Doyle, Dixon, & Moore, 2003). The main focus of disability management in the employment setting is preventing or minimizing the impact of the disability on the employer and employee and assisting in job retention (Bruyère, 2006). Employers utilizing these services often either contract with external third-party case managers to provide these disability management services, or they hire internal disability management providers. Disability management specialists can assist employers in assessing the needs of their aging workforce and developing programs to retain older workers (Dixon, Richard, & Rollins, 2003). Employers, as well as the disability management service providers who may be assisting them, also need to be aware of possible attendant mental health considerations in the aging process (Swett & Bishop, 2003), and of the unique needs of people with existing disabilities as they age (Larkin, Alston, Middleton, & Wilson, 2003).

As employers look to retain the experience and company-specific skills of older workers, and the federal government considers incenting older Americans to retire later in life, more focus needs to be placed on workplace practices to engage older workers, including effective disability management. One interesting international example is the Agemasters initiative of the Finnish company Abloy Oy, part of the multinational Assa Abloy Group. The national government set strong financial incentives for companies to keep older workers actively on payroll longer—for any employee retiring before the age of 63, the company is required to pay 100% of his or her (otherwise government-provided) pension. Abloy Oy responded by creating a holistic approach to older employee engagement and disability management that includes, among its mature worker benefits, a free-of-charge fitness facility just for employees 50 and over, additional time off for those over the age of 57 who take an annual fitness test, a personal fitness plan developed in consultation with the company's physiotherapy staff, the option to participate in the employee-led (company-funded) Agemasters' Club lectures and outings, and up to eight complimentary massages per year. The company also developed customized training of younger managers to increase their effectiveness with older workers (Young, 2007, pp. 35–41).

One or Many: Considering Differences by Disability Type

Those advocating for better employment outcomes for persons with disabilities face a difficult task in balancing the degree to which they address individuals with disabilities as a group, and the degree to which they focus on the distinct differences that are associated with specific disabilities. Successful workplace accommodation and job match require a highly individualistic approach; we otherwise risk considering all people with disabilities as having similar needs and desires and thus minimizing their individualistic choice and career needs. Stereotypes and misperceptions about people with certain disabilities are already prevalent in the workplace, and painting people with disabilities with too broad a brush in the employment process risks further reinforcement of these erroneous stereotypes. For example, according to Thakker and Solomon (1999), only 17% of managers surveyed had recruited, interviewed, or hired a person with a psychiatric disability in the past two years, while 42% had recruited, interviewed, or hired people with physical disabilities. Razzano, Cook, Burke-Miller, et al. (2005), in their pooled analysis of 24 months of data from eight supported-employment programs, demonstrated that employment outcomes for people with mental illness varied by the severity of psychiatric symptoms, after controlling for various demographic and study-condition variables. Co-occurring disabilities or medical conditions also had a negative impact on outcomes. Chapter 5, Figure 2 makes the variation in workplace outcomes for individuals with different disabilities clear.

Using charge data to gauge workplace experience also reveals variation by disability type. For example, Bjelland et al. (2010), in their research using EEOC disability employment charge data, found that behavioral and medical impairment charge categories are more often cited as the issue of termination than other categories, while orthopedic impairment charges are more frequently cited as issues of reasonable accommodation. In addition, more than 55% of charges brought on the basis of chemical sensitivity cite reasonable accommodation as an issue, a higher rate than any other basis.

Individual Factors and Compounding Challenges

Disability type is only one dimension of individual diversity to consider. As is true of all people, people with disabilities are not one-dimensional and often have compounding factors in their efforts to secure successful workplace outcomes. A person with a disability may also face employment challenges associated with being a parent of young children, the stigma of having had multiple breaks in employment, or a need to find employment near accessible public transportation. All dimensions of diversity (including but not limited to gender, race/ethnicity, and sexual orientation) that are often discussed in regard to employment outcomes also come into play in the work experiences of people with disabilities. The interaction of varying individual characteristics and employment barriers is important to keep in mind. We consider just a few here.

Veterans

According to the 2010 Employment Situation of Veterans, 23 million Americans in the civilian noninstitutionalized population in 2010 were military veterans. About 25% of Gulf War-era II veterans (those who served in the U.S. military any time after September 2001), and 13% of all veterans, reported having a service-connected disability in July 2010. A service-connected disability is one that has been determined by the Department of Veterans Affairs (VA) to be the result of disease or injury incurred or aggravated during military service. Note that a veteran can receive disability compensation for a wide range of conditions, and many veterans with a service-connected disability do not report having one of the six ACS functional or activity-limitation disabilities. The percentage of the overall veteran population employed in 2010 was 49.4%, while 46.4% of veterans with a service-connected disability were employed (Bureau of Labor Statistics, 2011b).

The Society for Human Resource Management (SHRM) surveyed over 1,000 members of SHRM to determine attitudes and practices concerning veterans with disabilities. Over 60% reported that they were unaware of resources available to employers to recruit qualified veterans with disabilities, such as the Tip of the Arrow Foundation, the VetSuccess Program, and the Wounded Warrior Program. Over 50% of respondents stated that they had not used recruitment sources to target applicants who are veterans, nor had they hired a veteran who disclosed a disability either before or after time of hire. Only 12% stated that they intended to do so in the next 12 months. Meanwhile, nearly 75% of organizations responded that, in general, "veterans with disabilities perform on the job as well as any other employee. These results validate the high potential of the veteran pool of candidates" (Society for Human Resource Management, 2011).

The Department of Veterans Affairs reports that for every soldier killed in Iraq and Afghanistan, 8 to 16 are hurt or disabled (Bilmes, 2007). Many of these injured veterans will want to return to work, and their return may be challenging for employers to deal with effectively. Cornell University research documents that issues of reasonable accommodation arise frequently among people who charge discrimination with the basis of post-traumatic stress disorder, one of the common impairments of returning veterans (Bruyère, von Schrader, et al., 2011). Such findings make a compelling argument for better preparation of American workplaces to more effectively accommodate this and other common impairments for returning veterans, such as traumatic brain injury. Proactive preparation to accommodate these issues will greatly heighten the likelihood that we can successfully reabsorb and retain these returning veterans in our workforce.

Criminal Records

Being an ex-offender is a compounding factor that can make successful employment outcomes even more challenging for people with disabilities. According to the Bureau of Justice, "Nearly a third of State inmates and a quarter of Federal inmates reported having some physical impairment or mental condition. . . . 12% of State inmates and nearly 6% of Federal inmates reported having a learning or speech disability. . . . Nearly 12% of State inmates and 11% of Federal inmates reported a hearing or vision problem" (Marushack & Beck, 2001, p. 1). The data on mental illness offer wide-ranging estimates of prevalence. A small-scale study using detailed methods of assessment found that 14.5% of male inmates and 31% of female inmates had some form of serious mental illness (Steadman, Osher, Robbins, Case, & Samuels, 2009), while other sources report that closer to half of all inmates demonstrate either a history of mental illness or current symptoms (56% of state prison inmates and 45% of federal prison inmates) (James & Glaze, 2006).

Background checks for criminal records are commonplace among hiring employers due to greater access to criminal record databases and diminishing costs for conducting such searches. This is one of several "job applicant screening practices that may differentially impact people with disabilities, potentially maintaining or increasing the [employment] gap" (von Schrader, Malzer, Erickson, & Bruyère, 2011, p. 10).

Substance Abuse

Another compounding factor is substance use. This process begins early—many studies indicate that youth with disabilities use alcohol and other drugs at higher rates than their nondisabled peers, and that substance use correlates with negative future employment and education outcomes (Hair, Park, Ling, & Moore, 2009; Hollar & Moore, 2004). Smoking, substance use, and other high-risk behaviors are also related to lower probabilities of employment and participation in postsecondary education for youth with disabilities (Bray, Zarkin, Dennis, & French, 2000; Bryant, Samaranyake, & Wilhite, 2000; Hair et al., 2009). Substance abuse is a common secondary issue among people with psychiatric disabilities, with some estimates indicating that up to half of all people with severe mental illness also have drug- or alcohol-abuse histories (Drake, Becker, & Bond, 2003). Razzano et al. (2005) found that having a co-occurring substance abuse problem was a barrier to achieving competitive employment for people with mental illness in vocational rehabilitation programs.

Race/Ethnicity

Culture is another factor that affects the employment outcomes of people with disabilities. While disabilities are found among people of all racial/ethnic groups, disability prevalence and service enrollment does vary across racial/ethnic communities (McCallion, Janicki, & Grant-Griffin, 1997). People who identify as Native American, for example, have a historically higher prevalence of disability. This higher rate of disability among minority groups in general has many social and cultural explanations, such as exposure to health risks or limited access to culturally stigmatized treatments (Ni, Wilkins-Turner, Liebert, Ellien, & Harrington, 2011). Studies on the lower rates of enrollment in state services by cultural minorities have reported "a greater reliance on filial piety, greater availability of extended family supports, suspicion of formal structures, and cultural beliefs that one should take care of one's own" (McCallion et al., 1997, p. 348).

McCallion et al.'s study offers a framework through which to examine the possible effects of cultural differences on the experiences of people with disabilities. The study examines older families from different cultural groups caring for adults with developmental disabilities who often avoid contact with service systems because of certain cultural values. The findings showed that perceptions of caregiving and disability differed between families of different cultural heritage, and that some cultural perceptions "present a caregiving picture different from that on which current services are based," thus discouraging the use of disability services (McCallion et al., 1997, p. 355). The impact of migration is another important issue for minority families with a member who has a disability. Being an immigrant reduces the size of the family network available to give support, but it may also increase concerns over seeking social service help due to legal status and historic discrimination.

The case of Native Americans is especially intriguing. The 2008 ACS reported that 18.0% of working-age American Indians and Alaskan Natives had disabilities, which was the highest prevalence among all races. This rate is compared to 14.1% for African Americans and 10.1% for whites (Erickson, Lee, & Von Schrader, 2010). This disparity in the rate of disability prevalence among Native Americans in comparison to other racial groups also translates into a socioeconomic disparity. The employment rate of working-age whites (ages 21 to 64) with disability in the United States was 41.1% in 2008, while employment of Native Americans with disability was only 36.8% (Erickson, Lee & Von Schrader, 2010). Ni et al. (2011), concerned that there is "a special challenge for Native Americans with disability to find employment" (p. 41), surveyed nearly 900 members of the tribal rolls of four eastern tribes. While they found significant differences in the disability rates between male and female tribal members, employment rates were not significantly different. In evaluating the challenges tribal members faced in finding or keeping a job, they noted that "disability was a common reason among men and home responsibilities was common among women" (p. 49). Over half of tribal members with disabilities were employed (56%), but knowledge and use of state vocational rehabilitation services was low. While 43% of those not currently working wanted to be employed, just 3% had sought help at VR agencies. As Ni et al. argue, consistent with the findings of other researchers, cultural stigmas and a lack of culturally relevant outreach often discourage people with disabilities from seeking services that more readily serve the majority population.

Gender

Gender inequity in the labor market is the topic of a large body of literature, beginning its modern era in the 1970s. The gender pay gap has narrowed in the United States over the past generation, but the gains flattened notably in the mid-1990s (Blau & Kahn, 2000).

The issue of gender also plays an important role in determining the employment experience of people with disabilities. In 2004, Ari Mwachofi conducted a study using case management data from vocational rehabilitation services (VRS) that mirrored a study conducted 30 years earlier on gender differences in access to and outcomes of VRS. The 2004 study found that while women had better educational outcomes than in 1974, they had "lower employment and earnings and greater dependence on needs-based public support than did men" (Mwachofi, 2009, p. 693). The study found that after controlling for all other factors, gender is "a significant predictor of earnings and employment outcomes" (p. 693), and that men with disabilities have a better chance of escaping poverty than women with disabilities. Gender is therefore a critical compounding factor for people with disabilities. As Mwachofi concludes, "women with disabilities face a double employment jeopardy, disability discrimination and sexism" (2009, p. 693).

Disability Management and Return to Work

Disability management is a broad term that captures activities ranging from proactive injury prevention to return-to-work interventions, all aimed at improving work outcomes for individuals and profitability for employers. As Rosenthal, Hursh, Lui, Isom, and Sasson (2007) state, "Disability managers are increasingly becoming skilled practitioners of outcome-based and evidence-based approaches to illness, injury, and disability as each relates to work and work productivity" (p. 83).

Recognized as a distinct practice as early as the 1970s, disability management has grown and evolved, spurred by financial interests and benefits accruing to both employers and individual workers. Large self-insured employers were among the first to recognize the cost savings from successful return-to-work programs for injured employees. The insurance industry then followed suit. Increasing evidence of the potential return on investment in broadened disability management has encouraged the adoption of safety practices, including ergonomics and ecological assessments, as well as the introduction of programs to promote wellness and disease management and reduce absenteeism, and even the development of specialized strategies for case management (Hursh, 1997; Rosenthal et al., 2007; Rosenthal, Hursh, Lui, Zimmerman, & Pruett, 2005).

Rosenthal et al.'s survey of disability management practitioners confirmed that disability managers are turning their attention to prevention, as employers increasingly expect them to "demonstrate a broader range and more specialized practice that includes an understanding of such advanced concepts as absence management, presenteeism, integrated benefit practice, productivity enhancement, and health and wellness paradigms" (2007, p. 82). Disability management, as a field, is putting increased emphasis on outcome-based and evidence-based practices to address the impacts of illness, injury, and disability on the workplace and productivity.

For change to be effective, leadership from top executives is imperative in articulating the importance of keeping people at work and returning them to work with supports as needed. Like all successful business practices, disability management approaches are most effective when they are imbedded into the organizational culture at all levels (Shrey & Lacerte, 1995). An incentive for employers to explore more effective disability management has been reductions in costs. Successful management of disability costs involves a variety of factors, including changing the corporate culture, restructuring financial incentives for return to work, and implementing injury prevention and reduction programs; the latter necessitates the cooperation of both employees and managers (Tweed, 1994). The key factor influencing the potential for reducing injury and lost time is the company's actual demonstrated behavior that it cares about its employees (Tweed, 1994).

Legislation Guiding Return to Work

Returning a person to work following the onset of a disability has been the focus of legislative acts and federal programs, including some of the workplace laws and considerations that employers say command a great deal of their focus, such as the Family Medical Leave Act, the Occupational Safety and Health Act, and workers' compensation.

The Family and Medical Leave Act (FMLA) requires employers of 50 or more people to allow eligible employees to take up to 12 work weeks of leave in any 12-month period if they or a member of their family have a "serious health condition." This leave can be taken throughout the year as needed, in increments as small as the employer's time-tracking system is able to record. Questions may arise about the interplay of FMLA leave and return-to-work efforts; leave can itself be an accommodation, but in some cases the FMLA's requirement that workers be returned to the same or an equivalent position can come into conflict with an employer's desire to accommodate a worker with "light duty" work. In addition, the FMLA allows employers to ask for certification of the serious health conditions for which employees are requesting leave, while the ADA puts restrictions on disability-related inquiries by employers.

The Occupational Safety and Health Act (OSHA) protects the rights of employees to a workplace free of recognized hazards. When a hazard is recognized, standards are developed against which workplace practices or conditions are measured. Often, those conditions are measured, or standards enforced, through inspections, which may include medical testing (for example, hearing tests) or examining medical records. This process again may seem to conflict with the ADA's restrictions on pre-employment physicals and medical inquiries, though OSHA testing requirements often take precedence over the ADA. OSHA may also conflict with the ADA in situations where a worker with a disability constitutes a "direct threat" to the health and safety of colleagues, in which case the employer is obligated to both protect the safety of other workers and accommodate (and protect the privacy of) a worker with a disability.

Workers' compensation programs are government-sponsored, employer-financed systems for compensating employees who incur an injury or illness in connection with their employment. These programs are governed by statutes at the state level, and they seem to rest on a very different principle of disability than the ADA and other civil rights legislation does. Disability rights laws are based on the assumption that disability does not mean the inability to work, while workers' compensation laws focus on the ways that impairments and injuries cause work limitations and decrease earning capacity. (This inconsistency is discussed further in the *Controversies* section that follows.)

While some government support programs are criticized for discouraging people with disabilities from returning to work for fear of losing their benefits, the last two decades have seen legislative attempts to remove some programmatic disincentives and barriers to gainful employment. One example is the Ticket to Work and Work Incentives Improvement Act (Ticket to Work). Passed in 1999, the Ticket to Work Act includes provisions designed to eliminate work disincentives. Specifically, it prohibits the use of work activity as a basis for review for individuals who are entitled to disability insurance benefits and who have received such benefits for at least 24 months. These provisions also allow for continuing disability reviews on a regularly scheduled basis that are not triggered by work activity, and termination of benefits if the individual has earnings that exceed the level considered as substantial gainful activity (SGA) (Social Security Legislative Bulletin, 1999).

Taking the holistic view across employer practices and governmental policies and programs, Bruyère, Golden, and Zeitzer (2007) conclude that the most effective return-to-work efforts include services and supports that are "consumer-driven; custom-tailored to meet individual needs; based on informed choice and consent; ensure legal rights; and provide encouragement and technical support to stakeholders involved in the employment process" (p. 85).

Differences in Employer Characteristics

Just as it is important to consider how the myriad of individual characteristics interact with disability to impact employment outcomes, research has also shown that it is important to consider the variation in employer characteristics. For example, larger organizations typically have more and richer human resources practices, including those practices related to increasing inclusion of people with disabilities. Also, job-skill demands and occupation types vary across industries, as do employment outcomes for people with disabilities. Here we further explore these differences.

Size: The Small Business Employer

The relative frequency of perceived discrimination varies by employer characteristics, with hiring allegations (as compared to other, non-hiring issues) more likely to be filed against small employers (those with between 15 and 100 employees). The higher rates of allegations against small employers come despite—or perhaps because of—their less frequent need to provide accommodations (McMahon et al., 2008). Bruyère, Erickson, and VanLooy (2006) compared the responses of HR managers from small businesses to those of larger firms and found that smaller companies were far less likely to have ever been asked to accommodate an employee, and that making changes to accommodate employees with disabilities was far more difficult for those companies. Smaller firms were also far less likely to have conducted training on disability-related topics—yet they found changing co-worker and supervisor attitudes much easier than did their counterparts at larger firms.

Because mid-sized and small businesses represent 99.7% of all U.S. employers, small employers are vital to any effort to improve employment outcomes (Kobe, 2007; Small Business Administration, 2009). According to the Small Business Administration (SBA) Office of Advocacy's figures (2009), America's 27.5 million small businesses employ more than half of the private workforce, generate more than half of the nation's gross domestic product, and are the principal source of new jobs in the U.S. economy, providing approximately 65% of the net new jobs added over the last 17 years. Small businesses also account for 51% of private-sector output, hire 43% of high-tech workers, and represent 97.5% of all U.S. exporters (Small Business Administration, 2009).

Small businesses hire a larger proportion of employees who are younger, older, women, or prefer to work part-time (Small Business Administration, 2003). They also provide 67% of workers with their first job and with initial on-the-job training in basic skills. This finding points to an excellent opportunity to provide job training, if not career-building opportunities, to youth with disabilities and older workers with disabilities who would like to work part-time to conserve strength and energy to sustain their employment well into their later working years. Other evidence also suggests that small employers are an important segment of the workforce to explore for job opportunities for people with disabilities. Small businesses pay 44% of the total U.S. private payroll and also account for 23% of federal prime contract dollars (Small Business Administration Office of Advocacy, 2004).

Surveys of smaller companies reveal interesting and perhaps conflicting observations regarding inclusion of employees with disabilities. The ADA covers employers of 15 or more employees, except in states that might have more stringent guidelines in related state legislation. In a survey conducted by the Heldrich Center for Workforce Development, workers in firms of 5 to 24 employees were less likely than those in firms employing more workers to say that their company was physically accessible (82% and 90%, respectively). In addition, 44% of these small employers (especially those that had no experience providing accommodations) reported that ensuring accessibility could be difficult or costly, compared to 32% of large firms. However, it seems that the actual experience of accommodating disabilities proves different, in that only 35% of firms that had actually hired people with disabilities agreed that doing so is expensive (Dixon, Kruse, & Van Horn, 2003).

Over 40% of respondents in an SHRM-sponsored survey of HR professionals indicated that their organizations made no effort, or very little effort, to recruit employees with disabilities (Lengnick-Hall, Gaunt, & Collison, 2003). It appears from the observed data that small businesses included in their sample were less likely to have a formal policy for hiring people with disabilities, and less likely to have shown an increase in the percentage of their workforce with disabilities in the last five years, but also less likely to have had an ADA complaint filed against them in the last 12 months. A Cornell University survey of HR professionals found similar results. This study also found that smaller companies were significantly less likely than larger companies to have made accommodations for employees with disabilities. However, when faced with a "need," smaller companies were as likely as larger ones to make the accommodation, doing so between 95% and 100% of the time (Bruyère, Erickson, & VanLooy, 2006).

Drury (1991) explains some of this apparent inconsistency by noting that small businesses have less experience with proactive disability management approaches, as they are less informed about these practices and also have limited resources to hire such services for their organizations. But business size can also be an asset. Since small businesses have less-formal work arrangements, they may also have more flexibility to allow for job modifications and/or accommodations for workers with disabilities. Fewer levels of management within smaller organizations mean workers have the opportunity to bring their concerns directly to the company's decision makers (Drury, 1991).

Bruyère, Erickson, and VanLooy (2006) stress the importance of training programs that take account of business size. Strides should be made to educate small businesses, which are "the most rapidly growing part of our national economy and therefore a potential source of employment for American job seekers with disabilities" (p. 194). Literature on the topic demonstrates that small businesses fear possible litigation and compliance costs of the ADA (Bruyère et al., 2006). Employers express concerns about costs, supervision issues, lowered productivity, and being "stuck" with a substandard employee (Peck & Kirkbride, 2001). However, the reality of the matter is that small businesses are actually far less likely to be asked to make an accommodation. And if an employee does request an accommodation, research has found that most actual accommodations for workers with disabilities are quite inexpensive (Job Accommodation Network, 1994).

Variation Across Industries

Similar methods to those used to study the impact of employer size on people with disabilities indicate that certain industries (manufacturing, finance, and public administration) have a larger proportion of ADA charges than expected, based on the number of labor force participants with disabilities in those industries (Bjelland & Webber, 2010).

Some researchers argue that one of the reasons for the employment gap between people with disabilities and people without disabilities is "job mismatch." This argument suggests that as the job requirements of some occupations and industries make employment of people with disabilities impossible or less productive, this narrows the employment opportunities to which people with disabilities can match their interests and skills. For example, according to Kruse, Schur, and Ali (2010), wheelchair users may not be able to perform the essential functions of manufacturing and service jobs that require good mobility, yet many may not have the education or training for white-collar jobs. People with disabilities are more likely to be employed in service and blue-collar jobs than in management-related and technical/professional occupations. The latter occupations, however, are predicted to be among the fastest-growing occupations in the next decade. As Kruse, Schur, and Ali point out, "Not only are people with disabilities underrepresented in most of the fastest-growing occupations, but also they are overrepresented in the fastest-declining occupations" (2010). Occupations in the textile industry, such as operators and tenders, are rapidly declining. Among these occupations, workers with disabilities represent 7.9% of workers, compared with the economy-wide average of 6.1%. Overall, workers with disabilities are overrepresented in 19 of the 20 declining occupations (Kruse, Schur, & Ali, 2010).

Nearly 70% of disability discrimination charges are filed in the manufacturing, retail, and services industries, while these three industries combined comprise roughly 57% of total employment. Whether this charge rate can be explained by the fact that people with disabilities are overrepresented in these sectors, or whether it is related to the nature of these industries, is not fully determined (Bruyère, von Schrader, et al., 2011).

Table 3   ADA Charges and Workers by Industry Group: 1993–2007 Combined

Industry	Number of Charges 1993–2007 Combined	Percent of Charges 1993–2007 Combined	Workers in Industry (2000 Average)	Employment Share of Industry (2000 Average)
Mining	2,452	0.70%	520,117	0.36%
Construction	8,415	2.40%	6,787,917	4.76%
Manufacturing	58,517	16.40%	17,265,083	12.11%
Trans., Comm., Elec., Gas, and Sanitary Services	30,333	8.50%	26,225,000	18.39%
Wholesale Trade	7,684	2.20%	5,932,967	4.16%
Retail Trade	54,652	15.40%	15,278,892	10.72%
Finance, Insurance, and Real Estate	22,230	6.20%	6,993,208	4.90%
Services	132,915	37.40%	48,808,833	34.23%
Public Administration	36,008	10.10%	20,790,417	14.58%
Total (excluding missing)	**355,837**	**100.00%**		

Note: Column 2 and 3 data from Cornell summary of the EEOC IMS files, June 2010; Column 4 and 5 data from BLS, Employment, Hours, and Earnings from the Current Employment Statistics survey (National), original data values, 2000.

The Federal Sector

While many employment challenges for people with disabilities in the federal government are similar to those in the private sector, differences exist (Brannick & Bruyère, 1999; Bruyère, 2000; Bruyère, Erickson, & Horne, 2002). Federal-sector supervisors surveyed in 1999 identified leadership from the top as the key to change efforts, just as their peers in private sector typically claim. "Visible top management commitment" was rated as the most effective means of reducing barriers to employment or advancement for people with disabilities, along with "skills training for employees with disabilities." However, responses of federal-sector and private-sector supervisors to a survey about policy and practice regarding employees with disabilities revealed notable differences (Bruyère, Erickson, & Horne, 2002).

For every accommodation specified in the survey, which included physical accommodations, workplace process accommodations, and communication accommodations, a greater share of public-sector supervisors reported that their organizations had provided the accommodation. The differences between the two sectors were statistically significant for each accommodation (Bruyère, 2000). Among those who had changes required by the ADA or the Rehabilitation Act, private-sector supervisors were generally more likely than public-sector supervisors to report that it was "difficult or very difficult" to make such changes, and they were generally more uncertain about aspects of the ADA (Bruyère, 2000).

One should not interpret the apparent greater prevalence of inclusionary practices in the public sector, however, as clearly identifying the public-sector workplace as more advantageous for persons with disabilities. Responding supervisors in the public sector also consistently answered "yes" more frequently when asked if their agencies had "experienced . . . disability claims under ADA" for the following list of charges: wrongful discharge, failure to provide reasonable accommodation, failure to hire, harassment, unfair discipline, failure to rehire, layoff, denied or reduced benefits, failure to promote, wage dispute, or suspension (Bruyère, 2000).

One difference in the supervisors themselves is worth noting. Almost half of private-sector supervisors responding had been with their organizations for five years or less. Among public-sector supervisors responding, nearly 60% had been with their organizations for 11 or more years, with almost 30% having been with their organizations over 20 years. This difference in length of tenure means that supervisors in the public sector have had more time to learn their organizations' policies and practices overall, including those relating to employees with disabilities (Bruyère, 2000).

Private-sector respondents were also more likely to work in smaller organizations. Forty percent of those responding were in organizations with fewer than 250 employees—double the share of public-sector respondents in organizations of this size (Bruyère, 2000). Also, almost three-quarters (73%) of public-sector supervisors responded that their employees were covered by collective bargaining agreements (union contracts). Just under one-quarter (23%) of responding private-sector supervisors reported that this was the case (Bruyère, 2000).

Controversies: Tough Issues to Discuss and Tougher to Address

Public Policy Goals and Incentives in Competition and Conflict

Perhaps there is no greater controversy at the core of employment outcomes for people with disabilities than that embodied in the question of "to what degree does a work-limiting disability limit work?" Defining disability in the context of determining and supporting one's ability to work has created policy dilemmas and prompted confused messages from the public sector. (For more on varying official definitions of disability, see Chapter 1.)

The Social Security program was founded to address the fundamental need for individuals who are unable to work to have financial assistance for living expenses. Since the founding of the Social Security program, policymakers and disability advocates have engaged in the following debate: If one's disability is so severe as to prevent work, then surely financial assistance for living expenses is needed. If, however, a person with a disability can work with accommodation, support, and training, then financial assistance for living expenses is not needed. But how much are "living expenses"? And who should bear what responsibilities regarding the costs of providing accommodation, support, and training to promote employment of people with disabilities?

From the time of the earliest legislation, the conflict was apparent. Applicants for disability benefits from Social Security were required to demonstrate a complete inability to work. Applicants seeking such support, however, were also all sent to state Vocational Rehabilitation (VR) programs, showing that Congress believed that even those whose medical conditions would never improve might, nevertheless, be able to engage in some form of employment (Golden, Zeitzer, & Bruyère, 2007).

The Americans with Disabilities Act and government-structured workers' compensation programs also show this dissonance. The ADA focuses on the removal of barriers through accommodation in the workplace on the premise that it is the barriers that individuals face, not their inherent disability status, that limits gainful employment. Workers' compensation, on the other hand, assumes that injuries and disabilities can and do permanently limit the ability to work. An employee's request for accommodation under ADA may be at odds with that employee's argument that she deserves workers' compensation because of a work-limiting injury (Bruyère & Reiter, in press; Geaney, 2004).

Social Security Disability Insurance (SSDI) Program

In considering employment outcomes of persons with disabilities, it is important to discuss in some detail the Social Security Disability Insurance (SSDI) program. Eligibility for SSDI is directly work-related, and SSDI is one clear example where public policy goals and incentives conflict. The role of SSDI is to protect workers and their families from poverty and lack of medical care in the event of a work-limiting disability. The controversy over SSDI is that the program provides strong incentives for beneficiaries to remain outside the labor force, and no incentives for employers to keep disabled employees on the job. Furthermore, as Autor and Duggan argue in their 2010 report *Supporting Work: A Proposal for Modernizing the U.S. Disability Insurance System*, it is increasingly clear that the cost of the SSDI program is unsustainable.

SSDI is one of the largest federal programs that provide assistance to people with disabilities. In December 2010, just under 9.4 million people received Social Security disability benefits as disabled workers, disabled widow(er)s, or disabled adult children; more than 8 million of these were American workers with disabilities (Social Security Administration, 2011, August, Chart 1 and Table 1). The Supplemental Security Income (SSI) program is another. Both are administered by the Social Security Administration, which uses the same process to determine whether an individual is considered "disabled" for the purposes of both programs (Social Security Administration, 2008).

SSDI, as its name suggests, is an insurance program to provide support if a work-active individual incurs a work-preventing disability. SSDI only pays benefits to qualifying individuals and certain members of their family if the individual is "insured." To be insured (covered) by SSDI, one must have worked at least half of the ten years preceding the disability onset and paid Social Security taxes. In contrast, eligibility for receipt of SSI benefits is determined by financial need (income and resource specifications) (Social Security Administration, 2011, July). SSI pays monthly benefits to the elderly, the blind, and people who have disabilities, limited assets, and very low income, and it does not require that an individual have previously worked and paid Social Security taxes. An individual receiving SSI will most likely also qualify for food stamps and Medicaid (Social Security Administration, 2011, May).

For either disability program, the Social Security Administration collects medical and other information about the individual applicant to make a decision about whether or not the person meets its definition of disability. The definition of disability under Social Security is distinct and strict. No benefits are payable for partial disability or for short-term disability (less than a year)—only those with a "total disability" that prevents work long-term are eligible for SSDI or SSI. Social Security was not intended to replace other means of support, such as workers' compensation, insurance, or personal savings (Social Security Online, 2011).

Therefore, the SSDI program provides benefits only to those who were employed but who can no longer work and are not expected to work in the future. A five-month waiting period to receive SSDI benefits is imposed by the Social Security Administration to try to "permit most disabilities to be corrected" or allow the individual to "show signs of probable recovery within less than 12 months after the onset of disability," either of which would disqualify one from SSDI eligibility (FirstStep, n.d.).

The "all-or-nothing" approach to work-limiting disabilities embodied in SSDI, since its inception, is at odds with more current notions (as well as other government policies, such as the ADA) of the abilities of people with disabilities to work. It is SSDI's current underlying financial situation, however, that is increasingly creating alarm among disability advocates and analysts. As Autor and Duggan (2010) show, SSDI's share of total Social Security outlays has nearly doubled since the late 1980s, increasing from 10% to almost 18% in 20 years. SSDI expenditures are now 30% greater than the revenue generated by the SSDI-dedicated payroll tax. According to the Trustees of the Social Security Administration, the SSDI Trust Fund will be exhausted by 2018.

Autor (2011) describes three factors that, when combined, have resulted in SSDI expenditures becoming "extremely high and growing unsustainably" (p. 1), namely: (1) an outdated concept of disability as incompatible with employability, even as technological advancements have lessened the share of strenuous physical activity at work, improved productivity-enhancing assistive devices, and prolonged life; (2) congressional relaxation of SSDI screening in the late 1980s; and (3) the business recession of the 1990s. It is the first of these factors that gets at the heart of the problem.

As discussed in Chapter 1, disability advocates as well as society at large have increasingly embraced and advanced the view that employment is not only feasible for most persons with disabilities, but important for individual self-esteem along with social and economic gain. The breakthrough legislation of the ADA powerfully drove this modern viewpoint into American workplaces through accommodation requirements. Yet the Social Security Administration's eligibility rules continue to define disability as incompatible with employment. Despite evidence that successful long-term return to work following a disability is enhanced by more immediate reengagement in the workplace, eligibility rules and a cumbersome appeals process make this difficult.

Concern over SSDI's impact on the ongoing employment of people with disabilities is amplified by the program's steeply mounting expenses that it cannot sustain. As Autor and Duggan (2010) state, "between 1989 and 2009, the share of adults receiving SSDI benefits doubled, rising from 2.3 to 4.6 percent of Americans ages twenty-five to sixty-four. . . . [At the same time] real annual cash transfer payments to SSDI recipients rose from $40 to $121 billion, and Medicare expenditures for SSDI recipients rose from $18 to $69 billion" (p. 2). The rising costs of the SSDI program due to the increasing number of people depending on SSDI and the undesirable adverse consequences of eligibility rules are two sides of the same coin. Difficult and controversial policy adjustments that would entice beneficiaries to remain in the workforce and employers to retain their employees following the onset of a disability will be necessary to address this growing challenge.

Interplay of State and Federal Agency Mission and Services

Although many disability-focused agencies and services operate at both the national and state levels, there are significant challenges across these agencies involving differing eligibility criteria, significantly different messages about the importance of employment in the lives of individuals with disabilities, and finally the relationship between organizations to create a seamless support system for the served individual. Each department or agency often makes independent decisions regarding an individual's program eligibility and services, the sequencing and interaction of which is at best slow and cumbersome, and at worst sends conflicting messages to people about the importance of work in their lives.

The interaction between the state agencies of mental health (MH), developmental disability (DD), and vocational rehabilitation (VR) exemplifies this problem. MH and DD agencies do not provide seamless services and ready referrals to their state VR partners consistently across states, resulting in many individuals finding themselves adrift in the community following their educational experience or return from hospitalization.

At the federal level, the Social Security disability determination process for SSI and SSDI benefits may also send the message to people with disabilities that it is better to focus on maintaining eligibility for benefits than to pursue work or return to work and jeopardize that possibility. Experts would describe best practice in return to work as a process that first and as quickly as possible determines vocational rehabilitation potential. Services to fulfill this potential should next be provided fully, with any award of permanent disability benefits being determined at the end of the process. The current practice is far from this ideal (Bruyère & Reiter, in press; Geaney, 2004).

"Ignoring" Those Not Living Independently

In discussing U.S. employment statistics of people with disabilities, researchers focus almost exclusively on those individuals captured by the official labor market statistics. These statistics ignore anyone living in "group quarters."[7] Group quarters (GQ) is the official term for both non-institutionalized group living arrangements (including college/university student housing, military barracks, emergency and transitional shelters, and group homes such as the YMCA/YWCA or workers' centers) and institutionalized living arrangements (including adult correctional institutions, juvenile facilities, nursing facilities/skilled nursing facilities, inpatient hospice facilities, residential schools for people with disabilities, and hospitals with patients who have no other usual home) (Brault, 2008, February, December). Those not in GQs are officially defined to be living in "households."

The controversy over the exclusion of GQs from labor market statistics occurs between those who consider GQ residents atypical individuals and those who want to look most broadly at the population of people with disabilities. The latter argue that the public at large includes GQ individuals within its scope of understanding, and spending on government programs does not exclude GQ individuals, and therefore analysis contributing to the public discourse surrounding employment outcomes for people with disabilities should include GQs as well. The official labor market numbers are deficient, according to this argument, because they represent only a subset of the population generally considered in broad public discourse and within government support systems.

It must be acknowledged that only a small minority, fewer than 3%, of the total U.S. population lives within group quarters (U.S. Census Bureau, 2001). In contrast, however, over 10% of males with disabilities and one-third of females with disabilities live in GQs (Stapleton, Honeycutt, & Schechter, 2009). The rate of disability and employment within each classification of living arrangement is, therefore, quite varied.

In public discourse and policy debate over the ability of persons with disabilities to support or not support themselves through paid employment (and be supported by family or government assistance programs if unable to support themselves), many argue that the total number of persons in all living arrangements should be always considered fully. As Brault concludes, "Whether an estimate is including the GQ population—in whole or in part—greatly affects the prevalence of disability and changes the understanding of who these people with disabilities are" (2008, February, p. 6).

Why Do Particulars of Data Collection Matter?

An understanding of the characteristics, economic status, and social participation of people with disabilities and those who use rehabilitation services is critical to evaluating the need for rehabilitation services and judging their performance. As Bruyère and Houtenville (2006) argue, this kind of understanding is especially crucial in these times of increasing fiscal pressure at the federal and local levels. The need to make a solid case for public support of rehabilitation services is especially dire as budget cuts and allocations are being considered at all levels of government and public spending. Disability statistics from national and administrative data sets can be a powerful tool for change when used in conjunction with rich qualitative information.

For example, statistics can be used to assess the need for disability employment services, advocate for services in discrete geographic regions, test hypotheses about various service delivery models, and observe similarities and differences in outcomes across a variety of service sectors. Large national data sources such as the Decennial Census, American Community Survey, and National Health Interview Survey, as well as administrative records from the Rehabilitation Services Administration,

Social Security Administration, and others, have the capacity to provide these statistics. Knowledge of these data sets and how they can be utilized to organize and evaluate service programs should be an integral part of the service planning, administration, and evaluation process.

Efforts to Integrate Disability Into Workforce Development Efforts

The Rehabilitation Act and related program services are under the umbrella of the Workforce Development system. The Rehabilitation Act of 1973 authorized a network of individual state vocational rehabilitation agencies to provide such services to people with disabilities. The Workforce Investment Act of 1998 (WIA) created a "One-Stop" system to serve every job seeker, with or without a disability, through a central location that provides access to multiple programs. This initiative was intended to improve efficiency and outcomes by consolidating all workforce preparation and employment services into a single, unified system.

To promote accessibility to One-Stop Centers for people with disabilities, WIA mandated a partnership between One-Stop Centers and the state vocational rehabilitation system. In practice, however, One-Stop Centers have continued to rely heavily on state VR agencies to provide needed services, rather than integrating people with disabilities into the workforce preparation system (Bruyère, Erickson, VanLooy, et al., 2006). Because One-Stop Centers remain unfamiliar with the job-seeking needs of people with disabilities, people with disabilities continue to be referred to disability-specific organizations, thwarting the original intent of WIA to integrate them into mainstream services. One-Stop Centers have not launched outreach to employers as effectively as needed to engage them on the subject of hiring employees with disabilities or make the significant business case for reaching out to customers with disabilities (Bruyère, Erickson, VanLooy, Hirsch, et al., 2006). Further education of employers by both One-Stop Centers and their VR agency partners is a much-needed continuing contribution to improving employment outcomes.

Set-Asides and Sheltered Workplaces

Community rehabilitation programs (CRPs) are an important part of vocational rehabilitation. As discussed in Chapter 1, controversy exists over CRPs using set-asides while simultaneously being eligible under Section 14(c) of the Fair Labor Standards Act (FLSA) to pay sheltered-workshop employees at rates below the minimum wage. While some government-provided incentives to employers to hire people with disabilities may be appropriate, organizations receiving set-asides that also utilize 14(c) can be criticized for, in some sense, being doubly benefitted at the expense of their employees with disabilities or taxpayers. This concern reached the point of legislative debate with the introduction of the Fair Wages for Workers with Disabilities Act of 2011, which would repeal Section 14(c) of the FLSA. The current repeal bill in the U.S. House of Representatives states, "many employers with a history of paying subminimum wages . . . claim that paying minimum wage to their employees with disabilities would result in [a] lack of profitability and forced reduction of their workforces, [yet they already] benefit from philanthropic donations and preferred status when bidding on Federal contracts." The Fair Wages for Workers with Disabilities Act of 2011 allows organizations employing majority workforces of people with disabilities to continue to be eligible for set-aside contracts, but it no longer allows them to pay employees with disabilities below minimum-wage standards.

Some critics further warn against the sheltered-workshop business model, in which CRPs can profit or be financially sustained in any way by matching their clients to in-house jobs that may be suboptimum for the client but profitable for the CRP as the employer. The concern is that CRPs, in advising people with disabilities about employment opportunities, might be tempted to engage in "predatory matching" if they can raise revenue from direct employment of these individuals in sheltered workshops.[8] In the critics' scenario, CRPs have the advantages of asymmetric information (a fuller range of information about employment opportunities than their clients), the trust of a "captive market" of clients, and a business model (through sheltered workshops) that is built on direct employment of those they are advising. Supporters of sheltered workshops argue that these workplaces offer opportunities that would not otherwise exist and provide employment to people who would otherwise go unemployed. These arguments are summarized succinctly in a 2009 ACCSES[9] Position Paper.

Wellness, Obesity Trends, and Workplace Implications

"Are the young becoming more disabled?" is the provocative title of Lakdawalla, Bhattacharya, and Goldman's study (2004). Their answer is yes. They point to a worsening U.S. obesity trend as a significant contributing factor. While the prevalence of disability has declined among the elderly, the reverse is true in younger age groups. Obesity tends to correlate with disability, and so the increase in youth obesity translates to rising prevalence rates. Between 1984 and 1996, "Disability has remained completely flat among the nonobese, even as it has risen by 151 per 10,000 among the obese" (p. 168). These authors calculate that roughly half of the increase in disability for those 18 to 29 years old is attributable to obesity. And for those 50 to 59 years old, an increase in the prevalence of disability has taken place only among those who are obese (Lakdawalla, Bhattacharya, & Goldman, 2004, p. 172).

The controversies over wellness, weight, and the workplace are multifold. Wellness and weight are considered "lifestyle choices" by many. Others suggest that individuals who make bad personal choices should not receive subsidized health care to treat conditions if the onset was preventable. Obesity also brings its own collection of negative workplace repercussions, such as less pay and lower employment probabilities (Cawley, 2007; Conley & Glauber, 2005). And, while employers have been subsidizing employee health care differently for smokers and nonsmokers for years, some employers have instituted new penalties for not maintaining a healthy weight (Ableson, 2011).

Employees with disabilities are not immune from the employment or workplace implications of the American wellness deterioration. Butcher and Park (2008) link the rise in obesity to declining employment rates among working-age men in the general population, and Karpur and Bruyère (2012) estimate higher health care costs associated with the prevalence of obesity among employees with disabilities. In particular, Karpur and Bruyère estimate that obesity "accounted for 27 to 41 percent of excess expenditures for people with various disability classifications compared to their nonobese peers with disabilities" (2012, p. 1).

Evidence on the return on investment that employers can reap from wellness programs is mounting, and leading-edge wellness practices among employers are spreading. (A lengthy, employer-focused discussion can be found in Rosen & Barrington, 2008.) In a review that analyzed 46 studies, Kuoppala, Lamminpää, and Husman (2008, p. 1216) concluded that the evidence supports promotion of work health as valuable to "employees' well-being and work ability and productive in terms of less sickness absences. Activities involving exercise, lifestyle, and ergonomics are potentially effective." In their meta-analysis, Baicker, Cutler, and Song (2010) find "that medical costs fall by about $3.27 for every dollar spent on wellness programs and that absenteeism costs fall by about

$2.73 for every dollar spent" (p. 304). The federal government is expanding its support for workplace wellness programs in an attempt to "improve employee health and contain health costs driven largely by chronic diseases." According to the U.S. Department of Health and Human Services (2011), $10 million will be awarded through competitive contract to seed the establishment and evaluation of comprehensive workplace health promotion programs.

Call, Gerdes, and Robinson (2009), however, raise the concern that employees with disabilities will be distinctly disadvantaged in the wellness game because, "as with most advancements in society, persons with disabilities largely have been left behind. That is, worksite wellness programs have been developed without taking into account the special needs of persons with disabilities" (p. 30).

Most workplaces do not house their own exercise facilities, but public fitness and recreation facilities are often not designed to be welcoming or accessible to people with disabilities (Rimmer, Riley, Wang, Rauworth, & Jurkowski, 2004; Rimmer & Rowland, 2008). Employers, as the brokers of employee discounts to local facilities, can play a role in improving access for and usage by their employees with disabilities.

Quotas Versus Equal Opportunities and Level Playing Fields

U.S. civil rights laws make it illegal to discriminate in the workplace against people with disabilities and other protected classes. Unlike laws passed in many other countries, these civil rights laws do not include any affirmative action or hiring quota requirements. According to Heyer (2008), the quota system is a part of a larger disability paradigm defined as a social welfare model. The social welfare model treats people with disabilities as people in need of special treatment for their conditions. It is underpinned by a medicalized view of disability with a doctrine of difference, or separate treatment. Consistent with the welfare model is the creation of separate social institutions (e.g., special schools or sheltered workshops) or parallel life paths for people with disabilities, including, in the opinion of some critics, employment quota schemes. More information about quota laws in other countries can be found in the World Health Organization's *World Report on Disability* chapter on employment (see Bruyère, Mitra, & VanLooy, 2011).

A quota is a specific number of members of a particular group that an employer is legally obligated to employ, or a certain percentage of that group that must be represented in the workforce (Thornton, 1998). Such laws make the implicit assumption that, without quotas, employers will not hire or retain workers with disabilities (Mont, 2004). However, dictating a quota does not mean it will be filled. In many countries the average quota fulfillment tends to run from 50% to 70% (Mont, 2004). Many employers operating in countries with quotas for employees with disabilities, for example, choose to build the annual fines for nonfulfillment into their cost structures rather than working rigorously to achieve them (CAHRS Working Group, 2011).

In contrast to the social welfare model, Heyer presents the civil rights model as a better representation of the U.S. paradigm. The civil rights model relies on equal employment *opportunity* instead of (mandated) separate educational services and employment. In this model, legislation is meant to provide a level playing field for people with disabilities, ensuring their right to be treated as equals (Heyer, 2008), but not guaranteeing equal outcomes.

While some advocates favor more aggressive mandates in representative hiring of people with disabilities (and other underrepresented minorities), U.S. opinion polls to date have shown the majority of the country opposed to "preferential treatment" in hiring (Pew Research Center, 2009). Furthermore, employer advocates ask: How can employers be held accountable for representation targets for employees with disabilities if employees do not want to self-disclose their disabilities? As discussed in Chapter 1, without an employee self-disclosing a disability to the employer, the employer may never know a given employee has a disability.

Federal Contractors

Even though civil rights legislation in the United States does not dictate it, many employers do operate under rules of affirmative action because they are federal contractors and therefore (indirectly) receive taxpayer monies. Under Executive Order 11246, signed by President Lyndon B. Johnson in 1965, covered employers who are federal contractors and subcontractors must take "affirmative action" to recruit and advance qualified minorities, women, persons with disabilities, and covered veterans (U.S. Department of Labor, n.d.).

According to Department of Labor instructions, "affirmative actions include training programs, outreach efforts, and other positive steps. These procedures should be incorporated into the company's written personnel policies. (A sample Affirmative Action Program [AAP] from the U.S. Department of Labor can be found at http://www.dol.gov/ofccp/regs/compliance/pdf/sampleaap.pdf.) Employers with written affirmative action programs must implement them, keep them on file, and update them annually" (U.S. Department of Labor, n.d.). How to take advantage of the benefits of affirmative action programs targeting people with disabilities, without creating the unintended consequences of a quota system, will remain a continuing challenge to the disability policy and business communities.

The Department of Labor's Office of Federal Contract Compliance Programs (OFCCP) enforces these contractual obligations of those who do business with the federal government. It emphasizes that companies must create numerical goals, but must not establish quotas. The OFCCP states that as part of required affirmative action programs, "numerical goals are established based on the availability of qualified applicants in the job market or qualified candidates in the employer's workforce" (U.S Department of Labor, 2002). The OFCCP goes on to assert, however, that these "numerical goals do not create set-asides for specific groups, nor are they designed to achieve proportional representation or equal results." Critics question how progress can be expected, since the "Executive Order and its supporting regulations do not authorize OFCCP to penalize contractors for not meeting goals [and the sections of the Code of Federal Regulations covering affirmative action programs] at 41 CFR 60–2.12(e), 60–2.30, and 60–2.15 specifically prohibit quota and preferential hiring and promotions under the guise of affirmative action numerical goals" (U.S. Department of Labor, 2002).

Advocates for people with disabilities point out that the more inclusive the culture, the more willing employees with disabilities will be to self-disclose their disability status. Therefore, holding employers accountable for specific representation targets for employees with disabilities can incent employers to create a workplace environment more inclusive of people with disabilities, encouraging more employees to self-disclose without concerns of negative consequences. This view appears to be winning favor among policymakers. As of this writing, the OFCCP is proposing new regulations that will increase the enforcement of these laws, which historically have not been as heavily enforced as needed (Affirmative Action and Nondiscrimination Obligations of Contractors, 2011).

The OFCCP's proposed rule would strengthen the affirmative action requirements established in Section 503 of the Rehabilitation Act of 1973, obligating federal contractors and subcontractors to ensure equal employment opportunities for qualified workers with disabilities. The proposed regulatory changes detail specific actions contractors must take in the areas of recruitment, training, record keeping, and policy dissemination—similar to those that have long been required to promote workplace equality for women and minorities. In addition, the rule would clarify OFCCP's expectations for contractors by providing specific guidance on how to comply with the law (Affirmative Action and Nondiscrimination Obligations of Contractors, 2011). The most controversial aspect of the proposed regulations, if adopted as proposed, is that they would "establish a national utilization goal of 7% for the employment of individuals with disabilities in each job group of the [federal] contractor's workforce," although "a utilization range between 4% and 10% in lieu of a single national utilization goal" is under serious consideration (U.S Department of Labor, 2011a).

While the outcome of the proposed changes to Section 503 regulations is as yet undetermined, renewed attention to these issues strongly suggests that federal contractors will face increased pressure on affirmation action.

Employers' Efforts at Changing Culture

Business owners and executives and advocates for people with disabilities disagree over the degree of effort and resources employers are actually spending on workplace inclusion of people with disabilities. Employers point to the cost of complying with government regulations related to people with disabilities and their own proactive diversity and inclusion practices. Leading companies argue that they are aware that being inclusive of diversity promotes productivity and business success, and that it is in employers' own best interests to create diverse and inclusive workplaces (Creary, 2008).

Advocates and academic scholars, on the other hand, focus on the large number of workplace discrimination claims made by people with disabilities (see earlier sections on U.S. EEOC charge data) and evidence of employers' halfhearted attempts at workplace-culture change. Bagenstos (2006) notes that dispute resolution procedures and diversity training make employers "appear to be invested in achieving workplace equality" (p. 29), but little if any evidence exists that such procedures and/or training actually result in equal treatment. Krawiec (2009) similarly suggests that employee training practices may in fact be mere "cosmetic compliance" on the part of employers who are more interested in "staving off more onerous mandatory performance-based rules than at reforming behavior" (p. 147), and that anti-harassment compliance structures have proliferated among employers despite the lack of evidence of effectiveness (Krawiec, 2003).

Litigation and Diversity Training

The authors, in working directly with large and small organizations, have collaborated with individual executives from the top of organizations down through mid-level management who are committed to improving the workplace inclusiveness and success of employees with disabilities. Many companies that stand out for being leaders in their commitment to advancing the employment outcomes of people with disabilities are recognized through awards by credible advocacy organizations. And yet, disparities on a national scale continue.

Sherwyn, Heise, and Eigen (2001) discuss how, in the realm of sexual harassment charges, common interpretations of the law create an "incentive for employers to devise a subtle system that satisfies the courts but discourages complaints" (p. 1294). For example, employers might not want to institute a 24-hour hotline for reports of discrimination or misconduct within the organization because it could increase the likelihood that employees will actually report discrimination.

But it is not just actual workplace experience that drives discrimination lawsuits. Koesnadi and Kleiner (2002) assert that today's litigious environment can be attributed to incremental legal changes and a natural evolution in the implementation of these rules. The revolution in employment liability litigation over the last decade can be traced to key changes in the federal Civil Rights Act of 1991 and the institution of the ADA employment provisions (Title I) in 1992, which gave plaintiffs advantages in discrimination cases.

Gutman (2009) examined recent precedents in EEO case law relating to personnel selection to identify potential legal pitfalls for employers and HR managers. These mistakes can be costly, but they can be avoided if policies and practices are in place. The assistance of experts may be required to develop good procedures, but in many cases, in-house training on EEOC-recommended practices is enough to prevent problems from occurring.

Choosing interventions carefully is imperative to ensure that resources are effectively targeted. For example, while researchers like Bisom-Rapp (2001) conclude that there is, in fact, no scientific basis for the conclusion that harassment training improves tolerance among employees or greatly improves the culture in the workplace, others caution that employers need to more strategically (and purposefully) target the training they provide.

Changing laws and litigation trends suggest that employers will need to continue to ratchet up their preemptive action against chargeable offenses or face further escalation of discrimination lawsuits. Koesnadi and Kleiner (2002) state that employees need training on company policies, existing laws, and how to recognize problems and contain them. Hirsh and Kmec (2009), who investigated hospitals' receipt of discrimination charges, found that *who* is trained is significant. They found that diversity training that targeted management reduced the likelihood of employees filing discrimination charges. But training "that raise[d] employees' rights awareness" and targeted employees broadly made it more likely the employer would receive a discrimination charge (p. 512). They conclude that "disaggregating diversity training according to who receives it is crucial for monitoring training's effectiveness and its capacity to reduce employment discrimination" (p. 529).

The fact that training can reduce bias and therefore reduce discrimination charges if it targets managers, but can also increase discrimination charges if it serves to increase awareness among a wider population of employees, illuminates workplace complexities that can create undesirable consequences. Employers may not be willing to spend more (on more litigation) in the short run as awareness is raised across all employees in order to weed out discriminatory practices broadly and truly improve workplace inclusiveness. The more expensive organizational change is, the more reluctant employers may be to embrace it in the many places in the employment process where such change is needed.

Solutions: Looking to Policymakers, Employers, and People With Disabilities Themselves

In the first half of this chapter, we have provided an overview of the problems and controversies that challenge people with disabilities, and also the public policy arena that is working to address these issues. Continuing economic disparities can be seen in workforce participation rates, pay gaps, compensation beyond wages and salary, and access to health care. Employment discrimination can be seen across industry sectors and business size, and it is expected to increase with the growing older-worker cohort. There are intersecting workplace regulations, such as employment nondiscrimination legislation (the ADA), workers' compensation, the FMLA, and occupational health and safety standards, that create challenges for employers and employees. And there are conflicting incentives to individuals to return to work, once on public benefits. In this latter part of our chapter, we discuss policy and government action as well as actions that employers can take to minimize the negative impact of some challenges while maximizing opportunities to make positive and sustainable change in the employment outcomes of people with disabilities.

Policies and Government Action

The Americans with Disabilities Act of 1990 and Amendments

The strongest single piece of federal legislation enacted in the United States to remove barriers to employment for persons with disabilities is the Americans with Disabilities Act of 1990. The legislation has two provisions— one that bans discrimination based on disability status and the other that requires employers to provide "reasonable accommodations" for employees with disabilities. As McMahon and Shaw (2005) state in their study on the ADA and workplace discrimination, while Title 1 of the ADA advances opportunities for people with disabilities, its character "is anti-discrimination, not affirmative action" (p. 137). The law requires employers to eliminate discriminatory policies and practices in their recruitment, hiring, and employment processes, but it does not require that they affirmatively recruit people with disabilities, nor is there a quota for hiring.

As discussed previously, an exception to this rule relates to requirements for federal contractors earning $10,000 or more. Federal contractors do have an affirmative action requirement under Section 503 of the Rehabilitation Act, which has been in place since the law was passed in 1973 and is enforced by the U.S. Department of Labor's Office of Federal Contract Compliance Programs (OFCCP).

Although the ADA has been in place over 20 years now and is the strongest piece of employment disability nondiscrimination legislation we have, the question continues to be raised as to whether the ADA has been an effective solution. Feedback from employers would suggest that the ADA's reasonable accommodation provisions have moved workplaces along in response to accommodation requests of applicants and workers with disabilities. Less than 10 years after the implementation of the ADA, a 1998 survey of HR representatives conducted by Cornell and SHRM found that the majority of employers reported making accommodations to the recruitment process and to the workplace. For example, most employers surveyed had made existing facilities physically accessible (80%), been flexible in the application of HR policies (79%), and restructured jobs or modified work hours (67%). Employers also reported changing interview questions (80%), making recruiting and interviewing locations accessible (76% and 79%), and changing the wording of their job applications (73%).

The majority reported that making changes to promote physical access and restructure job processes was easy or very easy, though much higher numbers reported difficulty providing information access for people with visual and hearing disabilities (Brannick & Bruyère, 1999). These HR representatives also reported that supervisors' lack of knowledge of accommodations was a barrier to employment for people with disabilities. However, the top barriers, as they perceived them, were a lack of experience and skills in the applicant or employee with a disability as well as the attitudes/stereotypes held about people with disabilities. Hernandez, Keys, and Balcazar's review of employer attitudes toward people with disabilities found that "although employers are supportive of the ADA as a whole, the employment provisions in particular evoke misgivings" (2000, p. 13). There is an expressed gap between employer attitudes toward people with disabilities and the actual willingness to hire them. The review found, however, that this gap narrows with employers that have had prior work contact with people with disabilities through vocational programs and supported employment programs. In other words, with familiarity comes comfort and objectivity.

So, although it appears that some gains have been made in terms of employers' response to making accommodations when requested, there are still significant issues with supervisor knowledge of accommodations and also attitudes of managers and co-workers toward people with disabilities. In addition, the labor force participation of people with disabilities in the United States has not increased since the passage of the ADA, or at least its impact has been mixed, and some researchers argue that the ADA may even have had a negative impact. Some, like Kaye (2003), argue that there is cause for some optimism, and that one must take into consideration the changing size and composition of the population of people with disabilities. He argues that there are a large number of people with disabilities who are not part of the workforce altogether, since they are either physically unable to work or are not actively looking. If one examines the effect of the ADA on working-age adults with disabilities who are actively searching for jobs, Kaye suggests that the policy had a noticeably beneficial effect. However, like many other scholars, Kaye focuses the debate on the definition of disability used in the major data sources and/or the confounding effect of changes in other policies, especially the Social Security programs, as discussed previously in the Controversies section.[10] Blanck (1997, 2000) also discusses the importance of assessing the economic impact of the ADA in terms of workplace accommodation costs and the benefits reaped from the employment of qualified workers with disabilities, as well as conducting a more in-depth analysis of the labor force participation of people with disabilities. These studies, Blanck argues, will aid in long-term improvement and implementation of the ADA.

Another issue that arises in assessing the ADA involves judging how well employers and policymakers understand what the law entails. Hernandez, Keys, and Balcazar (2003) conducted an ADA Knowledge Survey of college undergraduates, ADA experts, and private- and public-sector representatives, the results of which demonstrate part of the problem with ADA implementation. While ADA experts scored significantly higher than undergraduates (who will themselves soon be entering the workforce), private- and public-sector representatives demonstrated little ADA knowledge. Efforts were made early on to address this issue with the implementation of a national network of information providers funded by the U.S. Department of Education. The ADA National Network provides information, guidance, and training on the ADA, tailored to meet the needs of business, government, and individuals at local, regional, and national levels. The ADA National Network consists of 10 Regional ADA National Network Centers located throughout the United States that provide personalized, local assistance to ensure that the ADA is implemented wherever possible. These centers, now in existence for over 20 years, are not enforcement or regulatory agencies, but a helpful resource supporting the ADA's mission to make it possible for everyone with a disability to live a life of freedom and equality (see http://www .adata.org for further information).

Better Enforcement of Civil Rights Legislation

Better enforcement of the existing legislation protecting against disability discrimination, such as the employment provisions of the Americans with Disabilities Act, may assist in minimizing employment discrimination for people with disabilities. Employment discrimination charges are filed with the EEOC, and research confirms that stronger and more consistent enforcement of these regulations is needed.

Moss, Burris, Ullman, Johnsen, and Swanson (2001) looked at differences in outcomes of employment disability discrimination cases, depending on the investigating EEOC office. These authors suggest that many of the problems identified were related to the lack of resources available to sufficiently pursue ADA charge investigations, which they refer to as an EEOC "unfunded mandate." Moss and Johnsen (1997) found that many charges were given extensive, thoughtful investigations, but that there were numerous problems with the process of categorizing complaint information. Other problems included understaffing of EEOC field offices, insufficient investigative time, and inadequate funds to perform required investigations.

Moss et al. (2001) analyzed EEOC charge data to develop a framework that accounts for many contributing factors that affect the filing of employment discrimination charges under the ADA. Their intent was to develop a model to explain the impact of the EEOC's administrative process on outcomes such as overall benefit rates and the dollar amounts won. The location of the office where the charge was filed was found to have a significant impact on outcomes. Individuals who believe that they have been the victims of workplace discrimination on the basis of their disability may file a charge at the administrative level, either with the EEOC or with a state or local Fair Employment Practice Agency (FEPA). The statute bars individuals from pursuing a judicial remedy unless they have first exhausted their administrative remedies.

Outcomes tend to be related to whether a charge is filed with the EEOC or a FEPA office. Individuals who file with a FEPA receive beneficial outcomes more frequently. However, those who receive benefits at a FEPA have lower rates of monetary benefit as compared to those who receive benefits after an EEOC investigation (Moss, Ullman, Johnsen, Starrett, & Burris, 1999).

Evaluations of Public Policy and Related Initiatives to Improve Employment Outcomes

As mentioned previously, there have been attempts to assess and measure the impact of the employment provisions of the Americans with Disabilities Act. It is important also to look more broadly at other factors that can impact successful employment outcomes, such as the service delivery system that assists in preparing people for the workforce and in actually placing people with disabilities in jobs. Apart from the ADA, which represents a transformative change in the system of support for people with disabilities, other initiatives represent relatively small-scale tweaks to the existing system.

Most of the interventions, for example, focus on the individual rather than the employer. They are designed to help develop the net value of work to the individual and assist him or her in the job search process. There are a few public policy pieces and funded initiatives that focus instead on increasing the likelihood that employers will hire people with disabilities, such as the ADA provisions, the former Projects with Industry initiatives,[11] and select activities conducted by states under the Comprehensive Employment System Medicaid Infrastructure Grants.[12]

Although the evaluation of these initiatives has generated much useful information, certain shortcomings—such as a lack of adequate data and low participation rates—prevent a full assessment of the impact that these programs have on employment. Another reason why the evaluation might have limitations is that some studies have short time frames but seek understanding of outcomes that are longer term. Some studies also focus on measuring participant experiences, but lack broader analysis of reasons for participation/nonparticipation and benefits external to the program.

Several initiatives have sought to evaluate the work of federal and state agencies that promote the employment of people with disabilities. Livermore and Goodman (2009) offer a comprehensive summary of 27 federally sponsored programs and policies specifically designed to improve employment of adults with disabilities, along with various efforts to evaluate their effectiveness. Based on this review, certain observations can be made about how these initiatives try to overcome barriers to employment for people with disabilities.

In their review of programs aiming to improve the employment situation of people with disabilities, Livermore and Goodman observed that "few of the initiatives reviewed were able to rigorously demonstrate positive impacts on employment, and many of the initiatives were not sustained after the special funding for them ceased" (2009, p. 18). On the other hand, they found that greater attention is being paid to the employment issues surrounding people with disabilities. Livermore and Goodman suggest two complementary strategies that might promote initiatives toward the employment of people with disabilities and effectively transform the system: undertaking bolder initiatives and generating better evidence on the impact of these initiatives. Bolder initiatives would "intervene early, before workers with disabilities have left the labor force and entered onto Social Security Disability Insurance (SSDI) rolls, and before youth with disabilities have entered a lifetime of dependency on Social Security Insurance (SSI)" (Livermore & Goodman, 2009, p. 19).

Tables 4 and 5 are adapted from Exhibit 1 of Livermore and Goodman (2009). In our adaptation, we combine and condense the information from Exhibit 1 and the detailed information on each program contained in the rest of the report into one comprehensive table. The column for "more effective" contains a condensed adaptation of the analyses that conclude a positive outcome of a specific policy/initiative, and the column for "less effective" contains a condensed adaptation of the analyses reaching a negative conclusion.

Table 4   Evaluations of the American with Disabilities Act (ADA) of 1990

More Effective	Less Effective	Neutral
Houtenville and Burkhauser (2004) analyzed people with more long-term disability. They found that the decline in employment for this group began before the ADA and was more closely linked to the expansion of eligibility criteria for disability benefits under SSDI and SSI.	Acemoglu and Angrist (2001) found that employment rates decreased for men with disabilities in the 21–39 age category in 1992, and for women with disabilities in 1992. The largest decrease in employment was among mid-sized companies, because smaller companies were exempt and larger companies could more easily absorb costs related with ADA enforcement.	Kruse and Schur (2003) analyzed Survey of Income and Program Participation (SIPP) data and found that alternative definitions of disability produced different conclusions on the effect of ADA on employment.
Goodman and Waidman (2003) suggested that the recession in the 1990s factored into the decrease in employment rates.	DeLeire (2000a, 2000b) analyzed data from SIPP, controlled for demographic characteristics, industry, and occupation, and found that employment rates for people with disabilities were steady until 1989 and began to fall from 1990 onwards. Employers were avoiding hiring people with disabilities so as not to incur accommodation costs.	The National Council on Disability (2007), in a study based on a review of publicly available documents and data, concluded that while people with disabilities were experiencing less discrimination and more accommodation, they did not appear to be experiencing increases in hiring.

(Continued)

(Continued)

More Effective	Less Effective	Neutral
Hotchkiss (2004a) analyzed SIPP and CPS data and concluded that the apparent decline in employment was partly due to nondisabled individuals who were not in the labor market being reclassified as disabled, rather than an increase of people with disabilities leaving the workforce.		
Jolls and Prescott (2004) found that the negative effect of ADA was mostly in states that had no pre-ADA law or had laws that did not require employers to make accommodations. They also found that these negative effects disappeared after a few years.		

Source: Adapted from G. Livermore & N. Goodman, *A review of recent evaluation efforts associated with programs and policies designed to promote the employment of adults with disabilities*, Exhibit 1, Washington, DC: Mathematica Policy Research, February 2009. Compiled by the authors.

Another study offering evaluation of community-based rehabilitation programs was conducted by Menz, Hagen-Foley, and Gerber (2005). The study was designed to provide SSA with a solid understanding of the capabilities of community-based rehabilitation organizations and suggest ways these organizations may help Social Security beneficiaries return to work or begin working (p. 3). The results stress the importance of constant reassessment and development of practices as well as finding alternatives that give consumers the ability to choose options that are in their best interests.

(Text continued on page 112)

Table 5 Evaluation of Programs and Policies Designed to Promote the Employment of Adults With Disabilities

Program/Initiative & Year(s) Implemented	Target Population	More Effective	Less Effective
		Legislation	
Balanced Budget Act (1997)	Working people with disabilities		
Ticket to Work and Work Incentives Improvement Act (1999)	People with disabilities, with a particular emphasis on SSI/DI beneficiaries		
Workforce Investment Act (1998)	Adults, dislocated workers, and youth	No formal evaluation of the impact of WIA on access to services or the employment outcomes of people with disabilities has been conducted. However, based on outcome measures of entered employment rate, quarterly earnings of employed, and employment retention rate, the project met its 2005 targets.	

(Continued)

Program/Initiative & Year(s) Implemented	Target Population	More Effective	Less Effective
Centers for Medicare and Medicaid Services (CMS)			
Demonstration to Maintain Independence and Employment (various years since 2000)	Working adults with disabilities or potentially disabling conditions	Research Triangle Institute (RTI) evaluation of DC program found that within two years of its inception, the program had reached its enrollment cap and had a waiting list. The program improved access to treatment for non-HIV related conditions because participants received coverage for the full range of Medicaid services.	Because of its design, the demonstration in DC is unlikely to provide information on the impact of providing improved access to health care on the employment of individuals with HIV/AIDS.
Medicaid Buy-In Programs (various years since 1992)	Working adults with disabilities		The goal of Medicaid Buy-In programs is to increase employment among people with disabilities by eliminating the risk that employment will cause an individual to lose access to public health insurance. Although studies indicate that Buy-In enrollees increase their earnings, on average, there is no strong evidence that these programs *caused* the increase in employment.

Program/Initiative & Year(s) Implemented	Target Population	More Effective	Less Effective
Medicaid Infrastructure Grants (Various years since 2001)	Adults and transition-age youth with disabilities		
Department of Education (ED)			
Federal/State Vocational Rehabilitation Services Program (1973)	People with disabilities who want to work	Program Assessment Rating Tool (PART) assessment concluded that the VR program was performing adequately based on the annual performance goals.	
Projects with Industry (1968)	People with disabilities who want to work	According to the annual Government Performance and Results Act (GPRA) indicators, on average, PWI projects were closest to meeting their employment targets during 2004 and 2005, and exceeded the earnings increase targets in each year from 2003 to 2005.	RTI found that the percentage of persons served who exited into employment and the average hourly earnings of those individuals were comparable to those of the VR services program.
Systems Change/State Partnership Initiative (1998)	SSI/DI beneficiaries and others with disabilities who want to work		Despite the strength of the design, evaluators found the following limitations: insufficient follow-up period, lack of control over administrative data, problems implementing random assignment study designs, and contamination of control groups.

(Continued)

(Continued)

Program/Initiative & Year(s) Implemented	Target Population	More Effective	Less Effective
		Department of Labor (DOL)	
Customized Employment Grants (2001–2003)	People with disabilities who want to work	Westat (Elinson & Frey, 2005) reported that the customized employment process can be effective in helping some hard-to-serve individuals with disabilities find better employment.	In the absence of information on a comparison or control group, it is not possible to gauge the strength of Westat's findings (Elinson & Frey, 2005).
Disability Employment Grants (1998 and 2002)	People with disabilities who want to work	Across the 15 Disability Employment Grants, 47% of participants entered employment, thereby achieving the DOL's GPRA program's goal for 1998 of a 47% placement rate.	Employment outcomes achieved by participants varied substantially depending on personal characteristics, however.
Disability Program Navigator (various years since 2003)	One-Stop users with disabilities	Findings from a phone survey indicated high satisfaction with DPN. The most significant advantages noted were improving interagency coordination, program/service access, and availability of benefits counseling.	
Work Incentive Grants (2000-2004)	One-Stop users with disabilities	WIG evaluations identified the Disability Program Navigator as a promising approach to addressing many of the systematic barriers faced by people with disabilities in using the One-Stop system.	There were, however, several key obstacles to success of the program, including the state of the economy, staff turnover, service coordination, and employer interest and investment.

Program/Initiative & Year(s) Implemented	Target Population	More Effective	Less Effective
		Internal Revenue Service (IRS)	
Barrier Removal Tax Deduction (1976; amended in 1990)	Businesses of any size	Through interviews and literature reviews, the General Accounting Office (GAO) found some indication that employers do take tax incentives into consideration, but could not determine if the incentives directly helped people with disabilities find or retain employment.	Based on analyses of IRS data for 1999, GAO found that only a very small share of corporations or individuals with business affiliations used the two business tax provisions for which IRS data were available.
Disabled Access Tax Credit	Small businesses		
Work Opportunity Tax Credit (1996)	Businesses of any size		
		Department of Veteran Affairs (VA)	
Vocational Rehabilitation and Employment Program (from 1918 in various forms)	Veterans with service-connected disabilities	A 2006 PART assessment concluded that the VR&E program was performing adequately based on the annual performance goals.	The general conclusions of the 2004 Task Force were that the VR&E program had not been a priority of the VA, had limited capacity to manage its growing workload, and must be redesigned for the 21st century employment environment.

(Continued)

(Continued)

Program/Initiative & Year(s) Implemented	Target Population	More Effective	Less Effective
		Social Security Administration (SSA)	
Accelerated Benefits Demonstration (2007)	Uninsured DI beneficiaries in the Medicare 24-month waiting period		
Benefit Offset National Demonstration (Pending)	DI beneficiaries		
Benefits Planning and Assistance and Outreach/ Work Incentives Planning and Assistance (2001)	SSI and DI beneficiaries	From the Tremblay et al. (2004) study, there was some evidence that benefits counseling had a positive impact on the earnings of SSA disability beneficiaries in Vermont. Although there are some limitations associated with the study in attempting to draw conclusions about the effectiveness of the program, the findings of a significant positive impact cannot be completely discounted.	

Program/Initiative & Year(s) Implemented	Target Population	More Effective	Less Effective
Employment Support Representatives/Area Work Incentive Coordinators (2000)	SSI and DI beneficiaries	The SSA (2001) ESR evaluators concluded that the position was a success. The feedback from beneficiaries and staff of community organizations who were surveyed indicated overwhelming appreciation with the single point of contact and responsiveness of ESRs.	
Florida Freedom Initiative (2005)	Adult SSI recipients with developmental disabilities		FFI program enrollment lagged far below expectations. GAO (2008b) noted that evaluation of the FFI program was deemed infeasible with so few participants.

Source: Adapted from G. Livermore & N. Goodman, *A review of recent evaluation efforts associated with programs and policies designed to promote the employment of adults with disabilities*, Exhibit 1, Washington, DC: Mathematica Policy Research, February 2009. Compiled by the authors.

(Text continued from page 104)

Studies such as that conducted by Mullins, Roessler, Schriner, Bellini, and Brown (1997) discuss vocational rehabilitation programs through the prism of counselor efficacy. The study emphasizes the necessity of having counselors who are "proactive, empowering, and creative," and stresses that a counselor's attitude and method of practice affects the success of the client to a great degree. Strauser, Lustig, Keim, Ketz, and Malesky (2002) examined differences in career thoughts between people with disabilities and people without. They suggest that counselors should not assume that people with disabilities will have inappropriate or unreasonable ideas regarding their careers, but should instead take an individual approach to dealing with an advisee's career issues. Another study, by Szymanski (1999), discusses the increased job stress of today's labor market and how it may be exacerbated by disability stress. The study emphasizes the role of counselors in helping people with disabilities deal with job distress and plan appropriate strategies to overcome it, as well as in working with employers to minimize unhealthy levels of stress in the workplace.

Many efforts are also designed to make information about disability and employment resources more readily available to people with disabilities, in order to ease the complexity of the service system they encounter. While all of the initiatives are sponsored in some way by federal regulations and dollars, the onus for change is on the state and local entities to design and implement these federal initiatives. Many programs also combine health and vocational support in order to promote employment.

Balcazar, Keys, Davis, Lardon, and Jones (2005) examine an intervention designed to promote goal attainment among vocational rehabilitation (VR) consumers, and to explain the benefits and challenges of vocational training. Eighty-nine individuals with disabilities receiving VR services were randomly assigned to receive either "help-recruitment training plus follow-along support from counselors, help-recruitment training only, follow-along support only, or active treatment (regularly offered VR services)" (p. 40). After more than one year of follow-up, people who had received the combination of training and follow-along support attained more goals than the other participants.

Most of the reviewed initiatives focus on individuals who have already left the labor market, while few initiatives focus on early intervention or preventing labor force withdrawal. This finding may be due, in part, to the fact that until someone seeks the assistance of VR services, she is difficult to "locate" for inclusion in a study.

Seamless and Aligned Service Delivery Systems

There are many programs and initiatives to support the employment of people with disabilities, and there are just as many data systems for recording programs and outcomes—few of which "speak" to each other. This lack of integrated data across service delivery systems for people with disabilities reflects the minimal coordination among agencies that serve individuals with disabilities. In New York State, an effort is underway to improve this coordination through the implementation of a cross-agency integrated database. Previously, each agency had its own case-management system, and no single method for integrating all of these data systems was in place. Such an integrated system can provide a much more complete and accurate picture of the progress of the comprehensive employment system toward successful employment of people with disabilities. Such a data system can also afford agency administrators the ability to see duplication of resources, and it allows for the measurement of key outcomes and indicators across state agencies and service providers in order to better inform decision makers as they implement policies related to employment, rehabilitation services, and health care supports (Vilhuber & von Schrader, 2010).

There have been other efforts to bring different data sources together in one place for policymakers and others to improve decision making. The Institute for Community Inclusion at the University of Massachusetts has collected data from state intellectual/developmental disability agencies, the vocational rehabilitation system, and community organizations in order to describe trends in day and employment services for individuals with developmental disabilities. This project aims to provide a consolidated listing of current day and employment services for individuals with developmental disabilities and to identify factors that influence individual outcomes on a state and national level. The project's Web site, at www .statedata.info, makes a great deal of this information accessible to the public.

Employers convened in 2006 by the National EmployAbility Partnership (NEP) of the National Organization on Disability (NOD) stressed that a single point of contact would improve their outreach to organizations assisting employment of people with disabilities (PWDs). According to the resulting report, "Employers complained that the myriad of suppliers of employment services for PWDs was confusing and overburdened their time. How could they know which providers were [most] responsive to employers' needs?" (Whiting, 2007, p. 2).

One alignment solution is suggested by Autor and Duggan (2010). They propose adding a "front end" to the SSDI program by offering "workplace accommodations, rehabilitation services, partial income support, and other services to workers who suffer work limitations, with the goal of enabling them to remain in employment" (p. 5). In addition, they argue for financial incentives for employers to accommodate workers who become disabled, in order to prevent the movement of these workers into the SSDI system. Their proposal aims to support workers in the event of disability while discouraging them from overusing SSDI benefits, and it rewards employers that have a history of low claim costs by charging them lower rates. They model their proposed program after the U.S. workers' compensation and private unemployment insurance systems, essentially proposing universal private disability insurance.

While such a program would undoubtedly have added costs and complexities, its long-term benefits and sustainability could outweigh these considerations. If this program could return the employment rate of people with disabilities to its 1988 level, "close to one million working-age individuals would return to the work force" (Autor & Duggan, 2010, p. 8). By supporting work, the program might at least slow inflows into the SSDI program. This proposal builds on an existing model of insurance, while still keeping the best key elements of the SSDI program intact.

Educating for the Jobs in Demand

A long-term issue for people with disabilities involves getting timely access to appropriate training for jobs currently available and emerging in the economy. The U.S. Department of Labor's Employment Training Administration (USDOLETA) has designed several initiatives to build the capacity of its Workforce Development System to support job seekers with disabilities. USDOLETA administers the Disability Employment Initiative (DEI) to improve the education, training, and employment opportunities and outcomes of persons with disabilities who are unemployed, underemployed, and/or receiving Social Security disability benefits. USDOLETA also administers the Disability Program Navigator to provide seamless, comprehensive, and integrated access to services to help people with disabilities "navigate" complex rules and other challenges to employment. Information about the program and its initiatives is available at http://www.doleta.gov/disability.

The Rutgers University Heldrich Center for Workforce Development evaluated these initiatives by conducting a survey of service recipients of the USDOL Workforce Development System. Major areas for improvement highlighted by the survey of disability-specific agencies include performance management, accessibility, and outreach to job seekers and employers (Funaro & Dixon, 2002).

Studies have revealed that employers perceive that people with disabilities lack the requisite skills and prior experience needed for jobs for which they are recruiting (Bruyère, Erickson, & Horne, 2002). Biased perceptions of the capabilities of people with disabilities, as well as a lack of opportunity for people with disabilities to get the right training and skills preparation needed and to receive direct placement in real jobs in the community, has been a longstanding mismatch. For example, middle-skill jobs that require training in vocational schools, related on-the-job experience, or an associate's degree still appear in abundance and are consistently the most common group of occupations advertised monthly (Wright, Woock, Spector, & Barrington, 2010). In addition, many individuals with disabilities are not being prepared for the current growth industries identified by USDOLETA: advanced manufacturing, aerospace, automotive, biotechnology, construction, energy, financial services, geospatial, health care, hospital, information technology, retail, and transportation (U.S. Department of Labor, 2011b).

Are individuals with disabilities sufficiently represented among this strong employment segment? New data sources, such as the Bureau of Labor Statistics Job Openings and Labor Turnover Survey (JOLTS), The Conference Board Help Wanted OnLine (HWOL), and the Cornell University Labor Dynamics Institute (LDI), will continue to better clarify the trends in demand for various occupations, and the areas where service providers may best direct persons with disabilities seeking new careers.

Economic Development and Workforce Development Initiatives

While the aforementioned discussion has focused on the importance of getting people with disabilities the right skills and training to fit into the available pool of jobs in a local community's economy, another important part of this matching process involves probing the interests and aptitudes of the individual with a disability. The specific person's natural preferences and abilities have been an increasing focus in the disability career development process.

Over the past few decades, research from a variety of fields has presented evidence of the importance of employment to people with psychiatric disabilities. The 1997 National Health Interview Survey reports the employment rate for people with a wide array of mental disorders to be 37.1% (Harris, Hendershot, & Stapleton, 2005, p. 72). The employment rate for people with schizophrenia and related disorders is 22%. Supported employment, which may include on-the-job or community supports needed to sustain employment, has emerged as a beneficial practice for people with psychiatric disabilities, enabling them to gain employment and participate effectively in the workplace (Kiernan, 2000).

Cook and O'Day (2006) describe the Employment Intervention Demonstration Program (EIDP) as a model for how to effectively support people with psychiatric disabilities in employment settings. The EIDP was designed as a multi-site, randomized, controlled trial of the effectiveness of supported employment (SE) for people with psychiatric disabilities in eight locations across the United States. Clients assigned to SE groups were helped to obtain jobs directly (rather than being provided with lengthy assessment, training, and counseling services) and then given ongoing support to maintain and improve their earnings. During the two-year follow-up period, participants in the EIDP earned over $3.5 million and worked more than 850,000 hours. Participants assigned to an SE group were also more likely to attain competitive employment and earn more money than the control group participants. As Cook and O'Day (2006) report, "people with severe mental illness who received well-integrated and coordinated vocational and clinical services had significantly better employment outcomes than those who received non-integrated services" (p. 2).

In the earlier-mentioned study, the positive results of integrated employment services were not affected by the personal characteristics, diagnoses, work histories, receipt of SSA disability income, and functioning levels of the individuals with a disability. The more an individual participated and received vocational services, the better the employment outcome achieved. Supported employment models that integrated both vocational services and clinical psychiatric services, such as medication management and individual therapy, were more effective than models with low levels of service integration (see also Szymanski & Hanley-Maxwell, 1996). Cook and O'Day argue for a model for funding and service systems that is designed both to assist mental health consumers in obtaining employment quickly and to provide them with ongoing support, thereby heightening the likelihood that many more people with mental illness and limited skills can achieve increased levels of earnings over sustained periods.

Bond (1984) also assessed the financial and social advantages of psychosocial rehabilitation programs and stressed the importance of long-term follow-up for examining employment benefits. Bond and Dincin's study (1986) on accelerated employment also found that artificially limiting the time of prevocational training by involving members in transitional employment offers better results for their involvement in a competitive workplace. Bond, Dietzen, McGrew, and Miller (1995) reaffirmed this finding, reporting from their own research that prevocational training is not as effective as an early entry into competitive employment, coupled with intensive support. Bond et al. (2000) assessed the efficacy of supported employment programs and created a checklist to measure their implementation. They reported that, while supported employment programs were almost equally implemented among the states examined, their emphasis varied based on funding influences, and they were therefore in constant need of self-assessment. Bond et al. (2001) found that within vocational training programs, people with mental disabilities who were placed in a competitive work group showed "higher rates of improvement in symptoms; in satisfaction with vocational services, leisure, and finances; and in self-esteem than did participants in a combined minimal work–no work group. The sheltered work group showed no such advantage" (p. 489).

Tax Incentives

Surveys have indicated that employers support federal tax incentives for companies that hire workers with disabilities (Dixon, Kruse, & Van Horn, 2003). Although employers report a desire for tax credits, and the U.S government has created a number of tax incentives to encourage employers to hire people with disabilities, it is unclear whether the incentives actually affect employer practices, or whether most employers are even aware of their existence (Lengnick-Hall, Gaunt, & Collison, 2003).

In the United States, employers can earn up to $2,400 per year for each qualified hire they make through the Work Opportunity Tax Credit. Nine categories of potential employees are targeted by this tax credit, including individuals receiving Temporary Assistance to Needy Families, veterans with service-connected disabilities, current SSI recipients, and people referred from state VR agencies, among others (U.S. Department of Labor, 2011c).

Eligible small businesses can claim the Disabled Access Tax Credit, which provides a tax credit of 50% of the cost of certain actions they take to make their services or locations accessible to people with disabilities, including removing barriers, providing qualified readers or interpreters, and modifying devices or equipment (Adaptive Environments, Inc., 1998; Internal Revenue Service, 2006). In addition, businesses of any size can deduct select expenditures necessary to make a facility or public transportation vehicle more physically accessible for people with disabilities (Joblinks Employment Transportation, 2009).

Awareness and Knowledge of Business Incentive Policies

While there are many government policies or regulations, such as tax incentives, that could be directed at employers, these measures will only be effective if employers are aware of and knowledgeable about them. Unfortunately, managers' lack of awareness is an additional barrier to employment for people with disabilities.

A 2002 survey conducted by SHRM to assess employers' familiarity with and use of government incentives for hiring people with disabilities found that HR departments are most often responsible for deciding to use such incentives, yet their knowledge level varies widely. Employers most often reported using tax credits that were not disability-specific, such as the Work Opportunity Tax Credit, the Welfare-to-Work Act, and the Veterans Job Training Act. Few respondents said their organizations used the incentive programs for hiring individuals with disabilities, and they were much less familiar with these programs (Lengnick-Hall et al., 2003).

Unfortunately, formal education of business professionals has not significantly helped to change this situation. In the 1990s, when today's mid-career business people were being educated, a survey of professors teaching employment communication courses found that fewer than half (45%) discussed disability disclosure. Additionally, only 6 of the 13 business communication textbooks evaluated in the survey (all published after 1991) included any mention of nondiscriminatory language appropriate to people with disabilities (Parry, Rutherford, & Merrier, 1996). The lack of effective educational and training programs for HR professionals is a central issue to the disparity in employment between people with disabilities and people without disabilities. Legislation like the ADA may aim to protect the rights of those with disabilities, but without the proper information on what complying with regulation entails or what beneficial incentives exist, many employers continue to be apprehensive about employing people with disabilities.

Nongovernmental Business-Focused "Solutions"

Incentives for better inclusion of people with disabilities in the labor market can come from nongovernmental parties as well. Some argue that entering the marketplace directly—as a self-employed entrepreneur—can be a promising path for people with disabilities to gain better economic opportunities. Others say that more professional recruitment services could direct employers to talented professionals with disabilities.

Entrepreneurship, Self-Employment, and Supplier Diversity

Entrepreneurship is vital to the U.S. economy, and it has been the entry point to the American labor market for many immigrants, women, minorities, and other disadvantaged populations (Blanck, Sandler, Schmeling, & Schartz, 2000). For many people, being self-employed and/or building one's own business is the preferred alternative to excessive job demands or rigidity, workplace discrimination, or unemployment.

Many studies have examined women's motivation to be entrepreneurs or self-employed. Among the determinants prompting women to choose self-employment over wage-salary employment are a greater demand for flexibility, preference for a nonstandard work week, and ability to be covered under a spouse's health insurance (Lombard, 2001). These are some of the same concerns that are often noted as important considerations in the employment decisions of persons with disabilities.

Self-employment and small business experience is more prevalent among people with disabilities, at 11.9%, than among people without, at 9.8% (see Chapter 5, Table 7). But self-employment rates also differ substantially across ethnic and racial groups in the United States, even after removing the effects of other individual demographic characteristics, such as age, education, and immigration history (Fairlie & Meyer, 1996). This difference is true for persons with disabilities as well. In 2007, for example, 40% of immigrants with disabilities were self-employed, a greater proportion than their U.S.-born counterparts with disabilities (Xiang, Shi, Wheeler, & Wilkins, 2010).

The importance of self-employment for people with disabilities was recognized in 1998 by the Presidential Task Force on Employment of Adults with Disabilities, which recommended that the Small Business Administration actively support the development of small businesses by Americans with disabilities (Blanck et al., 2000). This recommendation came as increasing numbers of people with disabilities were choosing self-employment.

Entrepreneurship has many advantages for people with disabilities who want to work. Even after the passage of the ADA, discrimination has continued to be a problem. Self-employment bypasses the frustrating barriers in the job application and employment process. It gives workers with disabilities a chance to showcase their talents in ways that can change the attitudes of employers, and it serves as a demonstration of the potential benefits of changes in the workplace, such as flextime, job sharing, and telecommuting (Blanck et al., 2000).

But other than the personal work environment, what advantages are there for a disabled business owner in the sellers' market for goods and services? Supplier diversity is a stated goal of many businesses and is encouraged through policy at the federal, state, and local levels in the United States. Many corporations employ executives whose role is to promote purchasing of goods and services used in the primary business of the company from diverse suppliers, ensuring that the "firms' supply bases align with the diverse customer bases they serve and the diverse markets they seek" (The Conference Board, 2012).

The U.S. Business Leadership Network® (USBLN®), a national disability organization representing over 5,000 employers across North America, believes that a formal designation of businesses owned by disabled entrepreneurs will benefit self-employed individuals with disabilities. In 2010, the USBLN launched its own national certification program for disabled-owned businesses. The USBLN Disability Supplier Diversity Program® (DSDP®) offers businesses owned by individuals with a disability the opportunity to increase their access to potential contracting opportunities with major corporations, government agencies, and one another. Through the program, businesses can obtain Disability-Owned Business Enterprise Certification and get connected to a nationwide network of corporate and government procurement professionals, disability advocates, and other certified disability-owned businesses. With major corporations building "supplier diversity" into both their procurement and diversity strategies and policies, such a certification could provide disabled-owned small businesses with new opportunities to grow their business-to-business customer base.

Directing Employers to the Talent They Seek

Solutions that reduce the amount of energy employers have to expend on seeking out qualified candidates will encourage greater inclusion of people with disabilities in the workplace. In the case of seeking new employees, employers often express frustration that those in the business of directing talent to employers are not effectively promoting people with disabilities.

Recruitment is an annual occurrence on college campuses, yet employers complain that they find it challenging to proactively recruit students with disabilities because there is no single point of contact. A lack of coordination between offices of career services and offices serving students with disabilities on college campuses leaves visiting recruiters feeling that they cannot access the diverse talent they seek (CAHRS Working Group, 2011).

Similarly, for high-end executive positions, professional recruiting services often are not set up to help employers locate candidates with disabilities. For other underrepresented groups this is less the case. In addition to well-known private-sector "headhunters" that specialize in recruiting female and minority executives, professional organizations of women or minorities are more visible to employers than comparable professional organizations for people with disabilities (Whiting, 2007).

Advocacy groups for people with disabilities could encourage the flow of employers toward people with disabilities, especially for higher-level jobs, by easing the recruitment process for people with disabilities. Groups such as Emerging Leaders, a competitive program that places undergraduate and graduate students with disabilities in summer internships and leadership development opportunities, are beginning to move recruitment in this direction (Emerging Leaders, n.d.).

Employer-Based Action

Government policies to include people with disabilities in workforce development and training schemes, as well as to provide incentives for employers to hire people with disabilities, are important but not sufficient for making big-picture gains. It is also very important to understand what is driving the economy and employer actions in order to better determine where a synergistic match of interests between employers and advocates for people with disabilities can make longer-lasting impacts on the employment outcomes of people with disabilities.

To encourage employers to work proactively with disability advocates and public policymakers, instead of against them, in improving employment outcomes for people with disabilities, employers have to believe there is a "business case." This case is built on bottom-line factors, such as gaining access to a relatively untapped pool of available talent, building a realistic understanding of the job performance of people with disabilities, debunking myths on the cost of accommodations, constructively presenting risk mitigation that accompanies an inclusive workplace, achieving increased productivity from fuller employee engagement, and finding new revenue opportunities from better serving consumers with disabilities (CAHRS Working Group, 2011; Linkow, 2012).

Here we provide an overview of a variety of factors to consider in the employer's role in improving employment outcomes for people with disabilities.

Creating Change Inside the Workplace Walls

In the past, many best practices recommendations in both the rehabilitation and disability literature and the business management and HR literature have consisted of lists of interventions and programs offered by employers, without documentation of efficacy. Slowly, needed confirmation of which practices might indeed improve employment outcomes for people with disabilities is emerging. Research in the past 10 to 15 years has revealed useful information about the importance of specific workplace programs and practices, such as having central funds for accommodations, processes for requesting accommodations, educational and training programs on disability issues, and targeted recruiting practices for improving employment outcomes of people with disabilities (Able Trust, 2003; Bruyère, 2000; Bruyère et al., 2002; Bruyère,

Erickson, & VanLooy 2004; Lengnick-Hall, 2007). Gilbride, Stensrud, Vandergoot, and Golden (2003) identified 13 specific characteristics of employers open to hiring and accommodating people with disabilities. These characteristics fell into four major categories: person-to-job match, an engaging and inclusive workplace culture, employer experience with people with disabilities, and high-level executive support. These areas roughly line up with the major barriers identified in Bruyère (2000).

For vocational rehabilitation agencies, this finding means it is more important than ever to frame rehabilitation programs in terms of employer needs in order to ensure successful job placement. Fabian, Luecking, and Tilson (1995) offer recommendations to vocational rehabilitation agencies in their study titled "Personnel Perspectives on Hiring Persons with Disabilities." They suggest that agencies should also take on a more proactive role in terms of technical assistance and training in order to improve employment opportunities for people with disabilities. Kosciulek, Rosenthal, Vessell, Accardo, and Merz (1997) recommend that agencies assess customer satisfaction with their members and conduct local focus groups to assess employer needs. While certain models suggest that increasing informed consumer choice in the vocational rehabilitation process will lead to enhanced employment opportunities, more research is still needed to clarify factors that promote successful employment outcomes for people with disabilities (Kosciulek, 2007; Rumrill & Roessler, 1999).

In their meta-analysis looking at change inside the company walls, Harter, Schmidt, and Keyes (2003) conclude that "positive workplace perceptions and feelings are associated with higher business-unit customer loyalty, higher profitability, higher productivity, and lower rates of turnover" (p. 205). The outcome of these positive perceptions is captured in what HR practitioners call employee engagement, defined as "a heightened emotional and intellectual connection that an employee has for his/her job, organization, manager, or co-workers that, in turn, influences him/her to apply additional discretionary effort to his/her work" (Gibbons, 2007, p. 3). Heightened employee engagement, therefore, benefits the employer, but it also results in better workplace outcomes for the individual employee in the form of higher performance ratings and greater satisfaction with one's own work. These measures, in turn, would increase the likelihood of career advancement and higher earnings.

In their survey of 30,000 employees from 14 companies, Schur et al. (2009) found that employees with disabilities "report having less job security, being more closely supervised, and having lower levels of participation in decisions. . . . They are also less likely than their nondisabled peers to have received formal, company-sponsored training" (p. 397). As these workplace conditions (job security, independence, decision-making control, investment in job training) can all be associated with drivers of engagement, these findings are consistent with lower engagement among employees with disabilities.

Many of the necessary workplace conditions for a culture inclusive of people with disabilities (e.g., job empowerment, participation in decision-making, fair treatment, climate) are under the direct control of managers. The role and impact of the manager in fostering inclusion, minimizing employment disparities, implementing disability practices, and increasing engagement is central (The Conference Board, 2007). Certain federal contractors are required to file an annual EEO-1 Report with information about race/ethnicity and gender of employees. They rarely, however, include disability status. To rigorously pursue improved engagement of employees with disabilities, employers need to more actively analyze their internal culture and inclusion practices.

Employers Are Accommodating, but Not Universally

A 1998 survey of HR professionals conducted by Cornell and SHRM revealed that employers were accommodating employees with disabilities and were finding such accommodations relatively easy to make (Brannick & Bruyère, 1999; Bruyère, 2000; Bruyère et al. 2002). Gilbride, Stensrud, Ehlers, Evans, and Peterson (2000) surveyed 123 employers who had hired clients from vocational rehabilitation (VR) offices during 1997. The employers reported almost unanimously that they were glad they had hired a person with a disability, and 72% of midwestern employers and 38% of southeastern employers reported that they had provided accommodations for their employees with disabilities. In a study conducted in Florida of Chamber of Commerce members, nonmembers, and organizations considering Chamber membership, over 50% of the total sample of businesses had modified existing facilities or work schedules and restructured job requirements to accommodate workers with disabilities (Able Trust, 2003). Zwerling et al. (2003) found that nearly 16% of working Americans needed specific workplace accommodations, but 12% reported receiving such.

Related employer studies produced similar results that confirm that employers are making positive changes to their workplaces. They view hiring people with disabilities as an important strategic national business goal, and their experience working with people with disabilities confirms the good performance of these individuals (Lengnick-Hall, Gaunt, & Kulkarni, 2008; Unger, 2002). Lengnick-Hall et al. (2008) conducted semi-structured interviews with 38 executives across a broad array of industries and geographic regions and found that, while informants could articulate reservations about hiring people with disabilities, they also identified many reasons why hiring this population made good business sense. Reasons given were that many people with disabilities want to work and are not currently employed, that society is better off when more people with disabilities are employed, and that employers are advantaged in a global economy. Perspectives from supervisors also have shown that they are quite satisfied with the work performance of people with disabilities and find their performance to be similar to that of their nondisabled coworkers (Unger, 2002).

There are very few empirical studies regarding the benefits of accommodation, but research indicates that employer accommodation gets employees back to work after injury and keeps them at work if they become disabled while employed, assisting in the retention of incumbent workers with disabilities (Burkhauser, Butler, & Kim, 1995; Burkhauser, Butler, & Weathers, 1999; Butterfield & Ramseur, 2004; Fabian, Edelman, & Leedy, 1993). Schartz, Hendricks, and Blanck (2006) found that when employers provided estimates of direct and indirect costs and benefits of accommodation, the majority (60%) reported a positive net benefit, while 18% reported a negative net benefit.

Other research, however, indicates that employers may view the provision of accommodations as more of a barrier than they did at the time of earlier studies (Dixon, Kruse, & Van Horn, 2003; Domzal, Houtenville, & Sharma, 2008). In an employer survey conducted by Dixon, Kruse, and Van Horn (2003), 40% of respondents reported that it was difficult and costly to provide accommodations to workers with disabilities. This attitude was more prevalent among respondents who had no prior experience in doing so. Not knowing how much accommodations will cost and the actual cost of accommodations were cited by respondents in another employer survey as major concerns associated with hiring people with disabilities (Domzal et al., 2008).

"E" Everything: Accessibility and Productivity in the Online World of Work

Electronic and online tools and documents have become more than just a convenience. They are increasingly the *only* medium through which information and services are exchanged between employers and their employees and customers, as well as between co-workers and work collaborators. This development means that if people with disabilities are to be fully informed and equally productive in the workplace as their nondisabled peers, information technology (IT) accessibility of internal and external Web sites and Web-based processes is critical.

Adults with disabilities were more likely than those without disabilities to report that the Internet had significantly improved the quality of their lives (48% vs. 27%), which further stresses the importance of Web accessibility to all, regardless of disability (Bruyère, Erickson, & VanLooy, 2005). The Internet may be especially enabling for those with mobility-related impairments, allowing easy access to information. However, these technologies also have the potential to be significant barriers for those who have visual or hearing disabilities or limited dexterity, unless the applications are designed to be accessible.

A 2004 study commissioned by Microsoft found that 80% of working-age adults with mild disabilities were computer users, as were 63% of those with severe impairments. In comparison, 85% of people with no difficulties or impairments were computer users. This difference in rates of computer use was also found among people who used computers at work. Interestingly, however, this study found that adult students with mild disabilities currently attending school reported higher levels of computer use (at 53%) than either nondisabled (49%) or severely disabled students (44%) (Forrester Research, Inc., 2004).

Good practices in Web site accessibility are likely to result in overall improvements to an organization's Web site. Many accessibility guidelines address the usability of a site as well—something that benefits all users. In addition, many organizations that have worked to improve the accessibility of their Web sites have found that these efforts increase the public visibility and traffic of their sites. Search engines such as Google make use of the same features that improve accessibility. In fact, one expert likens Google to a blind Web user: "If Googlebot can't get to a page, it's not going to be indexed. . . . Google is blind. Google doesn't use a mouse. Google sometimes has trouble with javascript" (McGee, 2009). Correcting accessibility issues can improve a site's ranking with the major search engines, sending many more users to an organization's site.

Accessibility features are commonly used by many computer users, not just people with disabilities. The Microsoft study found that 40% of computer users were making use of built-in accessibility options and utilities such as display, keyboard, and sound adjustments, while 17% were using some form of assistive technology products such as touch screens, voice recognition, trackballs, and screen magnifiers (Forrester Research, Inc., 2004, p. 22). Most people (65%) reported that they were using assistive features and products not because of a disability or ongoing health issue, but because the feature or project enhanced their computing experience and made the computer easier to use, more comfortable, or more convenient (Forrester Research, Inc., 2004, p. 29).

A 2001 study examined the accessibility of more than 1,800 state and federal government Web sites and found that only 17% met standards of accessibility (West, 2001). That number had barely risen by 2008, when a follow-up study found that only 25% of federal Web sites and 19% of state Web sites were accessible to people with disabilities (West, 2008). According to ADA regulations, federal agencies' electronic and information technology is required to be accessible to people with disabilities. The law also requires telecommunications manufacturers to ensure that their equipment and services are accessible to people with disabilities (Bruyère, Erickson, & VanLooy, 2005).

In 2003, over 400 HR professionals were surveyed about HR processes and accessible IT. Nearly half of the respondents reported having made alterations to make a computer accessible to an employee with a disability, with larger companies being more likely to have made alterations. Only 10% felt computer use did not present a barrier to people with disabilities. Illustrating how employees with disabilities often need to be their own advocates and also lead their organizations into more inclusive practices, HR respondents rated employees with a disability as the most helpful internal resource they tapped to help address computer/Web accessibility issues (Bruyère, Erickson, & VanLooy, 2003, 2005).

A major area of concern is the accessibility of recruiting Web sites. The Internet has come to play a significant role in the employee recruitment process, and the fact that many company recruiting Web sites do not meet basic levels of accessibility is a great impediment to the inclusion of people with disabilities in the workforce.

Individuals with disabilities are just as likely to use the Internet to search for jobs as individuals without disabilities. However, in a 2000 assessment, only 18% of the 100 most heavily trafficked recruiting sites were found to meet top-priority accessibility requirements (Erickson, 2002). In the 2003 survey of HR representatives, just 13% of all respondents noted familiarity with guidelines for accessible Web design regarding their recruiting sites (Bruyère, Erickson, & VanLooy, 2003). This low level of familiarity highlights the importance of this issue.

The 2000 study evaluated 10 job boards and 31 corporate e-recruiting Web sites for accessibility. The evaluation used both a common automated assessment tool (used by sites to claim they had achieved accessibility) and a simulated application process designed to see if it would be possible for people with disabilities to successfully proceed through the entire job search and application process. None of the job boards passed the automated evaluation, and only 3 of 9 job boards and 3 of 12 corporate Web sites allowed a visually disabled user to complete a job application successfully. While Web-based recruiting offers great potential to many job applicants, especially those with mobility impairments, inaccessible sites could prevent people from finding or applying for open positions. Erickson (2002) concludes, "given the growth of online recruiting combined with the frequent access problems discovered in this study, there is a very real potential for a certain population of disabled individuals to be all but cut off from this most promising avenue for job searches and application" (p. 25).

Issues with information technology accessibility do not end after the recruitment process. Company policies and benefits information are increasingly distributed in electronic formats only. Online availability of benefits enrollment, policy manuals, and other processes is easier for many employees. But if these materials are not designed to be accessible, e-availability may become an obstacle for individuals with certain disabilities (Bruyère, Erickson, & VanLooy, 2003).

Respondents to the 2003 survey reported that about 80% used the Web for online benefits information dissemination, and around 60% for online benefits self-service (Bruyère, Erickson, & VanLooy, 2003). While having benefits information online can be a significant advantage for employers and for many employees, an inaccessible benefits system can deny some employees easy access to important information, updates, or the special elective benefits or "Plan Finder" tools enjoyed by other employees (Bruyère & Erickson, 2001).

Online employee training programs are another area where HR practices have been altered by the Internet. Like e-benefits and e-recruiting, e-learning has the potential to benefit people with disabilities by making instruction individual rather than institution-based and allowing training to happen anytime, anywhere. But accessibility barriers still make themselves felt in this arena. Rowland and Smith (1999) collected accessibility data from a random sample of 400 colleges, universities, and online learning institutions. The study found only 22% of the home pages to be free from any major accessibility errors.

Finally, apart from electronic recruiting, benefits, and training programs, the Internet has profoundly affected the core of work processes in most companies and organizations. Bruyère, Erickson, and VanLooy found that employee use of computers is extensive, with the majority of employees in organizations using computers, and a very large proportion working on computers more than half the workday (2005).

Job Fit: Retention, Advancement, and Match of the Individual to the Job

Employers have noted that the top barrier to employment of people with disabilities is a lack of experience and skills, followed by supervisor lack of knowledge regarding accommodations, and attitudes/stereotypes about people with disabilities. Federal HR managers reported similar concerns, as did federal supervisors (Brannick & Bruyère, 1999; Bruyère, 2000; Bruyère, Erickson, & Horne, 2002). People with disabilities also report experiencing significantly lower "fit" with their jobs once hired (Nishii & Bruyère, 2009), suggesting that job match may be a problem both prior to and after being hired. This finding suggests that job match remains a key issue for successful employment outcomes (Roessler, 2002).

Research suggests that the most important factors for retention of employees with disabilities include disability management and return-to-work programs (Brannick & Bruyère, 1999; Bruyère, 2000; Bruyère, Erickson, & Horne, 2002); employer accommodations (Burkhauser, Butler, & Gümüs, 2004; Burkhauser et al., 1999); and organizational mission, compensation levels, and the equitable treatment and engagement of employees (Habeck, Hunt, Rachel, Kregel, & Chan, 2010). Krause and Pickelsimer's study (2008) on return-to-work rates after five years for people with spinal cord injuries found that those who were actively looking for work were among the most successful at finding employment again. As for those who did not return to work within this five-year period, the study found that the most prominent reason preventing return to work was health condition, not disincentives or resources. Wehman, Targett, West, and Kregel (2005) describe return-to-work trends of people with traumatic brain injuries and come to similar conclusions about the importance of incorporating able people into the workforce through rehabilitation programs.

But retention and advancement of people with disabilities will also be influenced by their ability to perform their jobs well. Among the factors known to influence job performance are the motivating potential of the job (Hackman & Oldham, 1976; Humphrey, Nahrgang, & Morgeson, 2007); the fit of employee skills to the demands of the job (Cable & DeRue, 2002); and the level of negative strain experienced on the job (Kahn & Byosiere, 1992) in the form of work overload (Bliese & Castro, 2000; Lee & Ashforth, 1996), conflict (De Dreu & Weingart, 2003), and harassment (Raver & Nishii, 2010).

Advancement opportunities are also improved when good performance is fairly recognized and rewarded (Fried, Levi, Ben-David, Tiegs, & Avital, 2000; Gerhart, Trevor, & Graham, 1996; Mottaz, 1985; Williams, McDaniel, & Nguyen, 2006), and when individuals receive the support that they need to develop their careers through employee resource groups, high-quality relationships with supervisors (DiTomaso & Hooijberg, 1996; Gerstner & Day, 1997; Gomez & Rosen, 2001; McClane, 1991; Schyns, Paul, Mohr, & Blank, 2005), and mentoring relationships (Dreher & Cox, 1996; Kram, 1985). These factors could also be more likely to exist when an employee has a successful job fit, broadly defined. Fitting well in one's job can also mean fitting well with the management style of their boss and other mentors.

The broadest concept of job fit is sometimes defined as job "embeddedness." Embeddedness happens when employees experience *fit* with their jobs, co-workers, corporate culture, and off-the-job lives (work-life balance), but it also may include developing *links* to other people, groups, and organizations both on and off the job because of the work they do, as well as perceiving that they would have to *sacrifice* a lot if they left their jobs or community (Ellickson, 2002; Mitchell, Holtom, Lee, Sablynski, & Erez, 2001; Schur et al., 2005; Schur et al., 2009). The strength of this conceptualization of job embeddedness is that it takes into account the fact that employees often stay in their jobs because of factors that are not directly related to their jobs. The concepts of job embeddedness and employee engagement are closely linked.

Beyond the particular tasks and scope of work required in a specific job, job fit also includes broader dimensions, such as time of day worked or number of hours worked. Hotchkiss reveals that voluntary part-time employment had increased notably over the past 20 years among people with disabilities in comparison to their nondisabled peers (Hotchkiss, 2004b). She concludes that this part-time work is more attractive (a better fit) for financial considerations—in particular, the ability to keep health insurance through government-provided programs.

Broader Organizational Change

Schur et al. (2009) reported findings from a small sample of employers that suggest company climate and culture have a large influence on employees with disabilities. Hirsh and Kmec (2009) demonstrated that the existence of formalized HR structures, such as manager diversity training, lowers the likelihood of an organization receiving a discrimination charge, while the presence of an EEO unit and employee diversity training increases it, perhaps because of increased employee-rights awareness. Kalev, Dobbin, and Kelly (2006), examining corporate diversity programs more broadly, concluded that "the best hope for remedying [inequality in attainment at work] may lie in practices that assign organizational responsibility for change" (p. 611). Their research showed that "structures that embed accountability, authority, and expertise," such as affirmative action plans, diversity committees and task forces, and diversity managers and departments, "are the most effective means of increasing diversity" (p. 611). This conclusion supports the results of both Bruyère (2000) and Thakker and Solomon (1999), as well as business audience research (Creary, 2008).

Overall, this research suggests that the adoption of disability management practices alone is unlikely to stimulate broader change in organizational culture, and that more systematic attention to embedding inclusion as a strategic priority into the day-to-day activities of the organization may be necessary, although some research has suggested that HR representatives may feel that their organizations are doing an adequate job of creating inclusive work cultures (Unger et al., 2002). Since HR managers' reports and the actual experiences of employees can differ (Nishii & Wright, 2008), it is critical that research examines experiences of inclusion from the perspective of employees with disabilities.

Self-Advocating: Asking for Accommodation

The ADA does not require employers to inquire about employees' need for accommodation, so the provision of accommodations may be affected by the willingness of employees to request them. Little research has been done from the point of view of the employee in this area.

Importantly, not all employees who need accommodations to successfully perform their jobs request them. Allaire, Li, and LaValley (2003) found that while 98% of their sample faced barriers at work, only 38% requested accommodation. Balser (2007) found that only 72% of people with mobility-related disabilities requested accommodation. Baldridge and Veiga (2001, 2006) believe that employees' likelihood of requesting an accommodation depends heavily on the workplace culture and nature of the accommodation, because employees with disabilities consider workplace risks that could result from requesting accommodation. Findings from Frank and Bellini (2005) support this idea.

Zwerling et al. (2003), using a nationally representative sample of working Americans, found that only 12% reported receiving workplace accommodations, and that several specific impairments were less likely to be accommodated, including severe hearing problems, mental health, and alcohol abuse.

Self-advocating for accommodations is a somewhat paradoxical situation. If an individual does not ask for an accommodation at work, one will likely not be provided. However, for the individual to feel secure enough to ask, there needs to be a workplace culture of acceptance and inclusion. In a Cornell University/American Association of People with Disabilities study on disability self-disclosure in the workplace, respondents were asked to rate the importance of factors that might motivate them to disclose that they have a disability, and also factors that may be barriers to disclosure. About two-thirds of the respondents with disabilities rated the need for accommodation and supportive supervisor relationships as being very important to their decision to disclose their disability in their workplace. However, the culture of the workplace was also viewed as important, with high ratings for having a disability-friendly workplace and knowing that the employer was actively recruiting people with disability. Similarly, respondents were asked to rate factors in their decision not to disclose. Nearly three-quarters of people with a disability viewed risks of being fired/not hired as being important. Other factors most frequently rated as important were the fear of limited opportunities, the risk of losing health care, and the concern that the employer may focus on disability rather than ability (Von Schrader et al., 2011).

Managers' and Co-Workers' Attitudes Toward Individuals With Disabilities

Prior research has revealed that a vast majority of managers (70% or more, depending on the practice of interest) are unaware of their organization's disability practices (Nishii & Bruyère, 2009), suggesting that espoused practices may differ from those that are actually implemented by managers. Indeed, scholars have cautioned that managerial differences represent a large source of variation in the way that practices are executed (e.g., Bowen & Ostroff, 2004; Nishii & Wright, 2008). When individuals are left to their own discretion (purposefully or out of ignorance) to carry out policies and manage people, the overarching culture and the individuals' personal values and attitudes become more important than articulated policies.

Two nationally representative employer surveys on disability issues found that one-fifth of employers report that attitudes are a major barrier to the employment of people with disabilities (Bruyère, 2000; Dixon, Kruse, & Van Horn, 2003). A repeated finding of employer surveys is that "discriminatory or stereotyping attitudes in the workplace about people with disabilities continue to be a barrier to employment and advancement for people with disabilities" (Bruyère, Erickson, & Ferrentino, 2003, p. 1195). In assessing performance ratings, Colella et al. (1998) conclude that it is important to consider how stereotypes of job fit for persons with specific disabilities can impact personnel judgments.

Other experimental studies have reported that attitudes of supervisors and co-workers have a strong effect on the labor market experiences of those with disabilities, not only in terms of integration into the workplace, but in higher wage outcomes as well (Colella, 1996, 2001; Mank, Cioffi, & Yovanoff, 1999; Olson, Cioffi, Yovanoff, & Mank, 2001; Stone & Colella, 1996; Wehman, 2003). These studies have shown that employer attitudes toward disabilities vary by specific disability. More positive views were expressed about people with physical or sensory disabilities than about people with psychiatric or cognitive disabilities (Gilbride et al., 2000; Gouvier, Sytsma-Jordan, & Mayville, 2003;

Hernandez, Keys, & Balcazar, 2000; Unger, 2002). This hierarchy of attitudes was found in a literature review conducted in 1987 by Greenwood and Johnson and continues to be found in post-ADA studies (Callahan, 1994; Scheid, 1999). Some studies show that people with psychiatric or cognitive disabilities are more prone to having dysfunctional cognitions about their career incentives. However, there is no significant difference in how people with mental disabilities view their vocational identities as opposed to people with physical disabilities (Yanchak, Lease, & Strauser, 2005). A similar tendency to rank disabilities exists about the cause of the disability—whether the disability is perceived to be caused by factors under the control of the person with a disability. When an individual is believed to be responsible for his or her disability, "onset controllability" has been found to produce negative attitudes in employers (Florey & Harrison, 2000; Gouvier et al., 2003; Lee, 1996).

Yet studies have failed to show a strong correlation between employers' positive attitudes and actual willingness to hire (Scheid, 1999; Thakker & Solomon, 1999). The "exposure hypothesis"—the idea that people who have more contact with and exposure to people with disabilities have more positive attitudes—has repeatedly found support in the research (e.g., Diksa & Rogers, 1996; Dixon, Kruse, & Van Horn, 2003; Florey & Harrison, 2000; McFarlin, Song, & Sonntag, 1991; Morgan & Alexander, 2005; Schartz, Schartz, & Blanck, 2002; Smith, Webber, Graffam, & Wilson, 2004). While many researchers have called for more training and awareness programs for managers and employees (Brostrant, 2006; Younes, 2001), research on attempts to change the attitudes of managers and co-workers toward other underrepresented groups through training programs has found that their positive effect is often insignificant, and they may in fact generate a backlash (Kalev et al., 2006).

As discussed previously, Schur et al. (2009) surveyed 30,000 employees from 14 companies. In analyzing the workplace disparities reported by employees with disabilities, they discovered that corporate culture matters and varies across companies and workplaces. Employees with disabilities who worked in places that were ranked higher on measures of respect and fairness by *all* employees reported less inequity than those in workplaces where employees in general gave the culture of fairness and respect lower grades. In other words, workplaces that are responsive to the needs of *all* employees also are more responsive to, and provide a more positive environment for, employees with disabilities.

As attitudes do not necessarily become active practices, we need quantitative data on employer behaviors. Although a good deal of research since the implementation of the ADA has focused on employer attitudes and how to change them, less has been done to discover what employers are actually doing.

Attitudes and ADA Compliance

The attitude research that exists is based on the assumption that success of ADA employment provisions depends on the attitudes of employers (Hernandez, et al., 2000, 2003; Wittmer & Wilson, 2010).

Research that examines ADA compliance and attitudes as they relate to business size has been inconsistent. Unger (2002) found that research conducted prior to the implementation of the ADA reported small businesses as having less favorable attitudes toward people with disabilities in the workplace. However, studies of post-ADA implementation failed to identify a relationship between employer size and attitude.

Thakker and Solomon (1999) studied adherence to the ADA among managers. The most influential factor in determining adherence was the belief that one's organization was adhering to the ADA and was favorable toward individuals with disabilities, although managers' personal negative attitudes toward disabilities tended to make adherence less likely. This finding suggests that, overall, both organizational and managerial attitudes toward disability are important.

Baldwin (1997) argued that the ADA "implicitly assumes that employer discrimination is the main cause of disabled persons' disadvantages in the labor market," ignoring the fact that the difference in productivity between workers with and without disabilities is probably a more viable explanation for the hiring gap than prejudice (p. 37). In this respect, Baldwin argues that the ADA is insufficient and will not help the position of people with disabilities in the labor market.

The participants in a 2009 Delphi Study conducted by the Rehabilitation Engineering and Research Center on Workplace Accommodations also stressed the importance of creating a workplace where employers and co-workers are receptive to having employees with disabilities and are made aware of the invaluable contributions that such workers can bring (Moon & Baker, 2010). They also reiterated that "Many of the issues pertaining to workplace accommodations remain employer-side issues. . . . However, it is not enough to presume that employers are willing to make accommodations once they have received the appropriate facts and figures" (p. 36).

Many Gaps in Knowledge of What Happens in the Workplace

The overall scarcity of empirical information on employer behaviors and practices led the Interagency Committee on Disability Research to conduct a summit meeting in 2006 on "Employer Perspectives on Workers With Disabilities," focused on the future direction of disability employment research. A second conference, in 2008, had as its theme "Strengthening the Intersection of Demand-Side and Supply-Side Disability Research (U.S. Department of Labor, Interagency Committee on Disability Research, 2007, 2008). Loprest (2007), assessing the state of the science in research on employment for people with disabilities, concluded:

> For some demand-side analysis, information about and from employers is critical. But employer data can be more difficult to access than data on individuals with disability. To increase demand-side research, we may need to improve access to employer data through partnerships with employers and employer groups to access existing data, targeted collection of new data, or new ways to use existing individual data sources. (p. 31)

Setting a Higher Bar: Lack of Causal Evidence

Little research exists regarding how company policies and practices (and the corresponding attitudes of employers, supervisors, and co-workers) affect in a *causal* way the employment opportunities of people with disabilities (Blanck & Schartz, 2005). While employers report their impressions that such things are important, little is known about how these policies and practices actually *cause* improvement in the opportunities of people with disabilities they are meant to benefit. To date, research utilizing reports provided by HR managers about disability management practices has made an implicit assumption that these policies/practices should aid in the advancement and retention of people with disabilities. However, line managers are often unaware of these practices (Nishii & Bruyère, 2009).

Certain employers may have higher percentages of people with disabilities in their workforces, and may have more positive attitudes about disability within their organizations, but little quantitative data demonstrate that specific practices actually contribute to better outcomes (McCary, 2005; U.S. Equal Employment Opportunity Commission, 2005).

Better-Integrated Data

The integration of an employer's benefit programs can be positive for employees and help the employer manage costs (Quick, 2011). Further, integrating data across benefit programs can allow an organization to better manage its resources, measure its own efforts, and benchmark itself to similar organizations (Disability Management Employer Coalition, 2009). Employers who have integrated data across programs such as disability, sick leave, workers' compensation, return to work, and productivity data have gained valuable insights into managing resources for better outcomes. Examples can be found in the "Integrating and Reporting Metrics" area of the Disability Management Employer Coalition (2009) report.

The analysis of data across several disability-related programs can, for example, improve understanding of when an employer is "cost shifting from one program to another or is truly performing better or worse across all absence and disability programs" (Disability Management Employer Coalition, 2009, p. 231). Some larger employers are using integrated data to benchmark themselves against peer companies. For example, the Employer Measures of Productivity, Absence, and Quality (EMPAQ) system (see www.empaq.org) that was developed by the National Business Group on Health allows participants to benchmark in the areas of short-term disability, long-term disability, workers' compensation, group health, family and medical leave, incidental and total absence, employee assistance programs, and health management programs (National Business Group on Health, 2009).

Improving Empowerment and Increasing Self-Identification

There is a business adage: "What gets measured, gets done." Outcomes related to improving recruitment, retention, and advancement of employees with disabilities are rarely measured within the workplace walls. If the adage holds, then until more numerical goals are set and data collected regarding employees with disabilities, employers will not be driving much change.

Why is there a lack of internal workplace data on employees with disabilities, which may underpin the lack of managerial investment in and awareness of disability-related issues? In the authors' confidential conversations with employers, executives explained that the confidentiality requirements of the ADA and the Health Insurance Portability and Accountability Act (HIPAA; see http://www.hhs.gov/ocr/hipaa for further information) often make employers perceive that tracking disability and health-related information is illegal. The perception that they are not allowed to collect data related to the hiring, retention, and advancement of individuals with disabilities makes it easier for employers to justify a lack of accountability. The OFCCP's newly proposed standards for federal contractors may clarify the freedom that employers have to provide employees with opportunities to self-disclose their disability status, similar to gender and racial/ethnic identities.

Conclusion

The United States has just endured the worst employment recession since the Great Depression of the 1930s. The same can be said for many other significant economies around the globe. Policymakers and scholars, as well as household breadwinners, have been left reflecting on what will be the future of work and how to maximize employment opportunities.

Against this backdrop, the share of the population with a disability is growing. Members of the baby-boom generation are aging into their senior years. Advances in medical and scientific knowledge and techniques have increased survival rates, along with understanding, accommodation, and treatment of disabilities. In addition, enhancements in technology increasingly offer expanded opportunities to address workplace accommodation needs in a cost-effective manner.

A looming question is "Who pays?" State and federal government programs are facing greater financial constraints. The pressure to balance governmental budgets by reducing spending on social programs will likely not abate anytime soon. There is only one possible response to reconcile the colliding forces of more people with disabilities and pressure for less government spending—increase the quantity and quality of employment opportunities for people with disabilities.

This volume attempts to address these compelling issues. The first chapter of this volume provided an overview of the meaning of work, varying definitions of disability, the challenge for people with disabilities in finding work in the American labor market, and increasing global awareness of these issues. In Chapter 2, we document continuing employment disparities across a number of dimensions, provide an overview of current controversies in public policy and service provision, and discuss legislative, employer-focused, and advocacy-origination solutions to these challenges.

Notes

1. "Targeted disabilities" are those disabilities that the federal government, as a matter of policy, has identified for special emphasis. The targeted disabilities are deafness, blindness, missing extremities, partial paralysis, complete paralysis, convulsive disorders, mental retardation, and distortion of limb and/or spine (U.S. Equal Employment Opportunity Commission, 2008).

2. In academic research, the term "wage" is often used generically to represent total pay in the form of either salary or wages. It can include bonus pay as well. A wage gap does not typically include compensation such as the value of health care benefits or pension. In capturing these kinds of remuneration in addition to wage and salary pay, it would be more common to use the term "compensation."

3. Precisely, in September 2011, 30.6% of employer costs for employee compensation were non-wage/non-salary costs. This ratio is calculated quarterly in the Employer Costs for Employee Compensation report, part of the U.S. Bureau of Labor Statistics' Employment Cost Trends (see http://www.bls.gov/ncs/ect).

4. Schur et al. (2009) did measure total compensation in very "chunky" grouping using a five-point scale. See Table 4, Row 2, p. 393.

5. The U.S. Census Bureau broadly classifies health insurance coverage as private coverage or government coverage. People were "uninsured" if, for the entire year, they were not covered by any type of health insurance. Over 30% of Hispanics and 20% of blacks are uninsured in the United States. Just under 12% of whites are uninsured. See also U.S. Census Bureau (2010), Table 8, Figure 8, and Table C-2.

6. Currently, the Cornell University Employment and Disability Institute is analyzing the specific provisions and requirements within the health care reform legislation that impact employer practices and people with disabilities.

7. The U.S. has nine major official data sources of survey data and statistics regarding persons with disabilities: the U.S. Decennial Census of the Population, American Community Survey (ACS), Behavioral Risk Factor Surveillance System (BRFSS), Current Population Survey (CPS), Medical Expenditure Panel Survey (MEPS), National Health and Nutrition Examination Survey (NHANES), National Health Interview Survey (NHIS), Panel Study of Income Dynamics (PSID), and Survey of Income and Program Participation (SIPP).

Only the U.S. Decennial Census and the ACS (beginning in 2006) poll persons living in both noninstitutionalized and institutionalized group quarters

(GQ), although the standard reports from these surveys, including labor market statistics such as employment and unemployment, reference only civilian noninstitutionalized persons. The MEPS surveys some institutional populations and the CPS includes some military quarters in its survey framework.

See Chapter 1 for further discussion of official U.S. labor statistics and underlying definitions.

8. The term "predatory matching" is an adaptation of the term "predatory lending," which describes unscrupulous activities by financial institutions, usually in low-income communities. The predatory piece in both terms refers to a situation where one party has an asymmetric information advantage over another and can benefit financially by exploiting that advantage (Golden and Barrington, Cornell University).

9. ACCSES is the American Congress of Community Support and Employment Services, which took its current form in 2007 following a merger with the Disability Support Providers of America (DSPA). ACCSES represents 80 partner disability service providers across the United States.

10. For more information on the debate over the effects of the ADA, see also Acemoglu & Angrist, 1998, 2001; Bagenstos, 2004; Beegle & Stock, 2003; Bound & Waidmann, 2000; Burkhauser, Daly, Houtenville, & Nargis, 2001; Burkhauser & Houtenville, 2010; Burkhauser, Houtenville, & Wittenburg, 2001; Burkhauser & Stapleton, 2003, 2004; Center & Imparato, 2003; DeLeire, 2000a, 2000b; Goodman & Waidman, 2003; Hotchkiss, 2004a; Houtenville & Burkhauser, 2005; Jolls & Prescott, 2004; Kruse & Schur, 2003; Lehman, 2006; Schwochau & Blanck, 2000.)

11. The purpose of this program is to create and expand job and career opportunities for individuals with disabilities in the competitive labor market. It accomplishes this goal by involving private industry partners to help identify competitive job and career opportunities and the skills needed to perform these jobs, and by creating practical job and career readiness and training programs and providing job placement and career advancement (see http://www2.ed.gov/programs/rsapwi/index.html).

12. Section 203 of the Ticket to Work and Work Incentives Improvement Act of 1999 directs the Secretary of the Department of Health and Human Services (DHHS) to establish the Medicaid Infrastructure Grant (MIG) Program. More information about the program can be found at http://www.hcbs.org/theme.php/5/Medicaid%20Infrastructure%20Grants.

References

Able Trust. (2003, October). *Dispelling myths of an untapped workforce: A study of employer attitudes toward hiring individuals with disabilities.* Retrieved from http://www.abletrust.org/news/Able_Trust_Employer_Attitudes_Study.pdf

Ableson, R. (2011, November 16). The smokers' surcharge. *New York Times*, p. B1. Retrieved from http://www.nytimes.com/2011/11/17/health/policy/smokers-penalized-with-health-insurance-premiums.html?_r=2&pagewanted=all

ACCSES. (2009). *The continuum of approaches necessary for enhancing employment opportunities for persons with the most significant disabilities: An analysis of and recommendations regarding disability employment issues that include center-based employment and Section 14(c) of the Fair Labor Standards Act* [ACCSES Position Paper]. Washington, DC: Author. Retrieved from http://www.accses.org/vendorimages/accses/090309FINALACCSESPositionPaper-Section14_c_.pdf

Acemoglu, D., & Angrist, J. (1998). *Consequences of employment protection? The case of the Americans with Disabilities Act* (Working paper 6670). Cambridge, MA: National Bureau of Economic Research.

Acemoglu, D., & Angrist, J. (2001). Consequences of employment protection? The case of the Americans with Disabilities Act. *Journal of Political Economy, 109*(5), 915–957.

Adaptive Environments, Inc. (1998). *Tax incentives for improving accessibility. The Americans with Disabilities Act fact sheet series.* Retrieved from http://www.employmentincentives.com/federal_incentives/documents/taxpack.pdf

Affirmative Action and Nondiscrimination Obligations of Contractors and Subcontractors Regarding Individuals with Disabilities, 76 Fed. Reg. 77056 (2011). Notice of Proposed Rulemaking.

AHIP Center for Policy and Research. (2009, October). *Individual health insurance 2009: A comprehensive survey of premiums, availability, and benefits.* Retrieved from http://www.ahipresearch.org

Allaire, S. H., Li, W., & LaValley, M. P. (2003). Work barriers experienced and job accommodation used by persons with arthritis and other rheumatic diseases. *Rehabilitation Counseling Bulletin, 46,* 147–156.

Allen, H., Woock, C., Barrington, L., & Bunn, W. (2008). Age, overtime, and employee health, safety and productivity outcomes: A case study. *Journal of Occupational and Environmental Medicine, 50*(8), 873–894.

Autor, D. (2011). *The unsustainable rise of the disability rolls in the United States: Causes, consequences, and policy options.* (Working paper 17697). Cambridge, MA: National Bureau of Economic Research.

Autor, D., & Duggan, M. (2010, December). *Supporting work: A proposal for modernizing the U.S. disability insurance system* [Paper jointly released by the Center for American Progress and the Hamilton Project]. Retrieved from http://www.hamiltonproject.org/papers/supporting_work_a_proposal_for_modernizing_the_u.s._disability_insuran

Bagenstos, S. (2004). Has the Americans with Disabilities Act reduced employment for people with disabilities? *Berkeley Journal of Employment and Labor Law, 25,* 527–563.

Bagenstos, S. (2006). The structural turn and the limits of antidiscrimination law. *California Law Review, 94*(1), 1–47.

Baicker, K., Cutler, D., & Song, Z. (2010). Workplace wellness programs can generate savings. *Health Affairs, 29*(2), 304–311.

Balcazar, F. E., Keys, C.B., Davis, M., Lardon, C. & Jones, C. (2005). Strengths and challenges of intervention research in vocational rehabilitation: An illustration of agency-university collaboration. *Journal of Rehabilitation, 71*(2), 40–48.

Baldridge, D. C., & Veiga, J. F. (2001). Toward greater understanding of the willingness to request an accommodation: Can requesters' beliefs disable the ADA? *Academy of Management Review, 26,* 85–99.

Baldridge, D. C., & Veiga, J. F. (2006). The impact of anticipated social consequences on recurring disability accommodation requests. *Journal of Management, 32,* 158–179.

Baldwin, M. L. (1997). Can the ADA achieve its employment goals? *The ANNALS of the American Academy of Political and Social Science, 549*(1), 37–52.

Baldwin, M., & Johnson, W. (2006). A critical review of studies of discrimination against persons with disabilities. In W. M. Rogers III (Ed.), *Handbook on the economics of discrimination* (pp. 119–160). Northhampton, UK: Edward Elgar Publishing.

Baldwin, M. L., & Schumacher, E. J. (2002). A note on job mobility among workers with disabilities. *Industrial Relations, 41,* 430–441.

Balser, D. B. (2007). Predictors of workplace accommodations for employees with mobility-related disabilities. *Administration and Society, 39,* 656–683.

Beegle, K., & Stock, W. A. (2003). The labor market effects of disability discrimination laws. *The Journal of Human Resources, 38*(4), 806–859.

Bilmes, L. (2007). *Soldiers returning from Iraq and Afghanistan: The long-term costs of providing veterans medical care and disability benefits.* Cambridge, MA: John F. Kennedy School of Government, Harvard University.

Bisom-Rapp, S. (2001). An ounce of prevention is a poor substitute for a pound of cure: Confronting the developing jurisprudence of education and prevention in employment discrimination law. *Berkeley Journal of Employment and Labor Law, 22*(1), 1–48.

Bjelland, M., Bruyère, S., von Schrader, S., Houtenville, A., Ruiz-Quintanilla, A., & Webber, D. (2010). Age and disability employment discrimination: Occupational rehabilitation implications. *Journal of Occupational Rehabilitation, 20,* 456–471.

Bjelland, M., & Webber, D. (2010). *EEOC allegations of discrimination: Time trends, the environment, and underlying characteristics.* Manuscript in preparation. Ithaca, NY: Cornell University Employment and Disability Institute.

Blanck, P. D. (1997). The economics of the employment provisions of the Americans with Disabilities Act: Part I—Workplace accommodations. *DePaul Law Review, 46*(4), 877–914.

Blanck, P. D. (2000). The economics of the ADA. In P. Blanck (Ed.), *Employment, disability, and the Americans with Disabilities Act: Issues in law, public policy, and research* (pp. 201–227). Chicago, IL: Northwestern University Press.

Blanck, P., Sandler, L., Schmeling, J., & Schartz, H. (2000). The emerging workforce of entrepreneurs with disabilities: Preliminary study of entrepreneurship in Iowa. *Iowa Law Review, 85*(5). Retrieved from http://ssrn.com/abstract= 382587

Blanck, P., & Schartz, H. (2005). Special issue: Corporate culture and disability. *Behavioral Sciences and the Law, 23,* 1–2.

Blau, F., & Kahn, L. (2000). Gender differences in pay. *Journal of Economic Perspectives, 14,* 75–99.

Bliese , P. D., & Castro, C. A. (2000). Role clarity, work overload and organizational support: Multilevel evidence of the importance of support. *Work & Stress, 14*(1), 65–73.

Bond, G. (1984). An economic analysis of psychosocial rehabilitation. *Pscyhiatric Services, 35*(4), 356–362.

Bond, G., Dietzen, L., McGrew, J., & Miller, D. (1995). Accelerating entry into supported employment for persons with severe psychiatric disabilities. *Rehabilitation Psychology, 40*(2), 75–94.

Bond, G., & Dincin, J. (1986). Accelerating entry into transitional employment in a psychosocial rehabilitation agency. *Rehabilitation Psychology, 31,* 143–155.

Bond, G. R., Picone, J., Mauer, B., Fishbein, S., & Stout, R. (2000). The Quality of Supported Employment Implementation Scale. *Journal of Vocational Rehabilitation, 14*(3), 201–212.

Bond, G. R., Resnick, S. R., Drake, R. E., Xie, H., McHugo, G. J., & Bebout, R. R. (2001). Does competitive employment improve nonvocational outcomes for people with severe mental illness? *Journal of Consulting and Clinical Psychology, 69*(3), 489–501.

Bound, J., & Waidmann, T. (2000). *Accounting for recent declines in employment rates among the working-aged disabled* (Working paper 7975). Cambridge, MA: National Bureau of Economic Research. Retrieved from http://www.nber .org/papers/w7975

Bowen, D. E., & Ostroff, C. (2004). Understanding HRM-firm performance linkages: The role of the "strength" of the HRM system. *Academy of Management Review, 29*(2), 203–221.

Brannick, A., & Bruyère, S. (1999). *The ADA at work: Implementation of the employment provisions of the Americans with Disabilities Act.* Alexandria, VA: Society for Human Resource Management.

Brault, M. (2008, February). *Disability status and the characteristics of people in group quarters: A brief analysis of disability prevalence among the civilian noninstitutionalized and total populations in the American Community Survey* [U.S. Census Bureau Staff Paper]. Washington, DC: U.S. Census Bureau

Housing and Household Economic Statistics Division. Retrieved from http://www.census.gov/hhes/www/disability/publications.html

Brault, M. (2008, December). *Americans with disabilities: 2005* (Household Economic Studies. Current Population Reports, No. P70–117). Washington, DC: U.S. Bureau of the Census. Retrieved from http://www.census.gov/prod/2008pubs/p70-117.pdf

Bray, J. W., Zarkin, G. A., Dennis, M. L., & French, M. T. (2000). Symptoms of dependence, multiple substance use, and labor market outcomes. *American Journal of Drug and Alcohol Use, 26*(1), 77–95.

Brostrant, H. L. (2006). Tilting at windmills: Changing attitudes toward people with disabilities. *Journal of Rehabilitation, 72*(1), 4–9.

Bruyère, S. (2000). *Disability employment policies and practices in private and federal sector organizations.* Ithaca, NY: Cornell University Program on Employment and Disability. Retrieved from http://digitalcommons.ilr.cornell.edu/edicollect/63

Bruyère, S. (2006). Disability management: Key concepts and techniques for an aging workforce. *International Journal of Disability Management Research, 1,* 149–158.

Bruyère, S., & Erickson, W. (2001). *E-human resources: A review of the literature and implications for people with disabilities.* Ithaca, NY: Cornell University, School of Industrial and Labor Relations Extension Division, Program on Employment and Disability.

Bruyère, S., Erickson, W., & Ferrentino, J. (2003). Identity and disability in the workplace. *William and Mary Law Review, 44*(3), 1173–1196.

Bruyère, S., Erickson, W., & Horne, R. (2002). *Survey of the federal government on supervisor practices in employment of people with disabilities.* Ithaca, NY: Cornell University, School of Industrial and Labor Relations Extension Division, Program on Employment and Disability. Retrieved from http://digital commons.ilr.cornell.edu/edicollect/65

Bruyère, S., Erickson, W., & VanLooy, S. (2003). *Accessible IT for people with disabilities: HR considerations.* Ithaca, NY: Cornell University, School of Industrial and Labor Relations Extension Division, Program on Employment and Disability. Retrieved from http://digitalcommons.ilr.cornell.edu/edicollect/68

Bruyère, S., Erickson, W., & VanLooy, S. (2004). Comparative study of workplace policy and practices contributing to disability nondiscrimination. *Rehabilitation Psychology, 49*(1), 28–38.

Bruyère, S., Erickson, W., & VanLooy, S. (2005). Information technology and the workplace: Implications for persons with disabilities. *Disability Studies Quarterly, 25*(2).

Bruyère, S., Erickson, W., & VanLooy, S. (2006). The impact of business size on employer ADA response. *Rehabilitation Counseling Bulletin, 49*(4), 194–206.

Bruyère, S., Erickson, W., VanLooy, S., Hirsch, E., Cook, J., Burke, J., . . . Morris, M. (2006). Employment and disability policy: Recommendations for a social sciences research agenda. In A. Heinemann & K. Hagglund (Eds.), *Handbook of applied disability and rehabilitation research.* New York, NY: Springer.

Bruyère, S., Golden, T., & Zeitzer, I. (2007). Evaluation and future prospect of U.S. return to work policies for Social Security beneficiaries. *Disability and Employment, 17,* 53–90.

Bruyère, S., & Houtenville, A. (2006). The use of statistics from national data sources to inform rehabilitation program planning, evaluation, and advocacy. *Rehabilitation Counseling Bulletin, 50*(1), 46–58.

Bruyère, S., Mitra, S., & VanLooy, S. (2011). Chapter 8: Employment and work. In *World Report on Disability and Rehabilitation* (pp. 235–257). Geneva: World Health Organization.

Bruyère, S., & Reiter, E. (in press). Disability policy and law. In V. Tarvydas & D. Maki (Eds.), *The professional practice of rehabilitation counseling.* New York, NY: Springer.

Bruyère, S., von Schrader, S., Bjelland, M., & Coduti, W. (2011). United States employment disability discrimination charges: Implications for disability management practice. *International Journal of Disability Management, 5*(2), 48–58.

Bryant, R. R., Samaranyake, V. A., & Wilhite, A. (2000). The effect of drug use on wages: A human capital interpretation. *American Journal of Drug and Alcohol Abuse, 26*(4), 659–682.

Bureau of Labor Statistics. (2011a). *Economic news release: Table A. Employment status of the civilian noninstitutional population by disability status and age, 2009 and 2010 annual averages.* Retrieved from http://www.bls.gov/news.release/disabl.a.htm

Bureau of Labor Statistics. (2011b). *Employment situation of veterans—2010* (U.S. News Release No. USDL-11–0306). Retrieved from http://www.bls.gov/news.release/pdf/vet.pdf

Bureau of Labor Statistics. (2011c). *Women in the labor force: A databook* (BLS Report 1034). Washington, DC: Author. Retrieved from http://www.bls.gov/cps/wlf-databook-2011.pdf

Burkhauser, R., Butler, J., & Gümüs G. (2004). Dynamic programming model estimates of Social Security Disability Insurance application timing. *Journal of Applied Econometrics, 19,* 671–685.

Burkhauser, R. V., Butler, J. S., & Kim, Y. W. (1995). The importance of employer accommodation on the job duration of workers with disabilities: A hazard model approach. *Labour Economics, 3*(1), 1–22.

Burkhauser, R., Butler, J., & Weathers, R., II. (1999). How policy variables influence the timing of Social Security Disability Insurance applications. *Social Security Bulletin, 64*(1), 52–83.

Burkhauser, R. V., Daly, M., Houtenville, A., & Nargis, N. (2001). *Employment of working-age people with disabilities in the 1980s and 1990s: What current data can and cannot tell us.* Ithaca, NY: Cornell University, Rehabilitation Research and Training Center for Economic Research on Employment Policy for Persons with Disabilities.

Burkhauser, R. V., & Houtenville, A. J. (2010). Employment among working-age people with disabilities: What current data can tell us. In E. M. Szymanski & R. M. Parker (Eds.), *Work and disability: Issues and strategies for career development and job placement* (3rd ed.) (pp. 49–86). Austin, TX: Pro-Ed, Inc.

Burkhauser, R. V., Houtenville, A., & Wittenburg, D. (2001). *A user guide to current statistics on the employment of people with disabilities.* Ithaca, NY: Cornell University/Urban Institute, Rehabilitation Research and Training Center for Economic Research on Employment Policy for People with Disabilities.

Burkhauser, R. V., & Stapleton, D. (2003). A review of the evidence and its implications for policy change. In D. Stapleton & R. V. Burkhauser (Eds.), *The decline in employment of people with disabilities: A policy puzzle* (pp. 369–405). Kalamazoo, MI: W. E. Upjohn Institute for Employment Research.

Burkhauser, R. V., & Stapleton, D. C. (2004). The decline in the employment rate for people with disabilities: Bad data, bad health, or bad policy? *Journal of Vocational Rehabilitation, 20*(3), 185–201.

Burton, J. F., & Spieler, E. A. (1998). Compensation for disabled workers: Workers' compensation. In J. F. Burton, T. Thomason, & D. E. Hyatt (Eds.), *New approaches to disability in the workplace.* Ithaca, NY: Industrial Relations Research Association/Cornell University Press.

Butcher, K., & Park, H. (2008). Obesity, disability, and the labor force. *Economic Perspectives, 1Q,* 2–16.

Butterfield, T., & Ramseur, J. (2004). Research and case study findings in the area of workplace accommodations provisions for assistive technology: A literature review. *Technology and Disability, 16,* 201–210.

Cable, D. M., & DeRue, D. S. (2002). The convergent and discriminate validity of subjective fit perceptions. *Journal of Applied Psychology, 87*(5), 875–884.

CAHRS Working Group. (2011). *Attraction, retention, and reward for employees with disabilities: Working group summary.* Ithaca, NY: Center for Advanced Human Resource Studies. Retrieved from http://www.ilr.cornell.edu/cahrs/research/upload/exec-summary_CAHRS-Working-GroupDisabilities10–14–11.pdf

Call, C., Gerdes, R., & Robinson, K. (2009). *Corporate and worksite wellness programs: A research review focused on individuals with disabilities.* Gaithersburg, MD: Social Dynamics LLC. Retrieved from http://www.dol.gov/odep/research/CorporateWellnessResearchLiteratureReview.pdf

Callahan, T. J. (1994). Manager beliefs about and attitudes toward the Americans with Disabilities Act of 1990. *Applied Human Resource Management Research, 5,* 28–43.

Cawley, J. (2007). The labor market impact of obesity. In Z. Acs & A. Lyles (Eds.), *Obesity, business, and public policy.* Cheltenham, UK: Edward Elgar.

Center, C., & Imparato, A. J. (2003). Redefining "disability" discrimination: A proposal to restore civil rights protections for all workers. *Stanford Law & Policy Review, 14,* 321.

Certification of Disability Management Specialists Commission. (2008). *CDMS certification guide.* Schaumburg, IL: Author.

Colella, A. (1996). Organizational socialization of newcomers with disabilities: A framework for future research. *Research in Personnel and Human Resources Management, 14,* 351–417.

Colella, A. (2001). Coworker distributive fairness judgments of the workplace accommodation of employees with disabilities. *Academy of Management Review, 26,* 100–116.

Colella, A., DeNisi, A. S., & Varma, A. (1998). The impact of ratee's disability on performance judgments and choice of partner: The role of disability-job fit stereotypes and interdependence of rewards. *Journal of Applied Psychology, 83,* 102–111.

Conference Board. (2007). *Middle managers: Engaging and enrolling the biggest roadblock to diversity and inclusion* (Executive Action Series, No. 234). New York, NY: Author.

Conference Board. (2012). *Supplier Diversity Leadership Council.* Retrieved from http://www.conference-board.org/councils/councildetail.cfm?coun cilid=183

Conley, D., & Glauber, R. (2005). *Gender, body mass, and economic status* (Working paper 11343). Cambridge, MA: National Bureau of Economic Research.

Cook, J. A., & O'Day, B. (2006). *Supported employment: A best practice for people with psychiatric disabilities.* Ithaca, NY: Cornell University Rehabilitation Research and Training Center on Employment Policy for Persons with Disabilities. Retrieved from http://digitalcommons.ilr.cornell.edu/edicollect/1230

Corthell, D. W., & McAlees, D. (1991). Aging America: Implications and impact on vocational rehabilitation. *American Rehabilitation, 17*(1), 27–33.

Creary, S. J. (2008). *Leadership, governance, and accountability: A pathway to a diverse and inclusive organization.* New York, NY: The Conference Board.

De Dreu, C. & Weingart, L. (2003). Task versus relationship conflict, team performance, and team member satisfaction: A meta-analysis. *Journal of Applied Psychology, 88*(4), 741–749.

DeLeire, T. (2000a). The wage and employment effects of the Americans with Disabilities Act. *The Journal of Human Resources, 35*(4), 693–715.

DeLeire, T. (2000b). The unintended consequences of the Americans with Disabilities Act. *Regulation, 23*(1), 21–24.

DeNavas-Walt, C., Proctor, B., & Smith, J. (2011). *Income, poverty, and health insurance coverage in the United States: 2010* (Current Population Reports, P60–239).

Washington, DC: U.S. Government Printing Office. Retrieved from http://www.census.gov/prod/2011pubs/p60-239.pdf

Diksa, E., & Rogers, E. S. (1996). Employer concerns about hiring persons with psychiatric disability: Results of the employer attitude questionnaire. *Rehabilitation Counseling Bulletin, 40*(1), 31–44.

Disability Management Employer Coalition (DMEC). (2009). *Tools of the trade: A compilation of programs and processes for the absence, disability, health and productivity professional.* San Diego, CA: Author.

DiTomaso, N., & Hooijberg, R. (1996). Diversity and the demands of leadership. *Leadership Quarterly, 7,* 163–187.

Dixon, C. G., Richard, M., & Rollins, C. W. (2003). Contemporary issues facing aging Americans: Implications for rehabilitation and mental health counseling. *Journal of Rehabilitation, 69*(2), 5–12.

Dixon, K. A., Kruse, D., & Van Horn, C. E. (2003, March). *Restricted access: A survey of employers about people with disabilities and lowering barriers to work.* New Brunswick, NJ: Rutgers University, Heldrich Center for Workforce Development. Retrieved from http://www.heldrich.rutgers.edu/sites/default/files/content/Restricted_Access.pdf

Domzal, C., Houtenville, A., & Sharma, R. (2008). *Survey of employer perspectives on the employment of people with disabilities: Technical report.* McLean, VA: Office of Disability and Employment Policy, U.S. Department of Labor.

Doyle, R. H., Dixon, C. G., & Moore, C. L. (2003). Expanding rehabilitation services to meet the legal needs of aging Americans. *Journal of Rehabilitation, 69*(2), 49–54.

Drake, R., Becker, D., & Bond, G. (2003). Recent research on vocational rehabilitation for persons with severe mental illness. *Current Opinion in Psychiatry, 16,* 451–455.

Dreher, G. & Cox, T. (1996). Race, gender, and opportunity: A study of compensation attainment and the establishment of mentoring relationships. *Journal of Applied Psychology, 81*(3), 297–308.

Drury, D. (1991). Disability management in small firms. *Rehabilitation Counseling Bulletin, 34*(3), 243–256.

Elinson, L., & Frey, W. (2005). *Evaluation of the disability employment policy demonstration programs: Task 10: Interim report on ODEP demonstration programs: Accomplishments and issues identified by the independent evaluation.* Report prepared for the Office of Disability Employment Policy, U.S. Department of Labor. Rockville, MD: Westat.

Ellickson, M. C. (2002). Determinants of job satisfaction of municipal government employees. *Public Personnel Management, 31,* 343–359.

Emerging Leaders. (n.d.). *Emerging Leaders: About us.* Retrieved from http://www.emerging-leaders.com/aboutUs.htm.

Erickson, W. (2002, September). *A review of selected E-recruiting websites: Disability accessibility considerations.* Ithaca, NY: Cornell University, School of Industrial and Labor Relations—Extension Division, Program on Employment and Disability. Retrieved from http://digitalcommons.ilr.cornell.edu/edicollect/95

Erickson, W., Lee, C., & von Schrader, S. (2009). *2008 disability status report: The United States.* Ithaca, NY: Cornell University Rehabilitation Research and Training Center on Disability Demographics and Statistics. Retrieved from http://www.disabilitystatistics.org

Erickson, W., Lee, C., & von Schrader, S. (2010). *Disability statistics from the 2008 American Community Survey (ACS).* Ithaca, NY: Cornell University Rehabilitation Research and Training Center on Disability Demographics and Statistics (StatsRRTC). Retrieved from http://www.disabilitystatistics.org

Fabian, E. S., Edelman, A., & Leedy, M. (1993). Linking workers with severe disabilities to social supports in the workplace: Strategies for addressing barriers. *Journal of Rehabilitation, 59*(3), 29–34.

Fabian, E. S., Luecking, R. G., & Tilson, G. P. (1995). Employer and rehabilitation personnel perspectives on hiring persons with disabilities: Implications for job development. *Journal of Rehabilitation, 61*(1), 42–49.

Fair Wages for Workers with Diabilities Act of 2011. H.R. 3086, 112th Congress. Retrieved from http://thomas.loc.gov/cgi-bin/bdquery/z?d112:h.r.3086:

Fairlie, R. W., & Meyer, B. (1996). Ethnic and racial self-employment differences and possible explanations. *Journal of Human Resources 31*(4), 757–793.

FirstStep. (n.d.). *Social Security Disability Insurance (SSDI)* [Interactive tool]. Retrieved from https://www.cms.gov/apps/firststep/content/ssdi-qa.html

Florey, A., & Harrison, D. (2000). Responses to informal accommodation requests for employees with disabilities: Multistudy evidence on willingness to comply. *Academy of Management Journal, 43,* 224–233.

Forrester Research, Inc. (2004). *Accessible technology in computing: Examining awareness, use, and future potential.* Cambridge, MA: Author. Retrieved from http://www.microsoft.com/enable/research/phase2.aspx

Frank, J. J., & Bellini, J. (2005). Barriers to the accommodation request process of the Americans with Disabilities Act. *Journal of Rehabilitation, 71*(2), 28–39.

Fried, Y., Levi, A. S., Ben-David, H. A., Tiegs, R. B., & Avital, N. (2000). Rater positive and negative mood predispositions as predictors of performance ratings of ratees in simulated and real organizational settings: Evidence from U.S. and Israeli samples. *Journal of Occupational and Organizational Psychology, 73*(3), 373–378.

Funaro, A., & Dixon, K. A. (2002). *How the One-Stop System services people with disabilities: a nationwide survey of disability agencies.* New Brunswick, NJ: Rutgers University, Heldrich Center for Workforce Development.

Geaney, J. (2004). The relationship of workers' compensation to the Americans with Disabilities Act and Family and Medical Leave Act. *Clinics in Occupational and Environmental Medicine, 4,* 273–293.

Gerhart, B., Trevor, C., & Graham, M. E. (1996). New directions in compensation research: Synergies, risk, and survival. In G. R. Ferris (Ed.), *Research in personnel and human resource management* (Vol. 14, pp. 143–203). Bingley, UK: Emerald Group. Retrieved from http://www.emeraldinsight.com/books.htm?issn=0742-7301

Gerstner, C. R., & Day, D. V. (1997). Meta-analytic review of leader-member exchange theory: Correlates and construct issues. *Journal of Applied Psychology, 82,* 827–844.

Gibbons, J. (2007). *Finding a definition of employee engagement* (Conference Board Executive Action Series, No. 236). New York, NY: The Conference Board.

Gilbride, D., Stensrud, R., Ehlers, C., Evans, E., & Peterson, C. (2000). Employers' attitudes toward hiring persons with disabilities and vocational rehabilitation services. *Journal of Rehabilitation, 66*(4), 17–23.

Gilbride, D., Stensrud, R., Vandergoot, D., & Golden, K. (2003). Identification of the characteristics of work environments and employers open to hiring and accommodating people with disabilities. *Rehabilitation Counseling Bulletin, 46*(3), 130–137.

Gobel, C., & Zwick, T. (2010). *Which personnel measures are effective in increasing productivity of old workers?* (ZEW Discussion Paper). Mannheim, Germany: Center for European Economic Research. Retrieved from ftp://ftp.zew.de/pub/zew-docs/dp/dp10069.pdf

Golden, T., Zeitzer, I., & Bruyère, S. (2007). *New approaches to disability in social policy: The case of the United States.* Ithaca, NY: Cornell University Employment and Disability Institute.

Gomez, C., & Rosen, B. (2001). The leader–member exchange as a link between managerial trust and employee empowerment. *Group and Organization Management, 26,* 53–69.

Goodman, N., Stapleton, D., Livermore, G., & O'Day, B. (2007). *The health care financing maze for working age people with disabilities.* Ithaca, NY: Cornell University, RRTC on Employment Policy for People with Disabilities. Retrieved from http://digitalcommons.ilr.cornell.edu/edicollect/1234

Goodman, N., & Waidman, T. (2003). SSDI and the employment rate of people with disabilities. In D. Stapleton & R. Burkhauser (Eds.), *The decline in employment of people with disabilities: A policy puzzle* (pp. 339–405). Kalamazoo, MI: W. E. Upjohn Institute for Employment Research.

Gouvier, W., Sytsma-Jordan, S., & Mayville, S. (2003). Patterns of discrimination in hiring job applicants with disabilities: The role of disability type, job complexity, and public contact. *Rehabilitation Psychology, 48*(3), 175–181.

Greenwood, R., & Johnson, V. A. (1987). Employer perspectives on workers with disabilities. *Journal of Rehabilitation, 53*(3), 37–45.

Gutman, A. (2009). Major EEO issues relating to personnel selection decisions. *Human Resource Management Review, 19*(3), 232–250.

Habeck, R., Hunt, A., Rachel, C. H., Kregel, J., & Chan, F. (2010). Employee retention and integrated disability management practices as demand side factors. *Journal of Occupational Rehabilitation, 20*(4), 443–455. doi:10.1007/s10926-009-9225-9

Hackman, J. R., & Oldham, G. R. (1976). Motivation through the design of work: Test of a theory. *Organizational Behavior and Human Performance, 16,* 250–279.

Hair, E. C., Park, J. M., Ling, T. J., & Moore, K. A. (2009). Risky behaviors in late adolescence: Co-occurrence, predictors, and consequences. *Journal of Adolescent Health, 45,* 253–261.

Harris, B. H., Hendershot, G., and Stapleton, D. C. (2005). *A guide to disability statistics from the National Health Interview.* Ithaca, NY: Cornell University Rehabilitation Research and Training Center on Disability Demographics and Statistics. Retrieved from http://digitalcommons.ilr.cornell.edu/edicollect/186

Harter, J., Schmidt, F., & Keyes, C. (2003). Well-being in the workplace and its relationship to business outcomes: A review of the Gallup Studies. In C. Keyes & J. Haidt (Eds.), *Flourishing: The positive person and the good life* (pp. 209–224). Washington, DC: American Psychological Association.

Healthcare.gov. (2010, June 27). *Increasing choice and saving money for small businesses* [News release]. Retrieved from http://www.healthcare.gov/news/factsheets/2010/06/increasing-choice-and-saving-money-for-small-businesses.html

Healthcare.gov. (2011). *People with disabilities and the Affordable Care Act* [Factsheet]. Retrieved from http://www.healthcare.gov/news/factsheets/2011/08/people-with-disabilities.html

Hernandez, B., Keys, C. B., & Balcazar, F. E. (2000). Employer attitudes toward workers with disabilities and their ADA employment rights: A literature review. *Journal of Rehabilitation, 66*(4), 4–16.

Hernandez, B., Keys, C. B., & Balcazar, F. E. (2003). The Americans with Disabilities Act Knowledge Survey: Strong psychometrics and weak knowledge. *Rehabilitation Psychology, 48*(4), 93–99.

Heyer, K. (2008). Rights or quotas? The ADA as a model for disability rights. In L. Nielsen & R. Nelson (Eds.), *Handbook of employment discrimination research: Rights and realities* (pp. 227–257). New York, NY: Springer.

Hirsh, C. E., & Kmec, J. (2009). Human resource structures: Reducing discrimination or raising rights awareness? *Industrial Relations, 48*(3), 512–532.

Hollar, D., & Moore, D. (2004). Relationship of substance use by students with disabilities to long-term educational and social outcomes. *Substance Use & Misuse, 39*(6), 929–960.

Hotchkiss, J. (2004a). A closer look at the employment impact of the Americans with Disabilities Act. *The Journal of Human Resources, 39*(4), 887–911.

Hotchkiss, J. (2004b). Growing part-time employment among workers with disabilities: Marginalization or opportunity? *Federal Reserve Bank of Atlanta Economic Review,* 25–40.

Houtenville, A., & Burkhauser, R. (2005). *Did the employment of people with disabilities decline in the 1990s, and was the ADA responsible? A replication and robustness check of Acemoglu and Angrist (2001).* Ithaca, NY: Cornell University, Rehabilitation Research and Training Center for Employment Policy for Persons with Disabilities.

Humphrey, S. E., Nahrgang, J. D., & Morgeson, F. P. (2007). Integrating motivational, social, and contextual work design features: A metaanalytic summary and theoretical extension of the work design literature. *Journal of Applied Psychology, 92,* 1332–1356.

Hursh, N. (1997). Making a difference in the workplace. In W. Zimmerman (Ed.), *Strategies for success.* Port Alberni, BC: National Institute of Disability Management and Research.

Internal Revenue Service. (2006). *Form 8826 and instructions.* Retrieved from http://www.irs.gov/pub/irs-pdf/f8826.pdf

James, D., & Glaze, L. (2006, December). *Mental health problems of prison and jail inmates* (Bureau of Justice Statistics Special Report, NCJ 213600). Retrieved from http://bjs.ojp.usdoj.gov/content/pub/pdf/mhppji.pdf

Job Accommodation Network. (1994). *The president's committee on employment of people with disabilities: Quarterly report.* Alexandria, VA: Author.

Joblinks Employment Transportation. (2009). *Transportation for workers with disabilities: Widening your pool of potential talent.* Retrieved from https://www.disability.gov/viewResource?id=13459520

Jolls, C., & Prescott, J. J. (2004). *Disaggregating employment protection: The case of disability discrimination* (NBER Working Paper No. 10740). Retrieved from http://www.nber.org/papers/w10528

Kahn, R. L., & Byosiere, P. (1992). Stress in organizations. In M. D. Dunnette & L. M. Hough (Eds.), *Handbook of industrial and organizational psychology, Vol. 3* (pp. 571–650). Palo Alto, CA: Consulting Psychologists Press.

Kalev, A., Dobbin, F., & Kelly, E. (2006). Best practices or best guesses? Assessing the efficacy of corporate affirmative action and diversity policies. *American Sociological Review, 71*(4), 589–617.

Karpur, A., & Bruyère, S. (2012, January). *Workplace health promotion for people with disabilities: Healthcare expenditure among people with disabilities: Potential role of workplace health promotion and implication for rehabilitation counseling* [Working Paper]. Ithaca, NY: Rehabilitation Research and Training Center on Employer Practices, Cornell University ILR School.

Kaye, H. S. (2003). Employment and the changing disability population. In D. C. Stapleton & R. V. Burkhauser (Eds.), *The decline in employment of people with disabilities* (pp. 217–258). Kalamazoo, MI: W. E. Upjohn Institute for Employment Research.

Kiernan, W. E. (2000). Where are we now? Perspectives on employment of persons with mental retardation. *Focus on Autism and Other Developmental Disabilities, 15*(2), 90–97.

Kobe, K. (2007, April). *The small business share of GDP, 1998–2004* [Paper prepared for the Small Business Administration under Contract Number SBAHQ-05-M-0413]. Retrieved from http://www.sba.gov/advo/research/rs299tot.pdf

Koesnadi, G., & Kleiner, B. (2002). The need for training to avoid lawsuits. *Managerial Law, 44*(1/2), 25–30.

Kosciulek, J. F. (2007). A test of the theory of informed consumer choice in vocational rehabilitation. *Journal of Rehabilitation, 73*(2), 41–49.

Kosciulek, J., Rosenthal, D., Vessell, R., Accardo, C., & Merz, M. (1997). Consumer satisfaction with vocational rehabilitation services. *Journal of Rehabilitation, 63*(2), 5–9.

Kram, K. E. (1985). *Mentoring at work: Developmental relationship in organizational life.* Glenview, IL: Scott Foresman.

Krause, J. S., & Pickelsimer, E. (2008). Relationship of perceived barriers to employment and return to work five years later: A pilot study among 343 participants with spinal cord injury. *Rehabilitation Counseling Bulletin, 51*(2), 118–121.

Krawiec, K. (2003). Cosmetic compliance and the failure of negotiated governance. *Washington University Law Quarterly, 81,* 487–544.

Krawiec, K. (2009). The return of the rogue. *Arizona Law Review, 51,* 127–174.

Kruse, D., & Schur, L. (2003, January). Employment of people with disabilities following the ADA. *Industrial Relations, 42*(1), 31–66.

Kruse, D., Schur, L., & Ali, M. (2010). Disability and occupational projections. *Monthly Labor Review, 133*(10). Retrieved from http://www.bls.gov/opub/mlr/2010/10/art3exc.htm

Kuoppala, J., Lamminpää, A., & Husman, P. (2008). Work health promotion, job well-being, and sickness absences: A systematic review and meta-analysis. *Journal of Occupational & Environmental Medicine, 50*(11), 1216–1227.

Lakdawalla, D., Bhattacharya, J., & Goldman, D. (2004). Are the young becoming more disabled? *Health Affairs, 23*(1), 168–176.

Larkin, V. M., Alston, R. J., Middleton, R. A., & Wilson, K. B. (2003). Underrepresented ethnically and racially diverse aging populations with disabilities: Trends and recommendations. *Journal of Rehabilitation, 69*(2), 26–31.

Lee, B. (1996). Legal requirements and employer responses to accommodating employees with disabilities. *Human Resource Management Review, 6*(4), 231–251.

Lee, R. T., & Ashforth, B. E. (1996). A meta-analytic examination of the correlates of the three dimensions of job burnout. *Journal of Applied Psychology, 81,* 123–133.

Lehman, I. S. (2006). Minimum wage rates and employment of individuals with disabilities. *Journal of Rehabilitation, 72*(2), 50–57.

Lengnick-Hall, M. (2007). *Hidden talent: How leading companies hire, retain, and benefit from people with disabilities.* Westport, CT: Praeger.

Lengnick-Hall, M., Gaunt, P., & Collison, J. (2003). *Employer incentives for hiring individuals with disabilities.* Alexandria, VA: Society for Human Resource Management.

Lengnick-Hall, M. L., Gaunt, P. M., & Kulkarni, M. (2008). Overlooked and underutilized: People with disabilities are an untapped human resource. *Human Resource Management, 47*(2), 255–273. doi:10.1002/hrm.20211

Linkow, P. (2012). *Research Working Group on Improving Employment Outcomes for People with Disabilities.* New York, NY: The Conference Board.

Livermore, G., & Goodman, N. (2009, February). *A review of recent evaluation efforts associated with programs and policies designed to promote the employment of adults with disabilities.* Washington, DC: Mathematica Policy Research.

Lombard, K. V. (2001). Female self-employment and demand for flexible, nonstandard work schedules. *Economic Inquiry, 29*(2), 214–317.

Loprest, P. (2007). *Strategic assessment of the state of the science in research on employment for disabilities.* Washington, DC: The Urban Institute.

Mank, D. M., Cioffi, A. R., & Yovanoff, P. (1999). The impact of coworker involvement with supported employees on wage and integration outcomes. *Mental Retardation, 37*(5), 383–394.

Marushack, L., & Beck, A. (2001). *Medical problems of inmates, 1997.* (Special Report). Washington, DC: Bureau of Justice Statistics.

McCallion, P., Janicki, M., & Grant-Griffin, L. (1997). Exploring the impact of culture and acculturation on older families' caregiving for persons with developmental disabilities. *National Council on Family Relations, 46*(4), 347–357.

McCary, K. (2005). The disability twist in diversity: Best practices for integrating people with disabilities into the workforce. *Diversity Factor, 13*(3), 16–23.

McClane, W. E. (1991). Implications of member role differentiation: Analysis of a key concept in the LMX model of leadership. *Group and Organization Studies, 16*, 102–113.

McFarlin, D., Song, J., & Sonntag, M. (1991). Integrating the disabled into the workforce: A survey of Fortune 500 company attitudes and practices. *Employee Responsibilities and Rights Journal, 4*(2), 107–123.

McGee, L. (2009, August). *SEO and accessibility overlap.* Retrieved from http://www.communis.co.uk/blog/2009-08-06-seo-and-accessibility-overlap

McMahon, B. T., Roessler, R., Rumrill, P. D., Hurley, J. E., West, S. L., Chan, F., & Carlson, L. (2008). Hiring discrimination against people with disabilities under the ADA: Characteristics of charging parties. *Journal of Occupational Rehabilitation, 18*(2), 122–132.

McMahon, B. T., & Shaw, L. R. (2005). Foreword: Special issue on workplace discrimination and disability. *Journal of Vocational Rehabilitation, 23*(3), 137–145.

McMullian, J., & Shuey, K. (2006). Ageing, disability and workplace accommodations. *Ageing and Society, 26*, 831–847.

Mechanic, D., Bilder, S., & McAlpine, D. (2002). Employing persons with serious mental illness. *Health Affairs, 21*(5), 242–253. doi:10.1377/hlthaff.21.5.242

Menz, F. E., Hagen-Foley, D., & Gerber, A. (2005). *Community-based rehabilitation programs, phase II: Service, beneficiary, outcome, and organizational models and perceived barriers to pursuing work goals: Final report.* Urbana-Champaign, IL: University of Illinois, Disability Research Institute.

Mitchell, T. R., Holtom, B. S., Lee, T. W., Sablynski, C. J., & Erez, M. (2001). Why people stay: Using job embeddedness to predict voluntary turnover. *Academy of Management Journal, 44*(6), 1102–1121.

Mitra, S., & Kruse, D. (2008). *Disability and worker displacement.* Paper presented at the 2009 Annual Meeting of the Labor and Employment Relations Association, San Francisco, CA.

Mont, D. (2004). *Disability employment policy* (The World Bank, Social Protection Discussion Paper No. 0412). Retrieved from http://digitalcommons.ilr.cornell.edu/gladnetcollect/431

Moon, N., & Baker, P. (2010, February). *Workplace accommodations for people with disabilities: Results of a policy Delphi study* (Working Paper 02–2010). Atlanta, GA: Rehabilitation Engineering Research Center on Workplace Accommodations. Retrieved from http://www.workrerc.org/News/Papers/WorkplacePolicyDelphi.pdf

Morgan, R., & Alexander, M. (2005). The employer's perception: Employment of individuals with developmental disabilities. *Journal of Vocational Rehabilitation, 23*(1) 39–49.

Moss, K., Burris, S., Ullman, M., Johnsen, M., & Swanson, J. (2001). Unfunded mandate: An empirical study of the implementation of the Americans with Disabilities Act by the Equal Employment Opportunity Commission. *Kansas Law Review, 50*(1). Retrieved from http://ssrn.com/abstract=932059

Moss, K., & Johnsen, M. C. (1997). Employment discrimination and the ADA: A study, *Psychiatric Rehabilitation Journal, 21*(2), 111.

Moss, K., Ullman, M., Johnsen, M. C., Starrett, B. E., & Burris, S. (1999). Different paths to justice: The ADA, employment, and administrative enforcement by the EEOC and FEPAs. *Behavioral Sciences & the Law, 17*(1), 29–46.

Mottaz, C. (1985). The relative importance of intrinsic and extrinsic rewards as determinants of work satisfaction. *Sociological Quarterly, 26*, 365–385.

Mullins, J., Roessler, R., Schriner, K., Bellini, J., & Brown, P. (1997). Improving employment outcomes through quality rehabilitation counseling (QRC): Responding to the 1992 amendments. *Journal of Rehabilitation, 63*(4), 21–31.

Mwachofi, A. K. (2009). Gender differences in access and intervention outcomes: The case for women with disabilities. *Disability and Rehabilitation, 31*(9), 693–700.

National Business Group on Health. (2009). *EMPAQ annual report: Program year 2009: Executive summary.* Washington, DC: Author.

National Council on Disability. (2007). *The impact of the Americans with Disabilities Act: Assessing the progress toward achieving the goals of the ADA.* Washington, DC: National Council on Disability.

Ni, C., Wilkins-Turner, F., Liebert, D. E., Ellien, V., & Harrington, C. (2011). Native Americans with disabilities: A comparison of male and female eastern tribal members. *Review of Disabilities Studies, 7*(1), 41–53.

Nishii, L., & Bruyère, S. (2009). Protecting employees with disabilities from discrimination on the job: The role of unit managers. Paper presented as part of the panel *Workplace policies and practices minimizing disability discrimination: Implications for psychology,* at the 117th Annual Convention of the American Psychological Association, Toronto, Canada.

Nishii, L. H., & Wright, P. (2008). Variability at multiple levels of analysis: Implications for strategic human resource management. In D. B. Smith (Ed.), *The people make the place* (pp. 225–248). Mahwah, NJ: Lawrence Erlbaum Associates.

Olson, D., Cioffi, A., Yovanoff, P., & Mank, D. (2001). Employers' perceptions of employees with mental retardation. *Journal of Vocational Rehabilitation, 16*(2), 125–133.

Parry, L., Rutherford, L., & Merrier, P. (1996). Too little too late: Are business schools falling behind the times? *Journal of Education for Business, 71*(5), 293–299.

Peck, B., & Kirkbride, L. T. (2001). Why businesses don't employ people with disabilities. *Journal of Vocational Rehabilitation, 16*(2), 71–75.

Pew Research Center (2009). *Trends in political values and core attitudes: 1987–2009. Independents take center stage in Obama era.* Retrieved from http://www.people-press.org/files/legacy-pdf/517.pdf

Quick, E. (2011, March 25). Integrated disability management in a challenging economy. *SHRM Benefits.* Retrieved from http://www.shrm.org/hrdisciplines/benefits/Articles/Pages/DisabilityManagement.aspx

Raver, J. L., & Nishii, L. H. (2010). Once, twice, or three times as harmful? Ethnic harassment, gender harassment, and generalized workplace harassment. *Journal of Applied Psychology, 95*(2), 236–254.

Razzano, L. A., Cook, J. A., Burke-Miller, J. K., Mueser, K. T., Pickett-Schenk, S. A., et al. (2005). Clinical factors associated with employment among people with severe mental illness: Findings from the employment intervention demonstration program. *Journal of Nervous and Mental Disease, 193,* 705–713.

Rimmer, J., Riley, B., Wang, E., Rauworth, A., & Jurkowski, J. (2004). Physical activity participation among persons with disabilities: Barriers and facilitators. *American Journal of Preventive Medicine, 26*(5), 419–425.

Rimmer, J., & Rowland, J. (2008). Health promotion for people with disabilities: Implications for empowering the person and promoting disability-friendly environments. *American Journal of Lifestyle Medicine, 2*(5), 409–420.

Roessler, R. (2002). Improving job tenure outcomes for people with disabilities: The "3M" Model. *Rehabilitation Counseling Bulletin, 45*(3), 207–212.

Rosen, B., & Barrington, L. (2008). *Weights and measures: What employers should know about obesity* (Research Report R-1419–08-RR). New York, NY: The Conference Board.

Rosenthal, D., Hursh, N., Lui, J., Isom, R., & Sasson, J. (2007). A survey of current disability management practice: Emerging trends and implications for certification. *Rehabilitation Counseling Bulletin, 50*(2), 76–86.

Rosenthal, D., Hursh, N., Lui, J., Zimmerman, W., & Pruett, S. R. (2005). Case management issues within employer-based disability management. In F. Chan, M. Leahy, & J. Saunders (Eds.), *Case management for rehabilitation health professionals* (pp. 330–365). Lake Osage, MO: Aspen Professional Services.

Rowland, C., & Smith, T. (1999). Web site accessibility. *The Power of Independence (Summer Edition)*, 1–1. Outreach Division, Center for Persons with Disabilities, Utah State University.

Rumrill, P. D., Jr., & Roessler, R. T. (1999). New directions in vocational rehabilitation: A "career development" perspective on "closure." *Journal of Rehabilitation, 65*(1), 26.

Schartz, K. M., Hendricks, D. J., & Blanck, P. (2006). Workplace accommodations: Empirical study of current employees. *Mississippi Law Journal, 75*, 917–943.

Schartz, K., Schartz, H., & Blanck, P. (2002). Employment of persons with disabilities in information technology jobs: Literature review for "IT Works." *Behavioral Sciences and the Law, 20*, 637–657.

Scheid, T. (1999). Employment of individuals with mental disabilities: Business response to the ADA's challenge. *Behavioral Sciences & the Law, 17*, 73–91.

Schur, L. (2002). Dead-end jobs or a path to economic well-being? The consequences of nonstandard work for people with disabilities. *Behavioral Sciences and the Law, 20*, 601–620.

Schur, L., Kruse, D., & Blanck, P. (2005). Corporate culture and the experiences of persons with disabilities. *Behavioral Sciences & the Law, 23*(1), 3–20.

Schur, L., Kruse, D., Blasi, J., & Blanck, P. (2009). Is disability disabling in all workplaces? Workplace disparities and corporate culture. *Industrial Relations, 48*(3), 381–410.

Schwochau, S., & Blanck, D. (2000). The economics of the Americans with Disabilities Act, Part III: Does the ADA disable the disabled? *Berkley Journal of Employment and Labor Law, 21*(27), 271–313.

Schyns, B., Paul, T., Mohr, G., & Blank, H. (2005). Comparing antecedents and consequences of leader-member exchange in a German working context to findings in the U.S. *European Journal of Work and Organizational Psychology, 14*, 1–22.

Seshamani, M., & Montz, E. (2009). *Insurance at risk: Small business employees risk losing coverage.* Retrieved from http://www.healthreform.gov/reports/smallbusiness/index.html

Sherwyn, D., Heise, M., & Eigen, Z. (2001). Don't train your employees and cancel your 1–800 Harassment hotline: An empirical examination and correction of the flaws in the affirmative defense to sexual harassment charges. *Fordham Law Review, 69,* 1265–1304.

Shrey, D. E., & Lacerte, M. M. D. (1995). *Principles and practices of disability management in industry.* Winter Park, FL: GR Press, Inc.

Small Business Administration. (2003). About SBA. Retrieved from http://www.sba.gov/aboutsba

Small Business Administration. (2009, September). *Small Business Administration: Frequently asked questions.* Retrieved from http://www.sba.gov/advo/stats/sbfaq.pdf

Small Business Administration Office of Advocacy. (2004*). Small business by the numbers: Answers to frequently asked questions: United States.* Retrieved from http://www.sba.gov/ADVO/stats/profiles/02nation.pdf

Smith, K., Webber, L., Graffam, J., & Wilson, C. (2004). Employer satisfaction, job-match and future hiring intentions for employees with a disability. *Journal of Vocational Rehabilitation, 21*(3), 165–164.

Social Security Administration (2008). *Disability evaluation under Social Security.* (Blue Book, September 2008). Part 1: General Information. Retrieved from http://www.socialsecurity.gov/disability/professionals/bluebook/general-info.htm

Social Security Administration (2011, May). *Supplemental Social Security Income (SSI)* (SSA Publication No. 05–11000, ICN 480200). Retrieved from http://www.socialsecurity.gov/pubs/11000.html

Social Security Administration (2011, July). *Disability benefits* (SSA Publication No. 05-10029, ICN 456000). Retrieved from http://www.socialsecurity.gov/pubs/10029.html

Social Security Administration (2011, August). *Annual statistical report on the Social Security Disability Insurance program, 2010.* Washington, DC: Author. Retrieved from http://www.ssa.gov/policy/docs/statcomps/di_asr

Social Security Legislative Bulletin. (1999). *Congress passes the Ticket to Work and Work Incentives Improvement Act of 1999* (106–13R, December 3, 1999). Retrieved from http://www.ssa.gov/legislation/legis_bulletin_120399.html

Social Security Online (2011). *Disability planner: What we mean by disability.* Retrieved from http://www.ssa.gov/dibplan/dqualify4.htm

Society for Human Resource Management. (2011). *Recruiting veterans with disabilities: Perceptions in the Workplace SHRM Poll.* Alexandria, VA: Author. Retrieved from http://www.shrm.org/Research/SurveyFindings/Articles/Pages/Recruitingdisabledvets.aspx

Stapleton, D., Honeycutt, T., & Schechter, B. (2009). *Out of sight, out of mind: Including group quarters residents with household residents can change what we know about working-age people with disabilities* (MPR Report No. 6061–780). Princeton, NJ: Mathematica Policy Research.

Stapleton, D., & Liu, S. (2009, November). *Will health care reform increase the employment of people with disabilities?* (Policy Brief 09–04). Washington, DC: Mathematica Policy Research, Center for Studying Disability Policy. Retrieved from http://www.mathematica-mpr.com/publications/redirect_PubsDB.asp?strSite=PDFs/disability/healthcarereform.pdf

Steadman, H., Osher, F., Robbins, P., Case, B., & Samuels, S. (2009). Prevalence of serious mental illness among jail inmates. *Psychiatric Services, 60*(6), 761–765.

Stock, W., & Beegle, K. (2004). Employment protections for older workers: Do disability discrimination laws matter? *Contemporary Economic Policy, 22*(1), 111–126.

Stone, D. L., & Colella, A. (1996). A model of factors affecting the treatment of disabled individuals in organizations. *Academy of Management Review, 21*(2), 352–401.

Strauser, D. R., Lustig, D. C., Keim, J., Ketz, K., & Malesky, A. (2002). Analyzing the differences in career thoughts based on disability status. *Journal of Rehabilitation, 68*(1), 27–32.

Swett, E. A., & Bishop, M. (2003). Mental health and the aging population: Implications for rehabilitation counselors. *Journal of Rehabilitation, 69*(2), 13–18.

Szymanski, E. (1999). Disability, job stress, the changing nature of careers, and the career resilience portfolio. *Rehabilitation Counseling Bulletin, 42*(4), 279–289.

Szymanski, E. M., & Hanley-Maxwell, C. (1996). Career development of people with developmental disabilities: An ecological model. *Journal of Rehabilitation, 62*(1), 48–55.

Thakker, D., & Solomon, P. (1999). Factors influencing managers' adherence to the Americans with Disabilities Act. *Administration and Policy in Mental Health, 26*(3), 213–219.

Thornton, P. (1998). *Employment quotas, levies, and national rehabilitation funds for persons with disabilities: Pointers for policy and practice.* Geneva, Switzerland: International Labour Office. Retrieved from http://digitalcommons.ilr.cornell.edu/cgi/viewcontent.cgi?article=1083&context=gladnetcollect

Toosi, M. (2007). Employment outlook: 2006–16: Labor force projections to 2016—more workers in their golden years. *Monthly Labor Review,* November, 33–52.

Tremblay, T., Smith, J., Xie, H., & Drake, R. (2004). The impact of specialized benefits counseling services on Social Security Administration Disability Beneficiaries in Vermont. *Journal of Rehabilitation, 70*(2), 5-11.

Tweed, V. (1994). Simple answers to a complex problem: Common-sense disability-management strategies can have a lasting impact—cutting disability costs. *Business & Health, 12*(10), 57–60.

Unger, D. (2002). Employers' attitudes toward persons with disabilities in the workforce: Myths or realities? *Focus on Autism and Other Developmental Disabilities, 17*(1), 2–10.

Unger, D., Wehman, P., Yasuda, S., Campbell, L., & Greene, H. (2002). Human resource professionals and the employment of people with disabilities: A business perspective. In *Employers' views of workplace supports: Virginia Commonwealth University Charter Business Roundtable's national study of employers' experiences with workers with disabilities* (Chapter 2). Retrieved from http://www.worksupport.com/Main/employermanual.asp

U.S. Census Bureau. (2001, March 20). *Group quarters population by race and Hispanic origin: 2000 (PHC-T-7). Total population in households and group quarters by sex and selected age groups, for the United States: 2000. Table 1.* Retrieved from http://www.census.gov/population/www/cen2000/briefs/phc-t7/index.html

U.S. Census Bureau. (2010). *Income, poverty, health coverage in the United States, 2010* (Current Population Reports–Consumer income, P60–239). Retrieved from http://www.census.gov/prod/2011pubs/p60-239.pdf

U.S. Department of Health and Human Services (HHS). (2011, June 23). *$10 Million in Affordable Care Act funds to help create workplace health program* [Press release]. Washington, DC: Author. Retrieved from http://www.hhs.gov/news/press/2011pres/06/20110623a.html

U.S. Department of Labor (2002). *Office of Federal Contract Compliance Programs: Facts on Executive Order 11246—Affirmative Action.* Retrieved from http://www.dol.gov/ofccp/regs/compliance/aa.htm

U.S. Department of Labor (2011a). *Frequently asked questions: Section 503 of the Rehabilitation Act: Notice of Proposed Rulemaking (NPRM).* Retrieved from http://www.dol.gov/ofccp/regs/compliance/faqs/Section503_NPRM_faq.htm

U.S. Department of Labor. (2011b). *High growth job training initiative.* Retrieved from http://www.doleta.gov/BRG/JobTrainInitiative

U.S. Department of Labor. (2011c). *The Work Opportunity Tax Credit (WOTC): An employer-friendly benefit for hiring job seekers most in need of employment.* Washington, DC: Author. Retrieved from http://www.doleta.gov/business/incentives/opptax/PDF/WOTC_Fact_Sheet.pdf

U.S. Department of Labor. (n.d.). *Hiring: Affirmative Action.* Retrieved from http://www.dol.gov/dol/topic/hiring/affirmativeact.htm

U.S. Department of Labor, Interagency Committee on Disability Research. (2007, September). *Employer perspectives on workers with disabilities: A national summit to develop a research agenda.* Washington, DC: Author. Retrieved from http://www.icdr.us/documents/ISE_Report-Employer-Perspectives.pdf

U.S. Department of Labor, Interagency Committee on Disability Research. (2008, September). *Strengthening the intersection of demand-side and supply-side disability employment research: Toward a coordinated federal research agenda.* Washington, DC: Author.

U.S. Equal Employment Opportunity Commission. (2005). *Final report on best practices for the employment of people with disabilities in state government.* Retrieved from http://www.eeoc.gov/facts/final_states_best_practices_report.html

U.S. Equal Employment Opportunity Commission. (2008). *Improving the participation rate of people with targeted disabilities in the federal workforce.* Washington, DC: Author.

U.S. Equal Employment Opportunity Commission. (2010, April). *Facts about equal pay and compensation discrimination* (FSE/15, US EEOC Fact Sheet). Retrieved from http://www.eeoc.gov/eeoc/publications/index.cfm

Vilhuber, L., & von Schrader, S. (2010). *Data integration for the purpose of tracking employment outcomes of people with disabilities in New York State: Preliminary assessment.* Ithaca, NY: New York Makes Work Pay. Retrieved from http://www.nymakesworkpay.org/docs/Integrated%20Data%20Report%20Feb2010%20Final.pdf

Von Schrader, S., Malzer, V., Erickson, W., & Bruyère, S. (2011). *Emerging employment issues for people with disabilities: Disability disclosure, leave as a reasonable accommodation, use of job applicant screeners* (Report of a Cornell/AAPD Survey). Ithaca, NY: Cornell University, ILR School, Employment and Disability Institute. Retrieved from http://digitalcommons.ilr.cornell.edu/edicollect/1288

Wehman, P. (2003). Workplace inclusion: Persons with disabilities and coworkers working together. *Journal of Vocational Rehabilitation, 18*(2), 131–141.

Wehman, P., Targett, P., West, M., & Kregel, J. (2005). Productive work and employment for persons with traumatic brain injury: What have we learned after 20 years? *Journal of Head Trauma Rehabilitation, 20*(2), 115–127.

West, D. (2001). *State and federal e-government in the United States, 2001 report.* Retrieved from http://www.insidepolitics.org/egovt01us.html

West, D. (2008). *State and federal electronic government in the United States, 2008.* Retrieved from http://www.brookings.edu/~/media/Files/rc/reports/2008/0826_egovernment_west/0826_egovernment_west.pdf

Whiting, B. (2007, November). *Building bridges to better connect employers and providers of services to jobseekers with disabilities.* Report of a convening hosted by the Employability Advisory Board of the National Organization on Disability, New York City. Retrieved from http://www.nod.org/assets/downloads/Bridges_Convening_Rpt_FINAL_rev_for_NOD_website.pdf

Williams, M. L., McDaniel, M. A., & Nguyen, N. T. (2006). A meta-analysis of the antecedents and consequences of pay level satisfaction. *Journal of Applied Psychology, 91*(2), 392–413.

Wittmer, J., & Wilson, L. (2010). Turning diversity into $: A business case for hiring people with disabilities. *T + D, 64*(2), 58–62.

Wright, M., Woock, C., Spector, J., & Barrington, L. (2010). *Increasing U.S. business investment in postsecondary credentialing for new workforce entrants.* New York, NY: The Conference Board.

Xiang, H., Shi, J., Wheeler, K., & Wilkins, J. R. (2010). Disability and employment among U.S. working-age immigrants. *American Journal of Industrial Medicine, 53*(4), 425–434.

Yanchak, K. V., Lease, S. H., & Strauser, D. R. (2005). Relation of disability type and career thoughts to vocational identity. *Rehabilitation Counseling Bulletin, 48,* 130–138.

Younes, N. (2001). Getting corporations ready to recruit workers with disabilities. *Journal of Rehabilitation, 16*(2), 89–91.

Young, M. (2007). *Grey skies, silver linings: How companies are forecasting, managing, and recruiting a mature workforce* (Research Report R-1409-07-RR). New York, NY: The Conference Board.

Zwerling, C., Whitten, P., Sprince, N., Davis, C., Wallace, R., Blanck, P., & Heeringa, S. (2003). Workplace accommodations for people with disabilities: National Health Interview Survey Disability Supplement, 1994–1995. *Journal of Occupational and Environmental Medicine, 45*(3), 517–525.

Three

Chronology of Critical Events

Sara Furguson, Sara VanLooy,

Susanne M. Bruyère, and Linda Barrington

1526

Spanish humanist Juan Luis Vives proposes the coordination of charitable activities to promote communal and independent study of disadvantaged populations, including people with disabilities. He believes this will encourage rehabilitation for people with disabilities, but similar programs do not materialize until decades later.

1601

Elizabethan Poor Laws are established to aid the deserving poor, orphaned, and crippled. The Act for Relief of the Poor 1601 consolidates prior legislation and funds care by charging a "poor rate" on owners of property. Queen Elizabeth's government also divides the poor into three groups, with the disabled poor placed in the "helpless poor" grouping.

1648

George Dalgarno founds a two-handed means of communication for deaf people that is later used in the English schools of the early 19th century. Dalgarno later publishes *The Art of Signs* (1661), a book about universal language, and *The Deaf and Dumb Man's Tutor* (1680), a publication about deaf communication.

1651

In Germany, George Harsdörffer suggests that wax tablets may be used as a writing aid for the blind.

1662

The first American almshouse is founded in Boston for all people who are public charges, including petty criminals, "worthy" poor, vagrants, the sick, the mentally ill, and the disabled. In this and other early almshouses, criminals are housed in the same units as people with disabilities.

1711

Nicholas Saunderson invents the first tablet used to teach the blind how to write.

1760

The first public school for deaf children is founded in Paris by Charles Michel, Abbé de l'Epeé. Initially the school utilizes an oral method of instruction, but as enrollment increases the school transitions to a group manual method of instruction.

1773

The first American hospital to provide medical supervision for mentally ill patients is founded in Virginia. Hospitals play an important role in the evolution of concepts of rehabilitation as medical personnel realize that patient needs extend beyond medical treatment.

1812

The first educational institution for disabled children in America is established in Baltimore, Maryland. The school provides education to deaf and disabled children, and some families of deaf children are given opportunities to visit Scotland for specialized training.

1817

The first American public school for the deaf is established by Thomas Gallaudet in Hartford, Connecticut. Initially named the Connecticut Asylum at Hartford for the Instruction of Deaf and Dumb Persons, it later becomes known as the American School for the Deaf. Vocational education is added to his school's curriculum in 1822.

1824

Louis Braille invents the raised-point alphabet that has come to be known as Braille. This invention uses various combinations of twelve (eventually diminished to six) embossed dots in a system that enables blind people to read and write.

1830

The Decennial Census of the United States includes in its enumeration a count of individuals with disabilities for the first time. For each household a count is made of the total number of "white persons" and of "slaves and colored persons" who are "deaf and dumb" within three age categories: (1) under 14 years, (2) at least 14 and under 25 years, and (3) 25 years and upward. Additionally, for each household, a count is made of the total number of "white persons" and of "slaves and colored persons" who are blind. No age distinction is made (U.S. Census Bureau, 2011).

1831

Dr. Samuel Howe establishes the New England Asylum for the Blind, Boston's first school for the blind. Core principles of Howe's program include the training of blind young adults to assume places in the social and economic life of their communities, as well as an emphasis on education, especially in the areas of crafts and music. The school also opens an employment service for students in 1849.

1832

The Perkins Institute for the Blind opens in Massachusetts, with the goal of blending academic and vocational instruction into an integrated approach that teaches the whole child.

1833

The House of Commons in England makes its first appropriation for the education of children with physical disabilities. However, the education program focuses on industrial training and workshop production instead of general education.

1838

The Perkins Institute organizes the first known sheltered workshop for its blind students.

1839

Edouard Seguin opens the first school for children with severe retardation in France, and his methods for educating children with mental disabilities by using sensory training become famous throughout the world. In 1850 Seguin immigrates to the United States and establishes other teaching centers that use his methods.

1850

The Decennial Census of the United States first expands its enumeration of persons with disabilities to include cognitive disabilities. Each individual within a household is enumerated and categorized as "free" or "slave." For each inhabitant categorized as free, a note is made if the person is "deaf, dumb, blind, insane, idiotic, pauper, or convict." For each inhabitant categorized as slave, a note is made if the person is "deaf, dumb, blind, insane, or idiotic" (U.S. Census Bureau, 2011).

1855

The Syracuse State School opens with the help of Dr. Hervey Wilbur. The central mission of the school is to provide academic and vocational training to mentally retarded children who have potential for improvement.

1861

Civil War pensions are established by the U.S. Congress for soldiers who suffer war-related disabilities, as well as the widows and orphans of soldiers killed in action. Congress amends the law in 1862 to provide a maximum pension of $8 per month for total disability, with proportionately reduced awards for partial disability.

Congress passes the Morrill Act, which designates over 100,000 acres of federally owned land to western states for the founding of land grant colleges and other educational facilities, including institutions providing vocational rehabilitation services to people with disabilities.

1861–1865

The American Civil War wracks the United States. More than 30,000 Union veterans and an estimated 25,000 Confederate veterans return home with amputations by the end of the conflict, making many Americans aware of the need for disability vocational support (Barnes, 1991).

1869

The Charity Organizations Society is established in London. The institution, which encourages coordination of charitable services for the poor, a social-work approach to charity, and repression of begging, serves as an impetus to the founding of other charitable organizations.

The first wheelchair patent is registered with the United States Patent Office.

1870

The Decennial Census of the United States enumerates persons with disabilities (no longer as "free" or "slave") by noting if an individual is "deaf, dumb, blind, insane, or idiotic," thus eliminating "pauper, or convict" from the categorical agglomeration (U.S. Census Bureau, 2011).

1875

American Express establishes the first private pension plan offered by a U.S. company. The plan provides a lump sum payment to a worker who is temporarily unable to work or who must take early retirement because of disability.

1880

The Second International Congress on Education for the Deaf, held in Milan, Italy, declares that oral education is superior to sign language education and passes a resolution banning the use of sign language in schools. The National Association of the Deaf is founded in the United States to oppose this decision and advocate for the rights of the American deaf community to learn and use sign language.

The Decennial Census of the United States first expands its enumeration of persons with disabilities to list disabilities separately instead of in a categorical agglomeration. Also for the first time, the enumeration includes physical disabilities beyond blindness and deafness as well as an activity-related definition. The specific questions, each enumerated separately for each individual, include (1) Was, on the day of the enumerator's visit, the person sick or disabled so as to be unable to attend to ordinary business or duties? If so, what was the sickness or disability? (2) Was the person blind? (3) Was the person deaf and dumb? (4) Was the person idiotic? (5) Was the person insane? (6) Was the person maimed, crippled, bedridden, or otherwise disabled? (U.S. Census Bureau, 2011).

1881

The American Red Cross is founded. Originally established to help veterans with injuries and disabilities, the organization later expands to provide assistance to other disadvantaged groups or those suffering from the devastation of natural disasters.

1890

The Decennial Census of the United States modernizes its enumeration terminology relating to persons with disabilities and condenses the enumeration to two questions: (1) Is the person suffering from an acute chronic disease? If so, what is the name of that disease and the length of time affected? and (2) Is the person defective of mind, sight, hearing, or speech? Is the person crippled, maimed, or deformed? If yes, what was the name of his defect? (U.S. Census Bureau, 2011).

1891

Kansas establishes the first state "prevailing wage" law to mandate a minimum wage for all workers in the state.

1893

The Industrial School for Crippled and Deformed Children is established in Boston. It is the first American school specifically dedicated to providing training to children with physical disabilities.

1897

Spurred on by orthopedic surgeon Arthur J. Gillette, the state legislature of Minnesota provides the first-in-the-nation legislative support for the treatment, care, and education of physically disabled children.

1900

For the first time since 1820, the Decennial Census of the United States does not include questions enumerating persons with disabilities.

1902

Goodwill Industries is founded in Boston. The organization's initial objective is to service the poor by having the unemployed distribute goods to those in need. Initially, the Goodwill Industries workforce consists of workers who lost their jobs during economic downturn, but employment eligibility is gradually expanded to include people with disabilities.

1903

The Department of Commerce and Labor is established by an act of Congress. Ten years later, the department is divided into two separate departments, the Department of Commerce and the Department of Labor.

1904

The National Association for the Study and Prevention of Tuberculosis is founded to provide support to tuberculosis patients and advocate for legislation and vocational rehabilitation.

1906

Upton Sinclair's *The Jungle,* an account of the Chicago meatpacking industry, is published. It describes the human toll taken by the absence of governmental oversight for workplace safety and the injuries and disabilities that result.

1907

The Immigration Act of 1907 bars entrance to the United States for anyone with a "mental or physical defect . . . which may affect the ability of such aliens to earn a living."

Indiana becomes the first state to enact a eugenic sterilization law in state institutions. Twenty-four other states follow suit and enact similar laws.

1908

The federal government establishes the first national workers' compensation law. Under workers' compensation, employers are required to make provisions such that workers who are injured in accidents arising "out of or in the course of employment" receive medical treatment and payments (ranging up to roughly two-thirds of their wages) to replace lost income. Additional workers' compensation laws are adopted in many states between 1911 and 1920.

1910

The Decennial Census of the United States reinstates two questions enumerating persons with disabilities: (1) Is the person blind in both eyes? and (2) Is the person deaf and dumb? (U.S. Census Bureau, 2011).

1913

President William H. Taft signs the Organic Act to create the Department of Labor (DOL), which is responsible for occupational safety, wage and hour standards, unemployment insurance benefits, re-employment services, and some economic statistics.

1916

The National Defense Act of 1916 provides for an expanded army during peace and wartime, fourfold expansion of the National Guard, the creation of an Officers' and an Enlisted Reserve Corps, the creation of a Reserve Officers' Training Corps in colleges and universities, and access to vocational rehabilitation services. The act is expanded in 1920 to govern army reorganization efforts following times of war.

Psychologist Lewis Terman unveils the Stanford-Binet Intelligence Scale program of intelligence testing. Terman also proposes that intelligence testing be used to separate "feebleminded" students into special classes that focus on "concrete and practical" vocational instruction that will mold them into efficient workers.

1917

The Smith-Hughes National Vocational Education Act promotes vocational agriculture by providing federal funds for agricultural training and education.

The Red Cross Institute for Crippled and Disabled Men, America's first specialized trade school designed to train adults with disabilities, opens in New York City.

1918

The Soldiers Rehabilitation Act (Smith-Sears Act) provides vocational rehabilitation (VR) agencies, programs, and services for soldiers and supports the empowerment and economic self-sufficiency of people with disabilities through employment in careers, independence, and inclusion in American life.

Regina Dolan conducts the Wisconsin Industrial Commission Study, which analyzes the employability of workmen under the commission's review. After the study is complete, Dolan assists disabled workmen in finding employment and implements the first national vocational rehabilitation services as a full-time public employee.

1919

By this year, 43 states have established some form of workers' compensation programs.

The Ohio Society for Crippled Children is founded and later becomes the Easter Seals.

1920

The Fess-Smith Civilian Vocational Rehabilitation Act expands vocational rehabilitation programs to include all disabled civilians and establishes the current state-federal partnership arrangement for rehabilitation services, including counseling, training, prostheses, and placement services.

The Decennial Census of the United States again eliminates questions enumerating persons with disabilities.

1920s

Henry Ford, interested in the re-employment of returning veterans of World War I, instructs his plant managers throughout the country to make surveys of their communities and determine how many persons, in proportion to the population, have physical disabilities. These surveys result in Ford Motor Company instituting a policy of hiring 10% of its employees from the local pools of disabled workers. The Ford policy states, "The most direct way industry can help a man is by offering him a carefully selected job, a job which will make him self-supporting and restore his self-confidence and respect" (The Conference Board, 1945, p. 8).

1921

The National Society for Crippled Children develops several programs to assist people with disabilities, including diagnostic centers, workshops, rehabilitation centers, homebound programs, and more. The society also contributes to the vocational rehabilitation field through research on workplace issues, such as architectural barriers, that affect disabled workers.

1923

During a National Society for Vocational Education conference, a group of administrators of state vocational rehabilitation agencies meets. They call themselves the National Civilian Rehabilitation Conference and plan an organizational meeting the following year.

1924

The Veterans Bureau publishes a manual of procedure for the vocational rehabilitation of veterans of World War I. The document presents knowledge gained through research from 1918 to 1924.

1927

The Fourth National Conference on Vocational Rehabilitation is held in Memphis, Tennessee. The conference emphasizes technical and administrative considerations, unlike earlier national conferences that had devoted more time to the philosophical underpinnings of rehabilitation efforts.

The National Civilian Rehabilitation Conference approves The National Rehabilitation Association (NRA) as its official name.

New York Governor Franklin D. Roosevelt establishes the Warm Springs Institute Foundation, a facility for polio survivors. The foundation's self-proclaimed mission is "to employ individuals with disabilities to achieve personal independence." Roosevelt spent two-thirds of his personal assets to acquire the property and establish the facility, which later became the Roosevelt Warm Springs Institute for Rehabilitation, a model rehabilitation and peer counseling program.

1928

The Federal Board for Vocational Education issues "A Study of Rehabili-
tated Persons, a Statistical Analysis of the Rehabilitation of 6,391 Disabled
Persons." The report, directed by Tracy Copp, confirms that disabled people are capable of holding many different kinds of jobs with varied
mechanical and technical requirements.

1930

Focused on the worsening Great Depression, the Decennial Census of the
United States only enumerates persons with disabilities if their disability is
provided as a reason for why the individual is either "not at work" or "out
of job." Enumerators are instructed to be as specific as possible in the reason
recorded and a list of examples is provided to enumerators. The list
includes "sickness," "was laid off," "voluntary lay-off," "bad weather,"
"lack of materials," "strike," etc. in the case of the former; and "plant closed
down," "sickness," "off season," "job completed," "machines introduced,"
"strike," etc. in the case of the latter (U.S. Census Bureau, 2011).

1931

The Pratt-Smoot Act provides funding to the Library of Congress to
obtain and provide books and other materials for the use of adult blind
residents of the United States. This measure profoundly expands the
training and vocational rehabilitation possibilities available to people
with visual impairment.

1933

The Federal Emergency Relief Administration (FERA) is created. This
agency establishes a link between relief efforts and vocational rehabilitation programs. The FERA legislation includes an allotment of $70,000 per
month for vocational rehabilitation of disabled persons who are on relief
or eligible for relief.

1935

The Social Security Act is signed on August 14. The act establishes permanent authority for state and federal vocational rehabilitation programs. It

also gives money to states for aid programs covering aged individuals (Title I), unemployed workers (Title III), Aid to Families with Dependent Children (Title IV), Maternal and Child Welfare (Title V), public health services (Title VI), and the blind (Title X).

The League of the Physically Handicapped is established in New York City. Employing sit-ins, picket lines, and other demonstrations, the league protests discrimination against disabled people in federal works programs such as the Works Progress Administration. When the WPA stamps employment requests submitted by league members with "PH" for "Physically Handicapped," for example, 300 members hold a nine-day sit-in at the Home Relief Bureau of New York City. This protest action helps secure several thousand WPA jobs for people with disabilities.

The National Labor Relations Act becomes law. The NLRA stands as the established framework for labor relations in the United States. It protects workers from unfair labor practices by employers and requires employers to recognize and bargain collectively with unions that the workers elect to represent them.

1936

The Randolph-Sheppard Act is passed, creating a federal program to help blind persons establish and operate vending facilities in lobbies of federal office buildings and on other federal property.

1938

President Roosevelt signs the Fair Labor Standards Act, which establishes a national minimum wage, guarantees "time-and-a-half" for overtime in certain jobs, prohibits most employment of minors in "oppressive" workplace settings, and increases employment of blind workers in sheltered workshop programs.

1940

The American Federation of the Physically Handicapped is founded under the leadership of Paul Strachan. The group advocates for the end of job discrimination and the establishment of a National Employ the Handicapped Week.

The National Federation for the Blind is founded, with the mission of achieving widespread emotional acceptance and intellectual understanding of the capabilities of blind people. The NFB improves blind people's lives through advocacy, education, research, technology, and programs encouraging independence and self-confidence.

The 1940 census is the first to include a statistical sample with 5% of people asked additional questions. The Decennial Census of the United States, still reflecting the federal government's focus on mass unemployment, includes in the "long form" questionnaire asked of the 5% sample an enumeration of persons with disabilities only if their disability is provided as reason for why the individual is "not seeking work" and does not have "a job or business." Enumerators are instructed to "indicate whether engaged in home housework (H), in school (S), unable to work (U), or Other (Ot)" (U.S. Census Bureau, 2011).

1942

The state of Connecticut begins offering special rehabilitation clinics during the war; the clinics eventually expand to 18 states, and within three years more than 113 clinics are operational. A foremost objective of the clinics is to place qualified disabled persons into war production jobs.

1943

The Barden-LaFollette Act, also known as the Vocational Rehabilitation Act Amendments, is passed. The act adds physical rehabilitation to the goals of federally funded vocational rehabilitation programs and provides funding for certain health care services.

The Office of Vocational Rehabilitation is organized within the Federal Security Agency with two functional divisions—the Administrative Standards Division and the Rehabilitation Standards Division. This is followed by the establishment of eight regional offices.

The Welsh-Clark Act, also known as the World War II Disabled Veterans Rehabilitation Act, is passed on March 24, authorizing the Veterans Administration to carry out rehabilitation programs to help disabled individuals effectively readjust to the world of work.

1944

The Servicemen's Readjustment Act, better known as the GI Bill of Rights, is passed. The act provides tuition and subsistence for up to 48 months for veterans who undergo and complete training and vocational assessment/counseling services. However, while able-bodied veterans have full freedom to choose their school and major, their disabled counterparts cannot use federal funds to attend college unless they can prove the coursework has direct vocational relevance.

President Roosevelt announces his "Economic Bill of Rights." An essential part of this doctrine is the right of every individual to a useful and remunerative job in an atmosphere of economic security. To insure this right, Roosevelt's advisors set "full, and stable national productivity, income and employment" as the nation's postwar economic goal (U.S. Senate, 1966).

1945

The U.S. Congress passes House Joint Resolution 23, establishing the first week in October as "National Employ the Physically Handicapped Week." The purpose of this resolution is to encourage the employment of people with physical disabilities.

1946

Congress passes the Hospital Survey and Construction Act (also known as the Hill-Burton Act) authorizing federal grants to states for construction of hospitals, public health centers, and health facilities for the rehabilitation of people with disabilities. The act is designed to provide federal grants and guaranteed loans to improve and expand the physical plant of the nation's hospital system.

The Full Employment Act is passed, reaffirming the nation's commitment to full utilization of its material and human resources. The act specifically calls on the federal government to achieve high levels of employment and price stability.

1947

President Truman establishes the President's Committee on National Employ the Handicapped Week. The committee has responsibility for coordinating events and generating publicity for the week. Subsequently, in 1949, Congress authorizes an annual appropriation for the committee.

The Office of Vocational Rehabilitation announces formal cooperative agreements with 19 organizations interested in the welfare of people with disabilities. A variety of programs and relationships develop over the next two decades, building an impressive program of research, demonstration, and development.

Academic training in rehabilitation counseling emerges at institutions of higher learning across the country. Special summer courses in rehabilitation counseling are offered at Pennsylvania State College and Colorado Agricultural and Mechanical College. Ohio State University is the first to prepare a graduate-level curriculum in the discipline, and eventually 40 states offer degrees through in-service training institutes. In the first academic year (1947–1948), 581 counselors are trained.

Workers from Czechoslovakia and China visit rehabilitation activities and facilities in the United States under the auspices of the United Nations Relief and Rehabilitation Administration. From this time forward, the United States becomes increasingly active in exporting rehabilitation concepts and techniques.

Paralyzed Veterans of America is founded. The congressionally chartered organization works to maximize the quality of life for its members and all people with SCI/D (spinal cord injury and disease) as a leading advocate for health care, SCI/D research and education, veterans' benefits and rights, accessibility of facilities, sports programs, and disability rights.

The Labor-Management Relations Act is passed into law. Better known as the Taft-Hartley Act, this legislation is passed over President Truman's veto. The act, which is still in effect, is best known for rolling back union gains of the New Deal era. Taft-Hartley gives employees the right not to join unions (outlawing the closed shop), requires advance notice of a labor strike, authorizes an 80-day federal injunction in the event of strikes deemed to pose a threat to national health or safety, narrows the definition of unfair labor practices, specifies unfair union practices, restricts union political contributions, and requires union officials to take an oath pledging they are not Communists.

1948

The Rusk Institute of Rehabilitation Medicine is founded by Dr. Howard A. Rusk in New York City to work with injured veterans of World War II. Rusk's governing philosophy—that rehabilitation medicine provides care for the entire person, not just their illness or disability—becomes the basis for modern rehabilitation medicine.

A civilian arm of Paralyzed Veterans of America, called the National Paraplegia Foundation, is founded. The NPF quickly takes a leading role in advocating for disability rights.

The *Current Population Survey-Annual Social and Economic Supplement* is published for the first time. This collection, which includes disability-related data, is one of the longest-running nationally representative surveys in the United States. The CPS began in a simpler format as an effort to measure labor market conditions during the Great Depression of the 1930s.

1949

The National Foundation for Cerebral Palsy is founded by a group of parents of children with cerebral palsy who are determined to make the world a more accessible place for their children. The mission of the foundation, now known as the United Cerebral Palsy Foundation, is to advance the independence, productivity, and full citizenship of people with disabilities.

1950

Important augmentative and alternative communication (AAC) devices are invented, including picture boards and typewriters with switch-controlled scanning devices (Von Tetzchner & Martinsen, 2000). Augmentative and alternative communication strategies assist people with severe communication disabilities to participate more fully in their social roles, including interpersonal interaction, education, community activities, and employment. People with severe speech or language problems rely on AAC to supplement existing speech or replace speech that is not functional.

Mary Switzer is appointed the director of the U.S. Office of Vocational Rehabilitation, where she focuses on independent living. Fiercely committed to disability rights, Switzer becomes instrumental in the unanimous passage of the Vocational Rehabilitation Act of 1954.

Social Security Act Amendments of 1950 establish a federal-state program called Aid to the Permanently and Totally Disabled (APTD). This program, a prototype for the later Social Security Disability Income (SSDI) system, expands coverage to household employees working at least two days a week for the same person, along with nonprofit workers and the self-employed.

The National Association for Retarded Children, now known as The Arc (Association for Retarded Children), is founded. The Arc's vision is that every individual and family affected by intellectual disability in the United States has access to the information, advocacy, and skills they need to participate as active citizens of the American democracy and active members of their community. It provides an array of services and support for families and individuals.

1953

The new administration of President Dwight D. Eisenhower makes significant progress in the area of vocational rehabilitation. A variety of personnel are appointed to oversee the development of rehabilitation programs, and states become instrumental in the expansion and funding of such programs.

1954

The Social Security Act (Public Law 482) is passed into law on July 12. The bill enacts portions of President Eisenhower's health program, increasing and expanding federal aid for hospital construction to include hospitals for the chronically ill, nursing homes, diagnostic and treatment facilities, and rehabilitation facilities.

The Vocational Rehabilitation Act Amendments (Public Law 565) become law. The measure expands the provisions of the Vocational Rehabilitation Act to include people with physical disabilities and increases services for individuals with mental retardation and psychiatric handicaps. The act authorizes research and demonstration grants, extension and improvement grants, and funds for facility development. It also provides grants to colleges and universities to train rehabilitation counselors to work with individuals with disabilities.

1955

The National Council on Rehabilitation Education (NCRE) is founded to represent educators in the field of rehabilitation as well as institutions with rehabilitation programs. It begins advocating for up-to-date training and the maintenance of professional standards in the field of rehabilitation.

President Eisenhower issues Executive Order 10640, establishing the President's Committee on National Employ the Handicapped Week as a permanent organization, and renaming it the President's Committee on Employment of the Physically Handicapped.

1956

The Social Security Amendments of 1956 establish a Social Security Disability Insurance Trust Fund and provide for payments to eligible workers between the ages of 50 and 64 who become disabled.

1957

The National Health Interview Survey (NHIS), a nationally representative survey providing data on the health of the civilian, noninstitutionalized population of the United States, is administered for the first time. The survey, which is conducted by the National Center for Health Statistics (NCHS), Centers for Disease Control and Prevention (CDC), contains information on multiple aspects of health status, including activity limitations, injuries, health insurance, and access to and utilization of health care.

The document scanner is invented. This image-scanning process, first developed at the U.S. National Bureau of Standards, converts hard copies, such as paper documents and books, into digital forms that are more accessible to people with disabilities.

1958

The Social Security Amendments of 1958 extend Social Security Disability Insurance (SSDI) to dependents of disabled workers.

The American Psychological Association (APA) establishes its Division 22, an organization for psychologists concerned with the psychological and social consequences of disability. Division 22 members are among the pioneers helping psychology understand the world of work, and how work can be affected by disability.

The National Rehabilitation Counseling Association (NRCA) is founded to represent the concerns of practicing rehabilitation counselors. Most members are state/federal vocational rehabilitation employees.

1960

The Independent Living Movement begins. The Independent Living Movement is a struggle by people with disabilities to obtain full social and physical inclusion in their communities in areas including—but not limited to—employment and education. The movement emphasizes self-determination and equal opportunity for people with disabilities.

The Social Security Amendments of 1960 eliminate the age restriction for Social Security Disability Insurance (SSDI).

1961

The International Health Research Act is passed. U.S. experts in the professions related to rehabilitation and medicine develop programs to exchange ideas, methods, and skills with physicians and researchers from eight other countries. Approximately 61 American specialists eventually go abroad to provide assistance, while 48 international specialists travel from other countries to study and train in the United States.

President John F. Kennedy establishes the Presidential Panel on Mental Retardation and charges it with conducting an "intensive search for solutions" to the problems experienced by people with mental retardation. The panel's 1962 report contains 112 recommendations for new research, preventive health measures, strengthened educational programs, more comprehensive and improved clinical and social services, improved methods and facilities for care, a new legal and social concept of mental retardation, increased educational opportunities to learn about mental retardation, and public education and information programs.

The American Council of the Blind is formed. The council strives to improve the well-being of all blind and visually impaired people by serving as a representative national organization of blind people; elevating the social, economic, and cultural levels of blind people; improving educational and rehabilitation facilities and opportunities; cooperating with public and private institutions and organizations concerned with providing services for blind people; encouraging and assisting all blind persons to develop their abilities; and conducting a public education program to promote greater understanding of blindness and the capabilities of blind people.

The American National Standards Institute (ANSI) publishes *American Standard Specifications for Making Buildings Accessible to, and Usable by, the Physically Handicapped.* By 1973, 49 states have adopted some form of accessibility legislation based on these standards.

1962

The President's Committee on Employment of the Physically Handicapped (PCEPH) is renamed the President's Committee on Employment of the Handicapped (PCEH), reflecting an increased interest in employment issues affecting all people with disabilities—not just individuals with physical disabilities. President Kennedy's Executive Order 10994, which renamed the committee, also significantly expands its duties by instructing it to develop employment opportunities for people with both physical and mental disabilities. Congress recognizes this change in 1970 by passing Public Law 91–442, changing the name of National Employ the Physically Handicapped Week to National Employ the Handicapped Week.

1963

The Mental Retardation Facilities and Community Health Centers Construction Act (Public Law 8–164) is passed. This law calls for the establishment of research centers and training facilities relating to mental retardation. The measure also authorizes construction of community mental health centers, increased research regarding the education of children with disabilities, and training for individuals involved in educating people with mental disabilities.

President Kennedy calls for a reduction in the number of persons confined to residential institutions and urges that methods be found "to retain and return to the community the mentally ill and mentally retarded, and there to restore and revitalize their lives through better health programs and strengthened educational and rehabilitation services" (Kennedy, 1963).

South Carolina passes the first statewide architectural access code to ensure access for people with physical disabilities to all public and government-operated buildings.

1964

The National Rehabilitation Association releases a 26-page special "Report of Ten Years of Rehabilitation Progress under P.L. 565" featuring contributions from several leaders in the rehabilitation movement.

Physicist Robert Weitbrecht and two deaf colleagues invent the teletype, a machine that gives people with hearing impairments the ability to communicate more effectively. The advent of the teletype has a positive influence on the ability of deaf individuals to gain employment and increases the variety of jobs available to them.

President Lyndon B. Johnson signs the Civil Rights Act, which prohibits discrimination on the basis of race, religion, ethnicity, national origin, and creed in public accommodations, employment, and federally assisted programs. Gender and disability are not protected under the 1964 bill, but this act becomes the basis of future disability nondiscrimination legislation.

1965

The Medicaid and Medicare programs are implemented with the signing of the Social Security Amendments of 1965. The Medicare program is a social insurance program funded by the federal government that provides health insurance to people who are aged 65 or older or who meet other special criteria, while Medicaid provides medical coverage to the poor. This legislation also changes the definition of disability from "of long continued and indefinite duration" to "expected to last for not less than 12 months."

Vocational Rehabilitation Act Amendments provide for 6- and 18-month extended evaluations to determine if more severely handicapped individuals might benefit from vocational rehabilitation services. This act makes it possible to provide many rehabilitation services prior to formal acceptance into a program and eliminates economic-need criteria for any vocational rehabilitation service (though states still retain the option of employing economic-need tests for training and physical restoration). The law also creates the National Commission on Architectural Barriers to Rehabilitation of the Handicapped (NCABRH).

The Autism Society of America (ASA) is established. ASA works to increase public awareness about the day-to-day issues faced by people with autism, advocates for appropriate services for individuals across the lifespan, and provides the latest information regarding treatment, education, research, and advocacy.

Congress establishes the National Technical Institute for the Deaf in Rochester, New York, to educate deaf children.

1966

The President's Committee on Mental Retardation is established. Led by luminaries such as Elizabeth M. Boggs, the PCMR plays important roles in the passage of the Facilities Construction Act, which provides funds for service programs throughout the states, and the evolution of developmental disabilities research and advocacy efforts.

The Commission on Accreditation of Rehabilitation Facilities (CARF International) is founded as an independent, nonprofit accreditor of health and human services in the area of rehabilitation.

1967

The Vocational Rehabilitation Act Amendments of 1967 (Public Law 90–99) become law. This legislation authorizes funding for the construction of a national center for deaf and blind youths and adults and authorizes a system of project grants to benefit disabled migratory workers.

1968

The Architectural Barriers Act is signed into law on August 12. The act requires that facilities designed, built, altered, or leased with funds supplied by the United States federal government be accessible to all members of the public, including people with disabilities. The law generally does not apply to facilities that precede passage of the legislation, but alterations or leases undertaken after the law takes effect may be covered.

The Panel Study of Income Dynamics (PSID) begins with a sample of 4,800 families. These families are re-interviewed on an annual basis from 1968 to 1997, and re-interviewed biennially since then. The PSID collects data on economic, health, and social behavior, including the existence of disability.

A group of miners and widows of miners organizes the West Virginia Black Lung Association and successfully leads a campaign for legislation making this disabling occupational disease compensable under workplace safety laws. The group eventually becomes the National Black Lung Association.

1969

The National Assessment of Educational Programs (NAEP) is administered for the first time. Compiled by the Commissioner of Education Statistics within the U.S. Department of Education, the NAEP has been described by the National Research Council as "an unparalleled source of information about the academic proficiency of U.S. students, providing among the best available trend data on the academic achievement of elementary, middle, and secondary students in core subject areas" (National Center for Education Statistics, 1997).

The International Symbol of Access, also known as the Wheelchair Symbol, is introduced. Designed by Rehabilitation International, it quickly becomes the standard international symbol used to denote facilities that are accessible to people with disabilities.

The ARPAnet, the U.S. government computer network that is widely recognized as the first incarnation of the Internet, is formally commissioned.

Congress enacts the Federal Coal Mine Health and Safety Act, which marks the first time that Congress mandates that a major occupational disease must not only be compensated, but eradicated. The legislation also establishes a formal black lung benefits program.

1970

The Occupational Safety and Health Act is signed into law on December 29. OSHA applies to all employers, regardless of the volume of business they conduct or the number of people in their employ.

Several disability advocacy movements emerge, including the Rolling Quads, headed by Ed Roberts at the University of California-Berkeley; Disabled in Action at Long Island University in New York, led by Judy Heumann; and the Physically Disabled Students Program at UC Berkeley, developed by Ed Roberts, John Hessler, Hale Zukas, and others.

The Developmental Disabilities Services and Facilities Construction Act is passed. This act significantly expands the scope and purposes of the previous 1963 legislation. It gives states broad authority and responsibility for planning and implementing a comprehensive program of services for people with disabilities. It also offers local communities a strong voice in determining needs, establishing priorities, and developing a system for delivering services to citizens with disabilities.

The Urban Mass Transit Act, which requires that all new mass-transit vehicles be equipped with wheelchair lifts, becomes law. The American Public Transportation Association (APTA) delays full implementation for 20 years, however.

The Decennial Census of the United States updates the language and specificity of questions related to the ability of persons with disabilities to work in the "long form" questionnaire asked of a sample of the population. The three questions asked are (1) Does this person have a health or physical condition which limits the kind or amount of work he can do at a job? (2) Does the person's health or physical condition keep him from holding any job at all? and (3) How long has the person been limited in his ability to work? (U.S. Census Bureau, 2011).

1971

The Fair Labor Standards Act of 1938 is amended to bring people with disabilities (in addition to blindness) into the sheltered workshop system.

The National Center for Law and the Handicapped is founded at the University of Notre Dame in South Bend, Indiana—the first legal advocacy center for people with disabilities in the United States.

The landmark *Wyatt v. Stickney* decision is rendered. The plaintiffs in the class-action lawsuit argue that the conditions in Alabama's mental health facilities are inhumane, and that the patients lack appropriate individualized care. The District Court for the Middle District of Alabama agrees, and it uses the *Wyatt v. Stickney* decision to establish minimum standards of care and rehabilitation for people with mental retardation and mental illness. These standards are then widely emulated across the country.

1972

The Berkeley Center for Independent Living (CIL) is founded by Ed Roberts with funds from the Rehabilitation Administration. CIL becomes an influential support network that focuses on giving people with disabilities the knowledge and the tools to assert their civil rights.

Two court cases (*Mills v. Board of Education* and *PARC v. Pennsylvania*) strike down state laws in Washington, D.C., and Pennsylvania that exclude disabled students from public schools. In its decision in the *Mills* case, the District Court for the District of Columbia adopts "a presumption that among the alternative programs of education, placement in a regular public school class with appropriate ancillary services is preferable to placement in a special school class."

The 1972 Social Security Amendments create the Supplemental Security Income (SSI) program that provides stipends to low-income persons who are either aged 65 or older, blind, or disabled.

Parents of residents at Willow Brook State School in Staten Island, New York, the largest state-operated school for children with mental retardation in the United States, file suit in a protest against overcrowding and other deplorable conditions at the institution. A settlement is eventually reached in which thousands of residents are moved into community-based living arrangements. The school is finally closed in 1987.

Wolf Wolfensberger publishes *The Principle of Normalization in Human Services,* an enormously influential work which emphasizes the need to provide people with disabilities the same access to societal resources and opportunities that the general population enjoys.

1973

Section 503 of the Rehabilitation Act of 1973 prohibits discrimination and requires employers with federal contracts or subcontracts that exceed $10,000 to take affirmative action to hire, retain, and promote qualified individuals with disabilities. The measure also requires contractors and subcontractors to include a specific equal opportunity clause in each of their nonexempt contracts and subcontracts.

Section 504 of the Rehabilitation Act of 1973 states that "no qualified individual with a disability in the United States shall be excluded from, denied the benefits of, or be subjected to discrimination under" any program or activity that either receives federal financial assistance or is conducted by any executive agency or the U.S. Postal Service. Each federal agency has its own set of Section 504 regulations that apply to its own programs.

Section 504 also requires sheltered workshops to pay a "fair" or "commensurate" wage to disabled workers, but stops short of requiring the payment of the federal minimum wage.

The Architectural and Transportation Barriers Compliance Board is established under the Rehabilitation Act of 1973 and charged with enforcement of provisions of the Architectural Barriers Act of 1968.

Passage of the Federal Highway Act authorizes the release of federal funds for the construction of curb cuts. Under this measure, curb ramps are mandated at all intersections and midblock locations where pedestrian crossings exist.

1974

The first desktop computer designed for personal use is unveiled. This technological breakthrough greatly increases the independence and employment opportunities of people with disabilities.

The first Client Assistance Program (CAP) is established to provide representation and advocacy support for clients of state vocational rehabilitation services.

The Employment Retirement Income Security Act (ERISA) is enacted to protect the interests of employee benefit plan participants. This act establishes standards of conduct for plan fiduciaries and sets minimum standards for pension plans in private industry. Standards for vesting rules protect some employees forced to leave work prior to retirement age due to health conditions.

1975

The United Nations General Assembly adopts the Declaration on the Rights of Disabled Persons, which proclaims the equal civil and political rights of people with disabilities. As a resolution of the assembly, it is not binding on member nations, but it provides a framework that is frequently drawn on in subsequent years for the purposes of crafting international and domestic law. This is the first international document that attempts to define the term "disability."

The America Coalition of Citizens with Disabilities is founded. Created, governed, and administered by individuals with disabilities, the organization mounts a successful 10-city "sit-in" to force the federal government to issue long-overdue rules to carry out Section 504, the world's first disability civil rights provisions. The sit-ins occur across the country, from San Francisco to Washington, D.C., at major federal government buildings.

The Education for All Handicapped Children Act (EAHCA) passes, requiring free, appropriate public education in the least restrictive setting for children with disabilities. Under EAHCA, public schools must evaluate handicapped students and create an educational plan with parent input to emulate as closely as possible the educational experience of nondisabled students.

The Developmental Disabilities Assistance and Bill of Rights Act (DD Act) becomes law, ensuring that individuals with developmental disabilities are given the right to full integration and inclusion in the economic, political, social, cultural, religious, and educational sectors of their communities. The DD Act further ensures a role for individuals with developmental disabilities and their families in the design and administration of services and programs that promote independence, productivity, integration, and inclusion in the community.

The Association of Persons with Severe Handicaps (TASH) is founded by special education professionals in response to *PARC v. Pennsylvania*. The objective of this international association of people with disabilities, their family members, advocates, and professionals is to fight for inclusion of all people in all aspects of society.

The case of *O'Connor v. Donaldson* establishes that people cannot be institutionalized in psychiatric hospitals against their will unless they pose a threat to themselves or others.

Parent Training and Information Centers develop to help parents of children with disabilities exercise their rights under the Education for All Handicapped Children Act (EAHCA). These centers help parents participate more effectively in addressing their children's educational needs and work to improve outcomes for children and young adults with emotional, learning, cognitive, and physical disabilities.

1976

The Federal Communications Commission (FCC) authorizes reserving Line 21 on televisions for closed captioning.

The Expansion of Higher Education Act Amendments provide for services to physically disabled students entering college.

1977

The White House Conference on Handicapped Individuals is held to assess the current problems and potential of the disability rights movement. An estimated two-thirds of the conference attendees are people with disabilities; they are joined by parents, advocates, service providers, and researchers.

1978

Title VII of the Rehabilitation Act Amendments provides federal funds for the establishment of Independent Living Centers. The measure is based on the recognition that many individuals with severe disabilities who are unable to engage in vocational rehabilitation services may still benefit from other services that enable them to establish and maintain "independent living" lifestyles in local communities.

1979

The Independent Living Movement expands. Five regional conferences are held across the United States to introduce the concept of independent living and to provide directions for the establishment of independent living centers. Centers provide services and advocacy by and for persons with all types of disabilities in order to create opportunities for independence and help individuals achieve their maximum level of independent functioning within their families and communities.

1980

The Civil Rights of Institutionalized Persons Act is established to protect persons confined in state and local institutions (including patients in mental health facilities, prisoners in detention and jail settings, and elderly enrollees in nursing homes) against violations of their constitutional rights.

Disabled Peoples' International is founded in Singapore with the participation of advocates from Canada and the United States. Disabled Peoples' International is a network of national organizations or assemblies of disabled people, established to promote human rights of disabled people through full societal participation and equalization of opportunity and development.

Section 1619 of the Social Security Act Amendments of 1980 removes work disincentives for people with disabilities who receive Supplemental Security income (SSI).

The Decennial Census of the United States updates the language and specificity of questions related to the ability of persons with disabilities to work, asking: "Does this person have a physical, mental, or other health condition which has lasted for 6 or more months and which . . . (a) Limits the kind or amount of work this person can do at a job? (b) Prevents this person from working at a job? (c) Limits or prevents this person from using public transportation?" (U.S. Census Bureau, 2011).

1981

The United Nations General Assembly recognizes 1981 as the International Year of Disabled Persons. The General Assembly calls for national, regional, and international actions to support equalization of opportunities, rehabilitation, and disability prevention and formulates the UN's World Programme of Action Concerning Disabled Persons.

The Telecommunications for the Disabled Act is signed into law. The act mandates telephone access for deaf and hard-of-hearing people at public places like hospitals and police stations, requires that all coin-operated telephones be made hearing-aid compatible by January 1985, and approves state subsidies for production and distribution of telecommunication devices for the deaf (TDDs).

The Reagan administration terminates Social Security benefits for hundreds of thousands of disabled recipients as part of wider deficit-reduction measures. A variety of groups, including the Alliance of Social Security Disability Recipients and the Ad Hoc Committee on Social Security Disability, spring up to fight these terminations.

IBM's PC introduced. It will come to dominate the business computing market, making desktop computers widely available in the workplace.

1982

The National Council on Independent Living is formed to advocate on behalf of independent living centers and the independent living movement. NCIL represents thousands of organizations and individuals, including Centers for Independent Living (CILs), Statewide Independent Living Councils (SILCs), individuals with disabilities, and other organizations that advocate for the human and civil rights of people with disabilities throughout the United States.

The National Organization on Disability (NOD) is founded at the conclusion of the International Year of Disabled Persons to continue the momentum that has been established toward meeting the UN's goal of full societal participation of people with disabilities. Alan A. Reich is appointed the first president of the organization.

1983

The Job Accommodation Network (JAN) is founded by the President's Council on the Employment of the Handicapped. JAN's consultants offer one-on-one guidance on workplace accommodations, disability-related legislation, and self-employment and entrepreneurship options for people with disabilities. Assistance is available to private employers of all sizes, government agencies, employee representatives, service providers, and people with disabilities and their families.

Rehabilitation Act Amendments create the Client Assistance Program (CAP) to provide advocacy services for consumers of state vocational rehabilitation services and to publicize all services and benefits available under the Rehabilitation Act of 1973 and subsequent disability-related legislation.

1984

The Voting Accessibility for the Elderly and Handicapped Act is passed, mandating that all places of public polling be accessible to citizens who are elderly or have disabilities. It also mandates the availability of voting aids, such as instructions in large type, at poll sites.

The Survey of Income and Program Participation (SIPP) is administered for the first time. The primary purpose of SIPP, which is administered by the U.S. Census Bureau, is to collect information on the income and level of local/state/federal program participation of a nationally representative sample of households and individuals living in the United States. Each new fielding of the SIPP is called a "panel," and each panel includes several interviews conducted every four months over a period of at least 32 months. As of 2011, the Census Bureau had fielded 12 panels, with the most recent conducted in 2008.

The Behavioral Risk Factors Surveillance System (BRFSS) is introduced. This state-based system of health surveys collects information on health risk behaviors, preventive health practices, and health care access primarily related to chronic disease and injury. It is the world's largest ongoing telephone health survey system, tracking health conditions and risk behaviors in the United States on a yearly basis. States use BRFSS data to identify emerging health problems, establish and track health objectives, and develop and evaluate public health policies and programs.

One-quarter of the U.S. workforce is using computers at work.

Apple introduces the Macintosh 128K. Its operating system features the first widely available graphical user interface (GUI) on the consumer market, allowing users to interface with the computer with images rather than with text commands. While this makes computer use easier for many people, the graphical display renders previous systems of access for people with visual disabilities obsolete. As other makers of computer operating systems move to a similar visual interface over the next few years, new ways for users with visual disabilities to use computers at home and in the workplace must be explored.

1985

The Mental Illness Bill of Rights Act is passed, requiring states to provide protection and advocacy services for people with psychiatric impairments.

Microsoft introduces Microsoft Windows, in response to the growing interest in graphical user interfaces. It quickly comes to dominate the workplace computer environment.

1986

Congress passes the Employment Opportunities for Disabled Americans Act, which makes the Section 1619(a) and 1619(b) work incentives a permanent feature of the Social Security Act. The legislation also adds provisions to enable individuals to move back and forth among regular SSI, Section 1619(a), and Section 1619(b) eligibility status.

Congress amends Section 508 of the Rehabilitation Act of 1973, mandating that electronic and information technology developed, procured, maintained, or used by the federal government be accessible to people with disabilities.

The National Council on the Handicapped issues a report, *Toward Independence,* which cites the need for federal civil rights legislation for people with disabilities. A subsequent council report (*On the Threshold of Independence*) provides the first draft of the Americans with Disabilities Act.

1987

Justin Dart, Commissioner of the Rehabilitation Services Administration, is forced to resign after he testifies to Congress that "an inflexible federal system, like the society it represents, still contains a significant portion of individuals who have not yet overcome obsolete, paternalistic attitudes toward disability" (Disability History Timeline, 2002).

1988

The Fair Housing Act Amendments prohibit housing discrimination against people with disabilities and families with children and establish measures to ensure the architectural accessibility of new housing units and renovations for people with disabilities.

The Air Carrier Access Act is passed, prohibiting airlines from refusing to serve people with disabilities or charging them inequitably. The measure further stipulates various minimum levels of service and accommodations that must be provided to passengers with disabilities.

The Technology-Related Assistance for Individuals with Disabilities Act (TRAID) becomes law, authorizing federal funds to state projects to facilitate access to assistive technology. The overall purpose of TRAID is to provide financial assistance to states to help them develop consumer-responsive, cross-age, and cross-disability programs of technology-related assistance.

The Congressional Task Force on the Rights and Empowerment of Americans with Disabilities is created to build support for the passage of the Americans with Disabilities Act.

President Ronald Reagan signs Executive Order 12640 establishing the President's Committee on Employment of People with Disabilities, which is tasked with carrying out the provisions of the Rehabilitation Act. According to the executive order, the committee "shall provide advice and information as to the development of maximum employment opportunities for people who are physically disabled, mentally retarded, and mentally ill. To this end the Committee shall advise the President as to information that can be used by employers, labor unions, and national and international organizations, suggest programs for public education, and suggest methods of enlisting cooperation among organizations and agencies, Federal, State, and local officials, Governors' and local Committees on Employment of People with Disabilities, professional organizations, organized labor, and appropriate international organizations" (Reagan, 1988).

The Association for Persons in Supported Employment (APSE) is founded to provide integrated employment and career advancement opportunities for individuals with disabilities.

1989

Ted Henter and Rex Skipper produce JAWS (Job Access With Speech), a program for the MS-DOS operating system that will read the contents of a computer screen to a visually disabled user.

1990

The Americans with Disabilities Act of 1990 (ADA) is signed into law on July 26. Regarded as one of the most important legislative initiatives that protects people with disabilities from discrimination, the law prohibits job-related discrimination against "qualified individuals with disabilities" and requires that reasonable accommodations be provided by employers for people with disabilities. Disability is defined, for the purposes of the act, as "a physical or mental impairment that substantially limits a major life activity." Employers of 25 or more employees are covered as of July 26, 1992; employers of 15 or more are covered two years later.

The European Network on Independent Living (ENIL) forms to lobby within the European Economic Community (EEC), now the European Union, for personal assistance services and the promotion of the independent living philosophy among political parties and governments.

The Decennial Census of the United States expands the language and specificity of questions related to enumerating persons with disabilities in the "long form" questionnaire asked of a sample of the population, specifically asking: "Does this person have a physical, mental, or other health condition that has lasted for 6 or more months and which (a) Limits the kind or amount of work this person can do at a job? (b) Prevents this person from working at a job?" and, "Because of a health condition that has lasted for 6 or more months, does this person have any difficulty (a) Going outside the home alone, for example, to shop or visit a doctor's office? (b) Taking care of his or her own personal needs, such as bathing, dressing, or getting around inside the home?" (U.S. Census Bureau, 2011).

1991

Congress passes the Civil Rights Act of 1991 (CRA), overruling several Supreme Court decisions rendered in the late 1980s that had made it more difficult for plaintiffs to prevail in employment discrimination suits (and recover legal fees and costs even when they won their lawsuits). The CRA amends procedurally and substantively Title VII, the Age Discrimination in Employment Act (ADEA), and the Americans with Disabilities Act.

1992

The 1992 Amendments to the Rehabilitation Act state that all individuals with disabilities are presumed to benefit from vocational rehabilitation (VR) services in terms of an employment outcome unless the state VR agency demonstrates by clear and convincing evidence that the individual is incapable of doing so. Further, the amendments incorporate the independent living philosophy.

1993

The Family and Medical Leave Act (FMLA) is signed into law by President Bill Clinton on February 5. The FMLA establishes, for employers with 50 or more employees, a minimum labor standard with regard to leaves of absence for family or medical reasons. Under the FMLA, an eligible employee may take up to 12 work weeks of leave during any 12-month period for one or more of the following reasons: the birth of a child and to care for the newborn child; the placement of a child with the employee through adoption or foster care and to care for the child; to care for a spouse, son, daughter, or parent with a serious health condition; and in the event of a serious health condition that makes the employee unable to perform one or more of the essential functions of his or her job.

Nearly one-half of U.S. workers are required to use computers as part of their daily jobs.

1994

The National Health Interview Survey–Disability supplement (NHIS-D) is released. The NHIS-D is one of the most comprehensive data sources on people with disabilities in the United States. In addition to the broader disability questions used in the NHIS, the supplement contains questions that can assist in identifying disabilities, including questions about health conditions (both physical and mental), service receipt and program participation (e.g., SSI), activity limitations, and participation restrictions.

The supplement also contains extensive information about the different facets of the lives of people with disabilities, including the types of services people with disabilities receive, transportation issues facing working-age adults with disabilities, social activities of people with disabilities, vocational rehabilitation services, and disability accommodations.

1995

The American Association of People with Disabilities (AAPD) is founded in Washington, D.C. The AAPD has since become the largest national nonprofit cross-disability member organization in the United States, and it remains an advocate for economic self-sufficiency and political empowerment for all Americans with disabilities.

Freedom Scientific releases JAWS for Windows, in response to the growing popularity of the Microsoft Windows operating system over the older MS-DOS system. Three years in the making, it provides text-to-speech service, or communicates with a Braille display for visually disabled users.

1996

Section 255 of the Telecommunications Act of 1996 requires that manufacturers of telecommunications equipment and software ensure that such equipment be directly accessible to people with disabilities if that access is "readily achievable."

The Health Insurance Portability and Accountability Act (HIPAA) becomes law. Congress enacts this law to ensure continuation of health insurance coverage for workers and their families when they change or lose their jobs. The law also includes provisions to improve the security and privacy of health data.

Corinne Kirchner publishes one of the first criticisms of the use of work-limitation-based disability measures from the Current Population Survey in estimating the employment rates of working-age people with disabilities. Kirchner argues that falling employment rates in this population could be caused by a post-ADA change in the attitudes of people with disabilities that would lead those who were employed to be less likely to describe themselves as having a work limitation. She claims that this phenomenon artificially decreased the employment rates of those with disabilities who did report a work limitation.

1997

Section 4733 of the Balanced Budget Act (BBA), which becomes law on August 5, expands state options to provide Medicaid to working people with disabilities by creating a new optional eligibility category. Specifically, this legislation allows states to provide health insurance to qualified individuals with incomes up to 250 percent of the federal poverty level.

1998

Title I of the Workforce Investment Act (WIA) provides assistance to states in establishing statewide and local workforce investment systems to increase employment, retention, and earnings of participants. The objectives of the WIA include improving the quality of the workforce to sustain economic growth, improving productivity and competitiveness, and reducing dependency on welfare.

President Clinton signs Executive Order 13078 establishing a Presidential Task Force on Employment of Adults with Disabilities. The task force is charged with creating a coordinated and aggressive national policy to bring working-age individuals with disabilities into gainful employment at a rate approaching that of the general adult population.

The Persian Gulf War Veterans Act becomes law, authorizing the Veterans Administration (VA) to compensate Gulf War veterans for diagnosed or undiagnosed disabilities that are determined by the VA to be related to their military service in the Gulf War (such as exposure to a toxic agent, environmental or wartime hazard, or preventive medication or vaccine).

1999

The Ticket to Work and Work Incentive Improvement Act (TWWIIA) is passed on December 17. Crafted to modernize the employment services system for people with disabilities, TWWIIA includes five provisions—Ticket to Work and Self-Sufficiency Program, Expansion of Health Insurance Eligibility, Elimination of Other Work Disincentives, Demonstration

Project on Change in DI Benefits Schedule, and Work Incentives Outreach Program—that feature work incentives for people with disabilities. The act makes it possible for Americans with disabilities to join the workforce without fear of losing their Medicare or Medicaid coverage.

In *Olmstead v. LC and EW* the U.S. Supreme Court upholds the "integration mandate" of the Americans with Disabilities Act. The case was originally filed against the state of Georgia by plaintiffs who alleged that they were segregated in a psychiatric institution when, with proper supports, they could live a more normal, community-based life. After five years of litigation, the Supreme Court rules in favor of the plaintiffs, holding that the Americans with Disabilities Act requires that states place persons with disabilities in the most integrated setting appropriate to their disability.

The World Wide Web Consortium (W3C) publishes its first formal recommendations for accessibility, the Web Content Accessibility Guidelines (WCAG) 1.0. They consist of a set of guidelines on making Web-based content accessible, primarily for disabled users.

2000

The Decennial Census of the United States expands the language and specificity of questions related to enumerating persons with disabilities in the "long form" questionnaire asked of a sample of the population, specifically asking: "Does this person have any of the following long-lasting conditions: (a) Blindness, deafness, or a severe vision or hearing impairment? (b) A condition that substantially limits one or more basic physical activities such as walking, climbing stairs, reaching, lifting, or carrying?" and, "Because of a physical, mental, or emotional condition lasting 6 months or more, does this person have any difficulty in doing any of the following activities: (a) Learning, remembering, or concentrating? (b) Dressing, bathing, getting around inside the home? (c) If the person is 16 years or older, going outside the home alone to shop or visit a doctor's office? (d) If the person is 16 years or older, working at a job or business?" (U.S. Census Bureau, 2011). Concerns about the design of the survey and the enumeration methodology continue to raise questions about the accuracy of the disability statistics from the Census.

President Clinton signs legislation eliminating the retirement earnings test for people above the full-benefit retirement age. The earnings test previously required retirees to give up part of their Social Security benefits when they earned in excess of a certain amount. The test remains in place for beneficiaries below the full-benefit age.

The Consolidated Appropriations Act for fiscal year 2001 includes authorization for the establishment of an Office of Disability Employment Policy within the Department of Labor (DOL). Recognizing the need for a national policy to ensure that people with disabilities are fully integrated into the 21st-century workforce, the secretary of labor delegates authority and assigns responsibility to the assistant secretary for disability employment policy.

President Clinton signs Executive Order 13163, Increasing the Opportunity for Individuals with Disabilities to Be Employed in the Federal Government, on July 26, 2000, the tenth anniversary of the signing of the Americans with Disabilities Act. It calls for the federal government to hire 100,000 qualified individuals with disabilities over the next five years.

2001

Compliance with the Section 508 standards of the Rehabilitation Act developed by the Access Board becomes mandatory throughout the federal government. Under this mandate, all agencies are required to make electronic and information technology (from park kiosks to Web sites) accessible to people with disabilities.

President George W. Bush signs the New Freedom Initiative on February 1, as part of a nationwide effort to remove barriers to community living for people with disabilities. The initiative's goals are to increase access to assistive and universally designed technologies, expand educational opportunities, promote homeownership, integrate Americans with disabilities into the workforce, expand transportation options, and promote full access to community life. The employment measures of the initiative include funding for the promotion of telework for people with disabilities and full implementation of the Ticket to Work program.

In November the International Labour Organization (ILO) in Geneva adopts the ILO Code of Practice on Managing Disability in the Workplace, which was written to provide guidance on the recruitment of people with disabilities and their retention in the workforce.

2003

The International Classification of Functioning, Disability, and Health (ICF) is released. Designed as the World Health Organization's framework for measuring health and disability at both the individual and population levels, the ICF is officially endorsed by all member states, and is fully endorsed as the international standard to describe and measure health and disability.

The Panel Study of Income Dynamics (PSID) expands its disability-related questions to include specific medical conditions, Activities of Daily Living (ADLs), and Instrumental Activities of Daily Living (IADLs).

2005

The American Community Survey (ACS) is utilized by the U.S. Census Bureau for the first time. Since 2000, the ACS had been tabulating and publishing single-year estimates for specific areas with populations of 250,000 or more. In 2005, the ACS expands its sample size to cover all of the United States and the Commonwealth of Puerto Rico (U.S. Census Bureau, 2008). The ACS is conducted each year to gather national and state-level data on demographic, social, economic, and housing characteristics of the U.S. population. The survey includes six questions that are used to identify the population with disabilities. These questions replace those previously asked in the Decennial U.S. Census, which in 2010 no longer enumerates persons with disabilities.

2006

The Combating Autism Act, the first federal autism-specific law, is signed into law by President George W. Bush.

The General Assembly of the United Nations in New York adopts the Convention on the Rights of Persons with Disabilities on December 13. The purpose of the convention is "to promote, protect and ensure the full and equal enjoyment of all human rights by persons with disabilities." The convention, which was negotiated during eight sessions of an ad hoc committee of the General Assembly between 2002 and 2006, presents disability as a human rights issue rather than a social welfare issue.

2007

The United Nations Convention on the Rights of Persons with Disabilities, originally adopted in 2006, opens for signature on March 30. In its opening day the convention receives 82 signatories, 44 signatories to its Optional Protocol, and one ratification—the highest-ever number of signatories in history to a UN convention on its opening day. The convention enters into force on May 3, 2008.

2008

The Americans with Disabilities Act Amendments Act becomes law on September 25. The act emphasizes that the definition of disability should be construed in favor of broad coverage of individuals to the maximum extent permitted by the terms of the ADA and generally should not require extensive analysis. The act also makes important changes to the definition of the term "disability" in response to several Supreme Court decisions and portions of Equal Employment Opportunity Commission (EEOC) ADA regulations.

The U.S. Census Bureau changes the disability-related questions in the American Community Survey to provide higher-quality data on disability in the United States. Changes include better identification of specific portions of the population of people with disabilities, and more clearly defining disability as a functional limitation that may adversely affect a person's level of participation in work, recreation, and other activities.

President Bush signs the Genetic Information Nondiscrimination Act (GINA), which prohibits the improper use of genetic information in health insurance and employment. The act prohibits employers from using individuals' genetic information when making hiring, firing, job placement, or promotion decisions. The measure thus makes it illegal to discriminate on the basis of a person's likelihood of developing a disabling condition in the future.

2010

On the 20th anniversary of the signing of the Americans with Disabilities Act, President Barack Obama reinstates Executive Order 13163, which was signed by President Clinton in July 2000. The original executive order was a pledge to hire 100,000 federal employees with disabilities in the next five years, but it was never fully implemented. The reinstatement announcement calls for the federal government to become a model for the employment of people with disabilities, to design model recruitment and hiring strategies, and to develop mandatory training programs for both human resources personnel and hiring managers on the employment of people with disabilities.

References

Barnes, J. K. (1991). *The medical and surgical history of the Civil War.* Wilmington, NC: Broadfoot.

The Conference Board. (1945). *Reemployment of veterans* (Conference Board Reports: Studies in Personnel Policy No. 69). New York, NY: National Industrial Conference Board, Inc.

Disability history timeline. (2002). Philadelphia, PA: Temple University, Rehabilitation Research and Training Center on Independent Living Management. Retrieved from http://isc.temple.edu/neighbor/ds/disabilityrightstimeline.htm

Kennedy, J. F. (1963). *Special message to the Congress on mental illness and mental retardation.* Retrieved from http://www.presidency.ucsb.edu/ws/?pid=9546#axzz10XVT4fBr

National Center for Education Statistics. (1997). *The NAEP databases: An overview.* Retrieved from http://nces.ed.gov/pubs97/web/97045.asp

Reagan, R. (1988). Executive order 12640—President's Committee on Employment of People with Disabilities. 53 FR 16996, 3 CFR, 1988 Comp., p. 640. Retrieved from http://www.archives.gov/federal-register/codification/executive-order/12640.html

U.S. Census Bureau. (2008). Data dissemination. In *American community survey design and methodology* (p. 14-1). Retrieved from http://www.census.gov/acs/www/Downloads/survey_methodology/acs_design_methodology_ch14.pdf

U.S. Census Bureau. (2011). *History: Index of questions.* Retrieved from http://www.census.gov/history/www/through_the_decades/index_of_questions

U.S. Senate. (1966). *History of employment and manpower policy in the United States.* Prepared for a subcommittee of the Committee on Labor and Public Welfare, Senate, 88th Congress, Vol. 7, Part 1, p. 1.

Von Tetzchner, S., & Martinsen, H. (2000). *Introduction to augmentative and alternative communication* (2nd ed.). London, UK: Whurr.

Four

Biographies of Key Contributors in the Field

A large number of individuals have made significant contributions to the study of employment issues and the development of employment policies affecting people with disabilities. The biographical sketches in this chapter, presented in alphabetical order, profile some of those individuals and their contributions.

Sheila H. Akabas (1931–)

American professor of social work focusing on employment issues and disability policy

Sheila ("Shelley") H. Akabas was born Sheila Epstein in 1931. She married Aaron Akabas in the mid-1950s. Akabas attended Cornell University, earning a bachelor of science degree in 1951. She pursued graduate studies at New York University, earning a master's degree in business administration in 1956 and a Ph.D. in economics in 1970.

Akabas spent her early career helping labor unions to establish Membership Assistance Programs (MAP) and Employee Assistance Programs (EAP). She went on to create curricula for a number of schools of social work, with the goal of expanding services "to working men and women and to the many disadvantaged individuals who seek entry into the world of work."

Akabas joined the faculty of Columbia University's School of Social Work in 1969. During her long tenure there, she has consulted on disability and labor market policy with the United Nations, the World Rehabilitation Fund, and other groups throughout the world, including corporations, nonprofit organizations, and trade unions in the United States. Her work with the United Nations included the creation of disability policy in Bulgaria and the development of training policy for participation in competitive labor markets in Kazakhstan. Akabas served on the executive committee of the President's Committee on Employment of People with Disabilities for many years, and she was chair of the Technical Advisory Committee to the Dole Foundation for ten years.

Akabas is a co-founder and current director emeritus of the Columbia School of Social Work's Workplace Center, which has been widely recognized for its innovation in workplace practices. Akabas remains chair of the Social Enterprise Administration method of practice and the World of Work field of practice at Columbia. This position gives her the opportunity to mentor students in workforce management issues, employee assistance programs, collective bargaining, workplace discrimination and equal opportunity, and work and social welfare legislation.

In 2010 Akabas was presented with the Mark Moses Distinguished Fellowship Award from the National Network for Social Work Managers. She was recognized for her efforts to promote equality and justice in the workplace and further the employment of individuals with disability. Akabas has published many journal articles, book chapters, and books in her field, including *Work and the Workplace: A Resource for Innovative Policy and Practice* (2005) and *Disability Management: A Guide for Developing and Implementing Successful Programs* (1996).

Further Reading

Akabas, S. H. (1996). Supervisors as linch-pins in the employment of people with disabilities. *Journal of the California Alliance for the Mentally Ill, 6*(4), 17–19.

Akabas, S. H., & Gates, L. B. (2006). Older adults and work in the 21st century. In B. Berkman & S. D'Ambruoso (Eds.), *The Oxford handbook of social work in health and aging* (pp. 181–190). New York, NY: Oxford University Press.

Akabas, S. H., Gates, L. B., & Kantrowitz, W. (1996). Supervisors' role in successful job maintenance: A target for rehabilitation counselor efforts. *Journal of Applied Rehabilitation Counseling, 27*(3), 60–66.

CUSSW Full-Time Faculty Profile: Sheila H. Akabas. Retrieved from http://www.columbia.edu/cu/ssw/faculty/profiles/akabas.html

Gates, L. B., & Akabas, S. H. (in press). Accommodation as a social process. In I. A. Schultz & E. S. Rogers (Eds.), *Handbook of accommodation*. New York, NY: Springer. "Mark Moses Distinguished Fellowship Award." National Network for Social Work Managers. Retrieved from http://www.socialworkmanager.org/awards.php?id=mosesaward

Fabricio E. Balcazar (1956–)

Colombian-born psychologist specializing in transition and employment issues for minority populations with disabilities

Fabricio E. Balcazar earned a bachelor's degree in psychology from the Universidad de los Andes in Bogota, Colombia, in 1979. He then came to the United States to attend the University of Kansas on a Fulbright Scholarship. He earned a master's degree from the Department of Human Development in 1984 and completed a Ph.D. developmental and child psychology in 1987.

Balcazar is currently an associate professor in the Departments of Disability and Human Development in the College of Applied Health Sciences at the University of Illinois at Chicago (UIC). Over the course of his 25-year academic career, the main focus of his research has concerned the development of systematic approaches for promoting empowerment and effectiveness among individuals with disabilities, especially within minority groups and underserved populations.

Balcazar has served as principal or co-principal investigator in 17 grants totaling over $9.5 million since 1986. Some of his projects have involved the development and evaluation of approaches to vocational rehabilitation service delivery, interventions to aid in school-to-work transition planning for minority students with disabilities, and career development leading to employment opportunities. In 1995 Balcazar received an Outstanding Research Award from the American Rehabilitation Counseling Association (ARCA) for his work.

Balcazar currently serves as the director of the Center on Capacity Building for Minorities with Disabilities Research at UIC. In this role, he has led a team of researchers in the development of a transition model called the College Connection, which is being disseminated within the Chicago Public School District to support minority youth with disabilities as they move from high school to adult education training. Balcazar has also created training curricula and assessment instruments and served as a consultant and trainer to state and federal agencies, consumer advocacy groups, and Independent Living Centers.

A fellow of the American Psychological Association, Balcazar has published more than 60 articles in peer-reviewed journals. He also served as the co-editor of the 2010 book *Race, Culture, and Disability: Rehabilitation Science and Practice,* and as associate editor of the *Journal of Organizational Behavior Management* and the *Journal of Rehabilitation Psychology.*

Further Reading

Balcazar, F. E., Keys, C. B., Davis, M., Lardon, C., & Jones, C. (2005). Strengths and challenges of intervention research in vocational rehabilitation: An illustration of agency-university collaboration. *Journal of Rehabilitation, 71*(2), 40–48.

Fabricio Balcazar. Retrieved from http://www.ahs.uic.edu/ahs/php/content .php?type=7&id=55

Fabricio Balcazar. Retrieved from http://idhd.org/F_Balcazar.html

Hasnain, R., & Balcazar, F. E. (2009). Predicting community- versus facility-based employment for transition-aged young adults with disabilities: The role of race, ethnicity, and support systems. *Journal of Vocational Rehabilitation, 31,* 1–14.

Hernandez, B., Keys, C. B., & Balcazar, F. E. (2000). Employer attitudes toward workers with disabilities and their ADA employment rights: A literature review. *Journal of Rehabilitation, 66*(4), 4–16.

Hernandez, B., Keys, C. B., & Balcazar, F. E. (2002). The Americans with Disabilities Act: Strong psychometrics and weak knowledge. *Rehabilitation Psychology, 48*(4), 93–99.

Marjorie L. Baldwin (1949–)

American health economist focusing on work-related disability

Marjorie L. Baldwin received a bachelor of science degree from State University College at Oswego in 1971. She pursued graduate studies at Syracuse University, earning a master's degree in 1987 and a Ph.D. from the Maxwell School of Citizenship and Public Affairs in 1988. She joined the faculty of East Carolina University in 1989 as an assistant professor of economics. In 2002 she moved to Arizona State University (ASU), where she is currently a professor in the School of Health Administration and Policy and director of the Master's in Health Sector Management

(MHSM) program in the W.P. Carey School of Business. ASU is the first public university to offer an MHSM program that focuses specifically on urban health and related issues, including homelessness, mental health, and access to affordable health care.

A noted health economist, Baldwin has devoted much of her academic career to the study of work-related disability and workplace discrimination against people with disabilities. Baldwin has served as principal investigator in several major studies of the costs and outcomes of work-related disabilities, including projects supported by funding from the National Institute of Health and the National Institute on Disability and Rehabilitation Research. One of her best-known projects was the ASU Healthy Back Study, which was the largest study of work-related back injuries conducted in the United States. She has also conducted studies into the effects of stigma and discrimination on the work outcomes of people with mental disorders. In general, Baldwin's research has indicated that most people with disabilities want to work, but that their employment outcomes are often negatively affected by low wages and workplace discrimination.

Baldwin is the author of more than 40 articles and book chapters in the areas of employment and disability. A member of National Academy of Social Insurance, she also joined a panel of experts who advised the government of Dubai on a major revision of health insurance policy in that country. In 2009 Baldwin participated in a series of conference calls held by the official White House Health Reform Task Force to gather input for President Barack Obama's overhaul of the American health care system. One of her top priorities was to ensure that the proposed reforms took an integrated approach to mental and physical health. "Psychiatric conditions have been treated in a separate system, with different reimbursement rates, for far too long, helping to perpetuate the stigma of mental illness," she told the *ASU News*.

Following the passage of the Patient Protection and Affordable Care Act in 2010, Baldwin was frequently called upon to analyze the impact of the new health care reform law. Although she found the final legislation less than ideal and worried about its potential costs, she was pleased that it removed lifetime maximum benefit limits for people with disabilities and expanded health insurance coverage to low-income people and those with pre-existing conditions.

Further Reading

Baldwin, M. L. (1997). Can the ADA achieve its employment goals? *The ANNALS of the American Academy of Political and Social Science, 549*(1), 37–52.

Baldwin, M. L., & Johnson, W. (1993). The Americans with Disabilities Act: Will it make a difference? *Policy Studies Journal, 21*(4), 775–788.

Baldwin, M. L., Zeager, L. A., & Flacco, P. R. (1994). Gender differences in wage losses from impairments: Estimates from the Survey of Income and Program Participation. *The Journal of Human Resources, 29*(3), 865–887.

Butler, R. J., Johnson, W. G., & Baldwin, M. L. (1995). Managing work disability: Why first return to work is not a measure of success. *Industrial Relations Review, 48*(3), 452–469.

Marjorie Baldwin. Retrieved from http://wpcarey.asu.edu/directory/stafffaculty.cfm

Monroe Berkowitz (1919–2009)

American economist on disability issues

Monroe Berkowitz was born on March 19, 1919. A native of Wilkes Barre, Pennsylvania, Berkowitz earned his undergraduate degree (with high honors) from Ohio University in 1942. After a stint during World War II as a member of the staff of the War Labor Board, he worked for the United Auto Workers before entering Columbia University. Berkowitz earned his Ph.D. in economics from Columbia in 1951. He then joined the Department of Economics at Rutgers University, where he became a mainstay of the department. He remained at Rutgers for the next half-century (though fellowships also took him to India, New Zealand, England, and other parts of the world).

Berkowitz's life work focused on disability issues and their intersections with insurance, public and private rehabilitation, and economic policy. Specifically, he devoted his professional career to research into issues related to disability and workers' compensation, including the administration of such programs. A highly regarded expert on Social Security Disability Insurance (SSDI), he conducted important research into "early intervention" policies designed to provide an alternative to direct enrollment onto permanent SSDI or Supplemental Security Income (SSI).

Berkowitz's most important policy contribution in this regard was his "Ticket to Work" program for disability rehabilitation, which President Bill Clinton signed into law in 1999. This program was crafted to address the concern felt by many people with disabilities weighing a return to the work force about losing their SSDI health care coverage. The goal of Ticket to Work was to increase opportunities and choices for Social Security disability beneficiaries to obtain employment, vocational rehabilitation (VR), and other support services from public and private providers, employers, and other organizations.

Berkowitz also conducted research in the areas of national disability expenditures, cost-benefit analyses of vocational rehabilitation, and the economic impacts of permanent partial disability. He also worked extensively as a labor arbitrator. In 2006 he received the National Academy of Social Insurance Robert M. Ball Award for outstanding achievements in social insurance. Berkowitz died on November 15, 2009.

Further Reading

Berkowitz, M. (2003). The Ticket to Work program: The complicated evolution of a simple idea. In K. Rupp & S. H. Bell (Eds.). *Paying for results in vocational rehabilitation: Will provider incentives work for Ticket to Work?* Washington, DC: Urban Institute Press.

Berkowitz, M., & Hill, A. (1986). *Disability and the labor market.* Ithaca, NY: ILR Press.

Berkowitz, M., Johnson, W. G., & Murphy, E. H. (1976). *Public policy toward disability.* New York, NY: Praeger.

Berkowitz, M., & O'Leary, P. K. (2000). Persons with disabilities at work: The Atlantic City gaming casinos. *Journal of Disability Policy Studies, 11*(3), 152–160.

Monroe Berkowitz. Retrieved from http://econweb.rutgers.edu/sheflin/monroe_files/PROGRAM3.pdf

Peter D. Blanck (1957–)

American disability policy analyst and lawyer

Peter David Blanck was born on August 27, 1957, in Elmont, New York. A 1979 graduate (in psychology) of New York's University of Rochester, Blanck earned his Ph.D. in social psychology from Harvard University in 1982. Three years later he received his law degree from Stanford University, where he also served as a president of the *Stanford Law Review.*

Blanck spent the next several years working in private law practice and clerking for U.S. Appeals Court Judge Carl McGowan (D.C. Circuit). In 1993 he went to the University of Iowa, where he became a professor of law and professor of psychology. Blanck spent the next 13 years at Iowa as a professor in its College of Medicine, Department of Preventive Medicine and Environmental Health (1997–2006); College of Public Health,

Department of Occupational Medicine (1999–2006); and College of Law (2002–2006). He also served as director of the College of Law's Law, Health Policy and Disability Center from 2000 to 2006.

Since 2005 Blanck has been at Syracuse University, with appointments as a professor in the College of Law, College of Human Services and Health Professions, College of Arts and Sciences, School of Education, and the Maxwell School of Citizenship and Public Affairs. The year 2005 also marked the beginning of his tenure as chairman of the Burton Blatt Institute's Centers of Innovation on Disability.

Blanck's multi-faceted law career has focused in particular on the Americans with Disabilities Act (ADA), ADA amendments, and other laws/policies intended to guarantee the rights of individuals with mental and/or physical disabilities in institutional and community settings. In conjunction with his ADA work Blanck has received grants to study disability law and policy, represented clients before the U.S. Supreme Court in ADA cases, and testified before Congress. Blanck has also written widely on the ADA and related laws (Blanck is co-editor of the Cambridge University Press series *Disability Law and Policy*).

Other areas of interest for Blanck have included international disability and human rights law, law and ethics in behavioral sciences, the social and political history of disability policy, and social science experimental and field research methodologies. A former board member of the National Organization on Disability (NOD), the Disability Rights Law Center (DRLC), and Disability Rights Advocates (DRA), Blanck is a trustee of YAI/National Institute for People with Disabilities Network, a fellow at Princeton University's Woodrow Wilson School, a senior fellow of the Annenberg Washington Program, and chairman of the Global Universal Design Commission (GUDC), a non-profit organization dedicated to advancing sustainable and usable design practices in the building industry.

Further Reading

Ali, M., Schur, L., Kruse, D., & Blanck, P. (2010). What jobs do people with disabilities want? The same as anyone else. *Journal of Occupational Rehabilitation, 21*(2), 199–210.

Blanck, P. D. (1999). Empirical study of disability, employment policy, and the ADA. *Mental & Physical Disability Law Reporter, 23*(2), 275–80.

Blanck, P. D. (2000). The economics of the ADA. In P. Blanck (Ed.), *Employment, disability, and the Americans with Disabilities Act: Issues in law, public policy, and research* (pp. 201–227). Chicago, IL: Northwestern University Press.

Peter Blanck. Retrieved from http://bbi.syr.edu/blanck/

Schur, L., Kruse, D., & Blanck, P. (2005). Corporate culture and the employment of persons with disabilities. *Behavioral Sciences & the Law, 23*(1), 3–20.

Gary R. Bond (1944–)

American pioneer in the field of evidence-based practices for people with severe mental illness

Gary R. Bond attended Michigan State University, earning a bachelor of science degree in mathematics in 1966. He went on to attend the University of Chicago, earning a master's degree in psychology in 1972 and a Ph.D. in psychology in 1975. Bond was also a postdoctoral fellow at Stanford University in 1975.

Bond taught in the Department of Psychiatry and Behavioral Sciences at Northwestern University from 1977 until 1983. For most of that time, he also worked as director of research at the psychiatric rehabilitation agency Thresholds in Chicago. In 1983 Bond joined the faculty of Indiana University Purdue University, Indianapolis (IUPUI). During his tenure there, Bond held positions as associate professor, professor, chancellor's professor, and director of the Ph.D. program in Clinical Rehabilitation Psychology. Over the years, Bond took several sabbaticals to Dartmouth Medical School and the Dartmouth Psychiatric Research Center, and he left IUPUI for Dartmouth in 2009. Bond remains a chancellor's professor emeritus of psychology at IUPUI.

Bond's research has mainly involved two areas of rehabilitation approaches for people with severe mental illness. Assertive community treatment focuses on case management for people who suffer from mental illness as well as other difficulties, such as homelessness or addiction. Supported employment is an approach that concentrates on assisting people who suffer from severe mental illness in finding competitive employment. The development of fidelity scales is another area of interest to Bond. Fidelity scales are standardized methods for determining the effectiveness of program implementation. He also studies public policy as it relates to the provision of effective services to people with severe mental illness.

Bond is a two-time recipient of the Research Scientist Development Award from the National Institute of Mental Health (NIMH). He has consulted with mental health planners and researchers internationally, and he co-authored the textbook *Principles and Practice of Psychiatric Rehabilitation: An Empirical Approach* (2007).

Further Reading

Bond, G. R. (1998). Principles of the Individual Placement and Support Model: Empirical support. *Psychiatric Rehabilitation Journal, 22*(1), 11–23.

Bond, G. R., Resnick, S. R., Drake, R. E., Xie, H., McHugo, G. J., & Bebout, R. R. (2001). Does competitive employment improve nonvocational outcomes for people with severe mental illness? *Journal of Consulting and Clinical Psychology, 69*(3), 489–501.

Crowther, R. E., Marshall, M., Bond, G. R., & Huxley, P. (2001). Helping people with severe mental illness to obtain work: Systematic review. *British Medical Journal, 322*, 204–208.

Department of Psychology: Dr. Gary Bond. Retrieved from http://www.psynt.iupui.edu/People/Emeritus/Bond/index.html

Dilk, M. N., & Bond, G. R. (1996). Meta-analytic evaluation of skills training research for individuals with severe mental illness. *Psychiatric Services, 48*, 335–346.

Faculty Database: Gary R. Bond, Ph.D. Retrieved from http://dms.dartmouth.edu/faculty/facultydb/view.php?uid=3560

Susanne M. Bruyère

American academic focusing on employment issues for people with disabilities

Susanne M. Bruyère was born in upstate New York. She earned a Ph.D. in rehabilitation counseling and psychology from the University of Wisconsin at Madison in 1975, and a master's degree in public administration from Seattle University in 1979. In 1985 she joined the faculty at Cornell University, where she is currently professor of disability studies, associate dean of outreach in the School of Industrial and Labor Relations (ILR), and director of the Employment and Disability Institute (EDI) in the ILR's Extension Division.

Bruyère has described the main focus of her work as "getting people into the workforce and keeping them there." She is responsible for ILR's outreach activities, including the development and operation of programs and centers that provide research, training, and technical assistance to both employers and employees. As director of EDI, she oversees a multi-million dollar research, training, education, and information dissemination organization dedicated to improving employment opportunities and creating inclusive communities for people with disabilities. Bruyère is recognized as an expert in disability and rehabilitation, disability and inclusion, disability law, prevention of workplace disability, disability management, and nondiscrimination for persons with disabilities in employment.

Bruyère has served as project director and co-principal investigator of numerous research efforts—focusing on employment, disability, and nondiscrimination—funded by several federal agencies. One example is a four-year study funded by the U.S. Department of Education, National Institute on Disability and Rehabilitation Research (NIDRR), to analyze and improve employment practices under the Americans with Disabilities Act (ADA). She is also lead investigator of a similar study of federal agency equal employment and human resource practices for people with disabilities funded by the U.S. Department of Labor, Presidential Task Force on Employment of Adults with Disabilities.

Bruyère is a fellow in the American Psychological Association and a past president of its Division of Rehabilitation Psychology. She has also served as president of the National Council on Rehabilitation Education and the American Rehabilitation Counseling Association, and as a member of the boards of the National Association of Rehabilitation Research and Training Centers and of the Commission on Accreditation of Rehabilitation Facilities (CARF). She has published numerous journal articles and book chapters in the areas of disability and employment, and she is the co-author of *Volume 3: Employment and Work* in the *SAGE Reference Series on Disability*.

Further Reading

Bjelland, M., Bruyère, S., von Schrader, S., Houtenville, A., Ruiz-Quintanilla, A., & Webber, D. (2010). Age and disability employment discrimination: Occupational rehabilitation implications. *Journal of Occupational Rehabilitation, 20,* 456–471.

Bruyère, S. (2006). Disability management: Key concepts and techniques for an aging workforce. *International Journal of Disability Management Research, 1,* 149–158.

Bruyère, S., Erickson, E., & VanLooy, S. (2006). The impact of business size on employer ADA response. *Rehabilitation Counseling Bulletin, 49*(4), 194–206.

Colella, A., & Bruyère, S. (2011). Disability and employment: New directions for industrial/organizational psychology. In *American Psychological Association handbook on industrial organizational psychology, Vol. 1* (pp. 473–503). Washington, DC: American Psychological Association.

Faculty profile: Susanne M. Bruyère. Retrieved from http://www.ilr.cornell.edu/profiles/SusanneBruyere.html

Selected works of Susanne M. Bruyère. Retrieved from http://works.bepress
  .com/susanne_bruyere

Richard V. Burkhauser (1945–)

American economist specializing in poverty policy
as it relates to disability and old age

Richard Valentine Burkhauser was born on December 27, 1945, in Trenton,
New Jersey. He earned his bachelor's degree in economics from
St. Vincent College in Latrobe, Pennsylvania, in 1967. He earned his master's degree in economics from Rutgers University two years later. After a
two-year stint in the Peace Corps (1970–1972), during which time he
worked as a teacher in Jamiaca, Burkhauser received his Ph.D. in economics from the University of Chicago in 1976.

In 1979 Burkhauser joined the faculty of Vanderbilt University, where
he engaged in a wide range of scholarly research on U.S. economic policy, with a growing emphasis on policy issues affecting people with disabilities, the poor, elderly individuals, and other vulnerable citizens. He
continued in these realms of research after moving on to a professorial
position with the Department of Economics at the Maxwell School, University of Syracuse, in 1990. In 1998 he joined the Department of Policy
Analysis and Management (PAM) at Cornell University in Ithaca,
New York.

In addition to his ongoing teaching work, Burkhauser is co-principal
investigator of the Department of Education RRT Center for Economic
Research on Employment Policy for Persons with Disabilities, which is
exploring linkages between state and federal anti-discrimination and
workers' compensation laws related to people with disabilities and the
accommodation practices of existing and potential employers. He is also
co-principal Investigator on the RRT Center on Disability Demographics
and Statistics and a member of the RAND Financial Planning Research
Consortium (Social Security Administration).

Burkhauser, who has criticized many federal disability policies as
well-intentioned but counterproductive in terms of their impact on the
economic independence of people with disabilities, also maintains affilia-
tions with the Cato Institute, the American Enterprise Institute, and other
research institutions dedicated to free market and limited government
principles. In 2010 he became president of the Association for Public Policy Analysis and Management (APPAM).

Further Reading

Burkhauser, R. V., Butler, J. S., & Kim, Y. W. (1995). The importance of employer accommodation on the job duration of workers with disabilities: A Hazard Model approach. *Labour Economics, 3*(1), 1–22.

Burkhauser, R. V., & Houtenville, A. J. (2010). Employment among working-age people with disabilities: What current data can tell us. In E. M. Szymanski & R. M. Parker (Eds.), *Work and disability: Issues and strategies for career development and job placement* (3rd ed., pp. 49–86). Austin, TX: Pro-Ed, Inc.

Burkhauser, R. V., & Stapleton, D. C. (2004). The decline in the employment rate for people with disabilities: Bad data, bad health, or bad policy? *Journal of Vocational Rehabilitation, 20*(3), 185–201.

Burkhauser, R. V., & Wittenburg, D. C. (1996). How current disability transfer policies discourage work: Analysis from the 1990 SIPP. *Journal of Vocational Rehabilitation, 7*, 9–27.

John F. Burton, Jr. (1935–)

American scholar in the field of workers'
compensation and disability benefits

John F. Burton, Jr., is a nationally known expert in workers' compensation and disability benefits, employment law, and public policy. He earned a bachelor of science degree in industrial and labor relations from Cornell University in 1957. He pursued graduate studies at the University of Michigan, earning a law degree in 1960 and a Ph.D. in economics in 1965.

The following year Burton joined the faculty of the University of Chicago, where he taught until 1978, when he moved to Cornell University. Burton left Cornell in 1990, but he continues to hold the title of professor emeritus in Cornell's School of Industrial and Labor Relations. In 1990 Burton joined the faculty at Rutgers University. He served as dean of the School of Management and Labor Relations (SMLR) from 1994 to 2000, and since 2005 he has held the position of professor emeritus in SMLR.

Over the years, Burton has conducted research, served as a consultant, provided expert testimony, and assisted with the formulation of public policy in the areas of workers' compensation and disability benefits. He served as chair of the National Commission on State Workmen's Compensation Laws, which submitted its report to the President Richard Nixon and the U.S. Congress in 1972. He has served as a consultant to a number of jurisdictions, including Florida, Massachusetts, Michigan, New York, Oregon, Washington, and Ontario. A past president of the

Industrial Relations Research Association (now the Labor and Employment Relations Association), Burton is currently chair of the Study Panel on National Data on Workers' Compensation of the National Academy of Social Insurance (NASI).

Burton has published hundreds of articles and book chapters in his field of expertise. His 1987 book with Monroe Berkowitz, *Permanent Disability Benefits in Workers' Compensation*, received the Kulp Award from the American Risk and Insurance Association. He also served as editor of *John Burton's Workers' Compensation Monitor* from 1988 to 1997, and of the *Workers' Compensation Policy Review* from 2001 to 2008. Burton currently maintains a Web site, www.workerscompresources.com, devoted to providing up-to-date information about employment law.

Further Reading

Burton, J. F., & Spieler, E. A. (1998). Compensation for disabled workers: Workers' compensation. In J. F. Burton, T. Thomason, & D. E. Hyatt (Eds.), *New approaches to disability in the workplace*. Madison, WI: Industrial Relations Research Association/Cornell University Press.

John F. Burton, Jr. Retrieved from http://www.workerscompresources.com

Krueger, A. B., & Burton, J. F. (1990). The employers' costs of workers' compensation insurance: Magnitudes, determinants, and public policy. *The Review of Economics and Statistics, 72*(2), 228–240.

John Butterworth

American researcher specializing in expansion of employment opportunities for people with disabilities

John Butterworth has dedicated his 30-year career as an academic researcher, consultant, and trainer to improving employment opportunities and outcomes for people with disabilities. His primary interests in this field include organizational and systems change, person-centered planning, natural supports, and program management.

Butterworth earned a bachelor's degree from Bowdoin College, a master's degree from George Peabody College for Teachers, and a Ph. D. from the University of Connecticut. He is currently the coordinator of employment systems change and evaluation for the Institute for Community Inclusion (ICI). Affiliated with University of Massachusetts Boston (UMB) and Children's Hospital Boston, ICI is dedicated to promoting the inclusion of people with disabilities. Butterworth also holds the position of senior research fellow at UMB.

Butterworth has led numerous research projects aimed at collecting and analyzing employment data and developing and implementing integrated employment programs and services for people with disabilities. For instance, he is principal investigator of Access to Integrated Employment, a 20-year national data collection project on day and employment services for people with developmental disabilities. He has also played a leading role in the State of the States in Developmental Disabilities project, funded by the U.S. Department of Health and Human Services. This ongoing research project aims to assess the effectiveness of state and local agencies, and identify and catalog best practices, in promoting full inclusion of individuals with developmental disabilities in employment and community activities.

Butterworth serves on the staff of the CMS-funded Massachusetts Medicaid Infrastructure and Comprehensive Employment Opportunities initiative. He is also a member of the board of TASH/New England and a member of the advisory council for the Alliance for Full Participation (AFP). Butterworth has published extensively in his field, including the article "Entering Work: Employment Outcomes of People with Developmental Disabilities," which appeared in the *International Journal of Rehabilitation Research* in 2008.

Further Reading

Butterworth J., et al. (1996). Natural supports in the workplace: Defining an agenda for research and practice. *Journal of the Association of Persons with Severe Handicaps, 21*(3), 103–113.

Butterworth, J., Hagner, D., Helm, D., & Whelley, T. (2000). Workplace culture, social interactions, and supports for transition-age young adults. *Mental Retardation, 38*(4), 342–353.

Butterworth, J., & Strauch, J. (1994). The relationship between social competence and success in the competitive work place for persons with mental retardation. *Education and Training in Mental Retardation and Developmental Disabilities, 29*(2), 118–133.

John Butterworth. Retrieved from http://www.communityinclusion.org/staff .php?staff_id=2

Migliore, A., & Butterworth, J. (2008). Trends in outcomes of vocational rehabilitation services serving adults with developmental disabilities: 1995–2005. *Rehabilitation Counseling Bulletin, 52*(1), 35–44.

Claudia B. Center

American attorney who has championed
disability rights in the workplace

Claudia B. Center grew up in Milford, New Hampshire. She earned a bachelor's degree in government and African studies from Wesleyan University in Connecticut in 1987, and a law degree from the University of California, Berkeley, in 1991. Center entered professional life as an attorney in 1992 when she joined NARAL (National Abortion and Reproductive Rights Action League) Pro-Choice America, a nonprofit lobbying organization based in Washington, D.C., where she remained until 1995. During this time she was also a Fellow in the Women's Law and Public Policy program at Georgetown University. In 1995 Center moved to the Legal Aid Society-Employment Law Center (LAS-ELC) in San Francisco, where she rose to the position of senior staff attorney and director of the Disability Rights Program. In this position, Center has developed into one of the country's leading legal advocates for the rights of people with disabilities in the workplace.

In 1997 Center started the LIBRA (Lifting Invisible Barriers through Reasonable Accommodation) Project, which was incorporated into LAS–ELC's Disability Rights Program. She first made an impact at the state level in 2000 as the lead attorney in a successful push for disability rights amendments to California's Fair Employment and Housing Act. This experience served as a springboard to her most significant achievements, which have come from her ongoing efforts to clarify and expand the Americans with Disabilities Act (ADA) of 1990.

In 2001 Center represented Robert Barnett in arguing the *U.S. Airways, Inc. v. Barnett* case before the Supreme Court. The Court's decision marked a key victory in clarifying the scope of "reasonable accommodations" for disabled employees under the ADA. In 2003 she teamed with Andrew J. Imparato, president and CEO of the American Association of People with Disabilities, to write "Redefining 'Disability' Discrimination: A Proposal to Restore Civil Rights Protections for All Workers." In this important article, which appeared in the *Stanford Law & Policy Review*, they brought to light the need for ongoing vigilance in protecting the ADA, arguing that "federal courts have chipped away at the law's protected class by adopting overly narrow rules for the analysis of who meets the statutory definition of 'disability.'" Her continuing efforts in support of the ADA contributed significantly to the passage of the ADA

Amendments Act of 2008, which clarified and broadened the definition of "disability" in employment relations.

Center has earned national recognition for her work at LAS-ELC on behalf of people with disabilities of all types. In 2009 she received the Paul G. Hearne Award for Disability Rights, an honor given annually by the ABA Commission on Mental and Physical Disability Law.

Further Reading

Center, C. (2011). Law and job accommodation in mental health disability. In I. Z. Schultz & E. S. Rogers (Eds.), *Work accomodation and mental health* (pp. 3–32). New York, NY: Springer.

Center, C., & Imparato, A. J. (2003). Redefining "disability" discrimination: A proposal to restore civil rights protections for all workers. *Stanford Law & Policy Review, 14,* 321.

Claudia Center. Retrieved from http://www.las-elc.org/about-staff.html

Fong Chan

American educator and expert in the field of rehabilitation psychology and health research

Fong Chan attended Columbia College in Chicago for his undergraduate work before moving on to the University of Wisconsin at Madison, where he received his Ph.D. in Rehabilitation Psychology in 1983. Chan chose to stay in Madison as a professor and has risen to the position of director of clinical training in the Department of Rehabilitation Psychology and Special Education (RPSE), which is focused on "the educational and rehabilitation needs of persons with disabilities across the life span."

Chan has now been with RPSE for more than 25 years, but he has made an impact far beyond the university. From 1995 to 1999 he was the director of research for the Foundation for Rehabilitation Education and Research, providing inputs for counselor and case manager certifications. His research and writing have made him a leading expert in the field of rehabilitation for people with disabilities. His particular focus is in the area of "demand-side employment," helping prepare people with disabilities of all kinds for entry into the workforce, and educating employers to prepare them for hiring disabled employees. Chan has authored numerous articles and chapters for books in the fields of rehabilitation, counseling, and chronic illness and disability. He has also edited several textbooks, including *Understanding Psychosocial Adjustment to Chronic Illness and Disability: A Handbook for Evidence-Based Practitioners in Rehabilitation.*

More recently, Chan wrote a concept paper that led to initiation of a new project. A team of students led by Chan will serve as the research arm for the development of the Paths to Employment Resource Center (PERC). Planned for rollout by the end of 2011, PERC will be a web-based platform serving as a resource to aid in professional development, including technical assistance and training, for the state of Wisconsin's service providers and people with disabilities. In addition to these efforts and achievements, Chan is a Fellow in the American Psychological Association and a Distinguished Research Fellow with the National Institute on Disability and Rehabilitation Research. In 2010 he was awarded research honors at the American Rehabilitation Counseling Association annual conference.

Further Reading

Chan, F., Lee, G., Lee, E. J., Allen, C., & Kubota, C. (2007). Structural equation modeling in rehabilitation counseling research. *Rehabilitation Counseling Bulletin, 51,* 44–57.

Chan, F., Tarvydas, V., Blalock, K., Strauser, D., & Atkins, B. (2009). Unifying and elevating rehabilitation counseling through model-driven, diversity sensitive evidenced-based practice. *Rehabilitation Counseling Bulletin, 52*(2), 114–119.

Fong Chan. Retrieved from http://rpse.education.wisc.edu/?folder=content&pageName=2column&pageid=90

McMahon, B. T., Roessler, R., Rumrill, P. D., Hurley, J. E., West, S. L., Chan, F., & Carlson, L. (2008). Hiring discrimination against people with disabilities under the ADA: Characteristics of charging parties. *Journal of Occupational Rehabilitation, 18*(2), 122–132.

Judith A. Cook

American educator, psychiatrist, and expert on mental health

Judith A. Cook received her Ph.D. in sociology from Ohio State University. She then moved on to the University of Illinois at Chicago (UIC), where she completed a post-doctoral training program in clinical research sponsored by the National Institute of Mental Health (NIMH). Cook joined the faculty of UIC as a professor of sociology in psychiatry and also served as research director of the Thresholds National Research and Training Center on Long-Term Mental Illness in Chicago. She has risen to the position of director of the Center on Mental Health Service Research Program in UIC's Department of Psychiatry.

Under Cook's leadership, UIC has become one of the nation's leading research centers in the area of mental health and disability. The Department of Psychiatry includes two federally funded programs: the National Research and Training Center on Psychiatric Disability, which "promotes access to effective consumer-driven and community-based services for adults with serious mental illness"; and the Coordinating Center for the Employment Intervention Demonstration, which focuses on finding "new ways of enhancing employment opportunities and quality of life for mental health consumers." Cook also oversees UIC's Assertive Community Treatment (ACT) Training Institute. ACT is an established model for delivering mental health services to communities, and the institute seeks to enhance ACT services throughout the state of Illinois.

Cook's work at UIC has brought her national recognition as an expert in the mental health field. In 2002 she was tapped to participate in President George W. Bush's New Freedom Commission on Mental Health. She contributed a report to a commission subcommittee on the importance of employment and income supports to the process of rehabilitation or recovery from mental disorders. Cook also serves as a consultant with the U.S. Department of Labor, the Veteran's Administration, the National Institute of Mental Health, and other government agencies.

Cook has written extensively, with more than 150 published books, chapters, and peer-reviewed journal articles to her credit on a wide range of mental health topics, such as gender issues in mental health, the importance of self-determination in recovery, psychiatric rehabilitation, and women with HIV/AIDS. She has won numerous honors and awards, including the 2010 Researcher of the Year Award from UIC.

Further Reading

Cook, J. A., et al. (2005). Clinical factors associated with employment among people with severe mental illness: Findings from the employment intervention demonstration program. *Journal of Nervous and Mental Disease, 193*(11), 705–713.

Cook, J. A., & Burke, J. (2002). Public policy and employment of people with disabilities: Exploring new paradigms. *Behavioral Science and the Law, 20*(6), 541–557.

Cook, J. A., Leff, S., Blyler, C., Gold, P., Goldberg, R., Mueser, K., Toprac, M., et al. (2005). Results of a multi-site randomized trial of supported employment interventions for individuals with severe mental illness. *Archives of General Psychiatry, 62*(50), 505–512.

Cook, J. A., & Razzano, L. (2000). Vocational rehabilitation for persons with schizophrenia: Recent research and implications for practice. *Schizophrenia Bulletin, 26*(1), 87–103.

Judith A. Cook. Retrieved from http://www.psych.uic.edu/index.php?option=com_content&view=article&id=243:judith-a-cook&catid=54&Itemid=284

Judith A. Cook. Retrieved from http://www.socialinequities.ca/bio/judith-cook

Timothy R. Elliott (1956–)

American educator and expert in rehabilitation psychology

Timothy R. Elliott was born on November 7, 1956, in Montgomery, Alabama. He attended Freed-Hardeman University in Henderson, Tennessee, where he received his bachelor of science degree in 1979. He then moved on to Auburn University, completing his master's degree in rehabilitation counseling in 1982. He served a clinical internship with the Seattle Veteran's Administration Medical Center while working on his Ph.D. in counseling psychology, which he received from the University of Missouri-Columbia in 1987. He is married to Nancy Hampton Elliott and has two daughters, Natalie and Victoria.

Elliott began his professional career as an educator in 1987, when he joined the faculty of Virginia Commonwealth University as an assistant professor in the Department of Psychology. In 1993 he moved to the University of Alabama at Birmingham, where he established himself as a leading researcher and writer in the field of rehabilitation psychology. Elliott received the Fritz and Linn Kuder Early Career Scientist/Practitioner Award from the American Psychological Association (APA) in 1993, and he became a full professor in 2003. In 2006 Elliott joined the faculty of Texas A&M University, one of the top research universities in the country, as a professor in the Department of Educational Psychology and training director of the Counseling Psychology Doctoral Program.

Elliott has published hundreds of scholarly articles and book chapters in the area of rehabilitation psychology, and he partnered with Robert G. Frank to edit the groundbreaking resource *Handbook of Rehabilitation Psychology,* published in 2000. He has served as the editor of the journal *Rehabilitation Psychology* since 2005 and is on the editorial boards of several other journals. His work has been especially important in the area of understanding the personal, family, and community adjustments required in the wake of long-term disability and chronic illness. Elliott has also led a team of graduate students at Texas A&M in working to improve the mental and physical care provided to disabled veterans of the wars in Iraq and Afghanistan.

Elliott has received international recognition and numerous awards for his work. In 2009 he received the Roger G. Barker Distinguished Research Contribution Award, which is presented annually by the APA to an individual who has "made an outstanding lifelong contribution to rehabilitation psychology through empirical research, conceptual/theoretical development or both."

Further Reading

Elliott, T., Herrick, S., & Witty, T. (1992). Problem solving appraisal and the effects of social support among college students and persons with physical disabilities. *Journal of Counseling Psychology, 39*(2), 219–226.

Elliott, T., Kurylo, M., & Rivera, P. (2002). Positive growth following an acquired physical disability. In C. R. Snyder & S. Lopez (Eds.), *Handbook of positive psychology* (pp. 687–699). New York, NY: Oxford University Press.

Elliott, T., & Leung, P. (2005). Vocational rehabilitation: history and practice. In W. B. Walsh & M. Savickas (Eds.), *Handbook of vocational psychology* (3rd ed., pp. 319–343). New York, NY: Lawrence Erlbaum Press.

Peterson, D., & Elliott, T. (2008). Advances in conceptualizing and studying disability. In R. Lent & S. Brown (Eds.), *Handbook of counseling psychology* (4th ed., pp. 212–230). New York, NY: Wiley.

Timothy R. Elliott. Retrieved from http://people.cehd.tamu.edu/~telliott

Ellen S. Fabian

American educator dedicated to program and job development for people with disabilities

Ellen S. Fabian attended the University of Wisconsin at Madison, where she received a bachelor's degree in English in 1973 and a master's degree in rehabilitation counseling in 1981. Having developed a passion for psychiatric rehabilitation and counseling, she continued to pursue this field of study at the University of Maryland, where she received a Ph.D. in counselor education in 1988.

Fabian started her professional career in 1988 at George Washington University as an assistant professor in the Department of Human Services.

In 1990 she moved on to Pennsylvania State University as an assistant professor and coordinator of the Rehabilitation Counseling Program. The following year she was honored by the National Council on Rehabilitation Education with the New Career in Rehabilitation Education Award. At this time she also took a position as director of research with TransCen, Inc., a nonprofit organization based in Rockville, Maryland, focused on pursuing education and employment opportunities for people with disabilities.

In 1994 Fabian returned to the University of Maryland, joining the faculty as a research associate professor in the Department of Counseling and Personnel Services (CAPS), one of the top-rated departments of its kind in the United States. It is there that she established herself as a key figure in the field of rehabilitation counseling and program and employment development for people with disabilities. Fabian serves as director of the Rehabilitation Counseling Program and principal investigator of the Regional Rehabilitation Continuing Education Program for Community Rehabilitation Personnel.

Fabian has written dozens of book chapters, monographs, and peer-reviewed articles in her field. She also teamed with Richard Luecking and George Tilson, both of TransCen, Inc., to write two books on developing job opportunities for people with disabilities. She serves on the editorial boards of several journals and has been the editor of the *Journal of Applied Rehabilitation Counseling* since 2004. In 2010 she was elected president of the Maryland Rehabilitation Association.

Further Reading

Ellen S. Fabian. Retrieved from http://www.education.umd.edu/EDCP/staff_details.cfm?bio_id=204837909040820082

Fabian, E. S., Edelman, A., & Leedy, M. (1993). Linking workers with severe disabilities to social supports in the workplace: Strategies for addressing barriers. *Journal of Rehabilitation, 59*(3), 29–34.

Fabian, E. S., & Luecking, R. G. (1991). Doing it the company way: Using internal company supports in the workplace. *Journal of Applied Rehabilitation Counseling, 22,* 32–36.

Fabian, E. S., Luecking, R. G., & Tilson, G. P. (1995). Employer and rehabilitation personnel perspectives on hiring persons with disabilities: Implications for job development. *Journal of Rehabilitation, 61*(1), 42–49.

Luecking, R., Fabian, E., & Tilson, G. (2004). *Working relationships: Creating career opportunities for job seekers with disabilities through employer partnerships.* Baltimore, MD: Paul H. Brookes.

Dennis D. Gilbride

American educator and rehabilitation counseling specialist

Dennis David Gilbride attended Sonoma State University, a small college in the San Francisco area, receiving his bachelor of arts degree in psychology in 1978. He did his postgraduate work at the University of Southern California, achieving his master's degree in counseling psychology in 1980, followed by his Ph.D. in the same area in 1985. While working on his Ph.D., Gilbride also started his professional career in rehabilitation counseling by joining Intracorp, a case management service dedicated to helping employers to assist disabled workers in their entry and/or return to the workplace. He stayed with Intracorp from 1981 through 1989, working first as a rehabilitation counselor, then serving as psychological services director.

In 1989 Gilbride returned to the academic community, joining the faculty of Drake University in Des Moines, Iowa, as an assistant professor in the Department of Counseling and Rehabilitation. During his decade-long tenure at Drake, he received recognition from the National Rehabilitation Association by being named a Switzer Scholar in 1993, and he was promoted to associate professor in 1995. In 1999 Gilbride moved to Syracuse University's School of Education, which has long been considered a leader in the "inclusion movement" for people with disabilities in both education and employment. He initially accepted a position as associate professor of counseling and human services, and he became a full professor in 2005. Gilbride also serves as the coordinator of the Rehabilitation Counseling Program and as chair of the Department of Counseling and Human Services. Under his leadership, Syracuse University continues to be a national leader in the field, becoming one of the first universities to provide a disabilities studies program.

Gilbride is a nationally recognized expert in rehabilitation counseling and in developing strategies and programs for integrating people with disabilities into the workforce. He has written extensively in the field, with dozens of journal articles, book chapters, grants, and presentations to his credit, and serves on the editorial advisory boards of the *Rehabilitation Counseling Bulletin* and *Rehabilitation Education Journal.* In addition to his academic work at Syracuse, he frequently serves as a consultant, assisting employers and agencies in program and practices evaluation, and as a counselor to people with disabilities.

Further Reading

Dennis Gilbride. Retrieved from http://soe.syr.edu/about/member.aspx?fac=52

Gilbride, D., & Hagner, D. (2005). People with disabilities in the work place. In R. Parker, E. Szymanski, & J. Patterson (Eds.), *Rehabilitation counseling: Basics and beyond* (4th ed., pp. 281–305). Austin TX: ProEd.

Gilbride, D., Stensrud, R., Ehlers, C., Evans, E., & Peterson, C. (2000). Employers' attitudes toward hiring persons with disabilities and vocational rehabilitation services. *Journal of Rehabilitation, 66*(4), 17–23.

Gilbride, D., Stensrud, R., Vandergoot, D., & Golden, K. (2003). Identification of the characteristics of work environments and employers open to hiring and accommodating people with disabilities. *Rehabilitation Counseling Bulletin, 46*(3), 130–137.

Spirito-Dalgin, R., & Gilbride, D. (2003). Perspective of people with psychiatric disabilities on employment disclosure. *Psychiatric Rehabilitation Journal, 26*(3), 306–310.

Rochelle V. Habeck

American research expert on disability
and rehabilitation in the workplace

Rochelle Virginia Habeck attended Virginia Commonwealth University, receiving a master's degree in rehabilitation counseling. She continued her postgraduate work at the University of Wisconsin, receiving a Ph.D. in rehabilitation psychology. She joined the faculty of Michigan State University in 1982 as a professor in the Department of Counseling, Educational Psychology and Special Education. She stayed at MSU until 1999 and then returned to Virginia Commonwealth as a research consultant, a position she held until 2008. Habeck is also a Licensed Professional Counselor and a Certified Rehabilitation Counselor. She previously held positions as a counselor and program coordinator in the cancer rehabilitation center at the Medical College of Virginia and at the Wisconsin Clinical Cancer Center.

Habeck is now an independent research consultant with Habeck & Associates, based in Kalamazoo, Michigan. She has partnered with business, government, and educational organizations across the country on numerous projects addressing workplace issues related to disability and rehabilitation. She has also continued her working relationship with Virginia Commonwealth University, a nationally recognized Center of Excellence and member of the Association of University Centers on Disabilities, participating in a number of projects with VCU's Rehabilitation

Research and Training Center on Workplace Supports and Job Retention. The focus of many of these projects involves studying "those supports that are most effective for assisting individuals with disabilities maintain employment and advance their careers," she explained.

Habeck has written extensively on issues related to disability and rehabilitation, focusing especially on prevention and management of disabilities in the workplace, with dozens of articles, reports, and monographs to her credit. She also serves on the editorial boards for the *Journal of Disability Policy Studies*, the *Rehabilitation Counseling Bulletin*, and the *Journal of Vocational Rehabilitation*.

Further Reading

Amick, B., Habeck, R., Hunt, A., Fossel, A., Chapin, A., Keller, R., & Katz, J. (2000). Measuring the impact of organizational behavior on work disability prevention and management. *Journal of Occupation Rehabilitation, 10*(1), 21–38.

Habeck, R., et al. (1991). Employer factors related to workers' compensation claims and disability management. *Rehabilitation Counseling Bulletin, 34*(3), 210–226.

Habeck, R., Hunt, A., & VanTol, B. (1998). Workplace factors associated with preventing and managing work disability. *Rehabilitation Counseling Bulletin, 42*(2), 98–143.

Hunt, A., Habeck, R., Owens, P., & Vandergoot, D. (1996). Disability and work: Lessons from the private sector. In J. L. Mashaw, V. Reno, R. V. Burkhauser, & M. Berkowitz (Eds.), *Disability, work and cash benefits* (pp. 245–272). Kalamazoo, MI: W.E. Upjohn Institute for Employment Research.

Rochelle Habeck. Retrieved from http://www.worksupport.com/about_us/bio.cfm?id=88

Allen W. Heinemann

American educator and leader in the field of rehabilitation research

Allen W. Heinemann attended Washington State University, where he received his bachelor of science degree in psychology in 1977. After moving on to the University of Kansas for his post-graduate work, he began pursuing his lifelong interest in rehabilitation research. In 1980 he received his master's degree in clinical psychology, specializing in rehabilitation, followed two years later by his Ph.D., also in clinical psychology. His time at Kansas also included a training fellowship with the Rehabilitation Services Administration.

Heinemann has spent his entire professional career in the Chicago area, starting in 1982 when he joined the faculty of the Illinois Institute of Technology (IIT) as an assistant professor of rehabilitation programs in the Psychology Department. In 1984, while still with IIT, he started his association with the Rehabilitation Institute of Chicago (RIC), which is consistently recognized as one of the top rehabilitation hospitals in the United States. Following four years as a research consultant, Heinemann was appointed director of RIC's Center for Rehabilitation Outcomes Research, a position he has held ever since. In 1996 he added the title of associate director of research for the entire RIC. Meanwhile, he continued his academic career, moving to Northwestern University Medical School's Department of Physical Medicine and Rehabilitation in 1985. By 1999 he had achieved full professorship in both that department and in Northwestern's Institute of Healthcare Studies.

From these positions with RIC and Northwestern, Heinemann has established himself as a nationally recognized leader in the field of rehabilitation research. The main focus of his work involves the psychological and coping processes resulting from traumatic injuries and disabilities such as spinal cord injuries, substance abuse, and stroke. He has written and contributed to hundreds of books, articles, abstracts, reviews, and presentations. He has also edited two published books and serves on the editorial boards of a number of journals. Among the dozens of research projects he has led and participated in was the 2008 "Second Chances" study of the quality of life following stroke.

Heinemann has received frequent recognition for his work. His numerous awards include the Roger G. Barker Distinguished Research Contribution award from the Rehabilitation Psychology Division of the American Psychological Association in 2000. He is also a leading member of the American Congress of Rehabilitation Medicine, serving as president in 2004–2005 and also being designated as a Fellow in 2005 for his "significant contributions to the field of medical rehabilitation."

Further Reading

Allen W. Heinemann. Retrieved from http://www.ric.org/aboutus/people/doctors/results.aspx?doctorID=99

Allen W. Heinemann. Retrieved from http://www.feinberg.northwestern.edu/ihs/faculty-staff/heinemann-a.html

Boni-Saenz, A., Heinemann A. W., Crown D. S., & Emanuel, L. L. (2006). The business of employing people with disabilities: Four case studies. *Organizational Ethics, 3*(1), 3–16.

Hedrick, B., Pape, T. L.-B., Heinemann, A. W., Ruddell, J. L., & Reis, J. (2006). Employment issues and assistive technology use for persons with spinal cord injury. *Journal of Rehabilitation Research and Development, 43*(2), 185–198.

Heinemann, A. W. (1993). *Substance abuse and physical disability.* New York, NY: Haworth Press.

Smith, C., Edwards, J., Heinemann, A. W., & Geist, C. (1985). Attitudes toward and performance evaluations of workers with disabilities. *Journal of Applied Rehabilitation Counseling, 16,* 39–41.

H. Stephen Kaye

American researcher and leading advocate for accessibility for people with disabilities

H. Stephen Kaye attended Stanford University, receiving his Ph.D. in 1983. He has been involved in disability research since 1995, primarily as a member of the faculty at the University of California, San Francisco (UCSF), where he serves as an associate adjunct professor in the Institute for Health and Aging and the Department of Social and Behavioral Sciences. Kaye is also a leader in UCSF's Center for Personal Assistance Services (CPAS), where he has served as a co-principal investigator since 2003, and in UCSF's Disability Statistics Center, where he has held the position of research director since 2000.

Kaye has done critical work in analyzing the progress, and lack of progress, made by people with disabilities in America, especially in access to employment and technology. His report "Computer and Internet Use Among People with Disabilities," published in 2000 by the National Institute on Disability and Rehabilitation Research, showed that while people with disabilities potentially had the most to gain from using emerging computer technologies, they continued to lag far behind the rest of the population in actual use of those technologies, due primarily to lack of access. In the area of employment for the disabled, Kaye contributed a key and controversial chapter to the book *The Decline in Employment of People with Disabilities* in which he presented statistical evidence of the long-term impact of the 1990s recession on people with disabilities and their ability to return to work.

In numerous articles and reports, Kaye has pushed for ongoing vigilance to improve the status of people with disabilities in American society.

He argues that in spite of the passage of the Americans with Disabilities Act in 1990, people with disabilities continue to struggle to achieve equal access to jobs and services. More recently, he has focused his efforts on analyzing the cost and availability of long-term care and services for the chronically disabled.

Dr. Kaye has written and contributed to hundreds of articles and reports, and his work is frequently cited by peers and colleagues in the field of disability and rehabilitation. He has also served as program chair for the Disability Forum of the American Public Health Association.

Further Reading

H. Stephen Kaye. Retrieved from http://www.pascenter.org/about/bios.php

Kaye, H. S. (2003). Employment and the changing disability population. In D. C. Stapleton & R. V. Burkhauser (Eds.). *The decline in employment of people with disabilities.* Kalamazoo, MI: W. E. Upjohn Institute for Employment Research.

Kaye, H. S. (2009). Stuck at the bottom rung: Occupational characteristics of workers with disabilities. *Journal of Occupational Rehabilitation, 19*(2), 115–128.

William E. Kiernan (1945–)

American researcher and leading advocate for inclusion of people with disabilities in all walks of life

William E. Kiernan attended Boston University, where he received master's degrees in rehabilitation counseling and business administration, with a concentration in health care management. He went on to complete a Ph.D. in rehabilitation and special education at Boston College. Kiernan has maintained his connection with academia, serving for nearly 20 years as a research professor in the Graduate College of Education of the McCormack School of Policy Studies at the University of Massachusetts at Boston. It is in his association with the Institute for Community Inclusion (ICI), however, that he has made a major impact as an advocate for people with disabilities of all types.

ICI was first established in 1967, in response to President John F. Kennedy's challenge to the nation to improve support and training for people with mental retardation. It was one of the first institutions of its kind in the United States, and one of the first to be identified as a "University Center for Excellence in Developmental Disabilities." There are now 67 such institutions across the country. Kiernan has been involved with ICI for more than 35 years and now serves as director of the institute. He has also served as president of the Association of University Centers on Disabilities (AUCD).

With these positions as a platform, Kiernan has become a leading voice in advocating inclusion and equality in the community, in schools, and in the workplace for people with disabilities of all kinds. He is consulted frequently as an expert in developing training systems for people with disabilities and in assisting with the transition from disability to integral member of the community. He has also played an important role in helping communities overcome prejudices and misconceptions toward people with disabilities. He has been involved in program development across the United States and internationally, having served as a consultant in seven countries.

Kiernan has written extensively in the field of disability research and advocacy, with several books and more than 125 journal articles and reports to his credit. He has received national recognition and numerous awards for his work. In 2007 he received the Joseph M. Collins Human Service Award from the Massachusetts Association for the Blind, and in 2010 he was invited to attend the 20th Anniversary of the Americans with Disabilities Act celebration hosted by President Barack Obama.

Further Reading

Interview with William Kiernan, Institute for Community Inclusion. (2010, February 28). *Boston Sunday Review*. Retrieved from http://wn.com/william_kiernan_interview?orderby=rating

Kiernan, W. E. (1986). *Pathways to employment for adults with developmental disabilities*. Baltimore, MD: Paul H. Brookes Publishing Co.

Kiernan, W. E. (2000). Where are we now? Perspectives on employment of persons with mental retardation. *Focus on Autism and Other Developmental Disabilities, 15*(2), 90–97

Kiernan, W. E., et al. (1988). Employment environments and outcome for adults with developmental disabilities. *Mental Retardation, 26*(5), 279–288.

Kiernan, W. E., & Marrone, J. (1997). Quality of work life for persons with disabilities: Emphasis on the employee. In R. Schalock (Ed.), *Quality of life: Application to persons with disabilities* (pp. 63–78). Washington, DC: American Association on Mental Retardation.

Kiernan, W. E., & McGaughey, M. (1992). A support mechanism for the worker with a disability. *Journal of Rehabilitation, 58*(2), 56–63.

William E. Kiernan. Retrieved from http://www.communityinclusion.org/staff.php?staff_id=138

John F. Kosciulek

*American academic focusing on issues in
employment and work for people with disabilities*

John F. Kosciulek received his Ph.D. from the University of Wisconsin at Madison. He taught at the University of Missouri at Columbia's College of Education before joining the faculty of Michigan State University in 2001. He is currently a professor and director of the master's program in rehabilitation counseling in Michigan State's Department of Counseling, Educational Psychology, and Special Education.

A former National Institute on Disability and Rehabilitation Research Switzer Fellow, Kosciulek focuses his research on many areas of education, employment, and disability, including the development of disability policies, the delivery of rehabilitation services, school-to-career transition issues for students with and without disabilities, and the issues confronting family members of patients with brain injury.

Kosciulek is perhaps best known for introducing the Consumer-Directed Theory of Empowerment to rehabilitation services. This theory proposes that consumers of rehabilitation services be given greater control over the services they receive, so that in the process they will develop skills that will enable them to gain greater control over their lives and environment. "Many people with disabilities are often denied the opportunity to exercise choice and control over the most basic aspects of daily life," Kosciulek wrote in a 1999 article for the *Journal of Rehabilitation.* "Consumer direction is an approach to the development of disability policy and delivery of rehabilitation services whereby informed consumers have control and the opportunity to make choices. In a consumer-directed system, individuals with disabilities assess their own needs, determine how and by whom these needs should be met, and monitor the quality of services received."

Kosciulek has also been involved with a clinical rehabilitation counseling practice and in rehabilitation counselor education. The author of dozens of articles and book chapters, he has also served as co-editor of the professional journal *Rehabilitation Education.*

Further Reading

John Kosciulek. Retrieved from http://www.educ.msu.edu/cepse/faculty.asp

Kosciulek, J. F. (2000). Implications for consumer direction for disability policy development and rehabilitation service delivery. *Journal of Disability Policy Studies, 11*(2), 82–89.

Kosciulek, J. F. (2003). Empowering people with disabilities through career counseling. In N. C. Gysbers, M. J. Heppner, & J. A. Johnston (Eds.), *Career counseling: Process, issues, and techniques* (2nd ed.) (pp. 139–153). Boston, MA: Allyn & Bacon.

Kosciulek, J. F. (2007). A test of the theory of informed consumer choice in vocational rehabilitation. *Journal of Rehabilitation, 73*(2), 41–5.

Kosciulek, J. F., & Vessell, R. (1997). Consumer satisfaction with vocational rehabilitation services. *Journal of Rehabilitation, 63*(2), 5–9.

James S. Krause

*American disability researcher focusing on
rehabilitation and employment after spinal cord injury*

James S. Krause sustained a spinal cord injury at the age of 16 and is a tetraplegic. He attended the University of Minnesota, receiving his bachelor's degree in psychology in 1980 and his doctoral degree in 1990.

Krause began his research career at the Shepherd Center in Atlanta, one of the top rehabilitation centers in the nation for spinal cord injuries, working there from 1990 to 2000. In 2000 he joined the faculty of the Medical University of South Carolina, where he is professor and associate dean for clinical research in the College of Health Professions. He is currently the director of the Program for Movement, Exercise, and Rehabilitation Research at the university, and he also serves as scientific director of the South Carolina Spinal Cord Injury Research Fund, an organization that funds basic, applied, and interdisciplinary studies of spinal cord injury.

Krause's research focuses on various aspects of life after spinal cord injury, including its long-term effects on physical health, rehabilitation, work, and psychosocial development. He has been the principal investigator on 12 federal research studies of long-term outcomes of spinal cord injury, including a 35-year longitudinal study and others involving mortality studies, vocational opportunities, and secondary conditions. He also worked on studies for the Centers for Disease Control's National Center for Injury Prevention and Control, contributing to a study of traumatic brain injury and spinal cord injury for state health agencies. He has also been a contributing researcher and consultant in South Carolina, where he works with the South Carolina Spinal Cord Injury Association, and in Georgia, where he works as a consultant on the Georgia Model Spinal Cord Injury Systems Center.

Krause is also a prolific author, and he has published more than 90 articles and given more than 150 presentations in his field of expertise. He is the recipient of many awards, including the Garrett Early Career Award, the National Association of Rehabilitation Research and Training Centers Research Award, and the Patricia McCollom Memorial Research Award from the Foundation for Life Care Planning.

Further Reading

James Krause. Retrieved from http://www.musc.edu/chp/faculty/krause.htm

Krause, J. S. (1992). Employment after spinal cord injury. *Archives of Physical Medicine and Rehabilitation, 73,* 163–169.

Krause, J. S., & Anson, C. A. (1997). Adjustment after spinal cord injury: Relationship to participation in employment or educational activities. *Rehabilitation Counseling Bulletin, 40*(3), 202–214.

Krause, J. S., & Pickelsimer, E. (2008). Relationship of perceived barriers to employment and return to work five years later: A pilot study among 343 participants with spinal cord injury. *Rehabilitation Counseling Bulletin, 51*(2), 118–121.

Krause, J. S., Terza, J. V., Saunders, L. L., & Dismuke, C. E. (2010). Delayed entry into employment after spinal cord injury: Factors related to time to first job. *Spinal Cord, 48,* 487–491.

John Kregel

*American researcher focusing on
special education and disability policy*

John Kregel is currently a member of the faculty of the School of Education at Virginia Commonwealth University, in the department of Special Education and Disability Policy. He is the associate director of the university's Rehabilitation Research and Training Center on Workplace Supports and Retention. In his research, Kregel focuses on employment issues for people with disabilities, including Social Security, training, obtaining and maintaining employment, opportunities for advancement, and promoting economic self-sufficiency among working people with disabilities. He has also worked with veterans with traumatic brain injuries and spinal cord injuries as they attempt to return to work. In addition to working with adults with disabilities, Kregel has done research into improving post-secondary education and subsequent employment opportunities for adolescents with disabilities, including autism.

Kregel has published books and articles on the subject of employment for people with disabilities, and he has developed programs to help disabled people gain financial literacy to increase their self-sufficiency in money matters. He has testified before the U.S. Congress's Social Security Subcommittee of the House Ways and Means Committee on work issues, specifically incentives planning and assistance for people with disabilities so that they can find employment and reduce their dependence on Social Security benefits.

Further Reading

John Kregel. Retrieved from http://www.soe.vcu.edu/faculty/facpages/jkregel.html

Kregel, J., Wehman, P., & Banks, P. D. (1989). The effects of consumer characteristics and type of employment model on individual outcomes in supported employment. *Journal of Applied Behavior Analysis, 22*(4), 407–415.

Miller, L., & Kregel, J. (2008). The role of veteran's disability benefits in community reintegration and employment of service members with TBI. In P. Wehman, J. Kregel, & V. Brooke (Eds.), *Workplace supports and job retention: Promoting an employer driven approach to employment of people with disabilities.* Richmond, VA: Virginia Commonwealth University.

Wehman, P., & Kregel, J. (1998). *More than a job: Securing satisfying careers for people with disabilities.* Baltimore, MD: Paul H. Brookes.

Wehman, P., Targett, P., West, M., & Kregel, J. (2005). Productive work and employment for persons with traumatic brain injury: What have we learned after 20 years? *Journal of Head Trauma Rehabilitation, 20*(2), 115–127.

Douglas L. Kruse (1959–)

American economist focusing on the effects of disability on employment

Douglas L. Kruse was born on March 19, 1959, in Kearney, Nebraska. He received his bachelor's degree in economics from Harvard University in 1981, his master's degree in economics from the University of Nebraska in 1983, and his doctoral degree in economics from Harvard in 1988.

Kruse is currently a professor in the School of Management and Labor Relations at Rutgers University, where he is director of the Program for Disability Research. He is also a research associate with the National Bureau of Economic Research in Cambridge, Massachusetts. Kruse's research focuses on the effects of disability on employment. He has served on the President's Committee on Employment of People with Disabilities and was appointed by the governor of New Jersey to serve on the State Rehabilitation Council. He has also testified before the U.S. Congress on labor issues as they affect people with disabilities and is working with the U.S. Department of Labor Statistics on the design of new questions regarding disability for the monthly survey of employment.

Kruse is the recipient of several grants in the area of disability and employment. He served as the co-investigator for a five-year cooperative study with the Disability Research Institute and the Social Security Administration, in which he studied the impact of employment on people with disabilities receiving disability income. He was also co-investigator of a study for the National Institute on Disability and Rehabilitation Research that examined the political behavior of U.S. citizens with disabilities. As co-investigator for a study of computer use among disabled adults, he researched how computer technologies affect employment and earning power among mobility-impaired individuals.

Kruse has published many books and articles on disability and employment issues, including *Spinal Cord Injury: An Analysis of Medical and Social Costs,* and also serves on the board of reviewers of *Industrial Relations.* He is a member of the American Economic Association, the Labor and Employment Relations Association, and the Society for Disability Studies.

Further Reading

Blanck, P., Schur, L., Kruse, D., Schwochau, S., & Song, C. (2003). Calibrating the impact of the ADA's employment provisions. *Stanford Law and Policy Review, 14*(2), 267–290.

Douglas Kruse. Retrieved from http://smlr.rutgers.edu/DougKruse

Kruse, D. (1998). Persons with disabilities: Demographic, income, and health care characteristics. *Monthly Labor Review, 121*(9), 8–15.

Kruse, D., & Schur, L. (2003, January). Employment of people with disabilities following the ADA. *Industrial Relations, 42*(1), 31–66.

Schur, L., Kruse, D., & Blank, P. (2005). Corporate culture and the employment of people with disabilities. *Behavioral Sciences and the Law, 23,* 3–20.

David Mank

American researcher specializing in the employment of people with disabilities

David Mank received his bachelor's degree in psychology and English from Rockhurst College in 1975, his master's degree in special education from Portland State University in 1977, and his doctoral degree in special education and rehabilitation from the University of Oregon in 1985. While still a graduate student, Mank helped create Oregon's first free-standing supported employment program and worked in the specialized training program at the University of Oregon's Division of Special Education and Rehabilitation.

Mank is currently the director of the Indiana Institute on Disability and Community at Indiana University's Center for Excellence on Disabilities, and he is also a professor in Indiana's School of Education, Department of Curriculum and Instruction. The focus of his research is disability policy, especially in the area of education and supported employment of people with disabilities. As director of the Indiana Institute on Disability and Community, he coordinates research issues in disability across the life span, with projects focusing on early intervention; school improvement and inclusion; transition, employment, and careers; age-related change; autism spectrum disorders; planning and policy; and disability information and referral.

Mank has directed several major projects funded by federal and state agencies, as well as nongovernmental organizations. From 1996 to 1999, he served as project director of the Community Partnership Initiative for the U.S. Department of Education's Office of Special Education and Rehabilitation Services. From 1997 to 2002, he was the associate director of the National Supported Employment Consortium for the U.S. Department of Education's Rehabilitation Services Administration. From 1997 to 2003, he was the director of state appropriation for the Indiana Institute on Disability and Community. He also served as the project director of the program "The Impact of Employing People with Disabilities" for the Joseph P. Kennedy Jr. Foundation from 1996 to 1999.

A prolific author, Mank has written more than 100 articles or book chapters, and he serves on the editorial boards of *Mental Retardation, Journal of Disability Policy Studies,* and *The Journal of the Association for People with Severe Handicaps.* He is a member of the board of the Association of University Centers on Disabilities, where he served as president from 1999–2000. A founding board member of United States Association for Persons in Supported Employment, Mank received the Franklin Smith Award for National Distinguished Service from the Arc of the United States in 2001.

Further Reading

Brown, D. S., Bruyere, S. M., & Mank, D. M. (1997). Quality through equality: Total quality management applied to the implementation of Title I of the Americans with Disabilities Act. *Journal of Vocational Rehabilitation, 9*(3), 253–266.

David Mank. Retrieved from http://www.indiana.edu/~iuncate/facultyvita/dmank.html

Mank, D. M., Cioffi, A. R., & Yovanoff, P. (1999). The impact of coworker involvement with supported employees on wage and integration outcomes. *Mental Retardation, 37*(5), 383–394.

Mank, D., Cioffi, A., & Yovanoff, P. (2000). Direct support in supported employment and its relation to job typicalness, co-worker involvement, and employment outcomes. *Mental Retardation, 38*(6), 506–516.

Olson, D., Cioffi, A., Mank, D., & Yovanoff, P. (2001). Employers' perceptions of employees with mental retardation. *Journal of Vocational Rehabilitation, 16*(2), 125–133.

Brian T. McMahon (1951–)

American researcher focusing on workplace discrimination against people with disabilities

Brian T. McMahon was born in 1951 in Chicago, Illinois. He received his bachelor of science degree from Loyola University in 1972, his master's in rehabilitation counseling from the Illinois Institute of Technology in 1974, and his doctoral degree in rehabilitation psychology from the University of Wisconsin in 1977.

After receiving his Ph.D., McMahon worked as a health care administrator for several years. In 1988, when the early drafts of the Americans with Disabilities Act (ADA) came out, he considered the legislation so important that he decided to make its impact on employment and disability the focus of his career. In 1990 he joined the faculty of the University of Wisconsin at Milwaukee, where he taught until 1997. That year, he joined the faculty of Virginia Commonwealth University, where he holds appointments in four schools, including the Medical School's Department of Physical Medicine and Rehabilitation and the School of Allied Health Professions' Department of Rehabilitation Counseling. The focus of his research is workplace discrimination against people with disabilities as defined by the ADA, and he directs that research in collaboration with the U.S. Equal Opportunity Employment Commission (EEOC).

In 2003 McMahon, the EEOC, and researchers from 12 universities began a long-term study of workplace discrimination. Funded by the National Institute of Disability and Rehabilitation Research and housed at Virginia Commonwealth University, the project's researchers have profiled over 369,000 allegations of discrimination against people with disabilities, using data provided by the EEOC. This database of information is helping researchers to document and define workplace discrimination, "so that over time we can eliminate it entirely from our society," McMahon explained. The project's goal is to create a "flat earth" with all barriers removed, whether in architecture, attitude, or education. In 2007 McMahon and his colleagues received the Kevin Karr Innovative Rehabilitation System of the Year award for their contributions to the project and to the advancement of rehabilitation systems for people with disabilities.

In 2007 Virginia Commonwealth University's Department of Rehabilitation Counseling received a $4.25 million grant from the National Institute on Disability and Rehabilitation Research. The grant was used to establish the Coordination, Outreach, and Research Center at the university, with McMahon as its director. Its purpose is to continue to find ways to minimize workplace discrimination against people with disabilities through implementation of the ADA.

McMahon has served at the executive level for several national organizations in his field, including the American Rehabilitative Counseling Association and the American Counseling Association. He is also a prolific author and has written or co-written many articles in his field for professionals. He has also edited a book for general readers, *Enabling Lives*, which profiles some of the champions of the disability movement.

Further Reading

Brian McMahon (2009, June). The Disability Advocate. Retrieved from http:// rpse.education.wisc.edu/newsletter/post/Alumni-Profile-Brian -McMahon.aspx

Chan, F., McMahon, B. T., Cheing, G., Rosenthal, D., & Bezyak, J. (2005). Drivers of workplace discrimination against people with disabilities: The utility of attribution theory. *Work: A Journal of Prevention, Assessment, and Rehabilitation, 25*(1), 77–88.

Conyers, L., Boomer, K. B., & McMahon, B. T. (2005). Workplace discrimination and HIV/AIDS: The national EEOC ADA research project. *Work: A Journal of Prevention, Assessment, and Rehabilitation, 25*(1), 37–48.

McMahon, B. T., & Shaw, L. (2005). Workplace discrimination and disability. *Journal of Vocational Rehabilitation, 23*(3), 137–143.

McMahon, B. T., Shaw, L., West, S., & Waid-Ebbs, K. (2005). Workplace discrimination and spinal cord injury: The national EEOC ADA research project. *Journal of Vocational Rehabilitation, 23*(3), 155–162.

Frederick E. Menz (1941–)

*American academic researcher specializing in community
rehabilitation and employment of people with disabilities*

Frederick E. Menz was born on October 20, 1941, in Chicago, Illinois. He
received his bachelor's degree from Illinois State University in 1964. He
then moved to the University of Illinois, where he earned his master's
degree in guidance and counseling in 1967, and his Ph.D. in educational
psychology in 1970.

Menz began his career as a research associate in the education and testing department of the Educational Research Council of America, a position that combined his interests in educational measurement and statistics
and research evaluation. In 1972 he joined the faculty of the University of
Wisconsin-Stout, where he was director of the Research and Training Center for Community-Based Rehabilitation Programs, which was funded by
the National Institute on Disability and Rehabilitation Research. He was
also the director of the Continuing Education Center for Community-
Based Rehabilitation for the university, and also served as a fellow with
the Disability Research Institute and as a co-sponsor for the Institutes on
Rehabilitation Issues.

Early in his academic career, Menz focused on the training of rehabilitation professionals as well as on the development of community-level rehabilitation facilities and programs. More recently, his focus has shifted to
studying both the barriers confronting and the strategies assisting people
with disabilities and minorities as they seek to enter the workforce. To this
end, he was engaged in the development of models that helped predict the
opportunities for people with severe disabilities to find employment.

Menz has authored or co-authored more than 100 papers or book chapters in his area of expertise. He is also past president of the National Association of Rehabilitation Research and Training Centers Association and the
Association for the Education of Community-Based Rehabilitation Personnel. In 2004 he headed a focus group at the Stout Vocational Rehabilitation
Institute's Research and Training Center, collating data from 10 community
rehabilitation programs from across the United States in the preparation of
a study seeking to identify and implement programs to increase the opportunities for recipients of Social Security benefits to return to work.

In 1998 Menz received the award for Outstanding Researcher of the Year
from the National Council on Rehabilitation Education, which is given in
recognition of accomplishments in advancing the rehabilitation counseling

profession. In 2009 he received the Yvonne Johnson National Leadership Award from the National Rehabilitation Association. Now a professor emeritus, Menz continues to write, lecture, and consult in his field.

Further Reading

Menz, F. E., Hagen-Foley, D., & Gerber, A. (2005). *Community-based rehabilitation programs, phase II: Service, beneficiary, outcome, and organizational models and perceived barriers to pursuing work goals: Final Report*. Urbana-Champaign, IL: University of Illinois, Disability Research Institute.

Menz, F. E., Hansen, G., Smith, H., Brown, C., Ford, M., & McCrowey, G. (1989). Gender equity in access, services, and benefits from vocational rehabilitation. *Journal of Rehabilitation, 55*(1), 31–40.

Thomas, D., Menz, F. E., & Rosenthal, D. (2001). Employment outcome expectancies: Consensus among consumers, providers, and funding agents of community rehabilitation programs. *Journal of Rehabilitation, 67*(3), 26–34.

Richard T. Roessler (1944–)

American academic researcher focusing on rehabilitation education

Richard T. Roessler was born in 1944. He received his bachelor's degree from DePauw University, and his master's and doctoral degrees in education and psychology from Claremont Graduate School.

Roessler is currently professor emeritus at the University of Arkansas, where he was professor of rehabilitation education and research rehabilitation in the Department of Human Resources and Communication at the College of Education and Health Professions. His research has focused on several key areas in disability studies, including the adjustment to chronic illness and disability, employment placement, career development, and discrimination in employment for people with disabilities. He has done extensive research involving multiple sclerosis patients and the effect of the disease on employment.

Roessler is a member of the American Rehabilitation Counseling Association, the National Rehabilitation Association, and the National Council on Rehabilitation. He is also the recipient of grants from the National Institute on Disability and Rehabilitation Research, the National Multiple Sclerosis Society, the Social Security Administration, and the Rehabilitation Services Administration.

Roessler is the co-author of several books and many journal articles, including two books that are standard texts for graduate education in rehabilitation, *Foundations of the Vocational Rehabilitation Process* and *Case Management and Rehabilitation Counseling*. In addition, he is the co-author of *Life-Centered Career Education*, a textbook that is widely used in special education programs. He has received several awards for teaching, including the National Council on Rehabilitation's Distinguished Career in Rehabilitation Education Award and the American Rehabilitation Counseling Association's James Garrett Distinguished Career Award. Roessler continues to write and consult, and he is also a licensed psychologist, certified rehabilitation counselor, and licensed counselor.

Further Reading

Mullins, J., & Roessler, R. T. (1997). Improving employment outcomes through quality rehabilitation. *Journal of Rehabilitation, 63*(4), 21–31.

Richard T. Roessler. Retrieved from http://coehp.uark.edu/1624.php

Roessler, R. (2002). Improving job tenure outcomes for people with disabilities: The "3M" Model. *Rehabilitation Counseling Bulletin, 45*(3), 207–212.

Roessler, R. T., Rumrill, P. D., & Fitzgerald, S. M. (2004). Predictors of employment status for people with multiple sclerosis. *Rehabilitation Counseling Bulletin, 47*(2), 96–103.

Unger, D., Rumrill, P. D., Roessler, R. T., & Stacklin, R. (2004). A comparative analysis of employment discrimination complaints filed by people with multiple sclerosis and individuals with other disabilities. *Journal of Vocational Rehabilitation, 20*(3), 165–170.

Patricia Rogan (1956–)

American academic researcher focusing on education, transition, and employment issues in people with disabilities

Patricia Rogan was born on January 27, 1956, in Indianapolis, Indiana. She attended the University of Wisconsin, where she received her bachelor of science degree in special education in 1978, her master's degree in behavioral disabilities in 1985, and her doctoral degree in rehabilitation psychology and special education in 1987.

Rogan began her career in education in the public school system in Madison, Wisconsin, where she was a teacher of students with severe disabilities, a community vocational teacher, a transition coordinator, the coordinator of a community living project, and a consulting teacher. In 1987 Rogan joined the faculty of Syracuse University, where she was a professor in the Division of Special Education and Rehabilitation. In 1993 she joined the faculty of Indiana University, where she is currently an associate professor in the School of Education at the Indiana University Purdue University campus in Indianapolis. In addition to her duties at the Indianapolis campus, Rogan is a member of the reference faculty at the Institute for the Study of Developmental Disabilities at the main campus for Indiana University in Bloomington.

Rogan's research focuses on several areas of disability studies, including teacher training, secondary special education (especially in the urban environment), employment issues in disability, and transition issues for people with disabilities across the life span, especially in the area of the movement from school to work.

Rogan is a member of the National Association for Persons in Supported Employment and chair of the Indiana State Conversion Task Force. A prolific author, she has contributed to many professional publications and is also the co-author of three books, *Developing Natural Supports in the Workplace* and *Closing the Shop: Conversion from Sheltered to Integrated Work*, both with Steve Murphy, and *Make the Day Matter: Promoting Typical Lifestyles for Adults with Significant Disabilities*, with Pam Walker. She also serves on the editorial board of the American Association on Mental Retardation and is co-editor of the National TASH *Newsletter on Transition and Supported Employment*.

Rogan is the recipient of several major national grants. She is the principal investigator of the Urban Education Excellence Urban Teacher Residency for the U.S. Department of Education, and co-investigator of the Special Education Pre-Service Training Improvement Grant from the Department of Education's Office of Special Education Programs. She has also received many awards for her teaching, including the Indiana University Trustee's Teaching Award and the Faculty Colloquium on Excellence Teaching Award.

Further Reading

Migliore, A., Grossi, T., Mank, D., & Rogan, P. (2008). Why do adults with intellectual disabilities work in sheltered workshops? *Journal of Vocational Rehabilitation, 28*(1), 29–40.

Migliore, A., Mank, D., Grossi, T., & Rogan, R. (2007). Integrated employment or sheltered workshops: Preferences of adults with intellectual disabilities, their families, and staff. *Journal of Vocational Rehabilitation, 26*(1), 5–19.

Murphy, S. T., Rogan, P. M., & Rusch, F. R. (1996). Closing the shop: Conversion from sheltered to integrated work. *American Journal of Mental Retardation, 101*(3), 34–35.

Patricia Rogan. Retrieved from http://education.iupui.edu/soe/directory/facultydetail.aspx?id=24

Rogan, P., & Held, M. (1999). Paraprofessionals in job coach roles. *Journal of the Association for Persons with Severe Handicaps, 24*(4), 273–280.

Phillip D. Rumrill, Jr. (1968–)

American academic focusing on education and employment issues for people with disabilities

Phillip D. Rumrill, Jr. was born on July 24, 1968, in Keene, New Hampshire. He attended Keene State College, earning his bachelor's degree in psychology in 1989 and his master's degree in post-secondary counseling in 1991. Rumrill went on to earn his doctoral degree in rehabilitation from the University of Arkansas in 1993.

Rumrill began his academic career at the University of Wisconsin-Milwaukee in 1994 as an assistant professor in the Rehabilitation Counseling Program in the Department of Educational Psychology. In 1996 he joined the faculty of Kent State University, where he is a professor of Rehabilitation Counseling and the director of the Center for Disability Studies, an interdisciplinary center for research, community service, and training. Rumrill's research interests include implementation of the Americans with Disabilities Act (ADA), transition issues in education for people with disabilities, particularly those in higher education, and the employment issues of people with chronic diseases, including multiple sclerosis.

In his position as director of the Center for Disability Studies, Rumrill, who is blind, has developed job placement programs for students with disabilities at Kent State and has also helped the campus become more accessible and inclusive for students with disabilities. He has developed disability awareness programs at the university, including a Faculty Professional Development Institute to connect faculty and students with disabilities and to foster greater communication between them in such issues as education and employment.

Rumrill is a prolific author. He has written more than 150 professional journal articles and 40 book chapters, and he has developed measurement instruments and training manuals. He is also the author or co-author of nine books, including *Employment Issues and Multiple Sclerosis, Multiple Sclerosis: A Guide for Rehabilitation and Health Care Professionals, Research in Rehabilitation Counseling,* and *Research in Special Education.*

Rumrill is the recipient of 24 federal and private foundation grants. One recent grant from the U.S. Department of Education focuses on the ADA and examines the effectiveness of the Disability and Business Technical Assistance Centers in training personnel to implement the act, including discerning patterns of discrimination, as well as reporting and handling complaints. In recognition of his achievements, Rumrill was awarded the 2010 Distinguished Scholar Award from Kent State.

Further Reading

Phillip D. Rumrill, Jr. Retrieved from http://www.ehhs.kent.edu/can/dr__phil_rumrill.htm

Rumrill, P. D., Jr. (1999). Effects of a social competence training program on accommodation request activity, situational self-efficacy, and Americans with Disabilities Act knowledge among employed people with visual impairments and blindness. *Journal of Vocational Rehabilitation, 12*(1), 25–31.

Rumrill, P. D., Jr., & Roessler, R. T. (1999). New directions in vocational rehabilitation: A "career development" perspective on "closure." *Journal of Rehabilitation, 65*(1), 26.

Roessler, R. T., & Rumrill, P. D., Jr. (2003). Multiple sclerosis and employment barriers: A systemic perspective on diagnosis and intervention. *Work: A Journal of Prevention, Assessment and Rehabilitation, 21*(1), 17–23.

Roessler, R. T., Rumrill, P. D., & Fitzgerald, S. M. (2004). Factors affecting the job satisfaction of employed adults with multiple sclerosis. *Journal of Rehabilitation, 70*(3), 42–52.

Lisa A. Schur (1957–)

*American academic researcher focusing on
disability issues in employment and law*

Lisa A. Schur was born on December 17, 1957, in New York City. She received her bachelor's degree in sociology from Harvard University in 1981, her master's degree in political science from the University of California-Berkeley in 1984, her law degree from Northeastern University School of Law in 1987, and her doctoral degree in political science from the University of California-Berkeley in 1997.

Schur is an associate professor at Rutgers University in the Department of Labor Studies and Employment Relations. She combines her knowledge and expertise in law, political science, and labor relations in her work, which focuses on disability issues in employment and labor law, especially as they have been impacted by the Americans with Disabilities Act (ADA). She has examined several areas of disability and political participation among people with disabilities, including the effect of alternative work arrangements, the impact of workplace experience on political participation, and political activity among women with disabilities.

Schur has been the recipient of several major grants, including one from the Social Security Administration's Disability Research Institute that funded a 2001 study of alternative work arrangements for people with disabilities titled "Nonstandard Work Arrangements and Disability." She and her Rutgers colleague Douglas Kruse have co-authored several major studies of voter participation in people with disabilities, including "Empowerment Through Civil Participation: A Study of the Political Behavior of People with Disabilities." They launched the study in 1998, based on responses to a national survey conducted with people with disabilities, and conducted follow-up studies in 2000 and 2008. In their 2008 study, they showed that Americans with disabilities voted in record numbers in the presidential election of 2008, with 14.7 million people with disabilities casting ballots—a figure that is only 7 percentage points lower than that of Americans without disabilities who voted in the election.

Schur is the author of many professional papers and won the Best Article Award from *Political Research Quarterly* for her essay "Enabling Democracy: Disability and Voter Turnout" in 2002. She is a member of the American Bar Association, the American Political Science Association, the Industrial Relations Research Association, and the Society for Disability Studies.

Further Reading

Lisa Schur. Retrieved from http://smlr.rutgers.edu/LisaSchur

Schur, L. (2002). The difference a job makes: The effects of employment among people with disabilities. *Journal of Economic Issues, 36*(2), 339–347.

Schur, L. (2002). Dead-end jobs or a path to economic well-being? The consequences of nonstandard work for people with disabilities. *Behavioral Sciences and the Law, 20*, 601–620.

Schur, L. (2003). Barriers or opportunities? The causes of contingent and part-time work among people with disabilities. *Industrial Relations: A Journal of Economy and Society, 42*(4), 589–622.

Schur, L., Kruse, D., Blasi, J., & Blanck, P. (2009). Is disability disabling in all workplaces? Workplace disparities and corporate culture. *Industrial Relations: A Journal of Economy and Society, 48*(3), 381–410.

Robert (Bobby) Silverstein (1949–)

American attorney, policy analyst, and director of the
Center for the Study and Advancement of Disability Policy

Robert (Bobby) Silverstein was born on February 19, 1949, in New York, New York. He earned his bachelor's degree in economics from the Wharton School at the University of Pennsylvania in 1971 and his law degree from Georgetown University in 1974.

Silverstein has 30 years of experience working in the areas of disability, public policy, and health care practice. He began his legal career as a staff attorney for the U.S. Department of Labor in 1974, then joined the Lawyers Committee for Civil Rights Under Law in 1975. He worked as an attorney for the Office for Civil Rights in the U.S. Department of Health, Education, and Welfare, where he helped draft the Rehabilitation Act of 1973, Title VI of the Civil Rights Act of 1964, and Title IX of the Education Amendments of 1972. From 1987 to 1997, he served as counsel, staff director, and minority staff director to the U.S. Senate Subcommittee on Disability Policy, where he helped develop disabilities legislation and regulations. His work included drafting and implementing the Americans with Disabilities Act (ADA), the Rehabilitation Act, and the Individuals with Disabilities Education Act.

In 1997 Silverstein joined the faculty of the George Washington University Medical Center, where he was associate professor of health services management and policy in the School of Public Health, and also associate professor of health care sciences in the School of Medicine and Health Sciences.

In 2000 Silverstein became director of the Center for the Study and Advancement of Disability Policy, an organization that provides public education, leadership development and training, technical assistance, and information on public policy issues that affect people with disabilities. In 2007 he joined the law firm of Powers, Pyles, Sutter, and Verville as a principal, where he conducts a federal regulatory and legislative practice in disability, health care, employment, and civil rights.

Silverstein is the author of more than 75 professional papers on disability issues as they affect public policy. He is the recipient of many awards, including the Distinguished Services Award of the President of the United States, for his work on behalf of people with disabilities.

Further Reading

Center for the Study and Advancement of Disability Policy. *About the director.* (2007). Retrieved from http://www.disabilitypolicycenter.org/aboutdir.htm

Silverstein, R. (2000). Emerging disability policy framework: A guidepost for analyzing public policy. *Iowa Law Review, 85,* 1691–1798.

Silverstein, R. (2010). Anatomy of change: The need for effective disability policy change agents. *Archives of Physical Medicine and Rehabilitation, 91*(2), 173–177.

Silverstein, R., Julnes, G., & Nolan, R. (2005). What policymakers need and must demand from research regarding the employment rate of persons with disabilities. *Behavioral Sciences and the Law, 23*(3), 399–448.

David C. Stapleton (1950–)

American public policy researcher focusing on the impact of public policy on employment for people with disabilities

David C. Stapleton was born in 1950 in Massachusetts. He received his bachelor's degree from Dartmouth College, and his master's and doctoral degrees in economics from the University of Wisconsin.

Stapleton is currently a senior fellow with Mathematica Policy Research, a nonpartisan organization that conducts research and collects data for federal and state governments and national and international organizations. He directs Mathematica's Center for Studying Disability Policy and specializes in the impact of public policy on employment and income of people with disabilities, especially in the area of Social Security programs. He is the principal investigator for the Health and Human Services Center of Excellence for Comparative Effectiveness Research on Disability Services, Coordinated Care, and Integration; the Social Security Administration's Benefit Offset National Demonstration and its Ticket to Work Evaluation programs; and the Rehabilitation Research and Training Center's Disability Statistics and Demographics.

Prior to joining Mathematica, Stapleton was the director of the Institute for Policy Research at Cornell University, which is part of the Cornell Rehabilitation Research and Training Center for Economic Research on Employment Policy for Persons with Disabilities. At Cornell, he was co-principal investigator of a National Institute for Disability and Rehabilitation Research study.

A prolific author, Stapleton has published many professional papers and is also the author of several books in the area of disability studies, including *Counting Working-Age People with Disabilities: What Current Data Tells Us and Options for Improvement* and *Growth in Disability Benefits: Explanations and Policy Implications.* He is also a member of the Association of Public Policy Analysis and Management Program Committee.

Further Reading

David Stapleton. Retrieved from http://www.mathematica-mpr.com/About_ Us/Bios/dstapleton.asp

Goodman, N., & Stapleton, D. C. (2007). Federal program expenditures for working-age people with disabilities. *Journal of Disability Policy Studies, 18*(2), 66–78.

Stapleton, D. C., & Burkhauser, R. V. (2003). *The decline in employment of people with disabilities: A policy puzzle.* Kalamazoo, MI: W. E. Upjohn Institute for Employment Research.

Stapleton, D. C., & Burkhauser, R. V. (2004). The decline in the employment rate for people with disabilities: Bad data, bad health, or bad policy? *Journal of Vocational Rehabilitation, 20*(3), 185–201.

Robert H. Stensrud

American academic researcher focusing on employment issues in people with disabilities

Robert H. Stensrud received his bachelor's degree from Wartburg College, his master's degree from the University of Northern Iowa, and his doctoral degree in rehabilitation counseling from Drake University in 1983.

Stensrud began his career as a member of the faculty of St. Louis University in its Hospital Administration program, where he formed an organizational consulting practice that provided marketing, management consulting, development, and planning services to local hospitals, and also developed an executive assessment center, the Executive Performance Lab. While working at the university, Stensrud was also a rehabilitation counselor in a state mental institution and a manager in a community-based counseling center.

Stensrud joined the faculty of Drake University in 1988, where he is professor of counselor education at the school's National Rehabilitation Institute. Stensrud's research focuses on issues in employment for people with disabilities, including attitudes and expectations of employers, training, networking strategies, technology, cultural diversity, and other issues involving job placement and career development. In addition, he serves on the steering committee of the National Institute on Disability and Rehabilitation Research to develop best practices on disability and employment.

Stensrud has been the recipient of several federal grants to fund research into disability education programs, including a five-year study that began in 2009 and is funded by the U.S. Department of Education's Office of Special Education and Rehabilitative Services Training Program. The author of over 40 articles in professional journals on rehabilitation counseling, management, and related topics, Stensrud has also served as the manager of the Iowa Vocation Rehabilitation Services since 1998.

In 2006 Stensrud received the Iowa Governor's Award, which is the state's highest honor given to residents for enhancing empowerment and employment of people with disabilities. Currently, Stensrud is part of a leadership committee that is studying the issues of mentoring and transitioning for young people with disabilities for Iowa's Office of Disability Employment Policy. He is also a member of the Intergovernment Committee on Disability Research.

Further Reading

Gilbride, D., & Stensrud, R. (1999). Demand-side job development and system change. *Rehabilitation Counseling Bulletin, 42*(4), 329–342.

Gilbride, D., Stensrud, R., Ehlers, C., Evans, E., & Peterson, C. (2000). Employers' attitudes toward hiring persons with disabilities and vocational rehabilitation services. *Journal of Rehabilitation, 66*(4), 17–24.

Gilbride, D., Stensrud, R., Vandergoot, D., & Golden, K. (2003). Identification of the characteristics of work environments and employers open to hiring and accommodating people with disabilities. *Rehabilitation Counseling Bulletin, 46*(3), 130–137.

Stensrud, R. (2007). Developing relationships with employers means considering the competitive business environment and the risk it produces. *Rehabilitation Counseling Bulletin, 50*(4), 226–237.

Robert A. Stodden (1943–)

American academic focusing on the transition from post-secondary education to employment for youth with disabilities

Robert A. Stodden was born on August 22, 1943, in Temple, Texas. He received his bachelor's degree in education and psychology from Western Washington University in 1965, his master's degree in adolescent counseling and career guidance from California State University in 1974, and his doctoral degree in an interdisciplinary program in secondary special education and vocational rehabilitation from the University of Florida in 1976.

Stodden joined the faculty at the University of Hawaii in 1988, where he is a professor of special education and founder of the school's Center on Disability Studies, whose purpose is to improve access, participation, and performance for young people with disabilities in education and employment. At the university, he also serves as the director of the National Center for the Study of Postsecondary Education Supports as well as the National Technical Assistance Center for the Employment of Asian Americans and Pacific Islanders with Disabilities.

Stodden's research focuses on transition issues in education and employment for youth with disabilities, especially in the areas of high school to college, and college to work. He has been the director or principal investigator for more than 100 research and training projects funded by the U.S. Department of Education and the state of Hawaii. From 1995 to 1996, he served as a National Policy Fellow with the Joseph P. Kennedy Jr. Foundation, working with the U.S. Senate's Disability Policy Subcommittee on reauthorization of the Individuals with Disabilities Education Act. In that role, he helped draft the bill's language regarding transition service.

In 1998 Stodden headed a seven-year study for the National Center for the Study of Postsecondary Supports, Rehabilitation Research and Training Center at the University of Hawaii, which was funded the U.S. Department of Education's National Institutes of Disability and Rehabilitation Institutes. He was also principal investigator for the National Postsecondary Education Follow-up Study of Culturally and Linguistically Diverse Youth with Disabilities at the University of Hawaii, also funded by the U.S. Department of Education.

Stodden is past president of the Association of University Centers on Disability and won its Lifetime Outstanding Achievement Award in 2005. He is also a member and past president of the American Association of University Affiliated Programs, and a member of the board of directors of the International Council on Exceptional Children's division on mental retardation and developmental disabilities. He is also the author or co-author of many published papers and a speaker and presenter at national and international meetings in the area of special education.

Further Reading

Robert A. Stodden. Retrieved from http://www.rds.hawaii.edu/about/editors/editor01.php

Stodden, R. A. (2001). Postsecondary education supports for students with disabilities: A review and response. *Journal for Vocational Special Needs Education, 23*(2), 4–11.

Stodden, R. A., & Galloway, L. M. (2004). Secondary school curricula issues: Impact on postsecondary students with disabilities. *Exceptional Children, 70*(1), 9–25.

Tagayuna, A., Stodden, R. A., Chang, C., Zelenik, M., & Whelley, T. (2005). A two-year comparison of support provisions for persons with disabilities in postsecondary education. *Journal of Vocational Rehabilitation, 22*(1), 13–21.

David R. Strauser (1968–)

American academic researcher focusing on career development and employment of people with disabilities

David Ross Strauser was born on September 4, 1968. He did his undergraduate and graduate work at the University of Wisconsin, receiving his bachelor's degree in psychology in 1990, his master's degree in psychology in 1991, and his Ph.D. in rehabilitation psychology in 1995.

Strauser began his academic career at the University of Memphis, where he worked at the Center for Rehabilitation and Employment Research in the College of Education. His research focuses on the areas of career development and vocational behaviors in people with disabilities, including those with psychiatric and cognitive disabilities. He has also worked as a consultant to mental health and community-based rehabilitation programs in career and employment issues for people with disabilities. He is currently an associate professor at the University of Illinois's Department of Kinesiology and Community Health and also teaches in the university's Department of Special Education. His current research includes studies in the career development and employment of cancer survivors, and particularly young adult cancer survivors.

Strauser has written many professional articles in his field, and he has also given numerous papers and presentations in the United States and around the world. He has served as editor of the *Journal of Rehabilitation* and continues to serve on its board, as well as on the board of *Rehabilitation Counseling Bulletin*. Strauser is the recipient of several honors, including the Early Career Award from the National Center on Rehabilitation Education, the Certificate of Distinguished Service from the Alliance for Rehabilitative Counseling, and the 2004 Rehabilitation Service's Administration Community Award for Excellence in Education and Training.

A member of the American Counseling Association, the American Rehabilitation Counseling Association, and the National Rehabilitation Association, Strauser is the current president of the National Council on Rehabilitation Education and is also chair of the Commission on Rehabilitation Counselor Certification Scientific Advisory Committee.

Further Reading

David Strauser. Retrieved from http://wfnetwork.bc.edu/leaders_entry
.php?id=16820&area=All

Lustig, D. C., & Strauser, D. (2004). A living wage for individuals with disabilities:
Implications for rehabilitation professionals. *Journal of Rehabilitation, 70*(1), 3–4.

Lustig, D. C., & Strauser, D. R. (2007). The causal relationship between chronic
poverty and disability. *Rehabilitation Counseling Bulletin, 50*, 194–202.

Strauser, D. R., & Keim, J. (2002). The relationship between self-efficacy, locus of
control and work personality. *Journal of Rehabilitation, 68*(1), 3–5.

Strauser, D. R., Lustig, D. C., Keim, J., Ketz, K., & Malesky, A. (2002). Analyzing
the differences in career thoughts based on disability status. *Journal of
Rehabilitation, 68*(1), 27–32.

Edna M. Szymanski (1952–)

*American university president and researcher focusing on
vocational and career development in people with disabilities*

Edna M. Szymanski was born on March 19, 1952, in Caracas, Venezuela,
and raised in Philadelphia, Pennsylvania. She received her bachelor of science degree in biology from Rensselaer Polytechnic Institute in 1972, her
master's degree in rehabilitation counseling from the University of
Scranton in 1974, and her Ph.D. in special education and rehabilitation
counseling from the University of Texas at Austin in 1988.

Szymanski began her career in disability studies as a vocational evalua-
tor for a rehabilitation center, then worked as a counselor for the Office of
Vocational Rehabilitation for New York state. She joined the faculty of the
University of Wisconsin in 1989, where she was associate dean of the College of Education and chair of the Department of Rehabilitation Psychology and Special Education.

Szymanski has been a prolific author and researcher since graduate
school, with a focus on vocational and career development for people
with disabilities. She has written more than 100 professional articles and
book chapters, and she co-edited a widely used textbook in the rehabilitation field, *Work and Disability: Contexts, Issues, and Strategies for Enhancing
Employment Outcomes for People with Disabilities*, now in its third edition.

Szymanski has served on committees for the National Institute on Disability and Rehabilitation Research and has won many awards for her
research, including the American Rehabilitation Counseling Association's
James F. Garrett Award for a Distinguished Career in Rehabilitation

Research, the American Counseling Association Research Award, the Rehabilitation Education Researcher of the Year Award from the National Council on Rehabilitation Education and the McKinnon Foundation, the American Association for Counselor Education and Supervision Research Award, and the American Rehabilitation Counseling Association Distinguished Professional Award.

During her time at the University of Wisconsin, Szymanski realized that she had a gift for college administration, which she likened to the work of a rehabilitation counselor. "Our goal was to get the best possible match for the person and his or her environment," she explained. In 1999 she decided to pursue academic administration and moved to the University of Maryland, where she was dean and professor in the College of Education through 2006. In 2006 she was named senior vice president of academic affairs and provost at the University of Maine, Orono. In 2008 Szymanski was named president of Minnesota State University, Moorhood, where she serves as the school's first female president.

Further Reading

Edna Szymanski. Retrieved from http://www.mnscu.edu/about/presidents/profiles/szymanski.html

Hershenson, D. B., & Szymanski, E. M. (1999). Vocational and career development in rehabilitation. *Rehabilitation Education, 13,* 105–112.

Merz, M. A., & Szymanski, E. M. (1997). The effects of a vocational rehabilitation based career workshop on commitment to career choice. *Rehabilitation Counseling Bulletin, 41,* 88–104.

Szymanski, E. M. (1999). Disability, job stress, the changing nature of careers, and the career resilience portfolio. *Rehabilitation Counseling Bulletin, 42,* 279–289.

Szymanski, E. M., & Vancollins, J. (2003). Career development of people with disabilities: Some new and not-so-new challenges. *Australian Journal of Career Development, 12*(1), 9–16.

Paul Wehman

American academic focusing on the transition from education to adulthood and supported employment for people with disabilities

Paul Wehman received his bachelor's degree in business administration from Western Illinois University in 1970, his master's degree in general and experimental psychology from Illinois State University in 1972, and his Ph.D. in behavioral disabilities and rehabilitation psychology from the University of Wisconsin in 1976.

Wehman joined the faculty of Virginia Commonwealth University in 1976, and over the past 35 years he has pioneered the development of supported employment at the University. He has focused his research on expanding supported employment to people with severe disabilities, including those with mental retardation, traumatic brain injury, spinal cord injury, and autism. He has also written extensively on transition issues for young adults with disabilities, especially in the movement from school to employment.

Currently, Wehman is a professor in the Department of Physical Medicine and Rehabilitation at VCU, with a joint appointment in the Department of Teaching and Learning Rehabilitation Counseling. He is also director of the Rehabilitation Research and Training Center on Workplace Supports and Job Retention, and chair of the Division of Rehabilitation Research. Since joining VCU, he has been the principal investigator for many federally funded research grants, including the U.S. Department of Labor's Training and Technical Assistance Project on Self Employment and VCU's Diversity and Empowerment Project. He is responsible for a $6.25 million annual budget for the Research and Training Center, with fiscal and program oversight for over 20 federal grants and a staff of 65 researchers and staff.

Wehman is a prolific author, co-author, and editor, with more than 200 professional articles, 24 book chapters, and 40 books among his publications. He is also the editor-in-chief of the *Journal of Vocational Rehabilitation*. He is the recipient of many awards, including the Joseph P. Kennedy Jr. Foundation International Award in Mental Retardation, the Distinguished Service Award from the President's Committee on Employment for Persons with Disabilities, and the Mary Switzer Fellowship for the National Rehabilitation Association. In 2000 Wehman was named one of the 50 most influential special educators of the millennium by *Remedial and Special Education*. In 2006 he was elected a Life Long Emeritus Member of APSE: The Employment Network, and in 2007 he received the VCU School of Medicine Research Recognition Award.

Further Reading

Paul Wehman. Retrieved from http://www.worksupport.com/about_us/bio .cfm?id=48

Wehman, P. (2003). Workplace inclusion: Persons with disabilities and coworkers working together. *Journal of Vocational Rehabilitation, 18*(2), 131–141.

Wehman, P., Brooke, V., Green, H., Hewett, M., & Tipton, M. (2008). Public/Private Partnerships and employment of people with developmental disabilities:

Preliminary evidence from a pilot project. *Journal of Vocational Rehabilitation, 28*(1), 53–66.

Wehman, P., & Targett, P. (2006). Return to work for individuals with TBI: A supported employment approach. *Brain Injury/Professional: Vocational Issues in Traumatic Brain Injury, 3*(3), 8–10.

Wehman, P., Targett, P., Eltzeroth, H., Green, H., Brooke, V., & Barcus, J. M. (1999). Development of business supports for persons with mental retardation in the workplace. *Journal of Vocational Rehabilitation, 13*(3), 175–181.

George N. Wright (1921–2004)

American academic and pioneering figure in rehabilitation counseling education

George Nelson Wright was born on December 10, 1921, in Earlington, Kentucky, to James and Jennie Wright. After earning his bachelor's degree in social work from Indiana University in 1947, he began working as a rehabilitation counselor in West Lafayette, Indiana. He continued working in this field while completing his graduate education at Purdue University. He received his master's degree in 1954 and his doctoral degree in rehabilitation counseling in 1959. That year, he went to work for the National Epilepsy League in Chicago, where he was national director of programs until 1962.

In 1962 Wright joined the faculty of the University of Wisconsin-Madison. Over the course of a 30-year career at the university, he helped build the program in rehabilitation counseling into one of the best in the nation. Working in what is now called the Department of Rehabilitation Psychology and Special Education, Wright helped develop the Council on Rehabilitation Education, which is the accrediting agency for professional education programs in rehabilitation counseling. He was the director of the Rehabilitation Counselor Education Program at the university from 1962 to 1974, and he also served as the director of the Regional Rehabilitation Research Institute from 1963 to 1987.

Wright also took leadership roles in major organizations in his field, serving as president of the American Rehabilitation Counseling Association and of the rehabilitation psychology division of the American Psychological Association. He also worked as a consultant in the area of rehabilitation education on the national and international levels, advising the U.S. Veterans Administration and the Social Security Administration, as well helping to establish rehabilitation education programs in Israel, Saudi Arabia, Japan, Australia, and Nigeria.

Wright was also a published author, and one of his books, *Total Rehabilitation,* became a standard text in the field of rehabilitation. He also published extensively in the area of epilepsy rehabilitation and helped develop research-based instruments for the evaluation and accreditation of students in rehabilitation counseling programs. He was the recipient of many major awards in his field, including the Arthur A. Hitchcock Distinguished Professional Service Award, given by the American Association for Counseling and Development, and the Distinguished Career Contributions to Rehabilitation Psychology Award, given by the American Psychological Association.

Wright remained active as a consultant after his retirement from the University of Wisconsin in 1992, and he was a professor emeritus at the University at the time of his death on May 18, 2004. To honor his contributions to his field, the university established the George Wright Varsity Award, which is given annually to an alumnus of the school's doctoral program in rehabilitation psychology in recognition of outstanding contributions to the fields of rehabilitation counseling and rehabilitation psychology.

Further Reading

George Nelson Wright. (2001). *Contemporary Authors Online.* Farmington Hills, MI: Gale Group.

Memorial resolution of the faculty of the University of Wisconsin-Madison: On the death of Professor Emeritus George Nelson Wright. Retrieved from http://www.secfac.wisc.edu/senate/2006/1106/1944(mem_res).pdf

Wright, G. N. (1980). *Total Rehabilitation.* Boston, MA: Little, Brown.

Edward Yelin (1951–)

American academic focusing on employment and economic impact of chronic disease

Edward Yelin was born on June 13, 1951, in Newark, New Jersey. He received his bachelor's degree in public affairs from the University of Chicago in 1972, and his doctorate from the Department of City and Regional Planning at the University of California, Berkeley, in 1979.

Yelin is currently professor in residence of medicine and health policy in the Division of Rheumatology and Institute for Health Policy Studies at the University of California, San Francisco, where he is also director of the

Arthritis Research Group and the Work and Health Program. His research is focused on employment issues in patients with arthritis and other chronic diseases, and he has also researched health policy issues relating to patients with rheumatic diseases, asthma, pulmonary conditions, cancer, HIV, and mental illness. In the area of arthritis, Yelin has researched how changes in the health care system, especially the implementation of managed care programs, affect people who have the disease.

In the area of employment, Yelin has focused on both the social and economic effects of chronic disease, and has examined how changes in the overall economy, job loss, and poverty levels affect the general health of the population. He has been involved with several national studies in the area, including one for the Centers for Disease Control on the economic impact of arthritis in the United States, and one for the Social Security Administration on the economic impact of enabling people with impairments to continue work. Yelin is the director of the Effectiveness Center for the California Health Benefits Review Program, and he works with colleagues from several universities to study health insurance legislation for the state of California.

Yelin has written widely on topics in his field, including more than 50 professional papers. He is the recipient of several honors, including the Distinguished Scholar Award and the Clinical Scholar Science Award, both from the American College of Rheumatology, and the Clarke Award for Research from the Arthritis Foundation. In 1999 he was elected to the National Academy of Social Insurance.

Further Reading

Edward Yelin. Retrieved from http://coeh.berkeley.edu/people/faculty/yelin.htm

Yelin, E. H. (1997). The employment of people with and without disabilities in an age of insecurity. *Annals of the AAPSS, 549*(1), 117–128.

Yelin, E. H., & Katz, P. P. (1994). Labor force trends of persons with and without disabilities. *Monthly Labor Review, 177*(10), 36–42.

Yelin, E. H., & Trupin, L. S. (2002). Persons with disabilities and demands of the contemporary labor market. In G. S. Wunderlich, D. P. Rice, & N. L. Amado (Eds.), *The dynamics of disability: Measuring and monitoring disability for Social Security programs.* Washington, DC: National Academies Press.

Yelin, E. H., & Trupin, L. (2003). Labor force trends of persons with and without disabilities. *Monthly Law Review, 126*(5), 20–31.

Five

Annotated Data, Statistics, Tables, and Graphs

William Erickson, Sarah von Schrader,

Susanne M. Bruyère, and Linda Barrington

The following chapter presents data from several sources addressing key issues related to disability, employment, and work. We begin with a description of our primary sources of data in this chapter, including a discussion of how the definition of disability can impact estimates. We then present data on disparities between people with and without disabilities, first in terms of employment, and then with respect to income and poverty. We go on to examine, in more detail, people who are working, specifically their occupations, industries, and means of transportation to work. Among people in the labor market, we examine characteristics of perceived employment discrimination. Finally, we look at data from programs focused on people with disabilities who are likely out of the workforce, examining utilization and cost data from Social Security Administration programs, workers' compensation, and vocational rehabilitation.

Employment and Disability Data Sources

Much of the data that we present in this chapter compares people with disabilities to those without disabilities. In this section we highlight why it is important to clearly define how disability and employment are measured, as different data sources provide vastly different estimates of seemingly similar concepts. Note that throughout this chapter we limit the statistics based on national survey data to the non-institutionalized population. We deliberately exclude the institutionalized population (i.e., those residing in such places as correctional facilities or nursing homes) for whom employment is generally not a viable option.

Defining Disability

Before discussing the employment of persons with disabilities, it is imperative to understand who is actually defined as having a disability. However, as no single agreed-upon definition of disability exists, measurement of this concept is difficult. Programs and data sources often use different definitions and questions to determine disability status. Over 20 definitions of disability are used for purposes of entitlement to public or private income support programs, government services, or statistical analysis (Mashaw & Reno, 1996). These definitions identify various populations of persons with disabilities and, as a result, can lead to a wide range of prevalence rates. Who is defined as having (or not having) a disability can also have a significant effect on other measures of the identified population, including employment, income, and poverty rates. This makes it crucial to clearly understand the criteria and questions used to identify the population of persons with disabilities (see Weathers, 2009).

As a way to illustrate these potential differences, we provide a comparison of disability prevalence rates across six different national survey data sets. The five data sources shown in Table 1 were designed with specific purposes, and they use dissimilar methods, survey instruments, and sampling designs to identify the population with disabilities. Each of these factors can have a significant impact on the population identified as having a disability. In addition, each survey also provides only certain information and details regarding socioeconomic characteristics and status, such as employment and poverty rates, for the population with disabilities. Although most of the data presented in this chapter are based on the "working age" population, between the ages of 21 and 64, Tables 1 and 2

Table 1 Estimated Disability Population Size and Prevalence Rates by Data Source and Year (Noninstitutionalized Population Ages 25–61)

	Population	Prevalence Rate
2008 American Community Survey (ACS)	15,728,000	10.4
2003 ACS	17,146,000	11.9
2003 Current Population Survey Annual Social and Economic Supplement (CPS-ASEC)	11,155,000	7.8
2002 National Health Interview Survey (NHIS)	23,192,000	16.7
2002 Survey of Income and Program Participation (SIPP)	26,620,000	18.7

Source: Row 1 is from the authors' calculation of 2008 ACS Public Use Microdata Sample (PUMS). Rows 2–5 are adapted from "The disability data landscape," by R. R. Weathers II, 2009, in A. Houtenville, D. Stapleton, R. Weathers II, & R. Burkhauser (Eds.), *Counting working age people with disabilities: What current data tell us and options for improvement* (p. 43). Kalamazoo, MI: W. E. Upjohn Institute for Employment Research. Copyright 2009 by W. E. Upjohn Institute for Employment Research. Adapted with permission.

use the age range from 25 to 61, as this is the period in which most people have completed their schooling and have not yet reached the age of early retirement.

Even the same survey can have widely varying estimates over time due to changes in methodology and questions used. For example, the 2008 ACS survey uses a different sampling methodology than the 2003 ACS and, more importantly, includes a completely revised set of disability questions based upon a narrower concept of disability that results in the lower prevalence rate seen in Table 1 (10.4% compared with 11.9%). Typically, surveys using fewer disability questions are more likely to miss identifying certain disabilities that tend to fall through the cracks in the question set, resulting in a smaller number of persons identified as disabled. Surveys that use a larger number and greater variety of questions to identify disability, such as the Survey of Income and Program Participation (SIPP) with its broader definition (sometimes referred to as a "kitchen sink" approach), tend to identify more individuals with disabilities as they have fewer "cracks" in their definitions (Brault, 2008).

For the working-age population between the ages of 25 and 61, the highest population estimate is 26.6 million persons with disabilities based on the broader definition used in the SIPP; the lowest is 11.2 million based on a single, narrow "work limitation" definition of disability used in the Annual Social and Economic Supplement of the Current Population Survey (CPS-ASEC).

Defining Employment

Many methods exist to measure employment that can provide an indication of the level of attachment to the labor force. The three definitions of employment used by Weathers and Wittenburg (2009) in Table 2, arranged from the least to most attached, are the following:

Reference period employment: People are counted as employed if they reported working in the most recent week for persons in the ACS and CPS, two weeks in the NHIS, and the past month in the SIPP.

Any annual employment: Respondents are considered employed if they report having worked at least 52 hours (one hour per week) during the previous calendar year.

Full-time annual employment: Persons are counted as employed if they worked at least 35 hours per week and 50 or more weeks a year (including paid vacation, sick leave, and other paid leave).

Also known as the employment-to-population ratio, the *employment rate* is the percentage of the population that is employed. Table 2 demonstrates how employment rates vary across several different data sources by disability status for noninstitutionalized persons ages 25 to 61. It should be noted that *unemployment* rates are not included in this table, or anywhere in this chapter. The use of unemployment as a measure of attachment for persons with disabilities is problematic because the denominator used in that calculation only includes persons who are in the labor force (those currently employed, on layoff, or actively looking for work). This rate essentially excludes the large number of persons with disabilities who are discouraged workers and are thus no longer in the labor force, making unemployment a poor measure for this particular population (see Burkhauser, Houtenville, & Wittenburg, 2003, for more details on this issue).

Not surprisingly, the "any annual" employment rates are the highest of all three measures, as this measure is the easiest level of criteria to attain

Table 2 Estimated Employment Rates for Persons With and Without Disabilities, by Data Source (Noninstitutionalized Population Ages 25–61)

	Disability	No Disability
Reference Period Employment		
2003 ACS	39.3	79.5
2003 CPS-ASEC	19.6	81.4
2002 NHIS	47.3	83.3
2002 SIPP	48.9	82.4
Any Annual Employment		
2003 ACS	48.9	87.1
2003 CPS-ASEC	27.9	86.2
2002 NHIS	57.9	88.3
2002 SIPP	61.1	90.6
Full-Time Annual Employment		
2003 ACS	24.5	59.6
2003 CPS-ASEC	9.4	65.3
2002 NHIS	29.8	62.8
2002 SIPP	31.2	58.1

Source: Adapted from: "Employment," by R. R. Weathers II & D. C. Wittenburg, 2009, in A. Houtenville, D. Stapleton, R. Weathers II, & R. Burkhauser (Eds.), *Counting working age people with disabilities: What current data tell us and options for improvement* (pp. 114). Kalamazoo, MI: W. E. Upjohn Institute for Employment Research. Copyright 2009 by W.E. Upjohn Institute for Employment Research. Adapted with permission.

(i.e., anyone who has "reference period" or "full time annual" employment would also meet the "any annual" employment criteria). The effect of the definition of disability in the different data sets can also be seen, as even with the same measure of employment the rates vary significantly. For example, the reference period employment ranges from 19.6% for the 2003 CPS-ASEC to 48.9% for the 2002 SIPP. Perhaps not surprisingly, the population identified using the CPS-ASEC "work limitation" definition of disability has the lowest employment rate across all three measures of employment attachment.

As emphasized by the wide range of disability prevalence rates and employment rates across national survey data, it is important to clearly describe how people with disabilities are being measured when presenting data on disability and employment, so the reader is aware of who is (and is not) represented. Similarly, clearly defining what is meant by "employed" is crucial. It is from the intersection of the definitions of these two terms that the employment rate for people with disabilities is derived.

In this chapter, much of the data we present are from the American Community Survey (ACS) and the Current Population Survey (CPS). While not the only sources of disability and employment data, they are two rich sources. The ACS provides annual national, state, and local estimates of many key indicators, such as prevalence, employment, and poverty rates. The CPS provides national estimates of labor force characteristics on a monthly basis, as well as estimates of many more economic indicators annually. The following section describes the disability and employment measures on these surveys. For more information regarding the other data sources presented in Tables 1 and 2, see Weathers (2009).

The American Community Survey

A major source of the information in this chapter is the 2008 American Community Survey (ACS). The ACS is a continuous data collection effort conducted by the U.S. Census Bureau that is used to produce annual estimates at the national, state, and local levels on the characteristics of the United States population. As of 2010 it replaced the Decennial Census long form. The ACS has collected information on an annual basis since 2005 from approximately three million addresses in the United States, as well as a 2.5% sample of the population living in group quarters and 36,000 addresses in Puerto Rico. For more general information on the ACS, see the Census Bureau's related Web site at www.census.gov/acs.

From its first implementation, the ACS included the six questions used by the 2000 Decennial Census to identify the population with disabilities. In 2008, the U.S. Census Bureau implemented a new set of disability questions, making a conceptual break from the questions used in previous years. Note that as with most surveys, the disability questions are not mutually exclusive and people may report more than one disability type. The overall disability category used in the ACS is determined by a report of one or more of the six disabilities identified by the questions. The six questions asked in the 2008 ACS are as follows:

Hearing Disability (asked of all ages):

Is this person deaf or does he/she have serious difficulty hearing?

Visual Disability (asked of all ages):

Is this person blind or does he/she have serious difficulty seeing even when wearing glasses?

Cognitive Disability (asked of persons ages 5 or older):

Because of a physical, mental, or emotional condition, does this person have serious difficulty concentrating, remembering, or making decisions?

Ambulatory Disability (asked of persons ages 5 or older):

Does this person have serious difficulty walking or climbing stairs?

Self-Care Disability (asked of persons ages 5 or older)

Does this person have difficulty dressing or bathing?

Independent Living Disability (asked of persons ages 15 or older):

Because of a physical, mental, or emotional condition, does this person have difficulty doing errands alone such as visiting a doctor's office or shopping?

As Table 3 indicates, some disability types are more common than others. The most commonly reported disability type for the working-age (21–64) noninstitutionalized population is an ambulatory disability at 5.4%, followed by a cognitive disability, reported by 4.1% of people. Nearly half of the people with a disability (45.7%) report having two or more of the six disability types.

Disability prevalence rates vary substantially from state to state, as can be seen in the map in Figure 1. The states with the lowest disability prevalence rate are Minnesota (7.9%), New Jersey (7.7%), and Hawaii (7.2%). The three states with the highest prevalence rates are Kentucky (16.4%), Arkansas (16.6%), and West Virginia (18.7%). The rate was even higher in Puerto Rico, where more than one in five working-age persons reported a

Table 3   Disability Prevalence Rate by Disability Type (Noninstitutionalized Population, Ages 21–64, 2008 ACS)

Disability Type	Percent	Number
Any Disability	10.4	18,312,900
Visual	1.9	3,314,200
Hearing	2.3	3,990,400
Ambulatory	5.4	9,498,200
Cognitive	4.1	7,213,700
Self-Care	1.8	3,240,900
Independent Living	3.6	6,289,600

Source: From *2008 disability status report*, by W. Erickson, C. Lee, and S. von Schrader, 2010, Ithaca, NY: Cornell University Rehabilitation Research and Training Center on Disability Demographics and Statistics. Available from http://www.disabilitystatistics.org.

disability. These differences could be a reflection of differences in industries and common occupations between states; places with more heavy industry, mining, or agriculture may have higher rates of disability. Poverty and lack of access to quality health care may also be related to differences in state-level disability prevalence rates.

Current Population Survey

The Current Population Survey (CPS) is a monthly survey of about 50,000 households conducted by the Bureau of the Census for the Bureau of Labor Statistics, and is the primary source of labor force statistics for the U.S. civilian noninstitutionalized population. In June 2008, the CPS adopted the use of the six revised ACS disability questions on its Basic Monthly Survey, allowing the Bureau of Labor Statistics to report on the employment situation for people with and without disabilities each month. For more information the CPS, see http://www.census.gov/cps.

In addition to the Basic Monthly Survey, the CPS collects additional data using supplements, and in this chapter we examine data from the

Figure 1   Disability Prevalence Rates by State (Noninstitutionalized Population, Ages 21–64, 2008 ACS)

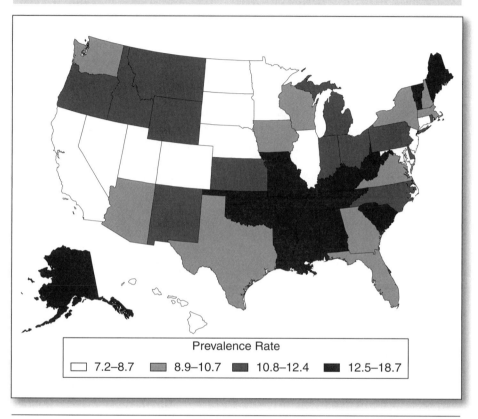

Source: Adapted from *2008 disability status report,* by W. Erickson, C. Lee, and S. von Schrader, 2010, Ithaca, NY: Cornell University Rehabilitation Research and Training Center on Disability Demographics and Statistics. Available from http://www.disabilitystatistics.org.

Annual Social and Economic Supplement (CPS-ASEC). This annual survey is conducted every March, and it utilizes a single disability screener question to identify what is referred to as a "work limitation disability." A work limitation is determined by the following question: "does anyone in this household have a health problem or disability which prevents them from working or which limits the kind or amount of work they can do? [If so,] who is that? Anyone else?" The CPS work limitation disability measure is valuable, as it is the only disability-related survey question that has been consistently asked on an annual basis and can be used to examine trends over time since 1981. The prevalence of disability (work limitation) among the working-age population (21–64) hovers around 8%, from 1981 to 2009, ranging from a low of 7.3% in 1989 to a high of 8.4% in 1994 (Bjelland, Burkhauser, von Schrader, & Houtenville, 2009).

Employment and Economic Disparities

Regardless of the definition of disability, major disparities in employment rates and other economic indicators demonstrate that people with disabilities are not faring well when compared to their nondisabled peers.

Employment Rates

According to the 2008 ACS (presented in Figure 2), the overall employment rate (defined earlier as the "reference period employment" rate) for persons with a disability is 39.5%, as compared to 79.9% for persons without a disability. This translates into a gap of 40.4 percentage points. Employment rates also differ by disability type. Persons with a hearing impairment have the highest employment rate of 56.0%, followed by those with visual impairment at 43.3%. Approximately one-quarter of persons reporting an ambulatory or cognitive disability are employed, while slightly fewer than one in five persons with a self-care or independent living disability are employed.

A more stringent employment criterion is to limit employment to those working full-time/full-year (FT/FY). FT/FY employment follows a similar pattern to "reference period" employment, with only one-quarter of persons with disabilities working FT/FY as compared to six out of ten persons without disabilities. Persons with a hearing disability have the highest FT/FY employment rate, followed by those with visual disability. Only about one in ten persons with self-care or independent living disabilities are employed FT/FY.

Comparing the "reference period" employment rate with the FT/FY employment rate reveals that employed persons with disabilities are more likely to work part-time and/or part-year than persons without disabilities. Approximately three-quarters of employed persons without disabilities work FT/FY, while six out of ten employed persons with disabilities work FT/FY.

The employment of persons with disabilities also varies within the United States. Table 4 highlights this by presenting state-level employment for those with and without disabilities. The state with the lowest employment rate for people with disabilities is West Virginia at 30.5%, which is less than half

Figure 2 Employment Rates by Disability Status and Type (Noninstitutionalized Population, Ages 21–64, 2008 ACS)

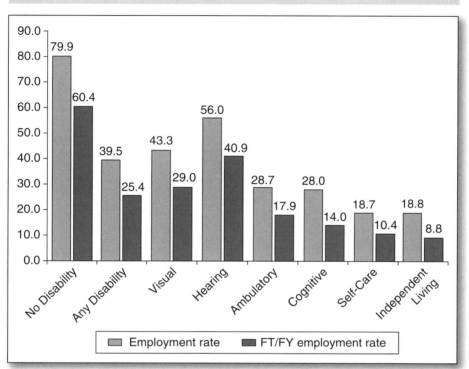

Source: Adapted from *2008 disability status report,* by W. Erickson, C. Lee, and S. von Schrader, 2010, Ithaca, NY: Cornell University Rehabilitation Research and Training Center on Disability Demographics and Statistics. Available from http://www.disabilitystatistics.org.

the rate for the state with the highest employment rate, South Dakota at 61.4%. It is important to be aware that the basic employment numbers do not tell the entire story, as the employment rates for persons without disabilities also vary by state. The employment *gap* between persons with and without disabilities varies widely between states, with the District of Columbia having the largest gap of 47.5 percentage points, and South Dakota having the smallest gap of 24.6 percentage points.

Another useful way to examine employment rates for persons with disabilities is to calculate the relative employment ratio. This ratio is derived by dividing the employment rate of persons with disabilities by the employment rate of those without disabilities. The relative employment ratios

Table 4   Employment Rate by Disability Status by State (Noninstitutionalized Population, Ages 21–64, 2008 ACS)

Location	People With Disabilities	People Without Disabilities	Location	People With Disabilities	People Without Disabilities
Alabama	33.1	78.1	Montana	43.7	81.0
Alaska	51.4	80.5	Nebraska	50.5	86.6
Arizona	42.4	78.2	Nevada	44.8	79.5
Arkansas	33.9	79.1	New Hampshire	46.4	84.6
California	37.2	77.3	New Jersey	41.7	81.3
Colorado	48.3	82.5	New Mexico	41.2	77.3
Connecticut	42.1	82.4	New York	36.2	78.9
Delaware	45.8	81.4	North Carolina	39.7	80.1
District of Columbia	33.1	80.6	North Dakota	60.2	87.0
Florida	36.6	78.4	Ohio	38.3	80.4
Georgia	40.8	79.2	Oklahoma	43.5	80.8
Hawaii	44.7	82.3	Oregon	41.2	79.0
Idaho	46.0	80.4	Pennsylvania	38.8	80.9
Illinois	39.5	80.0	Puerto Rico	25.0	59.4
Indiana	39.8	80.6	Rhode Island	39.8	81.4
Iowa	52.5	86.9	South Carolina	33.9	77.6
Kansas	51.3	85.0	South Dakota	61.4	86.0
Kentucky	30.8	77.0	Tennessee	35.6	79.1
Louisiana	36.6	77.6	Texas	42.9	79.6
Maine	39.5	81.4	Utah	45.9	80.1
Maryland	44.7	83.8	Vermont	48.8	84.0
Massachusetts	39.9	82.5	Virginia	41.5	82.6
Michigan	33.6	76.8	Washington	41.0	80.5
Minnesota	52.4	84.8	West Virginia	30.5	76.7
Mississippi	33.2	77.9	Wisconsin	45.1	84.3
Missouri	39.5	81.5	Wyoming	56.6	84.9

Source: From *2008 disability status report,* by W. Erickson, C. Lee, and S. von Schrader, 2010, Ithaca, NY: Cornell University Rehabilitation Research and Training Center on Disability Demographics and Statistics. Available from http://www.disabilitystatistics.org.

Figure 3 Relative Employment Ratio by State (Noninstitutionalized Population, Ages 21–64, 2008 ACS)

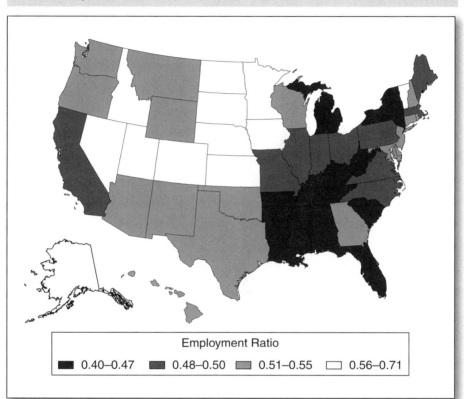

Employment Ratio
■ 0.40–0.47 ■ 0.48–0.50 ■ 0.51–0.55 □ 0.56–0.71

Source: Adapted from *2008 disability status report,* by W. Erickson, C. Lee, and S. von Schrader, 2010, Ithaca, NY: Cornell University Rehabilitation Research and Training Center on Disability Demographics and Statistics. Available from http:// www.disabilitystatistics.org.

presented in the map in Figure 3 demonstrate which states more equitably employ persons with disabilities. The states in black and dark gray employ persons with disabilities at half or less than half the rate of persons without disabilities, a ratio of 0.50 or less. The states shown in the two lighter colors employ people with disabilities at more than half the rate of those without. Note that even within the state with the best relative employment rate (South Dakota), working-age people with disabilities are only 71% as likely to be employed as a working-age person without disabilities.

While we know that people with a disability have significantly lower employment rates than their nondisabled peers, it is important to also consider those who are not employed. Figure 4 demonstrates that the percentage of

Figure 4   Employment Situation by Disability Status (Noninstitutionalized Population, Ages 21–64, 2008 ACS)

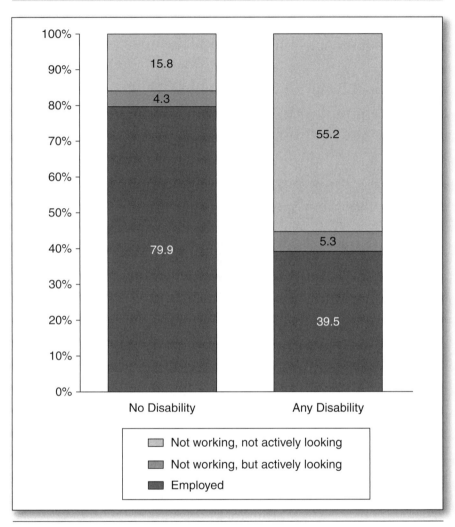

Source: Adapted from *2008 disability status report,* by W. Erickson, C. Lee, and S. von Schrader, 2010, Ithaca, NY: Cornell University Rehabilitation Research and Training Center on Disability Demographics and Statistics. Available from http:// www.disabilitystatistics.org.

people who are not working but are actively looking for work is similar for people with and without disabilities (5.3% and 4.3%, respectively). The major difference is in the proportion who are not working and are not actively looking for work, or are out of the labor force, with over 55% of people with disabilities falling into this category, compared to 15.8% of people without disabilities. This lower level of participation in looking for work is one reason why the typical measure of unemployment is problematic for people with disabilities. If a person is neither working nor actively looking for work, they are excluded from the unemployment calculation. The unemployment rate is the percentage of persons *in the labor force* who do not have a job:

$$\text{Unemployment Rate} = \frac{\begin{array}{c}\text{(Number of persons who do not have a job}\\ \text{but are actively looking for work)}\end{array}}{\text{(Number of persons in the labor force)}} \times 100$$

The number of persons in the labor force only includes people who have a job, are on layoff, or who actively searched for work in the last four weeks. The unemployment rate excludes "discouraged workers"—people who have given up trying to find work. People with disabilities who are not working may often fall into this category; unemployment figures may therefore exclude many persons with disabilities. This is not the case with the employment rate, the calculation of which includes all persons. Therefore, comparing employment rates between those with and without disabilities provides a more objective account of the employment situation for the population with disabilities than comparing unemployment rates.

Educational Attainment and Employment

Educational attainment is quite different between those with and without disabilities. Nearly one-quarter (23.9%) of working-age persons with disabilities have less than a high school education, as compared to 11.1% of persons without disabilities. At the other end of the spectrum, only 12.3% of working-age persons with disabilities have a bachelor's degree or higher education level, as compared to nearly one-third (30.6%) of those without a disability (Erickson, Lee, & von Schrader, 2010a).

Figure 5 demonstrates that with increased educational attainment, the employment rate for people with disabilities increases; while the employment gap between people with and without disabilities persists, it visibly narrows with higher educational attainment.

Veterans With Service-Connected Disability

There are over 13.1 million civilian working-age veterans in the United States, of whom approximately 2.2 million, or 16.9%, report a

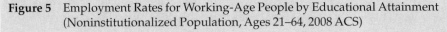

Figure 5   Employment Rates for Working-Age People by Educational Attainment (Noninstitutionalized Population, Ages 21–64, 2008 ACS)

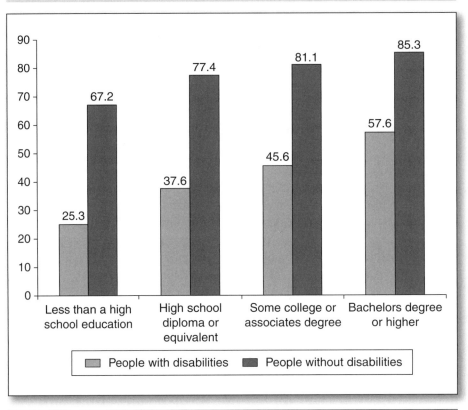

Source: Adapted from D*isability statistics from the 2008 American Community Survey (ACS),* by W. Erickson, C. Lee, and S. von Schrader, 2010, Ithaca, NY: Cornell University Rehabilitation Research and Training Center on Disability Demographics and Statistics. Available from http://www.disabilitystatistics.org.

"service-connected disability." A service-connected disability is one that has been determined by the Department of Veterans Affairs (VA) to be the result of disease or injury incurred or aggravated during military service. Note that a veteran can receive disability compensation for a wide range of conditions, and many veterans with a service-connected disability do not report having one of the six ACS disability types. The employment rate of civilian working-age veterans with a service-connected disability (64.2%) is significantly lower than that of veterans without a service-connected disability (77.3%) (authors' calculation based on analysis of the 2008 ACS Public Use Microdata Sample—PUMS).

Employment Rates Over Time

In June 2008, the Basic Monthly CPS began to include a set of six disability questions almost identical to those used in the 2008 ACS, with minor wording differences. These questions allow for monthly tracking of employment, labor force participation, and unemployment rates for people with and without disabilities, using the same disability measures as the ACS. In early 2010, the Bureau of Labor Statistics began releasing monthly data on the employment of people with disabilities in its high-profile monthly "Employment Situation" news release. Figure 6 presents monthly employment rates for men and women with and without disabilities based on these data.

Although the CPS Basic Monthly Survey now includes the ACS disability questions, the CPS-ASEC is valuable if one wants to look at employment rates and disparities for people with disabilities over a longer period of time, as it continues to include a work limitation measure that has been asked consistently on an annual basis since 1981. Research has indicated that while the employment rates for the work-limited population are significantly lower than for the population of people with disabilities defined by broader measures of disability, the employment trends are not significantly different (Burkhauser, Daly, Houtenville, & Nargis, 2002). Figure 7 demonstrates that the relative employment ratio (the ratio between the employment rate for people with disability and people without) has generally decreased over the last 20 years. In 2010, a working-age person with a work limitation disability was only 21% as likely to be employed as a working-age person without a disability. The relative employment ratio in 2008 calculated using the ACS disability measure was 0.49 compared to the CPS estimate in 2008 of 0.22. The difference here is driven primarily by the fact that people who report a work limitation are much less likely to be employed (17.7% in 2008) than people who report one of the six ACS disabilities (39.5% in 2008).

International Employment Rates

Figure 8 and Table 5 demonstrate that the low employment rate for people with disabilities is not an issue unique to the United States. While the measurement of disability and employment varies across the countries presented in Figure 8, it is clear that the rate of employment for people with disabilities is low and in several cases has fallen over time. Table 5 further demonstrates that people with disabilities are employed at a far lower rate than people without disabilities, with relative employment ratios ranging from a low of 0.28 in Poland, to a high of 0.72 in Finland.

Figure 6   Employment Rates (Not Seasonally Adjusted) of People Ages 16–64 With and Without Disabilities by Gender: June 2008–July 2010

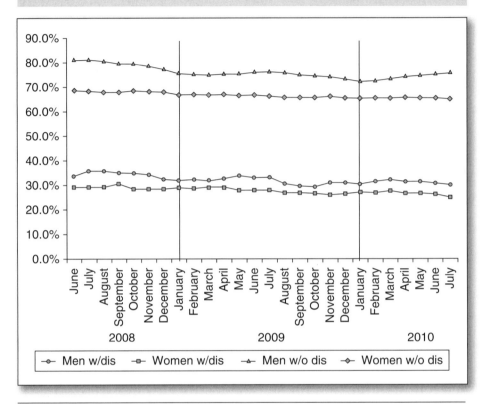

Source: Adapted from *Labor force statistics from the Current Population Survey,* Table A-6, by the Bureau of Labor Statistics, 2010. Retrieved from http://www.bls.gov/cps/cpsdisability.htm.

Note: A person with a disability has at least one of the following conditions: is deaf or has serious difficulty hearing; is blind or has serious difficulty seeing even when wearing glasses; has serious difficulty concentrating, remembering, or making decisions because of a physical, mental, or emotional condition; has serious difficulty walking or climbing stairs; has difficulty dressing or bathing; or has difficulty doing errands alone such as visiting a doctor's office or shopping because of a physical, mental, or emotional condition.

Income and Earnings Disparities

The previous section focused on the differences in the employment rates of people with and without disabilities. Related to this employment gap, there are also major income and earnings disparities. In the United States, for example, household income is lower for those households that include an individual with a disability, while the rate of poverty in those

Figure 7   Trend in Employment Rates of the Working-Age Population (21–64), 1981–2010

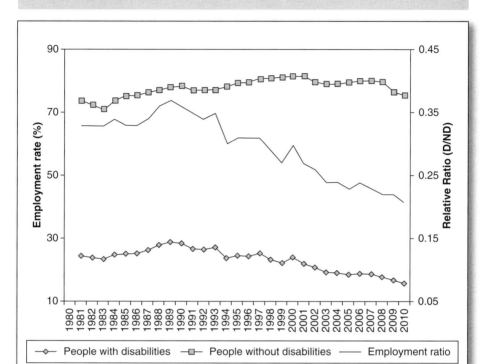

Source: From *2010 progress report on the economic well-being of working age people with disabilities* (p. 4), by M. Bjelland, R. Burkhauser, S. von Schrader, and A. Houtenville, 2011, Ithaca, NY: Rehabilitation Research and Training Center for Economic Research on Employment Policy for Persons with Disabilities.

Note: The population with disabilities is identified using the work limitation question: "[d]oes anyone in this household have a health problem or disability which prevents them from working or which limits the kind or amount of work they can do? [If so,] who is that? Anyone else?" Sample size reflects those ages 21–64 in the reference (survey) year.

households is higher. Important differences also exist in earnings between working people with disabilities and their nondisabled peers.

The median annual earnings for persons working full-time/full-year are shown in Table 6. The reason for limiting the numbers to FT/FY workers is to standardize the number of hours worked to produce the income, to the extent possible. It is important to remember that this criterion excludes all persons working part time and/or part of the year.

Figure 8 Employment Rates of Working-Age People With Disabilities in 27 OECD Countries

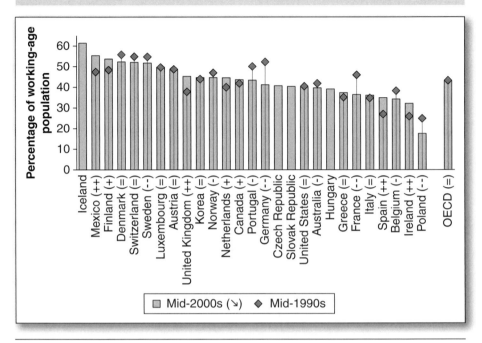

Source: Organisation for Economic Co-operation and Development, 2009. From *Sickness, disability, and work: Keeping on track in the economic downturn,* background paper presented May 14, 2009, Stockholm, Sweden (p. 12), by the Organisation for Economic Co-operation and Development. Copyright 2009 by Organisation for Economic Co-operation Development (OECD). Reprinted with permission.

Notes: (↘) in the legend relates to the variable for which countries are ranked from left to right in decreasing order.

(++)/(- -) refers to a strong increase/decline of 2% or more; (+)/(-) refers to a moderate increase/ decline between 0.75% and 2%; (=) refers to a rather stable trend between 0.75% and 0.75% per- centages refer to the annual average growth rate in employment rate of persons with a disability.

OECD refers to the unweighted average of the 27 countries; the mid- 1990s average is an estimate based from the 23 countries from which data are available.

Given this limitation, it is essential to examine this data in concert with the FT/FY employment levels. The median earnings of working- age people with disabilities who worked full-time/full-year in the United States are $35,600, a substantially lower total than the $40,700 earned by people without disabilities. The median income varies

Table 5   Relative Employment Ratio of People With Disabilities to Those
Without Disability

	Year	Relative Employment Ratio
Norway	2000	0.55
	2005	0.54
Poland	2000	0.31
	2004	0.28
Switzerland	2003	0.66
	2005	0.63
Australia	1998	0.55
	2003	0.50
Luxembourg	2002	0.69
Spain	1995	0.48
	2000	0.41
	2002	0.43
	2004	0.52
United Kingdom	1998	0.47
	2002	0.52
	2006	0.56
Denmark	2002	0.61
	2005	0.64
Finland	2005	0.72
Ireland	2005	0.44
Netherlands	2002	0.61
	2006	0.55

284 EMPLOYMENT AND WORK

Table 6 Median Annual Earnings of People Who Work Full-Time/Full-Year by Disability Status (Noninstitutionalized Population, Ages 21–64, 2008 ACS)

Disability Type	Median Earnings
No Disability	$40,700
Any Disability	$35,600
Visual	$32,600
Hearing	$40,700
Ambulatory	$33,900
Cognitive	$30,600
Self-Care	$35,600
Independent Living	$32,300

Source: From *2008 disability status report,* by W. Erickson, C. Lee, and S. von Schrader, 2010, Ithaca, NY: Cornell University Rehabilitation Research and Training Center on Disability Demographics and Statistics. Available from http://www.disabilitystatistics.org.

across disability types, with persons with hearing disabilities having the highest median income and those with cognitive disabilities having the lowest.

Median household income can be a better reflection of the economic status of persons, as it includes all households regardless of their individual employment status. Household income includes the total income of all household members from all sources, including any public assistance. The median income of households that include any working-age people with disabilities in the United States in 2008 is $39,600, compared to $61,200 for households that do not include any working-age people with disabilities. This is a significant income gap of $21,600. This means that typical households with working-age persons with disabilities have one-third less income than typical households without working-age persons with disabilities. As can be seen in Figure 9, significant variation exists across disability types, with households with hearing disabilities being much better off than households with any of the other disability types.

Figure 9   Median Household Income by Disability Status and Type
(Noninstitutionalized Population, Ages 21–64, 2008 ACS)

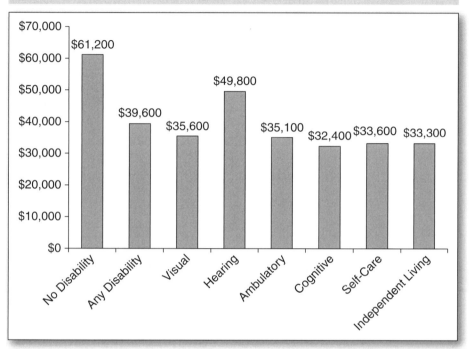

Source: From *2008 disability status report* (p. 41), by W. Erickson, C. Lee, and S. von Schrader, 2010, Ithaca, NY: Cornell University Rehabilitation Research and Training Center on Disability Demographics and Statistics. Available from http:// www.disabilitystatistics.org.

The calculation of poverty uses the sum of total income from each family member living in the household. The poverty threshold is adjusted for the family composition and takes into account the size of the family, the age of the householder, and the number of related children under the age of 18. Over one-quarter (25.3%) of working-age persons with disabilities are living in poverty in 2008. This poverty rate is over two and a half times higher than that of persons without disabilities (9.6%). As Figure 10 shows, persons with cognitive, self-care, and independent living disabilities have the highest poverty rates. Persons with hearing disabilities have much lower rates but still are nearly twice as likely to be in poverty as persons without any disability.

Figure 10   Poverty Status by Disability Status and Type (Noninstitutionalized Population, Ages 21–64, 2008 ACS)

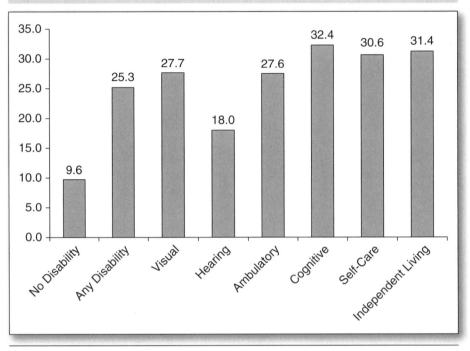

Source: Adapted from *2008 disability status report* (p. 43), by W. Erickson, C. Lee, and S. von Schrader, 2010, Ithaca, NY: Cornell University Rehabilitation Research and Training Center on Disability Demographics and Statistics. Available from http://www.disabilitystatistics.org.

Work and Disability

Where People With Disabilities Work

The data presented so far have highlighted the disparities in employment, income, and poverty for working-age people with disabilities as compared to their nondisabled peers. To look at this issue from another perspective, 5.5% of the workforce age 16 and over is composed of people with disabilities (U.S. Census Bureau, 2009). Table 7 provides more information about the jobs of employed people with disabilities and offers a comparison to the jobs of people without disabilities. People with disabilities are more likely to work for private, not-for-profit firms than people without disabilities (9.2% compared to 7.9%) and are more likely to be self-employed (11.9% compared with 9.8%). People with disabilities are far less likely to work in management, professional, and related

Table 7   Class, Occupation, Industry, and Mode of Transportation to Work for the Employed Population (Noninstitutionalized Population, Ages 16 and Over, 2009 ACS)

	With Disability	Without Disability
Employed Population Age 16 and Over	7,758,687	132,831,897
CLASS OF WORKER		
Private for-profit wage and salary workers	66.3%	70.8%
Employee of private company workers	63.1%	67.3%
Self-employed in own incorporated business workers	3.3%	3.5%
Private not-for-profit wage and salary workers	9.2%	7.9%
Local government workers	7.5%	7.8%
State government workers	5.0%	4.6%
Federal government workers	3.1%	2.5%
Self-employed in own not incorporated business workers	8.6%	6.3%
Unpaid family workers	0.3%	0.1%
OCCUPATION		
Management, professional, and related occupations	25.8%	36.3%
Service occupations	22.7%	17.5%
Sales and office occupations	25.0%	25.2%
Farming, fishing, and forestry occupations	0.8%	0.7%
Construction, extraction, maintenance, and repair occupations	9.4%	8.7%
Production, transportation, and material moving occupations	16.3%	11.6%
INDUSTRY		
Agriculture, forestry, fishing and hunting, and mining	2.4%	1.8%
Construction	6.8%	6.8%

(Continued)

Table 7   (Continued)

	With Disability	Without Disability
Manufacturing	10.5%	10.5%
Wholesale trade	2.6%	2.9%
Retail trade	13.1%	11.5%
Transportation and warehousing, and utilities	5.4%	5.0%
Information	1.9%	2.3%
Finance and insurance, and real estate and rental and leasing	5.2%	7.0%
Professional, scientific, and management, and administrative and waste management services	9.5%	10.7%
Educational services, and health care and social assistance	22.3%	22.7%
Arts, entertainment, and recreation, and accommodation and food services	9.2%	9.2%
Other services (except public administration)	5.9%	4.9%
Public administration	5.1%	4.8%
COMMUTING TO WORK		
Workers Age 16 and Over[1]	7,278,190	130,021,442
Car, truck, or van—drove alone	69.7%	76.5%
Car, truck, or van—carpooled	12.8%	9.9%
Public transportation (excluding taxicab)	5.8%	5.0%
Walked	3.6%	2.8%
Taxicab, motorcycle, bicycle, or other means	2.6%	1.7%
Worked at home	5.4%	4.2%

1. Only people who had worked during in the last week were asked this question; therefore, people who were employed but were away from work (e.g., on vacation) during the last week are not included.

Source: Adapted from American Factfinder, Table S1811: Selected economic characteristics for the civilian noninstitutionalized population by disability status. Data Set: 2009 American Community Survey 1-Year Estimates (U.S. civilian population ages 16 and older), by the U.S. Census Bureau, 2009. Retrieved from http://factfinder2.census.gov/faces/tableservices/jsf/pages/productview.xhtml?pid=ACS_09_1YR_S1811&prodType=table.

occupations (25.8% compared to 36.3%) and more likely to work in service or production, transportation, and material-moving occupations (16.3% compared to 11.6%). This raises an important issue of whether these occupations are more "disability friendly" or perhaps more likely to result in a disability.

Transportation can be a major barrier to work for many people with disabilities. People with disabilities are less likely to drive alone to work (69.7% compared to 76.5%). Working from home is a viable option for some jobs and may be a good alternative for people who face transportation issues, which may explain why people with disabilities are slightly more likely to work from home than persons without disabilities. The transportation issue, however, also poses a barrier to equitable access to a wide variety of potential occupations and positions.

Workplace Discrimination

Discrimination in hiring and in the workplace is one possible reason for the observed disparities in the employment of people with disabilities. Title I of the Americans with Disabilities Act of 1990 (ADA) made such discrimination illegal. The Equal Employment Opportunity Commission (EEOC) is charged with enforcing the ADA, along with other laws prohibiting employment discrimination. The EEOC maintains a database of discrimination charges filed with the EEOC (including charges filed with state and local Fair Employment Practice Agencies that contract with the EEOC), and the following data present information about these charges. It should be noted that the data include all charges filed, not only those determined to have merit by the EEOC. These charges represent perceived discrimination in the workplace, although it is important to note that not every case of perceived discrimination leads to a charge being filed. The EEOC data are not a perfect measure of the prevalence of employment discrimination, but provide useful insights regarding where in the employment process people with disabilities are perceiving discrimination.

Figure 11 presents the number of charges filed under various statutes prohibiting employment discrimination on the basis of disability (ADA), age (Age Discrimination in Employment Act or ADEA), sex (Title VII of the Civil Rights Act), and race (also Title VII) per 10,000 labor force participants in the protected class (labor-force adjusted charges of discrimination). The figure highlights that people with disabilities in the labor force are perceiving discrimination in the workplace at a much higher rate than other protected classes. Far more labor-force adjusted charges of

Figure 11   Number of ADA, ADEA, Title VII-Nonwhite, and Title VII-Female Charges per 10,000 People in the Labor Force With Protected Class Characteristics, 1993–2007

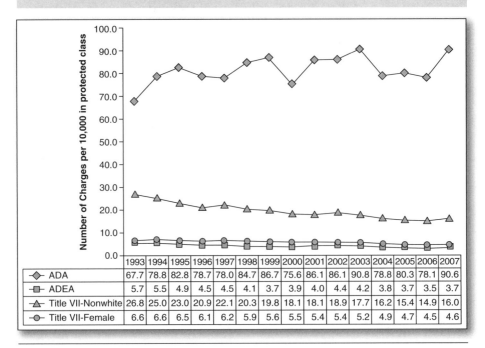

	1993	1994	1995	1996	1997	1998	1999	2000	2001	2002	2003	2004	2005	2006	2007
ADA	67.7	78.8	82.8	78.7	78.0	84.7	86.7	75.6	86.1	86.1	90.8	78.8	80.3	78.1	90.6
ADEA	5.7	5.5	4.9	4.5	4.5	4.1	3.7	3.9	4.0	4.4	4.2	3.8	3.7	3.5	3.7
Title VII-Nonwhite	26.8	25.0	23.0	20.9	22.1	20.3	19.8	18.1	18.1	18.9	17.7	16.2	15.4	14.9	16.0
Title VII-Female	6.6	6.6	6.5	6.1	6.2	5.9	5.6	5.5	5.4	5.4	5.2	4.9	4.7	4.5	4.6

Source: From "United States employment disability discrimination charges: Implications for disability management practice," by S. Bruyère, S. von Schrader, W. Coduti, and M. Bjelland, 2010, *International Journal of Disability Management, 5*(2), 48–58. © 2010 Australian Academic Press. Reprinted with permission.

Note: The number of charges represents the number of charges filed per 10,000 people in the base population where the ADA was cited (i.e., those charges filed based on the ADA alone or in combination with other statutes) and similarly for ADEA, Title VII–Nonwhite, and Title VII–Female. Estimates of the size of the labor force for each protected class were derived from the Annual Social and Economic Supplement to the Current Population Survey.

discrimination are filed under the ADA than any other statute. Over the 15-year period from 1993 to 2007, the average number of ADA charges per 10,000 people with disabilities in the labor force was 81.6. This compares to 4.3 ADEA charges per 10,000 people aged 40 and over in the labor force, 5.6 Title VII-Female charges per 10,000 females in the labor force, and 19.5 Title VII-Nonwhite charges per 10,000 nonwhite people in the labor force. The figure also demonstrates that while labor-force adjusted charge rates remain the same or decrease over the time period for charges filed under

ADEA, Title VII–Female, or Title VII–Nonwhite, the rate of ADA charges increases somewhat, though not monotonically.

Table 8 presents the basis (i.e., disability type) upon which ADA charges were filed from 1993 to 2007. It should be noted that more than one basis can be cited on a charge. The top five most common specific impairments cited on ADA charges are: orthopedic/structural back impairment (12.2%), nonparalytic orthopedic impairment (7.5%), depression (5.8%), diabetes (3.8%), and other psychiatric disorders (3.6%).

Table 9 presents ADA charges filed in the period 1993 to 2007 by issue (i.e., the reason a charge was filed). The most cited issue by far is Discharge, cited on 55.3% of charges—more than twice as many charges as the second most cited issue, Reasonable Accommodation (24.6%).

Who Is out of the Workforce?

Having discussed data related to people with disabilities in the workplace, we now turn our attention to that part of the American population with a disability or health-related condition that may prevent workforce participation. In this process we also present information on the public policy and service structures that support these individuals. Specifically, we provide information on those affected by workplace illnesses or accidents covered by workers' compensation regulations, those covered by Social Security Disability Insurance and Social Security Insurance, and those served by state vocational rehabilitation agencies.

Workplace Illness and Injuries and Workers' Compensation

Legislation has been in place for many years to protect the health and safety of workers and to specify employer responsibilities in the prevention of work-related injuries and illnesses, as well as the required reparation to employees in the event they are injured on the job. The Occupational Safety and Health Act of 1970 has at its core the idea that every worker has a right to a workplace that is free from recognized hazards. When a potential hazard is identified, the Occupational Safety and Health Administration (OSHA), a part of the Labor Department, develops a standard against which workplace practices or conditions should be measured. Unlike some other employment regulations, OSHA requirements apply universally to all employers, regardless of the volume of business they conduct or the number of people in their employ.

Table 8 Percentage of ADA Charges by Basis, Averaged Over 1993–2007

Basis	Percentage of Times Cited	Basis	Percentage of Times Cited
Other Disability	25.93	Multiple Sclerosis	1.18
Retaliation	13.11	Blood (Other)	1.08
Orthopedic/Structural Back Impairment	12.23	Gastrointestinal	0.91
Regarded as Disabled	9.86	Relationship/Association	0.85
Nonparalytic Orthopedic Impairment	7.54	Cumulative Trauma Disorder	0.84
Depression	5.75	Other Pulmo/Respiratory	0.80
Diabetes	3.75	Paralysis	0.77
Other Psychiatric Disorders	3.62	Brain/Head Injury (Traumatic)	0.70
Heart/Cardiovascular	3.57	Drug Addiction	0.68
Hearing Impairment	2.99	Post-Traumatic Stress Disorder	0.64
Record of Disability	2.92	Speech Impairment	0.62
Other	2.86	Mental Retardation	0.61
Other Neurological	2.67	Kidney Impairment	0.60
Cancer	2.43	Allergies	0.57
Other Anxiety Disorder	2.36	Cerebral Palsy	0.44
Vision Impairment	2.28	Schizophrenia	0.38
Missing Digits/Limbs	1.88	Chemical Sensitivity	0.27
Manic Depression (Bi-Polar)	1.78	Disfigurement	0.24
Epilepsy	1.62	Autism	0.05
Learning Disability	1.58	Tuberculosis	0.04
Asthma	1.55	Dwarfism	0.04
Handicap (Not ADA)	1.40	Cystic Fibrosis	0.03
Alcoholism	1.34	Genetic Discrimination	0.02
HIV	1.34	Alzheimer's	0.02

Source: From "Age and disability employment discrimination: Occupational rehabilitation implications," by M. Bjelland, S. Bruyère, S. von Schrader, A. Houtenville, A. Ruiz-Quintanilla, and D. Webber, 2009, *Journal of Occupational Rehabilitation, 20*(4), 456–471. © 2009 Springer Publications. Reprinted with permission.

Note: The percentage represents the fraction of charges filed citing that basis under the ADA (i.e., those charges filed based on the ADA alone or in combination with other statutes). It is important to note that a charge may cite more than one basis, therefore the sum of percentages over all bases will total more than 100%.

Table 9   Percentage of ADA Charges by Issue, Averaged Over 1993–2007

Issue	Percentage of Times Cited	Issue	Percentage of Times Cited
Discharge	55.30	Training	0.78
Reasonable Accommodation	24.64	Prohibited Medical Inquiry/Exam	0.67
Terms/Conditions	18.78	Union Representation	0.52
Harassment	12.18	Breach of Confidentiality	0.40
Hiring	8.16	References Unfavorable	0.27
Other	6.00	Job Classification	0.27
Discipline	5.19	Qualifications	0.24
Constructive Discharge	3.70	Exclusion	0.21
Promotion	3.47	Referral	0.16
Layoff	3.19	Seniority	0.16
Wages	3.00	Maternity	0.15
Demotion	2.77	Testing	0.14
Suspension	2.38	Segregated Facilities	0.11
Intimidation	2.09	Waivers	0.10
Reinstatement	2.06	Tenure	0.07
Assignment	1.93	Severance Pay Denied	0.06
Benefits	1.74	Early Retirement Incentive	0.03
Benefits—Retirement/Pension	0.95	Posting Notices	0.03
Retirement—Involuntary	0.85	Apprenticeship	0.02
Benefits—Insurance	0.84	Advertising	0.02
Recall	0.79		

Source: From "Age and disability employment discrimination: Occupational rehabilitation implications," by M. Bjelland, S. Bruyère, S. von Schrader, A. Houtenville, A. Ruiz-Quintanilla, and D. Webber, 2009, *Journal of Occupational Rehabilitation, 20*(4), 456–471. © 2009 Springer Publications. Reprinted with permission.

Note: The percentage represents the fraction of charges filed citing that issue under the ADA (i.e., those charges filed based on the ADA alone or in combination with other statutes). It is important to note that a charge may cite more than one issue, therefore the sum of percentages over all issues will total more than 100%.

Table 10 demonstrates that the incidence of illnesses and injuries in private industry has decreased since 2007; in fact, these rates have decreased annually since 1992 (Sengupta, Reno & Burton, 2010). While not all workplace injuries and illnesses that are reported result in a disability, the data do specify whether the injury or illness led to days away from work and/or job transfer or restriction, thus indicating a more serious condition. The goods-producing industries of manufacturing (2.3 cases with days away from work and/or job transfer or restriction per 100 full-time workers in 2009), construction (2.3), and natural resources and mining (2.2) have relatively high incidence rates, while trade, transportation, and utilities (2.4) has the highest rate among service-providing industries. Table 11 presents some of the more common types of workplace injuries that lead to days away from work, including sprains, strains, and tears (38.6% of all such injuries); bruises and contusions (8.7%); and cuts and lacerations (8.1%).

Workers' compensation is a social insurance program comprised of a collection of state systems designed to insure workers against the possibility of lost income due to injuries on the job (U.S. Social Security Administration, Office of Retirement and Disability Policy, 2007). Workers' compensation programs fulfill several social policy roles beyond earnings protection, in that they provide insurance coverage as well as reinforce occupational safety and health protections. Although all 50 states have some sort of workers' compensation laws, no single nationwide standard exists. Typically, workers' compensation premiums vary based on the employer's industry, size, and past losses (or "experience rating").

Workers' compensation is an important immediate source of income and medical care for workers who are injured on the job or contract a work-related illness. Workers' compensation programs paid $57.6 billion in benefits in 2008, with $29.1 billion of that total going to medical care and $28.6 billion for cash benefits (Sengupta, Reno, & Burton, Jr., 2010). Figure 12 presents benefits and employer costs per $100 of covered wages since 1980. For more information about workers' compensation, see the Social Security Administration's Web site at http://www.socialsecurity .gov/policy/docs/statcomps/supplement/2007/workerscomp.html.

Social Security Disability Insurance and Social Security Income

The Social Security Administration (SSA) implements the two benefit programs for eligible individuals with disabilities: Social Security Disability Insurance (SSDI) and Supplemental Security Income (SSI).

Table 10   Incidence Rates[1] of Nonfatal Occupational Injuries and Illness by Major Private Industry Sector and Selected Case Types, 2007–2009

Industry sector	Total Recordable Cases			Total Cases With Days Away From Work[2]		
	2007	2008	2009	2007	2008	2009
Private industry[3]	4.2	3.9	3.6	2.1	2.0	1.8
Goods producing[3]	5.4	4.9	4.3	2.9	2.6	2.3
Natural resources and mining[3,4]	4.4	4.1	4.0	2.5	2.5	2.2
Construction	5.4	4.7	4.3	2.8	2.5	2.3
Manufacturing	5.6	5.0	4.3	3.0	2.7	2.3
Service providing	3.8	3.6	3.4	1.9	1.8	1.7
Trade, transportation, and utilities[5]	4.9	4.4	4.1	2.8	2.6	2.4
Information	2.0	2.0	1.9	1.1	1.1	1.0
Financial activities	1.4	1.5	1.5	0.7	0.7	0.6
Professional and business services	2.1	1.9	1.8	1.0	1.0	0.9
Education and health services	5.2	5.0	5.0	2.4	2.3	2.2
Leisure and hospitality	4.5	4.2	3.9	1.7	1.6	1.6
Other services, except public administration	3.1	3.1	2.9	1.5	1.5	1.4

1. The incidence rates represent the number of injuries and illnesses per 100 full-time workers and were calculated as: (N/EH) x 200,000, where N = number of injuries and illnesses EH = total hours worked by all employees during the calendar year 200,000 = base for 100 equivalent full-time workers (working 40 hours per week, 50 weeks per year)

2. Days-away-from-work cases include those that result in days away from work with or without job transfer or restriction

3. Excludes farms with fewer than 11 employees.

4. Data for Mining (Sector 21 in the *North American Industry Classification System*—United States, 2007) include establishments not governed by the Mine Safety and Health Administration rules and reporting, such as those in Oil and Gas Extraction and related support activities. Data for mining operators in coal, metal, and nonmetal mining are provided to BLS by the Mine Safety and Health Administration, U.S. Department of Labor. Independent mining contractors are excluded from the coal, metal, and nonmetal mining industries. These data do not reflect the changes the Occupational Safety and Health Administration made to its recordkeeping requirements effective January 1, 2002; therefore, estimates for these industries are not comparable to estimates in other industries.

5. Data for employers in railroad transportation are provided to BLS by the Federal Railroad Administration, U.S. Department of Transportation.

Source: From *Occupational injuries and illnesses (annual) news release: Workplace injuries and illnesses—2009*, Table 7, by the Bureau of Labor Statistics, U.S. Department of Labor, 2010. Retrieved from http://www.bls.gov/news.release/archives/osh_10212010.htm.

Note: Because of rounding, components may not add to totals.

Table 11 Percent Distribution of Nonfatal Occupational Injuries and Illnesses Involving Days Away from Work[1] by Selected Injury or Illness Characteristics, 2008

Total [1,078,140 cases]	Private Industry [2,3,4]
Nature of injury or illness:	100.0
Sprains, strains, tears	38.6
Bruises, contusions	8.7
Cuts, lacerations	8.1
Punctures	1.2
Fractures	8.3
Heat burns	1.4
Carpal tunnel syndrome	0.9
Tendonitis	0.4
Chemical burns	0.5
Amputations	0.6
Multiple traumatic injuries	4.1

1. Days-away-from-work cases include those that resulted in days away from work, some of which also included job transfer or restriction.

2. Excludes farms with fewer than 11 employees.

3. Data for Mining (Sector 21 in the *North American Industry Classification System*—United States, 2002) include establishments not governed by the Mine Safety and Health Administration rules and reporting, such as those in Oil and Gas Extraction and related support activities. Data for mining operators in coal, metal, and nonmetal mining are provided to BLS by the Mine Safety and Health Administration, U.S. Department of Labor. Independent mining contractors are excluded from the coal, metal, and nonmetal mining industries. These data do not reflect the changes the Occupational Safety and Health Administration made to its recordkeeping requirements effective January 1, 2002; therefore, estimates for these industries are not comparable to estimates in other industries.

4. Data for employers in rail transportation are provided to BLS by the Federal Railroad Administration, U.S. Department of Transportation.

Source: From *Survey of occupational injuries and illnesses by selected characteristics news release: Nonfatal occupational injuries and illnesses requiring days away from work,* Table 6, by the Bureau of Labor Statistics, U.S. Department of Labor, 2008. Retrieved from http://www.bls.gov/news.release/archives/osh2_12042009.htm.

Note: Dash indicates data do not meet publication guidelines. Because of rounding and data exclusion of nonclassifiable responses, data may not sum to the totals.

Figure 12   Workers' Compensation Benefits* and Employer Costs** per $100 of Covered Wages, 1980–2008

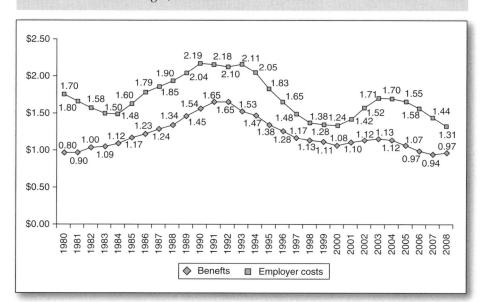

*Benefits are payments in the calendar year to injured workers and to providers of their medical care.

**Costs are employer expenditures in the calendar year for workers' compensation benefits, administrative costs, and/or insurance premiums. Costs for self-insuring employers are benefits paid in the calendar year plus the administrative costs associated with providing these benefits. Costs for employers who purchase insurance include the insurance premiums paid during the calendar year plus payments of benefits under large deductible plans during the year. The insurance premiums must pay for all of the compensable consequences of the injuries that occur during the year, including the benefits paid in the current as well as future years.

Source: From *Workers' compensation: Benefits, coverage, and costs, 2008,* by I. Sengupta, V. Reno, and J. Burton, Jr., 2010. Washington, DC: National Academy of Social Insurance. Retrieved from http://www.nasi.org/research/2010/report-workers-compensation-benefits-coverage-costs-2008. Copyright 2010 by National Academy of Social Insurance. Reprinted with permission.

To qualify for SSDI benefits, an individual must have been employed for a minimum period and paid Social Security taxes. The person must also have a medical condition that meets SSA's definition of disability, "the inability to engage in any substantial gainful activity by reason of any medically determinable physical or mental impairment which can be expected to result in death or which has lasted or can be expected to last for a continuous period of not less than 12 months." In contrast to workers' compensation, which provides benefits to individuals with a work-related injury or illness as soon as they are considered eligible, there is a five-month waiting period for cash benefits and a 24-month waiting period for health insurance (Medicare). Enrollment rates for SSDI roughly mirror what we see regarding prevalence rates across the states (higher prevalence rates tend to correspond with higher enrollment). Additionally, lower employment rates among people with disabilities are found in states with large numbers of SSDI beneficiaries.

Supplemental Security Income (SSI) is a means-tested program that provides an assured minimum income to aged, blind, and disabled individuals. Applicants must pass an income and resource test and must meet the same SSA disability standard as SSDI applicants.

The potential loss of cash benefits and medical care provided through the SSDI and SSI programs are an important reason why many people with disabilites who might be able to work with accommodation do not work. Each program treats the return-to-work process differently. Return to work under SSDI is complicated and poses more substantial risk to the beneficiary. By contrast, the SSI program has a gradual reduction in benefits.

Table 12 highlights the utilization and cost of the SSDI program. The total number of SSDI beneficiaries has increased consistently from 1983 to 2009. Table 13 presents the diagnostic groups of SSDI beneficiaries, with nearly one in three recipients having a diagnosis of "mental disorders."

Table 14 demonstrates the consistent increase in the total number of SSI recipients and total SSI payments from 1974 to 2009. Between the years 2000 and 2009, the number of recipients grew by over one million and the total payments increased by nearly $16 billion. Table 15 presents the diagnostic groups of working-age SSI recipients; as with SSDI, the most common diagnosis category is mental disorders (58.8%).

Vocational Rehabilitation

Vocational rehabilitation (VR) is a federal and state-sponsored program that provides grants to states to support a wide range of services designed to help individuals with disabilities prepare for and engage in gainful employment. The Rehabilitation Act of 1973, as amended, authorizes the allocation of federal funds for the administration and execution of vocational rehabilitation services at the state level. The goal of this law is to assist states with the operation of "comprehensive, coordinated, effective, efficient and accountable" vocational rehabilitation programs, including

Table 12 SSDI Total Beneficiaries, Worker Beneficiaries, and Total Monthly Benefits to Workers

Year	Total Beneficiaries	Worker Beneficiaries	Total Monthly Benefits to Workers (in Thousands of Dollars)	Year	Total Beneficiaries	Worker Beneficiaries	Total Monthly Benefits to Workers (in Thousands of Dollars)
1960	559,425	455,371	40,669	1985	3,289,485	2,656,638	1,285,281
1961	742,296	618,075	55,373	1986	3,380,480	2,728,463	1,331,217
1962	888,131	740,867	66,671	1987	3,453,414	2,785,859	1,415,774
1963	993,656	827,014	74,919	1988	3,507,707	2,830,284	1,498,635
1964	1,077,695	894,173	81,477	1989	3,583,451	2,895,364	1,609,822
1965	1,186,464	988,074	96,594	1990	3,712,763	3,011,294	1,768,232
1966	1,310,911	1,097,190	107,623	1991	3,925,472	3,194,938	1,946,995
1967	1,422,778	1,193,120	117,439	1992	4,236,080	3,467,783	2,171,179
1968	1,560,517	1,295,300	144,892	1993	4,529,466	3,725,966	2,390,952
1969	1,690,982	1,394,291	157,192	1994	4,796,313	3,962,954	2,621,098
1970	1,812,786	1,492,948	195,964	1995	5,044,388	4,185,263	2,853,512
1971	1,990,098	1,647,684	241,419	1996	5,264,321	4,385,623	3,087,040
1972	2,202,090	1,832,916	328,678	1997	5,400,781	4,508,134	3,253,069
1973	2,415,383	2,016,626	369,043	1998	5,605,272	4,698,319	3,444,338
1974	2,670,092	2,236,882	460,127	1999	5,798,776	4,879,455	3,679,597
1975	2,960,620	2,488,774	562,214	2000	5,972,468	5,042,333	3,965,291

(Continued)

(Continued)

Year	Total Beneficiaries	Worker Beneficiaries	Total Monthly Benefits to Workers (in Thousands of Dollars)	Year	Total Beneficiaries	Worker Beneficiaries	Total Monthly Benefits to Workers (in Thousands of Dollars)
1976	3,171,198	2,670,208	654,655	2001	6,208,847	5,268,039	4,290,449
1977	3,368,954	2,837,432	752,771	2002	6,491,494	5,539,597	4,621,852
1978	3,429,421	2,879,774	830,239	2003	6,830,714	5,868,541	5,054,332
1979	3,435,761	2,870,590	924,330	2004	7,167,375	6,197,385	5,540,703
1980	3,436,429	2,858,680	1,059,713	2005	7,503,405	6,519,001	6,113,106
1981	3,361,130	2,776,519	1,147,258	2006	7,803,692	6,806,918	6,655,048
1982	3,192,379	2,603,599	1,147,146	2007	8,118,382	7,098,723	7,127,082
1983	3,168,992	2,569,029	1,171,991	2008	8,528,164	7,426,691	7,895,536
1984	3,212,040	2,596,516	1,222,180	2009	8,945,376	7,788,013	8,288,762

Source: From *Annual statistical report on the Social Security Disability Insurance Program, 2009,* Table 3, by the U.S. Social Security Administration, 2010. Retrieved from http://www.ssa.gov/policy/docs/statcomps/di_asr/2009/index.html.

Table 13 Distribution of SSDI Worker Beneficiaries, by Diagnostic Group, December 2009

	Worker Beneficiaries	
	Number	Percent
Total	7,788,013	100
Congenital anomalies	13,614	0.2
Endocrine, nutritional, and metabolic diseases	278,565	3.6
Infectious and parasitic diseases	119,753	1.5
Injuries	330,708	4.2
Mental disorders		
Retardation	358,737	4.6
Other	2,220,390	28.5
Neoplasms	237,589	3.1
Diseases of the—		
Blood and blood-forming organs	19,977	0.3
Circulatory system	683,834	8.8
Digestive system	125,725	1.6
Genitourinary system	132,797	1.7
Musculoskeletal system and connective tissue	2,146,952	27.6
Nervous system and sense organs	734,496	9.4
Respiratory system	227,385	2.9
Skin and subcutaneous tissue	18,713	0.2
Other	18,030	0.2
Unknown	120,748	1.6

Source: From *Annual statistical report on the Social Security Disability Insurance Program, 2009,* Table 6: Distribution, by sex and diagnostic group, by the U.S. Social Security Administration, 2010. Retrieved from http://www.ssa.gov/policy/docs/statcomps/di_asr/2009/index.html.

Table 14   SSI Payments, Recipients, and Percent of Recipients Who Are Working Age, Selected Years 1974–2009

	Total Payments (in Thousands of Dollars)	Total Number of SSI Recipients	Percent of Recipients Who Are Working Age (18–64)
1974	5,096,813	3,996,064	37.6
1975	5,716,072	4,314,275	39.4
1980	7,714,640	4,142,017	41.8
1985	10,749,938	4,138,021	45.4
1990	16,132,959	4,817,127	50.9
1995	27,037,280	6,514,134	53.5
1996	28,252,474	6,613,718	54.0
1997	28,370,568	6,494,985	54.8
1998	29,408,208	6,566,069	55.5
1999	30,106,132	6,556,634	56.3
2000	30,671,699	6,601,686	56.7
2001	32,165,856	6,688,489	57.0
2002	33,718,999	6,787,857	57.1
2003	34,693,278	6,902,364	57.3
2004	36,065,358	6,987,845	57.5
2005	37,235,843	7,113,879	57.4
2006	38,888,961	7,235,583	57.4
2007	41,204,645	7,359,525	57.4
2008	43,040,481	7,520,501	57.6
2009	46,592,308	7,676,686	58.0

Sources: Adapted from *Annual statistical report on the Social Security Disability Insurance Program, 2009,* Table 4: Recipients, by age, and Table 2: Total payments, by eligibility category and source of payment, by the U.S. Social Security Administration, 2010. Retrieved from http://www.socialsecurity.gov/policy/docs/statcomps/ssi_asr/2009/table04.html and http://www.socialsecurity.gov/policy/docs/statcomps/ssi_asr/2009/table02.html.

Table 15   Percentage Distribution of All Working-Age (18–64) Blind and
Disabled SSI Recipients and Those Who Work, by Diagnostic Group,
December 2009

	All Blind and Disabled Recipients	Recipients Who Work[a]
Total		
Number	4,451,288	324,187
Percent	100	100
Congenital anomalies	0.8	1.9
Endocrine, nutritional, and metabolic diseases	3	1.1
Infectious and parasitic diseases	1.5	0.9
Injuries	2.6	1.4
Mental disorders		
Retardation	20.7	39.9
Schizophrenia	9.4	6.3
Other	28.7	21.2
Neoplasms	1.3	0.8
Diseases of the—		
Blood and blood-forming organs	0.4	0.4
Circulatory system	4.3	1.3
Digestive system	1	0.4
Genitourinary system	1	0.7
Musculoskeletal system and connective tissue	11.3	4.1
Nervous system and sense organs[b]	7.8	9.1
Respiratory system	2	0.8
Skin and subcutaneous tissue	0.2	0.1
Other	0.3	0.4
Unknown	3.8	9.2

a. Includes section 1619(b) participants.

b. Most disabled recipients classified as blind are included in this category. A few blind recipients with a primary impairment other than diseases of the eye are coded in other categories. Also, a few recipients are classified with diseases of the eye, but their impairment does not meet the definition of blindness.

Source: From *Annual statistical report on the Social Security Disability Insurance Program, 2009,* Table 42: Percentage distribution of all blind and disabled recipients and those who work, by the Social Security Administration, 2010. Retrieved from http://www.socialsecurity.gov/policy/docs/statcomps/ssi_asr/2009/table42.html.

Table 16 Vocational Rehabilitation Case Closures and Employment Outcomes: 2001–2008

	2001	2002	2003	2004	2005	2006	2007	2008
Total number of VR closures	639,979	643,415	650,643	654,040	616,879	617,149	600,188	609,625
Closures into an employment setting	233,684	221,031	217,557	213,431	206,695	205,791	205,447	202,297
Mean weekly earnings at closure from VR Services	$288	$273	$305	$312	$322	$335	$348	$362
Weekly hours worked at closure from VR Services	32.1	28.9	31.5	31.6	31.7	31.8	31.7	31.6
Closures with an Individualized Plan for Employment (IPE) but no employment outcome	151,355	146,572	154,700	171,642	149,534	146,347	139,061	147,948
Rehabilitation rate for all closures*	60.7%	60.1%	58.4%	55.4%	58.0%	58.4%	59.6%	57.8%
Percentage of all closures that were into employment	36.5%	34.4%	33.4%	32.6%	33.5%	33.3%	34.2%	33.2%

*Rehabilitation Rate = (# closures in employment) / (# closures in employment + # closures with an IPE not in employment).

Source: Adapted from *StateData: The national report on employment services and outcomes,* Tables 8 and 9 (p. 51), by J. Butterworth, F. Smith, A. Hall, and J. Winsor, 2010, Boston, MA: Institute for Community Inclusion (UCEDD). Retrieved from http://www.statedata.info. Copyright © 2010 by Institute for Community Inclusion. Adapted with permission.

vocational assessment, career counseling, job training, job development and placement, assistive technology, supported employment, and follow-along services (State Vocational Rehabilitation Services Program, 2001).

Once eligibility for VR has been established, an individual works with a VR counselor to develop an Individual Plan for Employment outlining, among other things, the desired employment outcome and the services needed to reach that outcome. A successful final outcome is defined as placement in an integrated employment setting at a prevailing wage rate, but outcomes such as becoming a homemaker or unpaid family worker may be considered successful vocational outcomes for some individuals. Successful closures are those with an employment outcome for a consumer within 90 days after VR services. An employment outcome includes closures into the following categories: integrated employment (including supported employment), self-employment, state agency-managed business enterprise, homemaker, and unpaid family worker.

The state and federal VR program serves approximately 1.2 million individuals with disabilities each year (Council of State Administrators of Vocational Rehabilitation, n.d.). Over 600,000 VR closures occur annually; approximately one out of three results in an employment outcome.

States are required to track outcomes of VR service closures, and these data are reported annually using the federal Rehabilitation Services Administration (RSA)-911 Case Service Report. Table 16 presents aggregate information on state VR agency case closures from 2001 to 2008. While the number of VR closures has decreased slightly over time, the percentage of closures into employment and the rehabilitation rate have remained fairly consistent from 2001 to 2008. When considering those VR closures that resulted in employment outcomes, a fairly consistent increase over time in earnings is apparent, while the weekly hours worked have remained steady.

Conclusion

In this chapter we have presented data from a wide variety of sources focusing on disability, employment, and work. The importance of how disability is defined and the effects of different disability definitions were demonstrated through comparisons of estimates among different data sources. Regardless of the disability definitions used, large disparities between persons with and without disabilities in terms of employment, income, and poverty status persist. This is not unique to the United States, as international data also show this effect. Among the employed, the distribution across occupations and industries differs between persons with and without disabilities. Equal Employment Opportunity Commission (EEOC) disability discrimination charge data provide evidence that a significant number of persons with disabilities perceive that they have been discriminated against by their employer or a potential employer. Finally, administrative data from SSA regarding SSI and SSDI show major increases in participation in these programs and in the associated costs over the period presented. The data presented in this chapter provide a backdrop for discussion about the issues related to the employment and economic well-being of the population with disabilities throughout this book.

References

Bjelland, M. J., Bruyère, S. M., von Schrader, S., Houtenville, A. J., Ruiz-Quintanilla, A., & Webber, D. A. (2009). Age and disability employment discrimination: Occupational rehabilitation implications. *Journal of Occupational Rehabilitation, 20*(4), 456–471. Retrieved from http://www.springerlink.com/content/g4503070w2x75028

Bjelland, M., Burkhauser, R., von Schrader, S., & Houtenville, A. (2009). *2009 progress report on the economic well-being of working age people with disabilities.* Ithaca, NY: Rehabilitation Research and Training Center for Economic Research on Employment Policy for Persons with Disabilities.

Brault, M. W. (2008, December). *Americans with disabilities: 2005 household economic studies* (Current Population Reports). Washington, DC: Department of Commerce, U.S. Census Bureau. Retrieved from http://www.census.gov/prod/2008pubs/p70-117.pdf

Bruyère, S., von Schrader, S., Coduti, W., & Bjelland, M. (2010). United States employment disability discrimination charges: Implications for disability management practice. *International Journal of Disability Management, 5*(2), 48–58. doi: 10.1375/jdmr.5.2.48

Burkhauser, R., Daly, M., Houtenville A., & Nargis, N. (2002). Self-reported work-limitation data: What they can and cannot tell us. *Demography, 39*(3), 541–555.

Burkhauser, R., Houtenville, A., & Wittenburg, D. (2003). A user's guide to current statistics on the employment of people with disabilities. In D. Stapleton & R. Burkhauser (Eds.), *The decline in the employment of people with disabilities: A policy puzzle* (pp. 23–86). Kalamazoo, Michigan: W. E. Upjohn Institute for Employment Research.

Butterworth, J., Smith, F. A., Hall, A. C., & Winsor, J. E. (2010). *StateData: The national report on employment services and outcomes.* Boston, MA: Institute for Community Inclusion (UCEDD). Retrieved from http://www.statedata.info

Council of State Administrators of Vocational Rehabilitation. (n.d.). *Public vocational rehabilitation program fact sheet*. Retrieved from http://www .rehabnetwork.org/press_room/vr_fact_sheet.htm

Erickson, W., Lee, C., & von Schrader, S. (2010a). *2008 disability status report: The United States*. Ithaca, NY: Cornell University Rehabilitation Research and Training Center on Disability Demographics and Statistics.

Erickson, W., Lee, C., & von Schrader, S. (2010b, March 17). *Disability statistics from the 2008 American Community Survey (ACS)*. Ithaca, NY: Cornell University Rehabilitation Research and Training Center on Disability Demographics and Statistics (StatsRRTC). Retrieved from http://www.disabilitystatistics.org

Mashaw, J., & Reno, V. (1996). *Balancing security and opportunity: The challenge of disability income policy* (Report of the Disability Policy Panel). Washington, DC: National Academy of Social Insurance. Retrieved from http://www.nasi.org/ research/1996/balancing-security-opportunity-challenge-disability-income

Organisation for Economic Co-operation and Development. (2006). *Sickness, disability and work: Breaking the barriers (Vol. 1): Norway, Poland, and Switzerland*. Paris, France: OECD Publishing.

Organisation for Economic Co-operation and Development. (2007). *Sickness, disability and work: Breaking the barriers (Vol. 2): Australia, Luxembourg, Spain, and the United Kingdom*. Paris, France: OECD Publishing.

Organisation for Economic Co-operation and Development. (2008). *Sickness, disability and work: Breaking the barriers (Vol. 3): Denmark, Finland, Ireland and the Netherlands*. Paris, France: OECD Publishing.

Organisation for Economic Co-operation and Development. (2009). *Sickness, disability and work: Keeping on track in the economic downturn—Background paper*. High-Level Forum, Stockholm, Sweden, May 14–15, 2009. Retrieved from http://www.oecd.org/els/disability/stockholmforum

Sengupta, I., Reno, V., & Burton, J. F., Jr. (2010). *Workers' compensation: Benefits, coverage, and costs, 2008*. Washington, DC: National Academy of Social Insurance. Retrieved from http://www.nasi.org/research/2010/report-workers-compensation-benefits-coverage-costs-2008

State Vocational Rehabilitation Services Program, 34 C. F. R. § 361.1 (2001).

U.S. Census Bureau. (2009). *American FactFinder, Table S1811: Selected economic characteristics for the civilian non-institutionalized population by disability status*. Retrieved from http://factfinder.census.gov/home/saff/main.html?_lang=en

U.S. Department of Labor, Bureau of Labor Statistics. (2008). *Survey of occupational injuries and illnesses by selected characteristics news release: Nonfatal occupational injuries and illnesses requiring days away from work. Table 6*. Retrieved from http:// www.bls.gov/news.release/archives/osh_10292009.htm

U.S. Department of Labor, Bureau of Labor Statistics. (2010). *Occupational injuries and illnesses (annual) news release: Workplace injuries and illnesses—2009. Table 7*. Retrieved from http://www.bls.gov/news.release/archives/osh_10212010 .htm

U.S. Department of Labor, Bureau of Labor Statistics. (2010). *Labor force statistics from the Current Population Survey. Table A-6*. Retrieved from http://www.bls.gov/cps/cpsdisability.htm

U.S. Social Security Administration. (2010). *SSI annual statistical report, 2009*. Retrieved from http://www.ssa.gov/policy/docs/statcomps/di_asr/2009/index.html

U.S. Social Security Administration, Office of Retirement and Disability Policy. (2007). *Workers' compensation program description and legislative history*. Retrieved from http://www.socialsecurity.gov/policy/docs/statcomps/supplement/2007/workerscomp.html

Weathers, R. R., II. (2009). The disability data landscape. In A. Houtenville, D. Stapleton, R. Weathers II, & R. Burkhauser (Eds.), *Counting working age people with disabilities: What current data tell us and options for improvement* (pp. 27–68). Kalamazoo, MI: W. E. Upjohn Institute for Employment Research.

Weathers, R., II, & Wittenburg, D. C. (2009). Employment. In A. Houtenville, D. Stapleton, R. Weathers II, & R. Burkhauser (Eds.), *Counting working age people with disabilities: What current data tell us and options for improvement* (pp. 101–144). Kalamazoo, MI: W. E. Upjohn Institute for Employment Research.

Six

Annotated List of Organizations and Associations

Sara Furguson, Sara VanLooy,

and Susanne M. Bruyère

This chapter provides an annotated list of organizations and associations that are involved in creating, supporting, or promoting employment programs and job opportunities for individuals with disabilities. The list is divided into the following categories: Private Organizations, Government Organizations, State Vocational Rehabilitation Agencies, and Regional ADA Centers.

Private Organizations

Ability Magazine/ABILITYJobs
ABILITY Mail Center
P.O. Box 10878
Costa Mesa, CA 92627

E-mail: info@abilityjobs.com

Web site: http://www.abilityjobs.com

This organization provides an electronic "classified" system that allows employers to recruit qualified individuals with disabilities and allows people with disabilities to locate employment opportunities and post their resumes. Ability *magazine provides information on locating qualified readers, interpreters, personal assistants, and assistive devices; on overcoming architectural, communication, and transportation barriers; and on performing job analysis, job modification, and job restructuring.*

AbilityLinks.org

26W171 Roosevelt Road

Wheaton, IL 60187

Telephone: (630) 909-7443

Fax: (630) 909-7441

Web site: http://www.abilitylinks.org

AbilityLinks is a Web-based community where job seekers with disabilities, inclusive employers, and service providers meet and gain access to valuable networking opportunities. Networking is accomplished through AbilityLinks.org, a free, nationwide job-opportunity Web site for persons with disabilities and inclusive employers, similar to niche Web sites set up to serve minorities, women, and ethnic groups protected by equal opportunity employment laws.

AbleData

8630 Fenton Street, Suite 930

Silver Spring, MD 20910

Telephone: (800) 227-0216

E-mail: abledata@macrointernational.com

Web site: http://www.abledata.com

AbleData provides objective information on assistive technology and rehabilitation equipment available from domestic and international sources to consumers, organizations, professionals, and caregivers within the United States. The organization serves the nation's disability, rehabilitation, and senior communities.

ADA National Network

Disability and Business Technical Assistance Center Hotline

Telephone: (800) 949-4232

Web site: http://www.adata.org

The ADA National Network provides information, guidance, and training on the Americans with Disabilities Act (ADA), to meet the needs of business, government, and individuals at local, regional, and national levels. The ADA National Network has ten regional ADA National Network Centers located throughout the United States that provide personalized, local assistance to ensure that the ADA is implemented properly (for contact information,

please see the Regional ADA Centers section of this chapter). ADATA does not hold enforce-
ment or regulatory power, but serves as a resource supporting the ADA's mission.

American Association of People with Disabilities

1629 K Street, NW, Suite 950
Washington, DC 20006
Telephone: (800) 840-8844
Web site: http://www.aapd.com
The American Association of People with Disabilities organizes people with disabilities
effectively to bring political, economic, and social change to society. Additionally, the
agency works to improve the hiring, retention, and promotion of people with disabilities in
employment. AAPD was founded in 1995 to help unite the diverse community of people
with disabilities, including their family, friends, and supporters, and to be a national voice
for change in implementing the goals of the Americans with Disabilities Act (ADA).

American Congress of Community Supports and Employment Services (ACCSES)

1501 M Street, 7th Floor
Washington, DC 20005
Telephone: (202) 466-3355
Fax: (202) 466-7571
Web site: http://www.accses.org
The mission of ACCSES is to promote and enhance community-based solutions that maxi-
mize employment and independent living opportunities for people with disabilities. ACCSES
works with government and other stakeholders to assure that services recognize and sup-
port the full potential of each person with a disability to enjoy a meaningful life. ACCSES
promotes openness and collaboration with the public.

American Council of the Blind

2200 Wilson Boulevard, Suite 650
Arlington, VA 22201
Telephone: (800) 424-8666
E-mail: info@acb.org
Web site: http://www.acb.org
The American Council of the Blind strives to improve the well-being of all blind and
visually impaired people by: serving as a representative national organization of blind
people; elevating the social, economic, and cultural levels of blind people; improving
educational and rehabilitation facilities and opportunities; cooperating with the public
and private institutions and organizations concerned with blind services; encouraging
and assisting all blind persons to develop their abilities; and conducting a public educa-
tion program to promote greater understanding of blindness and the capabilities of blind
people.

American Deafness and Rehabilitation Association (ADARA)
ADARA National Office
P.O. Box 480
Myersville, MD 21773
Web site: http://www.adara.org
The mission of ADARA is to facilitate excellence in human service delivery with individuals who are deaf or hard of hearing. This mission is accomplished by enhancing the professional competencies of the membership, expanding opportunities for networking among ADARA colleagues, and supporting positive public policies for individuals who are deaf or hard of hearing.

American Foundation for the Blind
2 Penn Plaza, Suite 1102
New York, NY 10121
Telephone: (800) AFB-LINE; (800) 232-5463
E-mail: afbinfo@afb.net
Web site: www.afb.org
The American Foundation for the Blind (AFB) is dedicated to addressing the critical issues of literacy, independent living, employment, and access through technology for the ten million Americans who are blind or visually impaired. AFB is a national nonprofit that expands possibilities for the more than 25 million people with vision loss in the United States. AFB's priorities include broadening access to technology; elevating the quality of information and tools for the professionals who serve people with vision loss; and promoting independent and healthy living for people with vision loss by providing them and their families with relevant and timely resources.

American Foundation for the Blind, National Employment Center
50 California Street, Suite 1500
San Francisco, CA 94111
Telephone: (415) 392-4845
E-mail: sanfran@afb.net
The AFB National Employment Center serves as an interface between employers, blind or visually impaired job seekers, and the rehabilitation professionals who serve them. The NEC conducts research, offers workshops, and directs advocacy efforts across the country. Additionally, NEC identifies and develops effective models to ease the transition from rehabilitation training to employment, provides help so that individuals losing their vision can retain their jobs, and offers training to employers and service-delivery professionals.

American Foundation for the Blind, National Technology Center
1000 Fifth Avenue, Suite 350
Huntington, WV 25701

Telephone: (304) 523-8651
Web site: http://www.afb.org

The AFB's National Technology Center (AFB TECH) has a database of 2,000 blind and visually impaired people who use adaptive equipment in various jobs. Employers are welcome to call for information. The center also evaluates high-tech products. AFB TECH's product evaluations can demonstrate how companies can get accessible products into the hands of people with vision loss to maximize profits. AFB TECH is the only organization of its kind to offer objective, comprehensive accessibility reviews of products for people who have lost some or all of their vision. AFB TECH can also help companies comply with Section 508 of the Rehabilitation Act, opening the door to government contracts.

American Institute for Managing Diversity

1200 West Peach Street, NW, Suite 3
Atlanta, GA 30309
Telephone: (404) 575-2131
Web site: http://www.aimd.org

AIMD works to advance diversity leadership through research, education, and public outreach. The institute provides pioneering and creative thinking on the issues of diversity and diversity management and serves as the desired destination for individuals and organizations around the world seeking access to a comprehensive array of resources on cutting-edge perspectives and approaches to diversity. AIMD has created unique learning environments for the public and produced research, tools, and information that will facilitate greater diversity management capability among organizations, communities, and the general public.

The Arc of the United States

1660 L Street, NW, Suite 301
Washington, DC 20036
Telephone: (800) 433-5255
Web site: http://www.thearc.org

The Arc promotes and protects the human rights of people with intellectual and developmental disabilities and actively supports their full inclusion and participation in the community throughout their lifetimes. The Arc's vision is that every individual and family affected by intellectual disability in the United States has access to the information, advocacy, and skills they need to participate as active citizens of the American democracy and active members of their community.

Association for People in Supported Employment (APSE)

451 Hungerford Drive, Suite 700
Rockville, MD 20850
Telephone: (301) 279-0060

Web site: http://www.apse.org
APSE is an international association that provides resources and information on how to utilize subsidized "supported employment" programs. The association also provides referral to state chapters which can then provide referral to supported employment programs in specific cities or areas. APSE advocates with federal, state, and local legislators for legislation promoting integrated employment. AFB's priorities include broadening access to technology; elevating the quality of information and tools for the professionals who serve people with vision loss; and promoting independent and healthy living for people with vision loss by providing them and their families with relevant and timely resources.

Barrier-Free E-recruitment: Employer's Forum on Disability
Nutmeg House
60 Gainsford Street
London SE1 2NY
United Kingdom
Telephone: (44) 020-7403-3020
Web site: http://www.barrierfree-recruitment.com
The Employers' Forum on Disability is an employers' organization working to the mutual benefit of employers and disabled people. The forum makes it easier to recruit, retain, and develop disabled employees and to welcome disabled customers. Barrierfree-recruitment. com is an interactive demonstration of what organizations need to do to achieve barrier-free e-recruitment for everyone. It has been produced by the Employers' Forum on Disability and with the support of the London Development Agency. The forum also assists employers to implement best practice on disability.

Brain Injury Association, Inc.
105 North Alfred Street
Alexandria, VA 22314
Telephone: (202) 296-6443
Web site: http://www.biausa.org
BIAUSA provides informational services and resources on traumatic brain injury. Additionally, the association offers employment-related publications on vocational rehabilitation, job-seeking skills, job placement, return-to-work and employment issues, and adaptive work behaviors for victims of brain injury. Local associations can be accessed for local information. Together with its network of more than 40 chartered state affiliates, as well as hundreds of local chapters and support groups across the country, the BIAA provides information, education, and support to people with traumatic brain injury.

Career Opportunities for Students with Disabilities
100 Dunford Hall
Knoxville, TN 37996-4010
Telephone: (865) 974-7148

Fax: (865) 974-6497

E-mail: amuir@cosdonline.org

Web site: http://www.cosdonline.org

Career Opportunities for Students with Disabilities (COSD) is a national professional association composed of 600 colleges and universities and over 500 major national employers. COSD's mission is to improve the employment rate of college students and recent graduates with disabilities on a national basis. COSD works with higher education institutions and assists them in developing collaborative relationships between the Disability Services and Career Services offices on campuses. COSD closely works with employers to identify innovative methods of recruiting and hiring college graduates with disabilities.

Connect-Ability

Telephone: (866) 844-1903

E-mail: info@connect-ability.com

Web site: http://www.connect-ability.com

Connect-Ability works to remove barriers that make it hard for job seekers with disabilities to find and keep jobs. The program's role is to offer information, tools, and technical assistance to job seekers and employers rather than provide direct job-placement services. The program does not directly provide services to match individuals with specific jobs. Instead, efforts are focused on removing the barriers that keep customers from finding one another. These barriers include, but are not limited to, low expectations, the transition from school to work, inadequate transportation, and the actual process of recruitment, hiring, and retention.

DisabilityWorks

Telephone: (312) 494-6713

Web site: http://www.disabilityworks.org

DisabilityWorks aims to increase the economic and employment opportunities of people with disabilities while meeting the workforce needs of businesses located in the state of Illinois by promoting a collaborative partnership between the private and public sectors. It also provides education and job matching for employers in Illinois in hiring individuals with disabilities in order to meet labor-market demands.

DisABLEDperson, Inc.

P.O. Box 230636

Encinitas, CA 92023-0636

Telephone: (760) 420-1269

E-mail: info@disabledperson.com

Web site: http://www.disabledperson.com

DisABLEDperson, Inc. is a public charity organization established in 2002 whose primary focus is disability employment. It offers resume posting, searchable job boards, and college scholarships for persons with disabilities. It is affiliated with Job Opportunities for

Disabled American Veterans (JOFDAV), which provides searchable resume, job posting, recruitment, and compliance resources for employers, as well as RecruitABILITY, an online recruitment application and community for students with disabilities transitioning from school to work.

DisaboomJobs

E-mail: info@disaboom.com

Web site: http://www.disaboomjobs.com

DisaboomJobs is a leading online resource for jobs for people with disabilities. The program allows employers to seek qualified people with disabilities for job openings in their inclusive workforce and view the resumes of candidates. Those seeking employment can search more than 600,000 jobs and showcase abilities to employers. The companies represented on DisaboomJobs are actively seeking to recruit and provide employment for people with disabilities as part of an inclusive workforce and anti-discrimination policies.

DiversityInc

Web site: http://www.diversityinc.com

DiversityInc's mission is to bring education and clarity to the business benefits of diversity. It also provides employer-focused information on the benefits of a diverse workforce, including individuals with disabilities. DiversityInc was founded in 1998 as a Web-based publication; a print magazine was launched in 2002.

Easter Seals Disability Services

233 South Wacker Drive, Suite 2400

Chicago, IL 60606

Telephone: (800) 221-6827; (312) 726-4258 TTY

Fax: (312) 726-1494

Web site: http://www.easterseals.com/site/PageServer?pagename=ntl_top_model_plan

The Easter Seals' Model Plan for the Employment of People with Disabilities compiles best practices for organizations to increase the hiring and retention of people with disabilities. It describes efforts that can be made by any organization to support the employment of individuals with disabilities.

Employment and Disability Institute

Cornell University School of Industrial and Labor Relations

101 ILR Extension

Ithaca, NY 14850

Telephone: (607) 255-7727; (607) 255-2891 TTY

Fax: (607) 255-2763

Web site: http://www.ilr.cornell.edu/edi

The Employment and Disability Institute (EDI), housed within the School of Industrial and Labor Relations (ILR) at Cornell University, conducts research and provides continuing education and technical assistance on many aspects of disability in the workplace. EDI contributes to developing inclusive workplace systems and communities in a variety of ways. The EDI team engages in research and produces scholarly articles, develops training materials, conducts training sessions domestically and internationally, and offers technical assistance on a wide array of disability-related matters.

Employment Resources, Inc.

4126 Lien Road, Suite 104
Madison, WI 53704
Telephone: (800) 710-9326
Fax: (608) 246-3445
Web site: http://www.eri-wi.org

ERI practices and promotes innovative services that advance employment opportunities, support personal choices, and enhance the well-being of individuals with disabilities. ERI provides employment and benefits counseling, assistive technology, and community outreach services to people with disabilities who are considering or pursuing employment.

Enable America

P.O. Box 3031
Tampa, FL 33601-3031
Telephone: (877) 362-2533; (813) 222-3212
Fax: (813) 222-3298
Web site: http://www.enableamerica.org

Enable America's objective is to increase employment among people with disabilities in the United States. To accomplish this goal, a two-pronged approach is utilized to reach all members of the disability community and the business community. The goal with this two-pronged approach is to embrace not only individuals with disabilities and the many organizations and service providers that support them, but also business leaders in their communities as well.

Epilepsy Foundation of America

8301 Professional Place
Landover, MD 20785-7223
Telephone: (800) 332-1000
E-mail: info@efa.org
Web site: http://www.epilepsyfoundation.org

The Epilepsy Foundation provides a wealth of information on employment concerns for those with epilepsy. The toll-free telephone number or Web site offers an ADA informational monograph and brochure, tips for employment interviewing and disclosure issues, information about local area employment programs or local epilepsy affiliates with employment programs, legal advocacy, and job discrimination issues.

ForEmployers.com

Institute for Community Inclusion/UMass Boston

100 Morrissey Boulevard

Boston, MA 02125

Telephone: (888) 886-9898

Web site: http://www.foremployers.com

ForEmployers.com uses technology and flexible design strategies (or universal design) to bridge the needs of the business community and the employment needs of people with disabilities. The site provides straightforward solutions and information that address everyday human resource issues, especially as they relate to current or future employees with disabilities.

GettingHired

1545 U.S. Route 206, First Floor

Bedminster, NJ 07921

Telephone: (866) 352-7481

Fax: (908) 470-2166

Web site: http://www.gettinghired.com

GettingHired aims to connect job seekers with disabilities, employers, advocacy organizations, and service providers. Services available to employers on a subscription-only basis include access and exposure to thousands of qualified job seekers and job matching. The initiative incorporates several unique free services designed to help people prepare for the workplace and build their careers.

Global Applied Disability Research and Information Network (GLADNET)

Telephone: (607) 255-2906

Web site: http://www.gladnet.org

The Global Applied Disability Research and Information Network (GLADNET) brings together research centers, universities, enterprises, government departments, trade unions, and organizations of and for persons with disabilities. The organization's main goal is to advance competitive employment and training opportunities for persons with disabilities. The GLADNET Association was established in 1997. GLADNET continues to work in close collaboration with the ILO Skills and Employability Department.

GLADNET is registered in Switzerland as an international not-for-profit organization and its administrative offices are in Ithaca, New York.

Hire Disability Solutions
327 East Ridgewood Avenue
Paramus, New Jersey 07652
Telephone: (800) 238-5373
E-mail: info@hireds.com
Web site: http://www.hireds.com
The mission of Hire Disability Solutions (HireDS) is to give all that want a chance to succeed, the opportunity to succeed. HireDS was founded in response to the increasing demand for services for individuals with disabilities. Additionally, HireDS aims to promote inclusion into the mainstream employment world. Through its educational campaigns surrounding employment law, education opportunities, and assistive technology, the company facilitates the success of individuals with disabilities and employers alike.

Hire Heroes USA
100 North Point Center East, Suite 200
Alpharetta, GA 30022
Telephone: (866) 915-HERO
Fax: (678) 248-8398
The mission of Hire Heroes USA (HHUSA) is to provide career placement assistance to returning service men and women. The HHUSA program works to provide transition assistance to Operation Iraqi Freedom and Operation Enduring Freedom veterans, specializing in the career placement of those injured or with any level of disability. HHUSA serves veterans from all branches of the military: Army, Navy, Air Force, Marines, National Guard, Reservists, and Coast Guard.

Hire Potential
Telephone: (888) 590-8808
Web site: http://www.hirepotential.com
Hire Potential provides consulting and staffing services for employers in meeting Office of Federal Contract Compliance Programs (OFCCP) and ADA compliance, implementing diversity initiative solutions, and ensuring Web site accessibility. Services focus on recruiting, hiring, and retaining individuals from the "untapped workforce," including individuals with disabilities.

International Association of Rehabilitation Professionals (IARP)
1926 Waukegan Road, Suite 1
Glenview, IL 60025-1770
Telephone: (888) 427-7722

Fax: (847) 657-6963
Web site: http://www.rehabpro.org
The International Association of Rehabilitation Professionals (IARP) provides a community for rehabilitation professionals in their quest for education and professional growth, thereby promoting effective, interdisciplinary services for persons with disabilities. IARP represents a diverse membership practicing in the fields of long-term disability and disability management consulting, case management and managed care, forensics and expert testimony, life care planning, and Americans with Disabilities Act (ADA) consulting.

Job Access
Asia Pacific Headquarters
1308 Prince's Building (13th & 14th Floors)
10 Chater Road
Hong Kong
Telephone: (852) 2877-8772
E-mail: info@jobaccess.com
Job Access strives to work as a true partner with its clients to tackle the many challenges of human resource management. In addition, the program offers recruitment services covering a broad spectrum of industries, specializing in information technology, telecommunications, and banking and finance, from middle to senior management positions.

Job Accommodation Network
Telephone: (800) 526-7234; (877) 781-9403 TTY
Web site: http://www.askjan.org
The Job Accommodation Network (JAN) is a leading source of free, expert, and confidential guidance on workplace accommodations and disability employment issues. JAN helps people with disabilities enhance their employability and shows employers how to capitalize on the value and talent that people with disabilities add to the workplace. JAN's consultants offer one-on-one guidance on workplace accommodations, the Americans with Disabilities Act (ADA) and related legislation, and self-employment and entrepreneurship options for people with disabilities. Assistance is available both over the phone and online.

Law, Health Policy, and Disability Center
280–1 Boyd Law Building
Iowa City, IA 52242-1113
Telephone: (319) 335-8469
Fax: (319) 335-9764
Web site: http://disability.law.uiowa.edu/index.htm
The Law, Health Policy, and Disability Center is an emerging leader in law, technology, education, and research. It is focused on improving the quality of life for persons living with disabilities. Based at the University of Iowa College of Law, with offices in Washington,

D.C., and elsewhere, the center concentrates on public policy and its impact on persons with disabilities, with an emphasis on employment, self-determination, and self-sufficiency.

Learning Disabilities Association of America

4156 Library Road
Pittsburgh, PA 15234-1349
Telephone: (412) 341-1515
Web site: http://www.ldanatl.org
The Learning Disabilities Association (LDA) provides support to people with learning disabilities, their parents, teachers, and other professionals. At the national, state, and local levels, LDA provides cutting-edge information on learning disabilities, practical solutions, and a comprehensive network of resources. Through its Annual International Conference as well as state affiliate conferences and workshops, LDA provides a forum for questions on learning disabilities and new technology and approaches for teaching individuals with learning disabilities.

National Association of Benefits and
Work Incentives Specialists (NABWIS)

12009 Shallot Street
Orlando, FL 32837
E-mail: nabwis@gmail.com
Web site: http://www.nabwis.org
The National Association of Benefits and Work Incentive Specialists (NABWIS) is comprised of the many and varied professionals providing assistance to individuals who receive disability benefits. Some of NABWIS' objectives are supporting the formation and development of state chapters for the promotion of the economic well-being of people with disabilities through knowledge regarding benefits and work incentives; cooperation with other organizations, both governmental and voluntary, including organizations of people with disabilities, in improving the economic status of people with disabilities; and ensuring the participation of people with disabilities in the activities and governance of the organization.

National Association of the Deaf

8630 Fenton Street, Suite 820
Silver Spring, MD 20910-3819
Telephone: (301) 587-1788; (301) 587-1789 TTY
Web site: http://www.nad.org
The National Association of the Deaf (NAD) is the premier civil rights organization of, by, and for deaf and hard-of-hearing individuals in the United States. In addition to advocacy, NAD offers a variety of employment services. These include improving access to early education and higher education; ensuring the availability and provision of vocational rehabilitation services; securing reasonable accommodations; fostering innovation and use of technology; and encouraging entrepreneurship.

National Business and Disability Council (NBDC)

201 I.U. Willets Road
Albertson, NY 11507
Telephone: (516) 465-1516
Web site: http://www.nbdc.com

The NBDC is a leading resource for employers seeking to integrate people with disabilities into the workplace and companies seeking to reach them in the consumer marketplace. Some areas of expertise include ADA compliance, building and product accessibility, reasonable accommodation, job analysis, recruitment, specialized equipment, and career development. NBDC also helps businesses create accessible work conditions for employees and accessible products and services for consumers.

National Center for Learning Disabilities

381 Park Avenue South, Suite 1401
New York, NY 10016
Telephone: (888) 575-7373
Web site: http://www.ncld.org

NCLD works to ensure that the nation's 15 million children, adolescents, and adults with learning disabilities have every opportunity to succeed in school, work, and life. Additionally, the center provides essential information to parents, professionals, and individuals with learning disabilities, promotes research and programs to foster effective learning, and advocates for policies to protect and strengthen educational rights and opportunities. NCLD has long provided national leadership in the shaping of public policy and federal legislation, working effectively to ensure that the voices of individuals with learning disabilities are heard by those in government.

National Empowerment Center

599 Canal Street
Lawrence, MA 01840
Telephone: (800) 769-3728; (800) 889-7693 TTY
Web site: http://www.power2u.org

The National Empowerment Center promotes recovery, empowerment, hope, and healing for people who have been labeled with mental illness. In addition, the center provides a variety of resources to those with mental illness and the community, including employment resources. The NEC keeps updated lists of consumer-run organization and advocacy groups in all 50 states. It is also active in the cross-disability movement and can help individuals network with independent living centers and disability rights groups across the country.

National Mental Health Consumers' Self-Help Clearinghouse

1211 Chestnut Street, Suite 1207
Philadelphia, PA 19107

Telephone: (800) 553-4539
Fax: (215) 636-6312
E-mail: info@mhselfhelp.org
Web site: http://www.mhselfhelp.org
The National Mental Health Consumers' Self-Help Clearinghouse is a consumer-run national technical assistance center serving the mental health consumer movement. It helps connect individuals to self-help and advocacy resources, and it offers expertise to self-help groups and other peer-run services for mental health consumers. The consumer movement strives for dignity, respect, and opportunity for those with mental illnesses. The clearinghouse works to foster consumer empowerment through its Web site, up-to-date news and information announcements, a directory of consumer-driven services, electronic and printed publications, training packages, and individual and onsite consultation.

National Public Website on Assistive Technology
Center for Assistive Technology and Environmental Access
Georgia Institute of Technology
490 Tenth Street
Atlanta, GA 30332-0156
Web site: http://www.assistivetech.net
Assistivetech.net provides access to information on assistive technology devices and services as well as other community resources for people with disabilities, employers, and the general public. This site is created and maintained through the collaboration of the Georgia Tech Center for Assistive Technology and Environmental Access (CATEA), National Institute on Disability and Rehabilitation Research (NIDRR), and Rehabilitation Services Administration (RSA).

National Spinal Cord Injury Association
1 Church Street, #600
Rockville, MD 20850
Telephone: (800) 962-9629
E-mail: info@spinalcord.org
Web site: http://www.spinalcord.org
The National Spinal Cord Injury Association is a national organization that has a network of chapters to help members with counseling, disability rights, and general advocacy. They maintain an extensive library and publish a quarterly magazine. At NSCIA, the goal is to educate and empower survivors of spinal cord injury and disease to achieve and maintain the highest levels of independence, health, and personal fulfillment. This is done by providing an innovative Peer Support Network and by raising awareness about spinal cord injury and disease through education.

Project HIRED
1401 Parkmoor Avenue, Suite 125
San Jose, CA 95126

Telephone: (888) 520-4572
E-mail: info@projecthired.org
Web site: http://www.projecthired.org
Project HIRED's mission is to assist individuals with disabilities to gain and sustain employment, in partnership with business and the community. Project HIRED offers an array of job placement, training, and employment services designed to promote self-sufficiency and independence, remove barriers, create opportunities, and help persons with disabilities get good jobs at competitive wages. Project HIRED is also a direct employer of people with disabilities in its HIRED Teams contract outsourcing division.

Recruit Military

422 West Loveland Avenue
Loveland, OH 45140
Telephone: (513) 683-5020
Fax: (513) 683-5021
Web site: http://www.recruitmilitary.com
RecruitMilitary is veteran-owned, operated, and advised. As the nation's leading military-to-civilian recruiting firm, they have established working relationships with industry associations, nonprofit organizations, and government agencies. Those relationships include re-seller arrangements by which the National Association of Manufacturers, the Employers Resource Association, and several other organizations make RecruitMilitary's online products available to their members.

Rehabilitation Engineering and Assistive Technology Society of North America (RESNA)

1700 North Moore Street, Suite 1540
Arlington, VA 22209
Telephone: (703) 524-6686
Fax: (703) 524-6630
E-mail: resnaTA@resna.org
Web site: http://www.resna.org
RESNA's goal is to maximize the health and well-being of people with disabilities through the use of technology. The purpose of RESNA is to contribute to the public welfare through scientific, literary, professional, and educational activities by supporting the development, dissemination, and utilization of knowledge and practice of rehabilitation and assistive technology in order to achieve the highest quality of life for all citizens. Professional development topics focus on the use of AT (devices and services) to facilitate the well-being of individuals with disabilities.

**Rehabilitation Research and Training Center on
Blindness and Low Vision (RRTC)**
108 Herbert South, Room 150 Industrial Education
Department Building
P.O. Drawer 6189
Mississippi State University
Mississippi State, MS 39762
Telephone: (662) 325-2001; (662) 325-8693 TDD
E-mail: rrtc@colled.msstate.edu
Web site: http://www.blind.msstate.edu
The RRTC's mission is to enhance employment and independent living outcomes for individuals who are blind or visually impaired through research, training, education, and dissemination. The RRTC provides quantitative and qualitative research, analyses of large databases, program evaluation, and knowledge development in the field of blindness and low vision. RRTC-MSU has worked with state and private agencies around the U.S. to serve the needs of people who are blind or have low vision since 1981.

Society for Human Resource Management (SHRM)
1800 Duke Street
Alexandria, VA 22314
Telephone: (703) 548-3440
Fax: (703) 535-6490
Web site: http://www.shrm.org
SHRM is a global HR professional organization that exists to develop partnerships with human resource professionals, media, governments, non-governmental organizations, businesses, and academic institutions, and to provide a community in which they can share expertise and create innovative solutions on people management issues.

U.S. Business Leadership Network
1501 M Street, NW, 7th Floor
Washington, DC 20005
Telephone: (202) 872-6739
E-mail: info@usbln.org
Web site: http://www.usbln.org
The USBLN maintains best practices in the employment and success of people with disabilities; the preparedness for work of youth and students with disabilities; marketing to consumers with disabilities; and contracting with vendors with disabilities through the development and certification of disability-owned businesses. Also, the organization strives to build workplaces where the talents of people with disabilities are fully utilized and valued.

Virginia Commonwealth University
Rehabilitation Research and Training Center
on Workplace Supports and Job Retention
1314 West Main Street
P.O. Box 842011
Richmond, VA 23284
Telephone: (804) 828-1851
Web site: http://www.worksupport.com

The purpose of the Virginia Commonwealth University RRTC on Workplace Supports and Job Retention is to study those supports that are most effective for assisting individuals with disabilities to maintain employment and advance their careers. The project helps those with disabilities as well as those who are unemployed, underemployed, or at risk of losing employment.

Virginia Commonwealth University
START-UP USA (Self-Employment Technical
Assistance, Resources, and Training)
1314 West Main Street
Richmond, VA 23284-2011
Telephone: (804) 828-1851
Web site: http://www.start-up-usa.biz

START-UP is a partnership between VCU and Griffin-Hammis and Associates with a main purpose of promoting self-employment as an effective employment outcome for individuals with disabilities. The partnership provides technical assistance and disseminates resources nationally to individuals interested in pursuing self-employment. Further, START-UP works to validate systems capacity-building strategies and systems change models for successfully increasing self-employment opportunities for individuals with disabilities.

Warriors to Work
7020 AC Skinner Pkwy, Suite 100
Jacksonville, FL 32256
Telephone: (904) 296-7350
Web site: http://www.woundedwarriorproject.org

The Wounded Warrior Project's Warriors to Work program helps individuals recovering from severe injuries received in the line of duty connect with the support and resources they need to transition into civilian life and build a career in the civilian workforce. Warriors to Work is a free service for the new generation of service men and women who have been injured in the line of duty.

Workplace Center
Columbia University, School of Social Work
1255 Amsterdam Avenue, 11th Floor

New York, NY 10027
Telephone: (212) 851-2256
E-mail: workplace@columbia.edu
Web site: http://www.workplacecenter.org
*The Center for Social Policy and Practice in the Workplace (Workplace Center) at Colum-
bia University is a cutting-edge service delivery, program development, research, training,
and consultation institute. As a nationally recognized center of innovation and best practice, it has assisted public and private employers on both an international and national
level to develop programs that are cost-effective and responsive to employee needs. The client base includes hospitals, social welfare organizations, major corporations, government
agencies, universities, and trade unions.*

WorkplaceDiversity.com LLC
26 Eastmans Road
Parsippany, NJ 07054
Telephone: (973) 992-7311
E-mail: service@WorkplaceDiversity.com
Web site: http://www.workplacediversity.com
*WorkplaceDiversity.com is a job search Web site for corporate recruiters who are seeking
experienced, diverse talent. Their main objective is to create a connection between companies that support diversity and experienced, distinct candidates by providing one location
for recruiters to post open positions. The site also provides for-fee job posting and searchable resumes for employers interested in a diverse workforce, including individuals with
disabilities. Employers may also create profiles.*

Government Organizations

Able Job Seekers Clearinghouse
P.O. Box 9046
Olympia, WA 98507-9046
Telephone: (866) 438-3292; (360) 438-3167
E-mail: ablejobseekers@esd.wa.gov
Web site: http://www.ablejobseekers.wa.gov
*The Able Job Seekers Clearinghouse has been implemented to provide employers with a single
source of contact to get ideas, resources, and assistance on issues related to serving applicants
and employees with disabilities. Sponsorship of and funding for this project comes from the
Department of Social and Health Services, Division of Vocational Rehabilitation.*

Employer Assistance and Resource Network (EARN)
Telephone: (866) 327-6669
E-mail: earn@earnworks.com

Web site: http://www.earnworks.com
The Employer Assistance and Resource Network works to improve the recruitment and hiring of people with disabilities. In addition, EARN provides free consulting services to employers and assists employers with understanding the useful business reasons for hiring people with disabilities. EARN connects employers with national networks of available job seekers through relationships with the Department of Veterans Affairs, the Council of State Administrators of Vocational Rehabilitation (CSAVR), and the Commission on the Accreditation of Rehabilitation Facilities (CARF).

National Collaborative on Workforce and Disability
4455 Connecticut Avenue, NW, Suite 310
Washington, DC 20008
Telephone: (877) 871-0744
Web site: http://www.ncwd-youth.info
The National Collaborative on Workforce and Disability (NCWD/Youth) was created to provide technical assistance to state and local workforce development systems who service youth with disabilities and other disadvantaged children. NCWD consists of experts in education, youth development, disability, employment, workforce development, and family issues.

National Council on Disability
1331 F Street, NW, Suite 850
Washington, DC 20004
Telephone: (202) 272-2004
Web site: http://www.ncd.gov
The National Council on Disability is a federal agency consisting of 15 members selected by the president to promote policies, programs, practices, and procedures that guarantee equal opportunity for individuals with disabilities. In addition, the agency works to give people with disabilities the opportunity to achieve economic self-sufficiency, independent living, and inclusion/integration into all areas of society. It provides advice to the president, Congress, and executive branch agencies.

National Institute on Disability and Rehabilitation Research (NIDRR)
U.S. Department of Education
400 Maryland Avenue, SW
Washington, DC 20202
Telephone: (800) 872-5327
Web site: http://www.ed.gov/offices/OSERS/NIDRR
The National Institute on Disability and Rehabilitation Research (NIDRR) provides leadership and support for a comprehensive program of research related to the rehabilitation of individuals with disabilities. All efforts are aimed at improving the lives of individuals

with disabilities from birth through adulthood. Some objectives of NIDRR include strengthening the federal commitment to assuring access to equal educational opportunity for every individual; and supplementing and complementing the efforts of states, the local school systems and other instrumentalities of the states, the private sector, public and private nonprofit educational research institutions, community-based organizations, parents, and students to improve the quality of education.

National Multicultural Institute
3000 Connecticut Avenue, NW, Suite 438
Washington, DC 20008-2556
Telephone: (202) 483-0700
Fax: (202) 483-5233
Web site: http://www.nmci.org
NMCI's mission is to work with individuals, organizations, and communities in creating a society that is strengthened and empowered by its diversity. NMCI holds conferences, offers individualized training and consulting interventions, and produces publications. Through the development of strategic initiatives, partnerships, and programs that promote an inclusive and just society, NMCI is at the forefront of global efforts to address critical and emerging issues in the diversity field.

National Technical Assistance and Research Leadership Center (NTAR)
30 Livingston Avenue
New Brunswick, NJ 08901
Telephone: (732) 932-4100 Ext. 6330
E-mail: NTAR@rci.rutgers.edu
Web site: http://www.ntarcenter.org
The NTAR Leadership Center promotes leadership to increase the employment and economic independence of adults with disabilities. Furthermore, NTAR promotes cross-agency and cross-system collaboration; advocates for a principle of universal design; assists with asset-building efforts; and develops customized employment strategies through flexibility of the workplace. NTAR focuses on using customized employment strategies to individualize the employment relationship between the job seeker and the employer to meet the needs of both and greatly improve employment opportunities for people with disabilities.

U.S. Equal Employment Opportunity Commission
131 M Street, NE
Washington, DC 20507
Telephone: (202) 663-4900
Web site: http://www.eeoc.gov
The U.S. Equal Employment Opportunity Commission (EEOC) is responsible for enforcing federal laws that make it illegal to discriminate against a job applicant or an employee because

of the person's race, color, religion, sex (including pregnancy), national origin, age (40 or older), disability, or genetic information. Also among the agency's duties are investigations of retaliation claims following an individual's involvement in a claim of discrimination.

U.S. Office of Personnel Management
1900 E Street, NW
Washington, DC 20415
Telephone: (202) 606-1800
Web site: http://www.opm.gov
The Office of Personnel Management works to encourage professional development and recognition opportunities, promote the fundamentals of public service, advocate innovative human resources practices, and develop the federal service workforce. Further, OPM helps individuals to understand federal disability hiring programs, learn about the ways of gaining access to reasonable accommodation, and more.

State Vocational Rehabilitation Agencies

This section, organized alphabetically by state, includes contact information for state agencies that provide vocational rehabilitation services to individuals with disabilities. Services can include counseling, advocacy, job training, job placements, and a variety of additional support services, including continuing, adult, and post-secondary education. For the Office of Vocational Rehabilitation Services in your state, consult a phone directory.

Alabama
Alabama Department of Rehabilitation Services
602 South Lawrence Street
Montgomery, AL 36104
Telephone: (334) 293-7500; (800) 441-7607; (334) 613-2249 TDD
Fax: (334) 293-7383
Web site: http://www.rehab.state.al.us/Home/default.aspx?url=/Home/Main

Alaska
Alaska Division of Vocational Rehabilitation
801 West 10th Street, Suite A
Juneau, AK 99801-1894
Telephone: (907) 465-2814; (800) 478-2815

Fax: (907) 465-2856
Web site: http://www.labor.state.ak.us/dvr/home.htm

Arizona
Arizona Rehabilitation Services Administration
1789 West Jefferson 2, NW
Phoenix, AZ 85007
Telephone: (602) 542-3332; (800) 563-1221
Fax: (602) 542-3778
Web site: http://www.azdes.gov/rsa

Arkansas
Arkansas Rehabilitation Services
1616 Brookwood Drive
P.O. Box 3781
Little Rock, AR 72203
Telephone: (501) 296-1600; (800) 330-0632; (501) 296-1669 TDD
Fax: (501) 296-1655
Web site: http://www.arsinfo.org

California
California Health and Human Service Agency Department
of Rehabilitation
721 Capitol Mall
Sacramento, CA 95814
Telephone: (916) 324-1313; (916) 558-5807 TTY
Web site: http://www.rehab.cahwnet.gov

Colorado
Colorado Division of Vocational Rehabilitation
1575 Sherman Street
Denver, CO 80203
Telephone: (303) 866-5700 V/TDD
Fax: (303) 866-4047
Web site: http://www.cdhs.state.co.us/dvr

Connecticut
Board of Education and Services for the Blind
Vocational Rehabilitation Division

184 Windsor Avenue
Windsor, CT 06095
Telephone: (860) 602-4000; (860) 602-4221 TDD
Web site: http://www.besb.state.ct.us

Bureau of Rehabilitation Services
Department of Social Services
25 Sigourney Street, 11th Floor
Hartford, CT 06106
Telephone: (860) 424-4844; (860) 424-4839 TDD/TTY
Web site: http://www.brs.state.ct.us

Delaware
Delaware Division of Vocational Rehabilitation
4425 North Market Street
P.O. Box 9969
Wilmington, DE 19809-0969
Telephone: (302) 761-8275; (302) 761-8275 V/TTY
Fax: (302) 761-6611
Web site: http://www.delawareworks.com/dvr/welcome.shtml

Delaware Health and Social Services
Division for the Visually Impaired (DVI)
1901 North DuPont Highway, Biggs Building
New Castle, DE 19720
Telephone: (302) 255-9800
Fax: (302) 255-4441
Web site: http://www.dhss.delaware.gov/dhss/dvi/index.html

District of Columbia
D.C. Rehabilitation Services Administration
810 First Street, NE, 10th Floor
Washington, DC 20002
Telephone: (202) 442-8663; (202) 442-8400
(Intake Services); (202) 442-8600 TTY/TDD
Fax: (202) 442-8742
Web site: http://dds.dc.gov/dds/cwp/view,A,3,Q,496870.asp

Florida
Division of Vocational Rehabilitation

2002-A Old Saint Augustine Road
Tallahassee, FL 32301
Telephone: (850) 245-3399; (800) 451-4327
Web site: http://rehabworks.org

Florida Division of Blind Services
325 West Gaines Street
Room 1114, Turlington Building
Tallahassee, FL 32399-0400
Telephone: (850) 245-0300; (800) 342-1828
Fax: (850) 245-0363
Web site: http://dbs.myflorida.com

Georgia
Georgia Department of Labor
Rehabilitation Services
148 Andrew Young International Boulevard
Suite 510, Sussex Place
Atlanta, Georgia 30303
Telephone: (404) 232-3910; (404) 232-3911 TTY
Web site: http://www.vocrehabga.org

Hawaii
Hawaii Vocational Rehabilitation and Services for the Blind
The State Kakuhihewa Building
601 Kamokila Boulevard, Room 515
Kapolei, HI 96707
Telephone: (808) 692-7715
Web site: http://www.hawaii.gov/dhs/self-sufficiency/vr

Idaho
Idaho Division of Vocational Rehabilitation
Agency of the State Board of Education
650 West State Street, Room 150
P.O. Box 83720
Boise, ID 83720-0096
Telephone: (208) 334-3390/(800) 856-2720
Fax: (208) 334-5305
Web site: http://www.vr.idaho.gov

Illinois
Department of Human Services
Office of Rehabilitation Services
623 East Adams Street
P.O. Box 19429
Springfield, IL 62794
Telephone: (800) 843-6154 (customers); (800) 447-6404 TTY; (800) 804-3833 (providers)
Web site: http://www.dhs.state.il.us/ors

Indiana
Division of Disability and Rehabilitative Services
402 West Washington Street C-453
P.O. Box 7083
Indianapolis, IN 46207-7083
Telephone: (317) 232-1252 (customers)
Fax: (317) 232-6478
Web site: http://www.in.gov/fssa/2328.htm

Iowa
Iowa Department for the Blind
524 Fourth Street
Des Moines, IA 50309
Telephone: (515) 281-1333; (800) 362-2587
Fax: (515) 281-1263
Web site: http://www.blind.state.ia.us

Iowa Vocational Rehabilitation Services (IVRS)
510 East 12th Street
Des Moines, IA 50319
Telephone: (515) 281-4211 V/TTY
Fax: (515) 281-7645
Web site: http://www.ivrs.iowa.gov

Kansas
Department of Social and Rehabilitation Services
915 Harrison Street Office Building
Topeka, KS 66612
Telephone: (785) 296-3959

Fax: (785) 296-2173
Web site: http://www.srskansas.org

Kentucky
Kentucky Office for the Blind
275 East Main Street
Frankfort, KY 40601
Telephone: (502) 564-4754; (800) 321-6668;
(877) 592-5463; (502) 564-2929 TDD
Fax: (502) 564-2951
Web site: http://blind.ky.gov

Kentucky Office of Vocational Rehabilitation
275 East Main Street
Frankfort, KY 40621
Telephone: (502) 564-4440; (800) 372-7172; (800) 372-7172 V/TTY
Web site: http://ovr.ky.gov

Louisiana
Louisiana Rehabilitation Services
627 N. Fourth Street
Baton Rouge, LA 70802
Telephone: (225) 219-2225; (800) 737-2958
Fax: (225) 219-4993
Web site: http://www.laworks.net/WorkforceDev/LRS/LRS_Main.asp

Maine
Maine Bureau of Rehabilitation Services
Division of Vocational Rehabilitation (DVR)
150 State House Station
Augusta, ME 04333-0150
Telephone: (800) 698-0150; (888) 755-0023 TTY
Fax: (207) 287-5292
Web site: http://www.maine.gov/rehab

Maryland
Maryland State Department of Education
Division of Rehabilitation Services
2301 Argonne Drive

336 EMPLOYMENT AND WORK

Baltimore, MD 21218-1696
Telephone: (410) 554-9442; (888) 554-0334; (410) 554-9411 TDD
Fax: (410) 554-9412
Web site: http://www.dors.state.md.us/dors

Massachusetts
Massachusetts Commission for the Blind
48 Boylston Street
Boston, MA 02116-4718
Telephone: (617) 727-5550; (800) 392-6450; (800)
392-6556; (800) 392-6556 TDD
Fax: (617) 626-7685
Web site: http://www.mass.gov/mcb

Massachusetts Rehabilitation Commission
Fort Point Place, Suite 600
27 Wormwood Street
Boston, MA 02210-1616
Telephone: (617) 204-3600; (800) 245-6543 V/TTY
Fax: (617) 727-1354
Web site: http://www.mass.gov/mrc

Michigan
Michigan Commission for the Blind
201 North Washington
P.O. Box 30652
Lansing, MI 48909
Telephone: (517) 373-2062; (800) 292-4200 (Lower Peninsula);
(800) 323-2535 (Upper Peninsula);
(517) 373-4025 TDD
Fax: (517) 335-5140
Web site: http://www.michigan.gov/lara/0,1607,7-154-28077_
28313---,00.html

Michigan Department of Labor and Economic Growth
Rehabilitation Services
201 N. Washington Square, 4th Floor
P.O. Box 30010
Lansing, MI 48909
Telephone: (517) 373-4026; (800) 605-6722; (888) 605-6722 TTY

Fax: (517) 335-7277
Web site: http://www.michigan.gov/mdcd/
0,1607,7-122-25392---,00.html

Minnesota
Department of Employment and Economic Development
Rehabilitation Services Branch
332 Minnesota Street, Suite E200
Saint Paul, MN 55101
Telephone: (651) 259-7366; (800) 328-9095; (651) 296-3900; (800) 657-3973
TTY
Fax: (651) 297-5159
Web site: http://www.deed.state.mn.us/rehab/vr/main_vr.htm

Mississippi
Mississippi Department of Rehabilitation Services
1281 Highway 51
Madison, MS 39110
Telephone: (800) 443-1000
Web site: http://www.mdrs.state.ms.us

Missouri
Missouri Division of Vocational Rehabilitation
3024 Dupont Circle
Jefferson City, MO 65109-0525
Telephone: (573) 751-3251; (877) 222-8963; (573) 751-0881 TDD
Fax: (573) 751-1441
Web site: http://dese.mo.gov/vr

Missouri Rehabilitation Services for the Blind
615 Howerton Court
P.O. Box 2320
Jefferson City, MO 65102
Telephone: (573) 751-4249; (800) 735-2966 TDD
Fax: (573) 751-4984
Web site: http://www.dss.mo.gov/fsd/rsb/index.htm

Montana
Montana Vocational Rehabilitation
111 North Sanders

P.O. Box 4210
Helena, MT 59604-4210
Telephone: (406) 444-2590 V/TDD; (877) 296-1197
Fax: (406) 444-3632
Web site: http://www.dphhs.mt.gov/dsd/mvr.shtml

Nebraska
Nebraska Department of Education
Vocational Rehabilitation
P.O. Box 94987
301 Centennial Mall, South
Lincoln, NE 68509-4987
Telephone: (402) 471-3644; (800) 742-7594
Fax: (402) 471-0788
Web site: http://www.vocrehab.state.ne.us

Nevada
Department of Employment, Training, and Rehabilitation
Rehabilitation Division
1370 South Curry Street
Carson City, NV 89703-5146
Telephone: (775) 684-4070 V/TDD; (775) 684-8400 TTY
Fax: (775) 684-4184
Web site: http://detr.state.nv.us/rehab/reh_index.htm

New Hampshire
Department of Education
Bureau of Vocational Rehabilitation
21 South Fruit Street, Suite 20
Concord, NH 03301
Telephone: (603) 271-3471 V/TTY; (800) 299-1647
Fax: (603) 271-7095
Web site: http://www.education.nh.gov/career/vocational/index.htm

Department of Education
Services for the Blind and Visually Impaired
21 South Fruit Street, Suite 20
Concord, NH 03301
Telephone: (603) 271-3537; (800) 581-6881; (603) 271-3471 V/TTY

Fax: (603) 271-3816
Web site: http://www.education.nh.gov/career/vocational/blind_visu.htm

New Jersey
New Jersey Department of Human Services
Commission for the Blind and Visually Impaired
153 Halsey Street, 6th Floor
P.O. Box 47017
Newark, NJ 07101
Telephone: (973) 648-2111
Fax: (973) 648-7364
Web site: http://www.state.nj.us/humanservices/cbvi/index.html

New Jersey Division of Vocational Rehabilitation Services
LWD Building, 10th Floor
John Fitch Plaza
P.O. Box 398
Trenton, NJ 08625-0398
Telephone: (609) 292-5987; (609) 292-2919 TTY
Fax: (609) 292-8347
Web site: http://lwd.dol.state.nj.us/labor/dvrs/DVRIndex.html

New Mexico
New Mexico Commission for the Blind
2905 Rodeo Park Drive, E, Building 4, Suite 100
Santa Fe, NM 87505
Telephone: (505) 476-4479; (888) 513-7968
Web site: http://www.cfb.state.nm.us

New Mexico Division of Vocational Rehabilitation
435 St. Michael's Drive, Building D
Santa Fe, NM 87505
Telephone: (505) 954-8500; (800) 224-7005
Fax: (505) 954-8562
Web site: http://www.dvrgetsjobs.com

New York
Commission for the Blind and Visually Handicapped
NYS Office of Children and Family Services

Capital View Office Park South Building, Room 201
52 Washington Street
Rensselaer, NY 12144-2796
Telephone: (518) 474-5686; (518) 473-1774; (518) 474-7501 TTY
Fax: (518) 486-5819
Web site: http://www.ocfs.state.ny.us/main/cbvh

Vocational and Educational Services for Individuals with Disabilities
1 Commerce Plaza
Albany, NY 12234
Telephone: (800) 222-JOBS
Fax: (518) 486-4154
Web site: http://www.vesid.nysed.gov

North Carolina
North Carolina Division of Services for the Blind
2601 Mail Service Center
Raleigh, NC 27699-2601
Telephone: (866) 222-1546
Fax: (919) 733-9769
Web site: http://www.dhhs.state.nc.us/dsb

North Carolina Division of Vocational Rehabilitation Services
2801 Mail Services Center
Raleigh, North Carolina 27699-2801
Telephone: (800) 689-9090; (919) 855-3579; (919) 733-7968
Web site: http://dvr.dhhs.state.nc.us

North Dakota
ND Disability Services Division
Vocational Rehabilitation
1237 West Divide Avenue, Suite 1B
Bismark, ND 58501-1208
Telephone: (701) 328-8950; (800) 755-2745; (701) 328-8968 TTY
Fax: (701) 328-8969
Web site: http://www.nd.gov/dhs/services/disabilities/index.html

Ohio
Ohio Rehabilitation Services Commission
400 East Campus View Boulevard

Columbus, OH 43235-4604
Telephone: (614) 438-1200 V/TYY; (800) 282-4536 (Ohio only)
Fax: (614) 438-1257
Web site: http://www.rsc.ohio.gov

Oklahoma
Department of Rehabilitation Services
3535 NW 58th Street, Suite 500
Oklahoma City, OK 73112-4815
Telephone: (405) 951-3400; (800) 845-8476
Fax: (405) 951-3529
Web site: http://www.okrehab.org

Oregon
Office of Vocational Rehabilitation Services (OVRS)
Department of Human Services
500 Summer Street, NE, E-87
Salem, OR 97301-1120
Telephone: (503) 945-5880; (866) 801-0130 TTY
Fax: (503) 947-5010
Web site: http://www.oregon.gov/DHS/vr

Pennsylvania
Department of Labor and Industry
Office of Vocational Rehabilitation
1521 North 6th Street
Harrisburg, PA 17102
Telephone: (800) 442-6351; (717) 787-5244; (717) 787-4885 TTY
Web site: http://www.dli.state.pa.us/landi/cwp/view
.asp?a=128&Q=168255&dsftns=1375

Rhode Island
Department of Human Services
Office of Rehabilitation Services
40 Fountain Street
Providence, RI 02903-1898
Telephone: (401) 421-7005; (401) 421-4016 TDD
Fax: (401) 222-3574
Web site: http://www.ors.ri.gov

Services for the Blind and Visually Impaired
40 Fountain Street
Providence, RI 02093-1898
Telephone: (401) 222-2300; (800) 752-8088 Ext. 2300; (401) 222-3010 TDD
Fax: (401) 222-1328
Web site: http://www.ors.ri.gov/SBVI.html

South Carolina
South Carolina Commission for the Blind
P.O. Box 2467
1430 Confederate Avenue
Columbia, SC 29202-0079
Telephone: (803) 898-8731; (800) 922-2222
Fax: (803) 898-8852
Web site: http://www.sccb.state.sc.us/

South Carolina Vocational Rehabilitation Department
State Office Building, 1410 Boston Avenue
P.O. Box 15
West Columbia, SC 29171-0015
Telephone: (803) 896-6500
Web site: http://www.scvrd.net

South Dakota
Division of Rehabilitation Services
East Highway 34, Hillsview Plaza
c/o 500 East Capitol
Pierre, SD 57501-5070
Telephone: (605) 773-3195
Fax: (605) 773-5483
Web site: http://dhs.sd.gov/drs

Tennessee
Department of Human Services
Vocational Rehabilitation Services
Citizens Plaza State Office Building
400 Deaderick Street, 2nd Floor
Nashville, Tennessee 37248-6000
Telephone: (615) 313-4891; (615) 313-5695 TTY

Fax: (615) 741-6508
Web site: http://tennessee.gov/humanserv/rehab/vrs.html

Texas
Texas Department of Assistive and Rehabilitative Services
Division for Blind Services
4800 North Lamar Boulevard, Suite 340
Austin, TX 78756
Telephone: (800) 628-5115
Web site: http://www.dars.state.tx.us/dbs

Texas Department of Assistive and Rehabilitative Services
Division for Rehabilitation Services
4800 North Lamar Boulevard
Austin, TX 78756
Telephone: (800) 628-5115
Web site: http://www.dars.state.tx.us/drs

Utah
Utah State Office of Rehabilitation
250 East 500, South
Salt Lake City, UT 84111
Telephone: (801) 538-7530; (800) 473-7530
Fax: (801) 538-7522
Web site: http://www.usor.utah.gov

Vermont
Division for the Blind and Visually Impaired
Department of Aging and Disabilities
Agency of Human Services
Weeks Building, 103 South Main Street
Waterbury, VT 05671-2304
Telephone: (802) 241-2210
Web site: http://www.dbvi.vermont.gov

Division of Vocational Rehabilitation
Department of Aging and Disabilities
Agency of Human Services
Weeks 1A, 103 South Main Street

Waterbury, VT 05671-2303
Telephone: (866) 879-6757 V/TTY
Web site: http://www.vocrehabvermont.org

Virginia
Virginia Department for the Blind and Visually Impaired
397 Azalea Avenue
Richmond, VA 23227-3697
Telephone: (804) 371-3140; (800) 622-2155 V/TTY
Fax: (804) 371-3351
Web site: http://www.vdbvi.org

Virginia Department of Rehabilitation Services
8004 Franklin Farms Drive
Richmond, VA 23229
Telephone: (804) 662-7000; (804) 662-9040; (800) 464-9950 TTY
Fax: (804) 662-9532
Web site: http://www.vadrs.org

Washington
Department of Services for the Blind
4565 7th Avenue, SE
P.O. Box 40933
Olympia, WA 98504-0933
Telephone: (800) 552-7103; (360) 725-3830; (206) 721-4056 TTY
Fax: (360) 407-0679
Web site: http://www.dsb.wa.gov

State of Washington, Division of Vocational Rehabilitation
4565 7th Avenue, SE
P.O. Box 45340
Olympia, WA 98504-5340
Telephone: (800) 637-5627; (360) 725-3636 V/TTY
Fax: (360) 438-8007
Web site: http://www.dshs.wa.gov/dvr

West Virginia
West Virginia Division of Rehabilitation Services
P.O. Box 50890, State Capitol

Charleston, WV 25305-0890
Telephone: (800) 642-8207
Web site: http://www.wvdrs.org

Wisconsin
Wisconsin Division of Vocational Rehabilitation
201 East Washington Avenue
P.O. Box 7852
Madison, WI 53707-7852
Telephone: (608) 261-0050; (800) 442-3477; (888) 877-5939 TTY
Fax: (608) 266-1133
Web site: http://www.dwd.state.wi.us/dvr

Wyoming
Wyoming Division of Vocational Rehabilitation
122 W. 25th Street
Herschler Building 2E
Cheyenne, WY 82002
Telephone: (307) 777-8650
Fax: (307) 777-5857
Web site: http://wyomingworkforce.org/vr

Regional ADA Centers

Regional ADA Centers were established to provide training, information, and technical assistance on the Americans with Disabilities Act (ADA) to businesses, consumers, schools, and state and local governments. Each center has a toll-free telephone line staffed by specialists who can answer specific questions on the ADA. Private businesses, individuals with disabilities, employers, architects, local government representatives, and other interested parties can call for advice and information on what is required, who is covered, and how to work through a disability-related question.

Great Lakes ADA Center
(Serving Illinois, Indiana, Michigan, Minnesota, Ohio, Wisconsin)
University of Illinois at Chicago
Department on Disability and Human Development
1640 West Roosevelt Road, Room 405

Chicago, IL 60608
Telephone: (312) 413-1407 V/TTY
Fax: (312) 413-1856
E-mail: http://www.adagreatlakes.org/WebForms/ContactUs
Web site: http://www.adagreatlakes.org

Great Plains ADA Center
(Serving Iowa, Kansas, Missouri, Nebraska)
University of Missouri/Columbia
100 Corporate Lake Drive
Columbia, MO 65203
Telephone: (573) 882-3600 V/TTY
Fax: (573) 884-4925
E-mail: brinkhoffj@missouri.edu
Web site: http://www.adaproject.org

Mid-Atlantic ADA Center
(Serving Delaware, District of Columbia, Maryland, Pennsylvania,
Virginia, West Virginia)
TransCen, Inc.
451 Hungerford Drive, Suite 700
Rockville, MD 20850
Telephone: (301) 217-0124 V/TTY
Fax: (301) 217-0754
E-mail: adainfo@transcen.org
Web site: http://www.adainfo.org

New England ADA Center
(Serving Connecticut, Maine, Massachusetts,
New Hampshire, Rhode Island, Vermont)
Institute for Human Centered Design
(formerly Adaptive Environments)
180-200 Portland Street, First Floor
Boston, MA 02114
Telephone: (617) 695-0085 V/TTY
Fax: (617) 482-8099
E-mail: adainfo@newenglandada.org
Web site: http://www.NewEnglandADA.org

Northeast ADA Center
(Serving New Jersey, New York, Puerto Rico, Virgin Islands)
Cornell University
201 Dolgen Hall
Ithaca, NY 14853-3901
Telephone: (607) 255-6686 V/TTY
Fax: (607) 255-2763
E-mail: dbtacnortheast@cornell.edu
Web site: http://www.dbtacnortheast.org

Northwest ADA Center
(Serving Alaska, Idaho, Oregon, Washington)
University of Washington
6912 220th Street, SW, #105
Mountlake Terrace, WA 98043
Telephone: (425) 248-2480
Fax: (425) 771-7438
E-mail: dbtacnw@u.washington.edu
Web site: http://www.dbtacnorthwest.org

Pacific ADA Center
(Serving Arizona, California, Hawaii, Nevada, Pacific Basin)
555 12th Street, Suite 1030
Oakland, CA 94607-4046
Telephone: (510) 285-5600 V/TTY
Fax: (510) 285-5614
E-mail: adatech@adapacific.org
Web site: http://www.adapacific.org

Rocky Mountain ADA Center
(Serving Colorado, Montana, North Dakota,
South Dakota, Utah, Wyoming)
Meeting the Challenge, Inc.
3630 Sinton Road, Suite 103
Colorado Springs, CO 80907
Telephone: (719) 444-0268 V/TTY
Fax: (719) 444-0269
E-mail: technicalassistance@mtc-inc.com
Web site: http://www.adainformation.org

Southeast ADA Center
(Serving Alabama, Florida, Georgia, Kentucky, Mississippi, North Carolina, South Carolina, Tennessee)
Project of the Burton Blatt Institute—Syracuse University
1419 Mayson Street
Atlanta, GA 30324
Telephone: (404) 541-9001 V/TTY
Fax: (404) 541-9002
E-mail: sedbtacproject@law.syr.edu
Web site: http://www.sedbtac.org

Southwest ADA Center
(Serving Arkansas, Louisiana, New Mexico, Oklahoma, Texas)
Independent Living Research Utilization
2323 South Shepherd Boulevard, Suite 1000
Houston, TX 77019
Telephone: (713) 520-0232 V/TTY
Fax: (713) 520-5785
E-mail: dlrp@ilru.org
Web site: http://www.dlrp.org

Seven

Selected Print and Electronic Resources

Sara Furguson, Sara VanLooy, and Susanne M. Bruyère

This chapter provides an annotated list of print and electronic resources pertaining to education, career development, employment opportunities, and workplace accommodations for individuals with disabilities.

Print Resources

Albrecht, G. L. (Ed.). (2005). *Encyclopedia of disability*. Thousand Oaks, CA: Sage.
This five-volume set aims to bring current knowledge and experience with disability across a wide variety of situations to both general and specialist readers.

Becker, D., & Drake, R. (2003). *A working life for people with severe mental illness*. New York, NY: Oxford University Press.
Becker and Drake provide a practical guide for therapists and rehabilitation counselors on effectively integrating work and employment goals into clinical treatment. This book describes a supported employment approach suitable for helping people with severe mental illness; it is the only approach with a strong empirical research base.

Berkowitz, M., & Hill, M. A. (Eds.). (1986). *Disability and the labor market: Economic problems, policies, and programs.* Ithaca, NY: ILR Press.

A collection of papers presented at a meeting on the economics of disability in Washington, D.C., this book won the Book of the Year award from the President's Committee on Employment of People with Disabilities. It offers a solid look at the state of policy and economic research in the years just before the passage of the ADA.

Burch, S. (Ed.). (2009). *Encyclopedia of American disability history.* New York, NY: Facts on File.

This comprehensive 3-volume set seeks to remove disability from the realm of medical pathology and allow the reader to understand disability topics in social and cultural terms. Aimed at high school and college readers, entries include issues, events, laws, people, and personal experiences, and contain multiple biographical sketches of people important in disability history.

Burkhauser, R., & Stapleton, D. (Eds.). (2003). *The decline in employment of people with disabilities: A policy puzzle.* Kalamazoo, MI: W. E. Upjohn Institute for Employment Research.

After the passage of the ADA in 1990, researchers looking at employment statistics saw that the employment rate for working-age people with disabilities declined during the 1990s but found little agreement about the cause of the decline. This book collects the viewpoints of a diverse group of contributors, paying special attention to the quality of the U.S. data used to calculate these statistics. The book begins with a documentation of the employment rate decline and ends by spelling out the implications of this decline for public policy. However, the bulk of the book provides a detailed examination of the various explanations for the puzzling decline in employment among the working-age population with disabilities.

Colker, R. (2005). *The disability pendulum: The first decade of the Americans with Disabilities Act.* New York, NY: New York University Press.

In tracing the effectiveness of the Americans with Disabilities Act of 1990, Colker argues that the landmark civil rights legislation has fallen short of its goal of ensuring equality of opportunity and access to people with disabilities. The book examines the shifting ground of legal decisions and societal attitudes that has impacted enforcement of the ADA and contributed to its failure to meet the aspirations of the disability rights movement.

Farkas, M., Sullivan Soydan, A., & Gagne, C. (2000). *Introduction to rehabilitation readiness.* Boston, MA: Boston University, Center for Psychiatric Rehabilitation. Retrieved from http://www.bu.edu/cpr/products/books/titles/introtoreadiness.html

Rehabilitation readiness helps people with serious psychiatric disabilities to actively assess their own willingness to engage in rehabilitation. Introduction to Rehabilitation Readiness *begins with a brief overview of psychiatric rehabilitation. The research background and context for the concepts involved in both assessing and developing psychiatric rehabilitation readiness are discussed.*

Hagglund, K., & Heinemann, A. (2006). *Handbook of applied disability and rehabilitation research.* New York, NY: Springer.
This book outlines the growing field of rehabilitation psychology with a look at research and practice. It offers recommendations for future research programs, policy changes, and clinical interventions, and seeks to demonstrate how much the field can evolve with the implementation of these changes. Employment topics include recommendations for a research agenda and evidence-based practices in vocational rehabilitation, while related topics include assistive technology selection and the importance of Internet accessibility.

Hotchkiss, J., (2003). *The labor market experience of workers with disabilities: The ADA and beyond.* Kalamazoo, MI: W. E. Upjohn Institute for Employment Research.
This book seeks to answer the question "What has the ADA accomplished?" and discover whether it serves as a statement of where we are rather than a prediction of where we are headed. Statistical analyses focus on two basic questions: How are disabled workers faring relative to nondisabled workers, and is their labor market experience improving? Specific attention is given to direct evidence of the existence of and changes in barriers to a positive labor market experience.

Houtenville, A. J., Stapleton, D. C, Weathers, R. R., & Burkhauser, R. V. (Eds.). (2009). *Counting working-age people with disabilities: What current data tell us and options for improvement.* Kalamazoo, MI: W. E. Upjohn Institute for Employment Research.
Working-age people with disabilities are often overlooked in discussions of the latest statistics on employment, income, poverty, and other measures. This book helps remedy that situation by providing a systematic review of what current statistics and data on working-age people with disabilities can and cannot tell us, and how the quality of the data can be improved to better inform policymakers, advocates, analysts, service providers, administrators, and others interested in this at-risk population.

Luecking, R. (2004). *Essential tools: In their own words: Employer perspectives on youth with disabilities in the workplace.* Minneapolis: University of Minnesota, Institute on Community Integration. Retrieved from http://ici.umn.edu/products/resourceguides.html
This resource guide is designed to help educators, transition specialists, workforce development professionals, family members, and youth to understand employers'

needs, circumstances, and perspectives as they establish work-based learning experiences. This publication, part of the "Essential Tools" series, features the experiences of employers in their own words. Eleven employers from various fields write about how they became involved in providing work experiences for youth with disabilities, what made it work, and what they recommend to individuals and organizations representing youth.

Mezey, S. (2005). *Disabling interpretations: The Americans with Disabilities Act in federal court.* Pittsburgh, PA: University of Pittsburgh Press.
Mezey, a political scientist, provides a review of federal court interpretations of the Americans with Disabilities Act of 1990. She describes how successive decisions narrowed the scope and impact of disability rights legislation and analyzes cases from across the federal judiciary.

Oakes, W. (2005). *Perspectives on disability, discrimination, accommodations, and law: A comparison of the Canadian and American experience.* New York: LFB Scholarly Pub.
This book summarizes the legislative frameworks for disability employment law in the United States and its nearest neighbor, comparing bases, definitions, and judicial responses.

O'Brien, R. (2001). *Crippled justice: The history of modern disability policy in the workplace.* Chicago, IL: University of Chicago Press.
O'Brien provides the first comprehensive intellectual history of disability policy in the workplace from World War II to the present. This book explains why American employers and judges have been so resistant to accommodating people with disabilities in the workplace.

Parker, R., Szymanski, E., & Patterson, J. (2004). *Rehabilitation counseling: Basics and beyond* (5th ed.). Austin, TX: Pro-Ed.
This textbook provides both a basic foundation for students beginning their journey into the profession of rehabilitation counseling and a broad-based reference for current practitioners. The contents overview the professional, historical, theoretical, research, and applied foundations of the rehabilitation counseling profession.

Riggar, T. F., & Maki, D. R. (2004). *Handbook of rehabilitation counseling.* New York, NY: Springer.
This textbook illustrates paradigms for professional practice, provides an overview of current knowledge and future trends in rehabilitation counseling, and aims to stimulate thinking that will lead to new research initiatives. Both settings (private and public) as well as services are addressed, including placement, advocacy, and case management. The text also contains elements of practice, including cutting-edge uses of technology and supervision, both clinical and managerial.

Rubin, S., & Roessler, R. (2008). *Foundations of the vocational rehabilitation process* (6th ed.). Austin, TX: Pro-Ed.

This book's 16 chapters present theoretical and practical assistance in translating current legislative mandates into action. It addresses involving individuals with severe disabilities in the rehabilitation process, adopting alternative approaches to vocational placement, providing independent living services, expanding services for those with developmental disabilities, and protecting the civil rights of people with disabilities.

Schultz, I., & Rogers, E. S. (2010). *Work accommodation and retention in mental health.* New York, NY: Springer.

Policymakers, employers, disability compensation systems, and rehabilitation and disability management professionals have lacked an evidence-based toolbox of best practices to accommodate and retain persons with mental health disabilities in the workplace. The need for workplace accommodations for persons with mental health disabilities has been growing and, based on epidemiological trends, is anticipated to grow even more in the future, leaving physicians, psychologists, occupational therapists, vocational rehabilitation professionals, disability managers, human resource professionals, and policymakers poorly prepared to face the challenge of integrating and maintaining persons with mental health disabilities in the workplace. The aim of this book is to close the gap between the needs of the professionals and networks that work with or study persons with mental health disorders in an employment context and the actual knowledge base in the field.

Stefan, S. (2001). *Unequal rights: Discrimination against people with mental disabilities and the Americans with Disabilities Act.* Washington, DC: American Psychological Association.

Unequal Rights *discusses how people with psychiatric disabilities or diagnoses experience discrimination and how antidiscrimination law protects (or does not protect) them. It is aimed at an audience of lawyers, therapists, and people with mental disabilities.*

Szymanski, E. M., & Parker, R. (Eds). (2010). *Work and disability: Contexts, issues, and strategies for enhancing employment outcomes for people with disabilities* (3rd ed). Austin, TX: Pro-Ed.

This book, now in its third edition, provides an updated picture of the legislative environment and other contextual matters affecting the employment of people with disabilities. It addresses vocational theories and research, counseling interventions, cultural issues, job development and placement, outreach to businesses, and supported employment topics.

Timmons, J., Podmostko, M., Bremer, C., Lavin, D., & Wills, J. (2005). *Career planning begins with assessment: A guide for professionals serving youth with educational and career development challenges.* Minneapolis: University of Minnesota, Institute on Community Integration. Retrieved from http://ici .umn.edu/products/resourceguides.html

This guide provides adults who work with youth with disabilities a solid understanding of the purpose, benefits, and limitations of assessment in relation to those youth and the workforce development system. It includes information on types of assessment tools and testing instruments, selecting and using appropriate assessment tools, and ethical and legal considerations in assessments.

Wehman, P., Inge, K., Revell, W. G., & Brooke, V. (2006). *Real work for real pay: Inclusive employment for people with disabilities.* Baltimore, MD: Brookes.

A collection of current best practices, employment theories, policies, and tools to support positive change in the workplace, Real Work for Real Pay *offers the prospect of real, inclusive employment for people with a variety of disabilities, and goes into great detail on the kind of groundwork and assistance needed to make that happen.*

World Health Organization. (2001). *The international classification of functioning, disability, and health: ICF.* Geneva, Switzerland: Author.

The International Classification of Functioning, Disability, and Health, known more commonly as ICF, is a classification of health and health-related domains. The ICF is WHO's framework for measuring health and disability at both individual and population levels. The ICF was officially endorsed by all 191 WHO member states in 2001 (Resolution WHA 54.21).

The ICF puts the notions of "health" and "disability" in a new light by acknowledging that every human being can experience a decrement in health and thereby experience some degree of disability. The ICF thus "mainstreams" the experience of disability and recognizes it as a universal human experience. By shifting the focus from cause to impact, it places all health conditions on an equal footing, allowing them to be compared using a common metric—the ruler of health and disability. Furthermore, ICF takes into account the social aspects of disability and does not see disability only as a "medical" or "biological" dysfunction. By including contextual factors, in which environmental factors are listed, ICF allows researchers to record the impact of the environment on the person's functioning.

Electronic Resources

Abilities! Retrieved from http://www.abilitiesonline.org

Founded as Abilities, Inc. in 1952, Abilities! has evolved into one of the world's foremost facilities for educating and training people with disabilities. The organization operates a number of programs that focus on empowering people with disabilities to be active, independent, and self-sufficient participants in society. These projects include the Kornreich Technology Center, which showcases state-of-the-art assistive technology; the Smeal Learning Center, a training facility that offers technology and multimedia resources; and the Global Institute, which identifies, researches, and promotes promising practices in special education and rehabilitation. In addition, Abilities! partners with Just One Break (JOB) to operate the National Business and Disability Council (NBDC) and the Emerging Leaders College Internship Program.

American College of Healthcare Executives. *Project SEARCH.* Retrieved from http://www.projectsearch.info/apps

Project SEARCH serves people with disabilities through innovative workforce and career development. Project SEARCH educates employers about the potential of this underutilized workforce while meeting their human resource needs. Project SEARCH provides employment and education opportunities for individuals with significant disabilities.

America's Heroes at Work. Retrieved from http://www.americasheroesatwork.gov

This project focuses on the employment challenges of returning service members living with Traumatic Brain Injury (TBI) and/or Post-Traumatic Stress Disorder (PTSD). Designed for employers and the workforce development system, this Web site offers information and tools to help returning service members affected by TBI and PTSD succeed in the workplace.

Association for People in Supported Employment. *Job Training & Placement Report.* Retrieved from http://www.apse.org/publications

APSE members receive an E-subscription to Job Training & Placement Report *(JTPR). JTPR has been serving supported employment professionals longer than any other publication of its kind. Each issue of JTPR consists of articles containing practical information to help readers keep up with industry trends and develop new strategies to increase employment opportunities for clients.*

Association for People in Supported Employment. *theAdvance.* Retrieved from http://www.apse.org/publications

APSE members receive four copies of theAdvance, the APSE E-newsletter, each year. Topics discussed in the Advance include Job Development; Job Creation; Job Supports; Customized Employment; SE Fundng; SE Values and Ethical Guidelines; Self-Advocacy; Transition from School to Work; Medicaid; State Employment First Initiatives; Social Security Work Incentives; Rehabilitation Act; and a myriad of other issues.

Career Perfect. *Work Preference Inventory.* Retrieved from http://www.careerperfect.com/content/career-planning-work-preference-inventory

The Work Preference Inventory is a 24-item inventory that helps users identify their preferred work style. The inventory is scored and printed. The quiz identifies qualities that an individual possesses and appropriate ways of utilization.

CareerKey. Retrieved from http://www.careerkey.org
This Web site provides expert help with career choices—career changes, career planning, job skills, and choosing a college major or educational program. The Career Key test is one of the few professional-quality career tests on the Internet. The results of scientific studies show that it measures what it is supposed to.

Centre for International Health and Development. Handicap International/ Healthlink Worldwide. *Source.* Retrieved from http://www.asksource.info
Source provides access to 25,000 resources relating to the management, practice, and communication of international health and disability issues. It includes both published and unpublished materials, many originating from developing countries. Source is a collaborative venture of the Centre for International Health and Development, Handicap International, and Healthlink Worldwide.

Cornell University, School of Industrial and Labor Relations, Employment and Disability Institute. *Disability & HR: Tips for Human Resource Professionals.* Retrieved from http://www.hrtips.org
This site contains a series of 36 searchable articles and 4 disability nondiscrimination and best-practices checklists designed in response to specific questions raised by HR professionals about managing disability issues in the workplace. Article topics include disability nondiscrimination regulations; management and HR practice; employment process; and accommodations of specific disabilities.

Cornell University, School of Industrial and Labor Relations, Employment and Disability Institute. *Disability Statistics.* Retrieved from http://www.ilr .cornell.edu/edi/disabilitystatistics
Disability Statistics offers 1981–2010 Current Population Survey (CPS) and Census 2000 disability statistics. The Annual Disability Status Reports provide policymakers, disability advocates, reporters, and the public with a summary of the most recent demographic and economic statistics on the noninstitutionalized population with disabilities.

Cornell University, School of Industrial and Labor Relations, Employment and Disability Institute. *ediONLINE.* Retrieved from http://www.ilr.cornell.edu/ edi/edionline/edionline.cfm
ediONLINE is the Employment and Disability Institute's vehicle for providing high-quality online training to managers, practitioners, advocates, and policymakers in the disability field in order to improve and enhance effectiveness in supporting employment outcomes and greater economic self-sufficiency for people with disabilities. These courses bridge the gap between policy and practice by providing users with practical applications, hands-on learning, leading-edge skills, and knowledge that they can immediately apply to their work.

Cornell University, School of Industrial and Labor Relations, Employment and Disability Institute. *Independence.* Retrieved from http://www.ilr.cornell.edu/edi/independence/default.htm
This Web-based resource brings together a wealth of information, with sections about public employment policy, research, and enabling programs and supports for people with disabilities. The information contributes to a better understanding of how public policy is reshaping the world of work, bringing society ever closer to the realization of full employment for people with disabilities.

Council of State Administrators of Vocational Rehabilitation. *Think Beyond the Label.* Retrieved from http://www.thinkbeyondthelabel.com
Think Beyond the Label is committed to making the business case for employing people with disabilities. It is a partnership of health and human service and employment agencies with federal grants, coming together to build a uniform national infrastructure and approach that connects businesses to qualified candidates with disabilities. The goal is to raise awareness that hiring people with disabilities makes good business sense.

Disability.gov. Retrieved from http://www.disability.gov
Disability.gov is managed by the U.S. Department of Labor in partnership with 21 other federal agencies. This award-winning Web site connects Americans with disabilities, their families, veterans, educators, employers, and others to thousands of resources from federal, state, and local government agencies, educational institutions, and nonprofit organizations. With just a few clicks, visitors can find critical information on a variety of topics, including benefits, civil rights, community life, education, emergency preparedness, employment, housing, health, technology, and transportation.

Employer Innovations Online. *Facilitating Practical Applications at the Workplace.* Retrieved from http://www.workplacementalhealth.org/Pages/EmployerInnovations/Search.aspx
Employer Innovations Online helps employers take action to address mental health at the workplace by providing case examples of successful corporate approaches. This site allows employers to search current approaches. Employers may search actual practices of leading employers in key areas, such as screening and education, Employee Assistance Programs, and disability management.

Equal Opportunity Publications. *CAREERS & the disABLED.* Retrieved from http://www.eop.com/mags-CD.php
CAREERS & the disABLED Magazine, *established in 1986, is the nation's first and only career-guidance and recruitment magazine for people with disabilities who are at undergraduate, graduate, or professional levels.*

Georgia State University. *IMPACT*. Retrieved from http://secureapp.netclubmgr
.com/ICS/CM/V2/Student/Club.aspx?uid=gastun&ClubId=12460
*IMPACT (Individually Motivated People Accepting Challenges Today) is a student
organization seeking students and faculty/staff who are interested in helping others
build confidence through advocacy. The focus is on the current changes that all
students are making, with an emphasis on the changes being made in the lives of
students with disabilities.*

Illinois Assistive Technology Program. *Workplace Technologies for People with
Disabilities.* Retrieved from http://www.iltech.org/workplacetechnologies.pdf
*This employment-focused guide describes how employers and service providers can
use assistive technology to make workplaces and service centers accessible to people
with disabilities. It contains illustrations of many different types of assistive technologies,
including descriptive text on the use of these technologies.*

InfoUse. Retrieved from http://www.infouse.com
*InfoUse uses the power of information, technology, and participatory research to
improve community equity, access, and outcomes. The program focuses on the
development of health, disability, and rehabilitation information using computer
technology. InfoUse researches and presents data on topics such as disability
statistics, program evaluation, policy, analysis, and interactive multimedia
production, and has produced interactive systems and materials for the U.S.
Department of Education, the U.S. Department of Health and Human Services, the
State of California, and others. This site offers links to many of their project sites.*

InfoUse. *Access to Disability Data*. Retrieved from http://www.infouse.com/
disabilitydata/home/index.php
*This site provides links to downloadable chartbooks published between 1996 and 2004
on special topics in disability, including overall numbers, work and disability, women
and disability, and mental health and disability.*

InfoUse. *Assistive Technology Data Collection Project*. Retrieved from http://www
.infouse.com/atdata
*InfoUse, in collaboration with the Research Triangle Institute, has designed and
implemented a Web-based reporting system for assistive technology data collection.
The Chartbook on Assistive Technology presents national estimates on the need for and
use of assistive technology. The project produces statistical estimates, by state, on the
need for and use of assistive technology.*

InfoUse. *Center for Personal Assistance Services: Economics and Workplace PAS*.
Retrieved from http://pascenter.org/workplace_pas/index.php
*For many working-age people with disabilities, there are many barriers that prevent
working or returning to work. Lack of personal assistance services (PAS) at work is*

one key barrier. There is little public funding for workplace PAS, and the ADA does not require employers to provide PAS. This site provides links to InfoUse research and resources on PAS.

InfoUse. *Open Futures: Role Models for Youth with Disabilities.* Retrieved from http://www.infouse.com/openfutures
Although people with disabilities often face barriers moving into the world of work, many do succeed. Many discover exciting jobs inspired by their interests and abilities. Each month Open Futures *introduces readers to three people with disabilities who believed in themselves and followed their dreams. It also provides a link to order CD-ROM and video versions of this series.*

InfoUse. *Vocational Rehabilitation & Independent Living: Employment Outcomes Partnership Project.* Retrieved from http://www.infouse.com/vr-il
This Web site presents the results of the Employment Outcomes Partnership project, which explored partnering between vocational rehabilitation (VR) agencies and independent living centers (ILCs). The VR-IL Directory provides the VR and IL communities as well as other consumer and professional groups with a resource guide to programs and practices that exemplify the best approaches to employment-focused collaboration. The Expert Panel, as well as the relevant literature, is also included on this site.

International Labour Organization. *ILO Publications on Work and Disability.* Retrieved from http://www.ilo.org/skills/lang-en/index.htm
Governments, employers' associations, and trade unions around the world are working to improve the quality and relevance of training and employment services in order to improve the employability of workers and the productivity and competitiveness of enterprises. The ILO has worked for over 50 years to promote skills development and employment opportunities for people with disabilities based on the principles of equal opportunity, equal treatment, mainstreaming into vocational rehabilitation and employment services programs, and community involvement.

Job Accommodation Network. *ADA Library.* Retrieved from http://askjan.org/links/adalinks.htm
This library includes links to the text of the ADA, the ADA Amendments Act, EEOC guidance about each title, and technical assistance manuals on each title.

Job Accommodation Network. *Ask JAN.* Retrieved from http://askjan.org
JAN's consultants offer one-on-one guidance on workplace accommodations, the Americans with Disabilities Act (ADA) and related legislation, and self-employment and entrepreneurship options for people with disabilities. Assistance is available both over the phone and online. Those who can benefit from JAN's services include private employers of all sizes, government agencies, employee representatives, and service providers, as well as people with disabilities and their families.

Job Accommodation Network. *JAN Video on Accommodations.* Retrieved from http://www.youtube.com/watch?v=SBbfVNcNlAg
This is a video on workplace accommodations and assistive technology from the Job Accommodations Network (JAN). A variety of possible workplace accommodations are discussed and demonstrated.

Job Accommodation Network. *Searchable Online Accommodation Resource (SOAR).* Retrieved from http://askjan.org/soar/index.htm
JAN's Searchable Online Accommodation Resource (SOAR) system is designed to let users explore various accommodation options for people with disabilities in work and educational settings.

Job Accommodation Network. *Universal Design & Assistive Technology in the Workplace.* Retrieved from http://www.askjan.org/media/udafact.doc
This fact sheet provides tips for choosing equipment that includes universal design features and for choosing assistive technologies that meet the specific accommodation needs of an employee with a disability.

JOBLINKS. *Transportation to Work—A Toolkit for the Business Community.* Retrieved from http://web1.ctaa.org/webmodules/webarticles//anmviewer.asp?a= 1442&z=5
This toolkit is a collection of online resources that guide company executives and human resources professionals in providing job-related transportation benefits to their employees while improving their companies' bottom line. The toolkit has a menu of options from which employers can select what will work well for their businesses, such as giving employees the opportunity to sign up for pre-tax commuter benefit deductions or assisting employees with disabilities with transportation to work.

Just One Break (JOB), Inc. Retrieved from http://www.justonebreak.com/Index .aspx
Just One Break (JOB) is a national nonprofit organization that is dedicated to increasing employment opportunities for individuals with disabilities. In partnership with Abilities!, JOB operates the National Business and Disability Council (NBDC), a business-to-business membership organization that provides services to employers to assist them in recruiting, retaining, and advancing workers with disabilities; and the Emerging Leaders College Internship Program, which matches college students with disabilities to the internship needs of employers wishing to diversify their workforce.

National Association of Colleges and Employers. *Jobweb.* Retrieved from http:// www.jobweb.com
Jobweb is a resource for students, employers, and parents on the job market and offers possible employment opportunities for recent graduates. A variety of resources are available on the market, job trends, minority employment guides, and more.

National Collaborative on Workforce and Disability. *Navigating the Road to Work: Making the Connection between Youth with Disabilities and Employment.* Retrieved from http://www.ncwd-youth.info
This site is a product of the National Collaborative on Workforce and Disability for Youth (NCWD/Youth), which assists state and local workforce development systems to better serve all youth, including youth with disabilities and other disconnected youth. It offers links to tools, checklists, guideposts, and other resources designed to help young people with disabilities get started on the road to work.

National Organization on Disability. *Harris Interactive Surveys.* Retrieved from http://nod.org/research_publications/nod_harris_survey
Since the 1980s, NOD has collaborated with the Harris Poll on numerous surveys on a variety of issues facing people with disabilities. The surveys enjoy wide coverage in the press, and results are frequently cited by policymakers and by the disability community.

New Jersey Business Leadership Network. *Accessible Employment.* Retrieved from http://www.accessibleemployment.org
AccessibleEmployment.org is a national job board dedicated to including disabled employees in today's workforce. The site is focused on closing the gap between employers searching for qualified workers and disabled candidates searching for employment.

Operation Confidence. Retrieved from http://www.operationconfidence.org
Operation Confidence is a grassroots nonprofit organization that provides job preparation workshops, searches for employment opportunities, and hosts career fairs for individuals with physical disabilities. Operation Confidence's Positive Redirection Team is a diverse group of very independent people (all wheelchair users) who are motivational speakers, mentors, life coaches, and consultants.

Program Development Associates. *DisabilityTraining.com.* Retrieved from http://www.disabilitytraining.com
This online tool is a source for over 600 disability videos, CDs, DVDs, and curricula. It features a variety of training resources and tools to address diversity issues in the workplace. It provides information and training on age, race, religion, sexual orientation, or gender discrimination. This one-stop shop makes it easy and convenient for both human service and human resources professionals who need educational resources on disability or diversity to achieve their training objectives.

San Diego State University. *Interwork Institute.* Retrieved from http://www.interwork.sdsu.edu
The San Diego State University Interwork Institute's activities focus on promoting the integration of all individuals, including those with disabilities, into all aspects of school, work, family, and community life. Education and research efforts involve

organizations and individuals in the United States, the Pacific Basin, Asia, South America, and Europe.

Sierra Group Foundation. *Employment Incentives Web Portal.* Retrieved from http://employmentincentives.com
The Employment Incentives Web Portal provides information on employment incentives for businesses, including tax credits, business loans and grants, vocational rehabilitation services, assistive technology information, and other financial advantages to encourage businesses to employ people with disabilities. The Sierra Group Foundation works toward this mission by investing resources in three focused areas: scholarships; researching adaptive technology for the workplace; and publishing research on employer best practices.

Training and Technical Assistance for Providers. *Personal Assistance in the Workplace: A Customer-Directed Guide.* Retrieved from http://www.t-tap.org/strategies/manuals/pasmanual.htm
This guide is a consumer-oriented resource on using Personal Assistance Services (PAS) in the workplace. The manual covers self-assessment, employers' perspectives, keys to being a workplace personal assistant, assistive technology, funding options, independent living, and employment services.

United Nations Secretariat, Division for Social Policy and Development. *UN Enable.* Retrieved from http://www.un.org/disabilities
The Division for Social Policy and Development of the United Nations Secretariat in New York is the focal point within the United Nations system on matters relating to disability. Within the division, the Secretariat for the Convention on the Rights of Persons with Disabilities provides support to the work of the ad hoc committee on a disability convention, and deals with promoting, monitoring, and evaluating the implementation of the World Programme of Action and the Standard Rules. It also prepares publications and acts as a clearinghouse for information on disability issues; promotes national, regional, and international programs and activities; provides support to governments and non-governmental organizations; and gives substantial support to technical co-operation projects and activities.

University of Buffalo. *Center for International Rehabilitation Research Information and Exchange (CIRRIE).* Retrieved from http://cirrie.buffalo.edu
CIRRIE facilitates the sharing of information and expertise in rehabilitation research between the United States and other countries through a wide range of programs. The site contains an international research database, information about international exchange programs, International Classification of Function, Disability, and Health (ICF) utilization, cultural competence information, and additional resources.

University of Massachusetts—Boston, Institute for Community Inclusion. *Real People, Real Jobs: Stories from the Front Line*. Retrieved from http://www.realworkstories.org

This site highlights the employment successes of people with Intellectual Disabilities/Developmental Disabilities (ID/DD) who are working in paid jobs in their communities. Through the use of innovative, front-line employment support practices, these individuals are earning money, forming networks, and contributing to their communities. This Web site allows visitors to learn more about these people and the promising practices that led to their success.

University of Massachusetts—Boston, Institute for Community Inclusion. *School Days to Pay Days: An Employment Planning Guide for Families of Young Adults With Intellectual Disabilities*. Retrieved from http://www.communityinclusion.org/pdf/DDS_booklet_F.pdf

Collaboratively designed by ICI and the Department of Developmental Services, this booklet will help families get started with the school-to-work transition process. Readers will learn about resources, services, and programs available for young adults with intellectual disabilities in Massachusetts; and find inspiration in the many success stories of young adults who have secured fulfilling employment with appropriate supports.

University of Massachusetts—Boston, Institute for Community Inclusion. *StateData: The National Report on Employment Services and Outcomes*. Retrieved from http://www.statedata.info

The ICI StateData.info Web site offers ready access to descriptive information on services and outcomes for state agencies that provide employment supports to individuals with disabilities. The target audiences include state agency personnel, policymakers, and advocates. The Web site automatically creates fully accessible graphics from underlying data.

University of Minnesota, Institute for Community Integration. *Essential Tools: Resource Guide Series*. Retrieved from http://ici.umn.edu/products/resourceguides.html

Essential Tools is a series of resource guides for family members, people with disabilities, and practitioners. Free downloadable publications include handbooks on transition from school to work, employer perspectives on employing youth with disabilities, career assessment guides, and mentoring information.

U.S. Department of Agriculture. *Target Discovery Series: How to Support the Employment of People With Disabilities*. Retrieved from http://www.dm.usda.gov/oo/target/discovery/index.html

Through this captioned video presentation from the U.S. Department of Agriculture's (USDA) TARGET Discovery Series, learn about the technology, organizations, hiring authorities, and best practices that can help increase the employment and advancement of people with disabilities—one of the biggest untapped resources in today's federal and private workplaces.

U.S. Department of Education, Office of Special Education and Rehabilitative Services. *Disability Employment 101.* Retrieved from http://www2.ed.gov/about/offices/list/osers/products/employmentguide/disabilityemployment101.pdf
This guide is a comprehensive analysis of hiring employees with disabilities that includes information about how to find qualified workers with disabilities, how to put disability and employment research into practice, and how to model what other businesses have done to successfully integrate individuals with disabilities into the workforce. Among other things, the guide provides information regarding Department of Education-funded vocational rehabilitation agencies, Disability and Business Technical Assistance Centers (DBTACs), and Centers for Independent Living (CILs).

U.S. Department of Labor, Employer Assistance and Resource Network (EARN). *EARNWorks Employer–Success Stories.* Retrieved from http://www.earnworks.com/employers/success/employer.asp
This is a collection of the experiences of organizations that have hired people with disabilities. Many of these accounts describe how several managers and employees with disabilities from private-sector businesses across a variety of industries worked together to find solutions that were highly effective in supporting their goals. These stories offer shared lessons, best practices, and personal insights to help employers in developing or enhancing business strategies.

U.S. Department of Labor, Employment and Training Administration. *Workforce³ One Project.* Retrieved from http://www.workforce3one.org
Workforce³ One is an E-learning, knowledge-sharing Web space that offers workforce professionals, employers, economic development and education professionals a dynamic network featuring innovative workforce solutions. Online learning events, resource information, and tools help organizations learn how to develop strategies that enable individuals and businesses to be successful in the 21st century economy.

U.S. Department of Labor, Office of Compliance Assistance Policy. *Employment Law Guide.* Retrieved from http://www.dol.gov/compliance/guide/index.htm
This guide, a companion to the elaws FirstStep Employment Law Advisor, describes the major statutes and regulations administered by the U.S. Department of Labor that affect businesses and workers. The guide is designed mainly for those needing "hands-on" information to develop wage, benefit, safety and health, and nondiscrimination policies for businesses.

U.S. Department of Labor, Office of Disability Employment Policy. *Customized Employment: Practical Solutions to Employment Success*. Retrieved from http://www.dol.gov/odep/pubs/custom/index.htm
This fact sheet describes ways to individualize or customize the relationship between a job seeker or employee and an employer in ways that meet the needs of both. It includes a description of the customized employment process and how to appropriately identify ways of customization.

U.S. Department of Labor, Office of Disability Employment Policy. *Diversifying Your Workforce*. Retrieved from http://www.dol.gov/odep/topics/Diversity AndInclusion.htm
Diversifying Your Workforce is a quick reference guide outlining the advantages of hiring people with disabilities, along with four simple steps to increasing the inclusiveness of your workforce. With numerous resources and Web links, the site is a helpful starting point for organizations looking to benefit from the talents of qualified individuals with disabilities.

U.S. Department of Labor, Office of Disability Employment Policy. *Diversity Includes Disability*. Retrieved from http://www.dol.gov/odep/topics/ DiversityAndInclusion.htm
This Web page provides information regarding how companies can support diversity, including employees with disabilities. The steps necessary to create a diverse workforce are outlined and explained. Additional resource information is also supplied.

U.S. Department of Labor, Office of Disability Employment Policy. *A New Day: We're Listening Webcasts*. Retrieved from http://www.dol.gov/odep/ disabilitylistening.htm
In early 2010, the U.S. Department of Labor's (DOL) Office of Disability Employment Policy (ODEP) and its federal partners held a series of six "Listening Sessions" across the country on the employment of people with disabilities. Each session provided an opportunity for members of the public to provide input to senior federal officials on better ways to employ all people with disabilities, including women, veterans, and minorities with disabilities, and what was currently working in their communities to increase employment among people with disabilities. Summary reports in Word format and recorded video and audio programs of these sessions are available.

U.S. Department of Labor, Office of Disability Employment Policy. *Roadmaps II*. Retrieved from http://www.dol.gov/odep/categories/employment_ supports/roadmaps.htm
The U.S. Department of Labor's Office of Disability Employment Policy (ODEP) has released a follow up to its Roadmaps for Enhancing Employment of Persons with Disabilities through Accessible Technology *(AT).* Roadmaps II *provides an overview of federally funded AT programs; a summary of some of the barriers that*

affect the use of AT by individuals with disabilities; and recommendations to increase the employment of individuals with disabilities though AT. The complete report can be downloaded in PDF or Word format.

U.S. Department of Labor, Office of Disability Employment Policy. *A World in Which People with Disabilities Have Unlimited Employment Opportunities.* Retrieved from http://www.dol.gov/odep/pubs/fact/diverse.htm
This fact sheet explores how businesses can enhance their competitive edge by hiring people with disabilities. The informational Web page provides data on methods that effectively increase the employment of people with disabilities by creating an inclusive work environment. It also provides a list of additional resources.

U.S. Equal Employment Opportunity Commission. *Americans with Disabilities Act (ADA) & Workers Placed by Temporary Agencies: Frequently Asked Questions.* Retrieved from http://www.eeoc.gov/policy/docs/qanda-contingent.html
This Web page provides guidance that explains the responsibilities of staffing firms and their clients in complying with requirements unique to the ADA, including reasonable accommodations and rules concerning disability-related questions and medical examinations.

U.S. Equal Employment Opportunity Commission. *Best Practices of Private Sector Employers.* Retrieved from http://www.eeoc.gov/eeoc/task_reports/best_practices.cfm
This report highlights noteworthy business practices by which employers are complying with their equal employment opportunity obligations and diversity objectives. The report identifies current best practices utilized in major businesses.

U.S. Equal Employment Opportunity Commission. *Enforcement Guidance on Reasonable Accommodation & Undue Hardship under the Americans with Disabilities Act (ADA).* Retrieved from http://www.eeoc.gov/policy/docs/accommodation.html
This U.S. Equal Employment Opportunity Commission (EEOC) enforcement guidance combines the Supreme Court decisions and EEOC's new regulations under Section 501 of the Rehabilitation Act.

U.S. Equal Employment Opportunity Commission, Leadership for the Employment of Americans with Disabilities (LEAD). *The ABCs of Schedule A for Applicants with Disabilities: Tips for Getting Federal Jobs.* Retrieved from http://www.dol.gov/odep/pubs/scheduleA/abc_Job_Applicants_ODEP_508 compliant.pdf
This simple guide advises Americans with disabilities on how federal hiring authorities work and how to use Schedule A to get through the federal hiring process.

U.S. Social Security Administration, Office of Employment Support Programs. *Employment Network Handbook for Employers: The Many Benefits of Hiring Workers with Disabilities*. Retrieved from http://www.socialsecurity.gov/work/documents/Employers_handbook_091808.pdf
The handbook provides information from the Social Security Administration's Office of Employment Support Programs on how to become an Employment Network (EN) under the Ticket to Work Program. As an EN, employers are offered a financial incentive to hire people with disabilities. Employers can recruit from hundreds of Social Security disability beneficiaries who want to work, and generate over $4,700 in income within the first nine months of a beneficiary's employment.

U.S. Social Security Administration, Ticket to Work Program. *Employing People with Disabilities*. Retrieved from http://www.socialsecurity.gov/work/envr.html#Employers
This site provides information about employing people with disabilities, including background on the Americans with Disabilities Act, tax incentives, referral services, and helpful links to the U.S. Department of Labor's Office of Disability Employment Policy.

Virginia Commonwealth University, Rehabilitation Research and Training Center on Workplace Supports and Job Retention. *VCU Business Roundtable*. Retrieved from http://worksupport.com/projects/project.cfm/18
The VCU Business Roundtable is a business forum for identifying and addressing factors that inhibit industries from employing workers with disabilities. Discussion topics include ways to enhance the productivity of people with disabilities and methods to create an inclusive work environment.

Virginia Commonwealth University, Rehabilitation Research and Training Center on Workplace Supports and Job Retention. *Worksupport.com Resources*. Retrieved from http://worksupport.com/resources/index.cfm
The VCU Workplace Supports RRTC is dedicated to studying supports that are most effective for assisting individuals with disabilities to maintain employment and advance their careers. The resources center contains articles, briefing papers, case studies, factsheets, and manuals on a wide variety of employment topics, downloadable for free.

WETA-TV. Public Broadcasting Station *LD OnLine*. Retrieved from http://www.ldonline.org
LD OnLine seeks to help children and adults reach their full potential by providing accurate and up-to-date information and advice about learning disabilities and ADHD. The site features hundreds of helpful articles, multimedia presentations, monthly columns by noted experts, first-person essays, children's writing and artwork, a comprehensive resource guide, very active forums, and a Yellow Pages referral directory of professionals, schools, and products.

What Can You Do? The Campaign for Disability Employment. Retrieved from http://www.whatcanyoudocampaign.org

The Campaign for Disability Employment is a collaborative effort between several disability and business organizations that seeks to promote positive employment outcomes for people with disabilities by encouraging employers and others to recognize the value and talent they bring to the workplace, as well as the dividend to be realized by fully including people with disabilities at work. People with disabilities can and do make important contributions to America's businesses every day. By implementing good workplace practices, like maintaining a flexible and inclusive work environment, businesses can capitalize on the talents of qualified people with disabilities, benefitting everyone.

Glossary of Key Terms

ACA *See* Affordable Care Act of 2010 (ACA)

Accommodation A modification or adjustment to a job or work environment that enables a qualified applicant or employee with a disability to participate in the application process or to perform essential job functions.

ACS *See* American Community Survey (ACS)

ADA *See* Americans with Disabilities Act of 1990 (ADA)

ADEA *See* Age Discrimination in Employment Act of 1967 (ADEA)

Affirmative Businesses Community-based employment training settings that are owned and operated by a Community Rehabilitation Program (CRP) and provide an intermediate employment step to competitive or individualized supported job placement for people with disabilities.

Affordable Care Act of 2010 (ACA) Also known as the Patient Protection and Affordable Care Act, this sweeping health care reform legislation requires that all Americans have health insurance; bars health insurance companies from discriminating based on pre-existing medical conditions, health status, or gender; prohibits lifetime limits on coverage; prohibits rescission (dropping) of customers by insurers; creates insurance exchanges; requires employers with 50 workers or more to offer health insurance benefits or pay a fee; expands Medicaid and provides premium assistance; and creates temporary insurance pools for consumers with pre-existing conditions until insurance exchanges open in 2014.

Age Discrimination in Employment Act of 1967 (ADEA) Legislation that prohibits discrimination in hiring, promotion, wages, termination, and other conditions of employment for persons aged 40 or older in the United States.

American Community Survey (ACS) A continuous data collection effort conducted by the U.S. Census Bureau that is used to produce annual estimates at the national, state, and local levels on the characteristics of the United States population.

Americans with Disabilities Act of 1990 (ADA) A sweeping civil rights law that prohibits discrimination against people with disabilities in employment, public transportation, public accommodations, and telecommunications, and requires employers to provide "reasonable accommodations" for employees with disabilities. Under Title I of this law, individuals are considered to have a disability if they have a "physical or mental impairment that substantially limits one or more major life activities" or are "regarded as having such an impairment."

Annual Social and Economic Supplement to the Current Population Survey (CPS-ASEC) A national survey conducted by the Bureau of the Census in March each year that collects data in addition to the monthly CPS; it utilizes a single disability screener question identifying what is referred to as a "work limitation disability."

Any Annual Employment A definition of employment that includes anyone who worked at least 52 hours anytime in a year (working an hour a week throughout the year or just one intense 52-hour work week in a whole year count the same).

Charge Data Records of individuals' claims, filed with the Equal Employment Opportunity Commission or a state or local Fair Employment Practices Agency, charging that an employers' actions violate the Americans with Disabilities Act (ADA) or other civil rights statutes that cover the employment of protected groups.

Civil Rights Act of 1964, Title VII Title VII prohibits employment discrimination on the basis of race, color, religion, sex, and national origin.

Community Rehabilitation Program (CRP)   Nongovernmental organizations that facilitate employment of people with disabilities through a range of work-related services and serve as a catalyst in the supply/demand employment matching process.

Compensation   Remuneration received for work, including wages and salaries as well as benefits such as health care, paid vacation, or unemployment taxation.

CPS   *See* Current Population Survey (CPS)

CPS-ASEC   *See* Annual Social and Economic Supplement to the Current Population Survey (CPS-ASEC)

CRP   *See* Community Rehabilitation Program (CRP)

Current Population Survey (CPS)   A monthly survey of about 50,000 households conducted by the Bureau of the Census for the Bureau of Labor Statistics; it is the primary source of labor force statistics for the U.S. civilian noninstitutionalized population.

Customized Employment   A process of finding an individual match between employee and employer. The skills and interests of an individual are matched with the employer's business needs, and a job may be customized or personalized to suit both parties.

Disability   Disability is a complex and multi-dimensional concept. National surveys have often been used to assist in identifying the population of people with disabilities; the disability definition included in these surveys varies. Currently, the major noninstitutional surveys in the United States (the American Community Survey, the National Health Interview Survey, and the Survey of Income Program Participation) all elicit information on sensory impairments, functional limitations, mental disabilities, limitations in activities of daily living (ADLs) or instrumental activities of daily living (IADLs), and work disabilities. People who report having one of these impairments or limitations are counted as "disabled" in these surveys. In 1965 Saad Nagi proposed a model of disability as a social construct, which views disability as an interaction between a person's health condition and the physical and social environment—making disability a function of society. Disability, under this paradigm, is a mismatch between an individual's abilities and the demands of the environment in which the individual lives and works. The World Health Organization (WHO) is working to reframe how disability is defined, more consistent with a social rather than a medical model of disability and impairment. The result has been the International Classification of Functioning, Disability, and Health (ICF), which includes measures of community participation and inclusion, rather than just impairment, in the model.

Disability Management   A workplace program that seeks to reduce the impact of injury and disability and to accommodate employees who experience functional work limitations; the term captures activities ranging from proactive injury prevention to return-to-work interventions, all aimed at improving work outcomes for individuals and profitability for employers.

Discouraged Worker   A person considered "marginally attached" to the workforce who reports that he/she did not look for work recently because he/she believes there are no jobs available.

Earned Income Tax Credits (EITC)   Tax credits for low-income workers, intended to provide an incentive to work.

EEOC   *See* Equal Employment Opportunity Commission (EEOC)

EITC   *See* Earned Income Tax Credits (EITC)

Employment Process   The various steps involved in being hired for a particular position that is appropriate to one's skills and abilities.

Employment Rate   Also known as the employment-to-population ratio, this figure is the number of employed people in a given group divided by the total number of people in that same group; the rate is calculated across all persons: those working, those actively seeking employment, and those neither employed nor seeking work.

EPA   *See* Equal Pay Act of 1963 (EPA)

Equal Employment Opportunity Commission (EEOC)   The U.S. federal government agency responsible for enforcing and interpreting several pieces of anti-discrimination legislation in the employment sector, including the Americans with Disabilities Act.

Equal Pay Act of 1963 (EPA)   A law that prohibits employers from discriminating on the basis of sex by paying lower wages to employees of one gender than it pays to employees of the other gender within the same establishment for equal work at jobs that require equal skill, effort, and responsibility, and that are performed under similar working conditions.

Executive Order 11246   Signed by President Lyndon Johnson in 1965, it requires employers who are federal contractors and subcontractors to take "affirmative action" to recruit and advance qualified minorities, women, persons with disabilities, and covered veterans.

Executive Order 13078   Signed by President Bill Clinton in 1998, it required the federal government to develop an accurate and reliable measure of the employment rate of people with disabilities, and to publish this figure as frequently as possible.

Fair Employment Practice Agency (FEPA)   Agencies responsible for enforcing state and local laws prohibiting employment discrimination.

Fair Labor Standards Act (FLSA)   The federal regulatory policy that most broadly defines the rules for employment of people in the United States, including standards for wages (e.g., minimum wage) and work hours (e.g., 40-hour work week).

Fair Wages for Workers with Disabilities Act of 2011   Proposed legislation that would repeal Section 14(c) of the Fair Labor Standards Act; the new law would continue to allow organizations employing majority workforces of people with disabilities to be eligible for set-aside contracts, but it would no longer allow them to pay employees with disabilities below minimum-wage standards.

Family and Medical Leave Act of 1993 (FMLA)   A law that establishes, for employers with 50 or more employees, a minimum labor standard with regard to leaves of absence for family or medical reasons. Under the FMLA, an eligible employee may take up to 12 work weeks of leave during any 12-month period due to a serious health condition that makes the employee unable to perform one or more of the essential functions of his or her job, or due to the employee's need to care for a spouse, son, daughter, or parent with a serious health condition.

FEPA   *See* Fair Employment Practice Agency (FEPA)

FLSA   *See* Fair Labor Standards Act (FLSA)

FMLA   *See* Family and Medical Leave Act of 1993 (FMLA)

FT/FY   *See* Full-Time/Full-Year Employment (FT/FY)

Full-Time/Full-Year Employment (FT/FY)   A strict definition of employment that includes only full-time year-round workers (those who work at least 35 hours a week and 50 or more weeks per year).

Function   The normal physiological action or activity of a body part, organ, or system.

GQ   *See* Group Quarters (GQ)

Group Quarters (GQ)   Institutions housing large numbers of people, such as nursing homes and prisons; residents are not included in U.S. employment statistics, whether they are actively working or not.

Impairment   A biomedical, underlying functional condition that is intrinsic to a person and constitutes the essential health component of disability; impairments may be sensory (difficulty in hearing or visual impairment), physical (difficulties in moving or standing up), or psychological (difficulty in coping with stress, depression, or memory loss).

Labor Force Participation Rate   The number of persons "in the labor force" divided by the number of persons in the population. The labor force includes people who have a job, who are on layoff, or who actively searched for work in the last four weeks.

Management Directive 715 (MD-715)   An Equal Employment Opportunity Commission policy that took effect on October 1, 2003, and set standards for establishing and maintaining an effective affirmative action program for the hiring, placement, and advancement of people with disabilities in the federal sector.

Marginally Attached   The relationship to the labor force of an individual who reports wanting a job, being available to work, and having looked for a job in the past 12 months but not during the four weeks immediately preceding the survey.

MD-715   *See* Management Directive 715 (MD-715)

National Health Interview Survey (NHIS)   A cross-sectional household interview survey that is the primary data source on the health of the civilian, noninstitutionalized population of the United States. It collects information to track health status, health care access, and progress toward achieving national health objectives and displays results based on socioeconomic and demographic characteristics.

NHIS   *See* National Health Interview Survey (NHIS)

Occupational Safety and Health Act of 1970 (OSHA)   A U.S. law designed to protect the rights of employees to working conditions that are safe, healthful, and free of recognized hazards.

OFCCP   *See* Office of Federal Contract Compliance Programs (OFCCP)

Office of Federal Contract Compliance Programs (OFCCP)   A section of the U.S. Department of Labor responsible for enforcing the contractual obligations relating to affirmative action and equal employment opportunity required of those who do business with the federal government.

OSHA   *See* Occupational Safety and Health Act of 1970 (OSHA)

Person-Centered Planning   An approach used to help people with disabilities plan for their futures. People with disabilities are put in charge of defining their own direction and choosing their own pathways based on their personal attributes, gifts, and talents. They are supported in accomplishing their goals by a team of individuals who care about them and help them to figure out where they want to go and how best to get there.

Poverty   A measure that compares the sum of total income from each family member living in the household to the appropriate poverty threshold given the household's composition. Poverty thresholds are adjusted to take account of the size of the family, the age of the householder, and the number of related children under the age of 18.

Preferential Hiring   Employment programs required by federal statutes and regulations designed to remedy discriminatory practices in hiring minority group members. These programs are intended to eliminate existing and continuing discrimination, to remedy lingering effects of past discrimination, and to create systems and procedures to prevent future discrimination. They are commonly based on population percentages of minority groups in a particular area and take into consideration such factors as race, color, sex, creed, and age.

Quota   A specific number of members of a particular group that an employer is legally obligated to employ, or a certain percentage of that group that must be represented in the workforce.

Reasonable Accommodation   Under the Americans with Disabilities Act, reasonable accommodation is any modification or adjustment to a job, an employment practice, or the work environment that makes it possible for a qualified individual with a disability to apply for, perform the essential functions of, and enjoy equal benefits and privileges of employment.

Reference Period Employment   A definition of employment that includes respondents who report having worked at all during a certain period, such as the most recent week, the past two weeks, or the past month (depending on the survey).

Rehabilitation Act of 1973   A U.S. law that prohibits discrimination on the basis of disability in federal agencies, programs, and employment, as well as in state and private programs that receive federal funding.

Relative Employment Ratio   A figure derived by dividing the employment rate of persons with disabilities by the employment rate of those without disabilities.

Schedule A   An exception to the usual federal hiring process provided by the U.S. Office of Personnel Management that allows a job to be filled noncompetitively by a person who is disabled and has a certification letter from a State Vocational Rehabilitation Office or the Department of Veterans Affairs.

Service-Connected Disability   A disability that has been determined by the Department of Veterans Affairs (VA) to be the result of disease or injury incurred or aggravated during military service.

Set-Aside Contracts   Government contracts that have been exempted from the normal competitive bid process and reserved to award to "worthy organizations" that employ a majority of individuals with disabilities.

Sheltered Employment   A form of employment in which individuals with disabilities are effectively removed from the general labor force and put into "protective environments" where the demands of competitive employment are minimized. Sheltered workplace businesses create goods and services that are sold in the marketplace, but often through specific contractual or outsourcing agreements with local businesses or government agencies. Many of these work environments have 14(c) wage certificates allowing them to pay sub-minimum wage.

SIPP   *See* Survey of Income and Program Participation (SIPP)

Social Security Disability Insurance (SSDI)   A federal government program that provides wage replacement income for individuals who have worked and paid Social Security taxes and become disabled according to Social Security criteria; its benefits are paid to disabled workers, their widows, widowers, and children, and eligible adults disabled since childhood.

SSDI   *See* Social Security Disability Insurance (SSDI)

SSI   *See* Supplemental Security Income (SSI)

Supplemental Security Income (SSI)   A federal government income supplement program that is designed to help low-income people who are elderly, blind, or disabled meet their basic needs for food, clothing, and shelter. It does not require that an individual have previously worked and paid Social Security taxes.

Supported Employment A form of employment in which individuals with disabilities are fully integrated within a competitive work environment, with supports of various sorts (i.e., a job coach, specialized training, transportation, or assistive technology) provided by specially trained Community Rehabilitation Program personnel.

Survey of Income and Program Participation (SIPP) A survey conducted by the Bureau of the Census to collect income data, labor force information, program participation and eligibility data, and general demographic characteristics to measure the effectiveness of existing federal, state, and local programs and to provide improved statistics on the distribution of income and measures of economic well-being in the United States.

Ticket to Work and Work Incentives Improvement Act of 1999 (TWWIIA) A federal government program intended to help pave avenues to employment for people with disabilities by eliminating work disincentives; it allows people with disabilities to join the workforce without fear of losing their Medicare or Medicaid coverage.

TWWIIA *See* Ticket to Work and Work Incentives Improvement Act of 1999 (TWWIIA)

Unemployment Rate The number of unemployed persons divided by the number of persons determined to be in the labor force.

United Nations Convention on the Rights of People with Disabilities Adopted in 2006 and put into effect on May 3, 2008, this international agreement reaffirms state parties' responsibility to take the appropriate measures to support persons with disabilities in order for them to "attain and maintain maximum independence, full physical, mental, social and vocational ability, and full inclusion and participation in all aspects of life."

U.S. Department of Labor's Employment Training Administration (USDOLETA) The agency that administers federal government job training and worker dislocation programs, federal grants to states for public employment service programs, and unemployment insurance benefits; it has designed several initiatives to build the capacity of its Workforce Development System to support job seekers with disabilities.

USDOLETA   *See* U.S. Department of Labor's Employment Training Administration (USDOLETA)

Vocational Rehabilitation (VR)   Services designed to help individuals with disabilities gain or regain their independence through employment or some form of meaningful activity and reintegration into society; VR includes such services as vocational guidance, job training, occupational adjustment services, and job placement.

VR   *See* Vocational Rehabilitation (VR)

Wage Gap   A disparity or difference in pay between two different groups.

WIA   *See* Workforce Investment Act of 1998 (WIA)

Work Limitation   A determinant of disability status used by the Annual Social and Economic Supplement of the Current Population Survey (CPS-ASEC); it asks whether respondents have a health problem or disability which prevents them from working or which limits the kind or amount of work they can do.

Work Opportunity Tax Credits   A federal tax incentive provided to private-sector businesses that hire employees from nine groups that have historically been discriminated against, including long-term welfare recipients, veterans, residents of certain communities, ex-felons, and vocational rehabilitation program referrals.

Workers' Compensation Programs   Government-sponsored, employer-financed systems for compensating employees who incur an injury or illness in connection with their employment.

Workforce Investment Act of 1998 (WIA)   Legislation that created a "One–Stop" system of job services and employment training to serve every job seeker, with or without a disability, through a central location that provides access to multiple programs.

Workplace Experience   What happens once an employee is on the job.

Index

Page references followed by (table) indicate a table; followed by (figure) indicate an illustrated figure.